KONG

THE HISTORY OF A MOVIE ICON
FROM FAY WRAY TO PETER JACKSON

RAY MORTON

APPLAUSE THEATRE & CINEMA BOOKS · NEW YORK

KING KONG: The History of a Movie Icon from Fay Wray to Peter Jackson
By Ray Morton

All photos in this book are from the personal collection of the author, except as follows: From the collection of M.F. Harmon: pages 178, 180, 192 (top), 196, 197, 199, 210 (bottom right), 212 (top), 213, 224, 231. From the collection of Barry Nolan: page 182. From the collection of Jim Welker: pages 204, 313 (top left), 314. From the collection of Angel Orona: pages 299, 300. Photofest: pages 319, 320, 323, 327.

Book design by Mark Lerner

Library of Congress Cataloging-in-Publication Data:
Morton, Ray, 1961–
  King Kong : the history of a movie icon from Fay Wray to Peter Jackson / by Ray Morton.
    p. cm.
  Includes bibliographical references.
  ISBN-13: 978-1-55783-669-4 (pbk. original)
  ISBN-10: 1-55783-669-8 (pbk. original)
  1. King Kong films—History and criticism. I. Title.

PN1995.9.K55M67 2005
791.43'75—dc22

                    2005022742

Applause Theatre & Cinema Books
19 West 21st St.
New York, NY 10010
Phone: (212) 575-9265
Fax: (212) 575-9270
Email: info@applausepub.com
Internet: www.applausepub.com

Applause books are available through your local bookstore, or you may order at www.applausepub.com
or call Music Dispatch at 800-637-2852

SALES & DISTRIBUTION

North America:
Hal Leonard Corp.
7777 West Bluemound Road
P. O. Box 13819
Milwaukee, WI 53213
Phone: (414) 774-3630
Fax: (414) 774-3259
Email: halinfo@halleonard.com
Internet: www.halleonard.com

Europe:
Roundhouse Publishing Ltd.
Millstone, Limers Lane
Northam, North Devon EX 39 2RG
Phone: (0) 1237-474-474
Fax: (0) 1237-474-774
Email: roundhouse.group@ukgateway.net

KING

KING KONG THE HISTORY OF A MOVIE ICON

FROM FAY WRAY TO PETER JACKSON

This book is dedicated to my parents.

To my father, Raymond J. Morton, Sr., who not only introduced me to Kong, but also to Carl Denham's favorite phrase: "Keep your chin up."

And to my mother, Rita K. Morton, for all of the love, patience, and understanding she has always shown toward a son whose obsession with apes (especially forty-foot-tall ones) she may not have always understood but never discouraged, even when the neighbors were looking at her funny.

CONTENTS

ACKNOWLEDGMENTS

I want to thank four people without whom this book would not have happened: The first is Stephen Tropiano—author, teacher, and friend—who was kind and generous enough to review my initial proposal and pass it on to more than a few of the right people. The second is June Clark of the Peter Rubie Literary Agency, who helped me find my way in the unfamiliar world of book publishing and who set this project up so quickly that it made my head spin. I also want to express my sincere appreciation to Michael Messina, my editor at Applause Books, who has been enthusiastic about, and extremely supportive of, this project every step of the way. Finally, I want to thank Tim Partridge. Tim did the initial contact work for many of the people who were interviewed for this book and conducted the interviews with several of the U.K.-based subjects. He has been a font of information concerning cinematography, special effects, and optical process work. He has also been a good and supportive friend.

In addition, I would also like to thank four people associated with the 1976 version of *King Kong*, who not only allowed me to interview them, but who also made themselves available for ongoing consultation, fact-checking, and support: Richard H. Kline, Barry Nolan, William Kronick, and Fred Sidewater.

I would also like to thank designer Mark Lerner, copy editor Richard Fumosa, and production editor Brian Black for all they did to bring the book to life. For their technical facilitation, research assistance, and support for various aspects of this project, I wish to than Carmen Apodaca, Ron Barbagallo, Steven Bingen, Frank Caruso, Lorenzo De Maio, Joy De Marchis, Rick Goldschmidt, Tara Johnson, Daryl Maxwell, Brian Morishita, Raymond J. Morton Sr., Rich Morton, Jean Sievers, Gary Smith, Robert Tieman, and Jim Welker.

I would also like to acknowledge the following institutions and businesses: The Margaret E. Herrick Library at the Academy of Motion Picture Arts & Sciences, The Glendale (California) Public Library, The Pasadena Public Library, The Los Angeles Public Library, The New Canaan (Connecticut) Public Library, Hollywood Book & Poster Company, Jerry Ohlinger's Movie Material Store, Larry Edmunds Bookstore, and Samy's Camera (Pasadena).

Tim Partridge would like to thank: Kevin H. Martin, James Philips, Sean Gilpin, Harrison Ellenshaw, Charles Finance, Jeff Okun, Jim Aupperle, Craig Barron, Geoff Leonard, M. David Mullen, A.S.C., Matthew Motyka, Manuel Alducin, Charles "Buckey" Grimm, Lukas Kendall, Jeff Bond, The International Cinematographers Guild, Mary O'Gara at R!ot Pictures, Dharmesh Chauhan, Donna Yeates, Naomi Carvey, Carrie Percival, Daniel Thackeray, and Kevin Cuffe.

Finally, I would also like to thank all of the wonderful people who agreed to be interviewed for this book. They are (in alphabetical order): Rene Auberjonois, Rick Baker, Jeff Bridges, Robin Browne, B.S.C., Terry Carr, Jeffrey Chernov, Peter Elliott, Brian Frankish, Michael Grossberg, Brian Kerwin, Richard H. Kline, A.S.C., William Kronick, Gary Martin, David McGiffert, Collin Miller, Alec Mills, B.S.C., Peter Murton, Barry Nolan, Jack O'Halloran, Robert Pergament, Carlo Rambaldi, Arthur Rankin, John Scott, Lorenzo Semple, Jr., Will Shephard, Ronald Shusett, and Fred Sidewater. My thanks also to those who agreed to be interviewed anonymously.

On a personal note, I would like to thank the members of my family for all of their love and support: Raymond and Rita Morton; Kathleen and Caitlin Bunting; Nancy, Jim, Kate, Maddie, and Carrie Lutian; Richard and Kendra Morton; William Morton; Ken Morton; Claire Morton, Andrew Morton; and Tom Morton.

I would also like to acknowledge my friends, who mean the world to me: M. F. Harmon (thirty years of dumb conversations and still going strong), Maggie Morrisette (mere thanks will never be enough); Tara, Kurt, and Mia Johnson; Carmen and Dan Apodaca and the entire Apodaca family; Sara Chovan, Arslan Aziz, and Mabel Chovan-Aziz; Ron Barbagallo; Terri Barbagallo; Dana Bowden and Dave Cullen; Peter Buonadonna; Jim DeFelice; Neil Feigeles; Brian Finn; Faith Ginsberg; Steven Ginsberg; Michael Larobina; Janet McKenney (who was there on 12/17/76); John and Ali Nelson; Angel Orona; Dorian Palumbo; Joe and Donna Romeo; David Shaw; Paul Van Bloem; Erin and Andrew Villaverde; Shelly Mellot, Misse Geatty, Andrew Schneider, and everyone at *Scr(i)pt*.

Finally I would like to thank Ana Maria Apodaca for her unwavering love and support, and for the occasional use of her Scrabble chips.

INTRODUCTION

I saw my first *King Kong* movie when I was about eight years old. It was the 1933 original, and I watched it on television while sitting with my father in the family room of our home in Glen Head, (Long Island) New York. My dad first saw the film on a double bill with *Gunga Din* at the Island Theatre in Hollis (Queens), New York City, in the summer of 1939 and, recalling it as one of the highlights of his young movie-going life, was eager for me to see it as well. Although Dad had described the film to me before it started, nothing could have prepared me for the experience of actually seeing the movie for the first time.

I was immediately captivated by this brilliant cinematic fairy tale about a monstrous giant gorilla found on a prehistoric island who falls in love with a beautiful young woman, is captured, brought to New York City in chains, escapes, and then makes a valiant last stand against a squadron of airplanes on top of the Empire State Building. It was simultaneously the strangest, scariest, most exciting, and most touching thing I had seen in my young life and I was completely bewitched by it. I remain so to this day.

A short time later, I got a chance to see *Kong*'s tragicomic sequel, *The Son of Kong* (thanks to WOR-TV, New York's Channel 9, which made a tradition of showing *Kong*, *The Son of Kong*, and *Mighty Joe Young* back to back to back every Thanksgiving, although what connection the station thought giant apes had to turkey and stuffing I could never understand). I also caught up with its two delightfully cheesy Japanese knock-offs: *King Kong Versus Godzilla* and *King Kong Escapes*. While I realized even then that there was a huge difference in quality between the original *Kong* and its various progeny, I loved them all and would watch them whenever they were on.

As obsessed as I was with these films, it was only after I came across a copy of Thomas G. Aylesworth's *Monsters from the Movies* in the library of St. Boniface Martyr School in Sea Cliff, New York, that I realized there was more to the story. One of the chapters in Aylesworth's slim volume described how *Kong* was made, which is the first time I discovered that the giant ape was actually an eighteen-inch-tall puppet brought to life by a magical process known as *stop-motion animation*. I found this information to be as fascinating as the film itself and began reading everything I could get my hands on to learn how *Kong* and its spinoffs were created. In the course of this reading I was introduced to amazing people such as Merian C. Cooper, Ernest Schoedsack, and Willis O'Brien. I also learned all about articulated armatures, optical printing, and why it's a bad idea to wrap miniature apes in rabbit fur.

My *Kong*-mania went into overdrive in November 1975, when an ad in the *New York Times* informed me that a spectacular remake of the original film was about to go into production. I was on the case from the start, collecting every piece of information I could about the new *Kong*. By the time I finally saw the film in December 1976 (after waiting outside the Ridgeway Theatre in Stamford, Connecticut, for four hours in the freezing cold with my sister Nancy so that we could be first in line on opening night), I knew all there was to know (or so I thought) about giant robotic gorillas, hydraulically-operated hands, and men in ingeniously designed monkey suits. In the years that followed, I continued my research and discovered that the stories behind the movies were often as intriguing, complex, and sometimes even as exciting as the films themselves. Eventually it occurred to me that these stories would make a good book, and so a few years ago I began formal work on this volume.

I began by talking to as many people as I could that were involved in the making of the various *Kong* films. Sadly, by the time I started, the only person still living that had worked on the original two movies was Fay Wray, who unfortunately passed away before I could meet her. Happily though, I was able to speak to a wide range of people associated with the other films. Conducting these interviews was a terrific experience—everyone I spoke to was extremely nice and incredibly generous with their time and with their memories. I not only got to meet some legendary people whose work I have always admired, but I made some wonderful new friends as well. I hope that all involved will accept this book as a tribute to their hard work and artistry and as thanks for all of the hours of entertainment and joy that their work has given to me (and to countless others) over the years. I supplemented the interviews with research conducted in libraries, archives, and on location in many of the places where the movies were made. I also rewatched all of the films a few dozen times, which didn't really seem like work.

The two biggest sections of this book focus on the creation of the two versions of *King Kong* that have been released to date—the 1933 original and the 1976 remake. The making of the original film has been well documented over the years, but there have always been a few gaps in the story. In the course of my investigations I came across some fascinating bits of information that filled in many of those gaps, especially those concerning the development of the initial concept and the original screenplay. The making of the 1976 *King Kong*— the biggest, most complicated King Kong film made to date—has been less well documented and much that has been written about the film has been at best inaccurate and at worst just plain wrong. I have done my best to ensure that the account contained herein is as complete and accurate as possible and hope that it will provide Kong fans with new insight into this underappreciated film.

The rest of the book is divided into chapters about the making of the two *Kong* sequels, the Japanese *Kong* films, movies that have been inspired by *Kong*, *Kong* productions that never made it to the screen, and a look at some of the merchandise the various films have spawned over the years. The book concludes with a look at the 2005 *King Kong* film directed by the man who made the cinematic *Lord of the Rings* trilogy—Peter Jackson.

I hope that you enjoy reading this book as much as I enjoyed writing it.

■ ■ ■

K.Pub-A21

CHAPTER 1

THE FATHER OF KONG

King Kong was the brainchild of Merian Coldwell Cooper—a remarkably intelligent and creative man who lived a life filled with adventures amazing enough to rival any he would later depict on screen. Short, muscular, and hot-tempered, Cooper was an imaginative, enthusiastic showman with a flair for the dramatic. He dreamed large and possessed both the talent and the tenacity to turn those dreams into reality. Applying his abilities to the three great passions of his life—exploration, aviation, and cinema— he achieved tremendous success and made significant and lasting contributions in all three fields. In doing so, he traveled to distant lands, flew in both World Wars, and helped found several airlines. He also wrote books and newspaper articles, introduced technical innovations that revolutionized the filmmaking process, produced several classic movies, and created an enduring cultural icon.

Merian C. Cooper: the man who created King Kong.

EARLY YEARS   Cooper was born to a wealthy family of southern plantation owners in Jacksonville, Florida, on October 24, 1893. When he was six years old, an uncle gave him a copy of the book *Explorations and Adventures in Equatorial Africa*, which was written in 1862 by French explorer Paul du Chiallu. The book kindled in young Cooper a passionate desire to travel to distant lands and explore the far-flung reaches of the earth. A story in one of the book's chapters about a tribe of ferocious giant gorillas that attacked a native village also caught his eye. An incident in which one of the apes carried a female villager off into the jungle especially intrigued him. While this depiction of gorillas as vicious, rampaging beasts is quite at odds with the shy and gentle nature of the real animals, it was very much in line with the popular conception of the time that characterized these noble, mysterious creatures as rapacious and terrifying monsters. Enthralled, the young Cooper began a life-long fascination with gorillas.

In 1911, Cooper received an appointment to the United States Naval Academy at Annapolis, Maryland. During his time there, he was more interested in airplanes and girls than he was in his studies and was asked to leave in the middle of his senior year. By then, World War I was raging in Europe and Cooper wanted to join the fight by enlisting in either the French or the British air service (since the United States was not yet involved in the war). To get to Europe, Cooper signed on as a seaman in the merchant marine and made his way to London, where he promptly jumped ship. Cooper was caught almost immediately and, lacking the proper passport, was shipped back to the United States. Following his return, Cooper became a reporter and wrote for a string of newspapers, including the *Minneapolis Daily News*, the *Des Moines Register-Leader*, and the *St. Louis Post-Dispatch*. Looking for adventure, he enlisted in the Georgia National Guard in 1916 and was sent to Mexico, where he took part in the campaign against Pancho Villa.

After the United States entered the war in 1917, Cooper joined the U.S. Army Signal Corps—Aviation Section as a pilot. After flying several successful missions, he went on a bombing run in a de Haviland DH-4 (a wooden airplane nicknamed "the Flaming Coffin"), which was attacked and set on fire by an enemy Fokker. Cooper's face and right arm were seriously burned; he considered jumping out of the plane (without a parachute) to escape the flames but decided instead to remain with his wounded observer. In a risky maneuver, he put his plane into a steep dive, which blew out the flames and enabled him to make a crash landing. Both Cooper and his observer were captured and taken to a German prison hospital for treatment. Although Cooper recovered, his injuries left scars that would remain with him for the rest of his life. He stayed in the prison hospital until a month after the Armistice, at which point he returned to his unit. Cooper was awarded the Distinguished Service Cross, but refused it on the ground that "We all took the same risks."

ERNEST B. SCHOEDSACK   After the war ended, Cooper joined the American Relief Organization to help bring food to the famine-stricken areas of Europe. Passing through Vienna in February 1919 on his way to a posting in

Warsaw, he struck up a friendship with a tall, lanky newsreel photographer named Ernest Beaumont Schoedsack. Born on a farm in Council Bluffs, Iowa, on June 8, 1893, Schoedsack had run away from home at the age of fourteen. Working his way around the country doing a series of odd jobs, Schoedsack ended up in Los Angeles, where he became a cinematographer for the Mack Sennett Studios. When the war began, Schoedsack joined the Signal Corps and became a frontline combat photographer. Following the war, Schoedsack stayed in Europe and joined the Red Cross relief mission to aid Polish refugees escaping from the Russo-Polish War (Poland was fighting to maintain its newly won independence in the face of a takeover attempt by the newly formed Soviet Union). An adventurous fellow in his own right, Schoedsack drove ambulances, ferried supplies and refugees across war-ravaged areas, and shot documentary footage of all aspects of the conflict.

In August 1919, Cooper went to Paris and helped found the Kosciusko Aerial Squadron—a group of American pilots that joined the Polish army to help in its fight for freedom. He flew over seventy strafing missions and was soon promoted to squadron commander. On July 13, 1920, he was again shot down behind enemy lines, severely injuring his leg in the process. Captured by the Bolsheviks, Cooper knew he would be killed if his captors knew he was the squadron leader, so he kept his true identity a secret. Five days after he was captured, Cooper escaped from Bolshevik headquarters. Hindered by his damaged leg, Cooper was recaptured two days later and sent to a prison in Moscow. Although Poland won its independence, and the war ended on October 12, 1920, Cooper was not released. Being an American, he was classified as a criminal rather than a prisoner of war. Instead he was sent to a work camp outside Moscow, where he remained until April 12, 1921, when he and two Polish soldiers escaped from the camp. Hiding out during the day and moving only at night, the three men traveled 500 miles across Russia through forests and swamps, stealing food, eluding authorities, and at one point even killing a Soviet soldier who threatened to expose them. After two weeks, the fugitives finally arrived at the Latvian border and made it across with the help of a professional smuggler. Back in Poland, Cooper was awarded the *Virtuti Militari* (Cross of the Brave), Poland's highest honor, as well as the Polish Service Medal. On his way home to the United States, Cooper once again encountered Schoedsack, who was now working as a newsreel cameraman in London.

Schoedsack went on to work for the Near East Relief mission during the Greco–Turkish War, while Cooper returned to New York City, where he wrote an autobiography called *Things Men Die For* and became a reporter and feature writer for the *New York Times*. In 1922, he joined an around-the-world expedition led by explorer and promoter Captain Edward A. Salisbury.

Cooper sailed with Salisbury through the Indian Ocean. When one of the expedition's cinematographers quit, Cooper suggested Schoedsack as a replacement. Schoedsack was hired and joined the team in Africa. Cooper and Schoedsack traveled with Salisbury through Abyssinia (now Ethiopia), shooting film and writing articles as they went. On the way to North Africa, however, *Wisdom II* was damaged in a monsoon, requiring the expedition to sail to Italy for repairs. While in dry dock, *Wisdom II* caught fire. The flames destroyed the ship and the expedition came to an end.

THE "NATURAL DRAMAS"   During the journey, Cooper and Schoedsack had grown dissatisfied with making travelogues and yearned to create something more exciting. They decided to work together, but rather than produce another straightforward documentary, they decided to make what they called a "natural drama." To make such a film, they would travel to an exotic land, shoot footage of real people and real events and then, through creative editing, shape that footage into a dramatic narrative that had all the thrills and excitement of a fictional adventure film. When they finished with Salisbury, the two formed Cooper-Schoedsack Productions, the slogan of which was "Keep It Distant, Difficult, and Dangerous." They decided that the subject of their first production would be a tribe of nomads and the adventures it encountered as it migrated to survive.

To fund the production, Cooper borrowed $10,000—half from his family and half from his friend Marguerite Harrison, a fellow reporter and adventurer who, much to Schoedsack's dismay, planned to accompany them on their trip. The trio journeyed to southern Persia (now Iran) and traveled with the Bakhtiari tribes as they made a perilous crossing over the snow-covered Zardeh Kuh Mountain in search of the grass they needed to keep their livestock alive. The forty-six-day trip was an arduous one, but the team managed to capture some spectacular footage, which they eventually edited into a film called *Grass: A Nation's Battle for Life* (1925). Cooper and Schoedsack found that they worked extremely well together, in part because their personalities were so complementary—Cooper was an enthusiastic dreamer who was constantly coming up with new and ever-more spectacular ideas, while Schoedsack was a practical realist who kept them reasonably tethered to the ground.

Cooper took *Grass* on the lecture circuit while Schoedsack accepted a job as a cinematographer on a New York Geological Society expedition to the Sargasso Sea and the Galapagos Islands. During the trip, Schoedsack met a former actress named Ruth Rose. The daughter of a playwright, Rose took a job as a research assistant with the New York Zoological Society during an actor's strike and eventually became an accomplished research technician. Rose was serving as the Galapagos expedition's official historian when she met Schoedsack. The two fell in love and were soon married. Meanwhile, Jesse L. Lasky, head of Paramount-Famous Players-Lasky, saw *Grass*. Impressed, he acquired it for distribution. The film premiered on March 30, 1925, at New York's Criterion Theater. The New York engagement made money, but the film did not do well in its national release, which was blamed on the fact that the film lacked a romantic subplot. Still, Lasky was impressed enough to finance another Cooper-Schoedsack adventure.

This time, the team decided on a jungle setting. They went to Siam (now Thailand) and made a film about a native family that finds a baby elephant, takes it home, and ties it to their house. When the baby's mother comes to free it, she brings along the rest of the herd, which stampedes and destroys the village before finally being subdued by the natives. Although it was still made in a documentary fashion, this new film was more fictionalized than *Grass* had been (the filmmakers staged many of the scenes, including the elephant stampede), an indication of the team's increasing interest in dramatic storytelling. *Chang* (the Lao word for elephant) opened at the Rivoli Theater in New York on April 28, 1927. The film was a huge hit and was nominated for an Academy Award, although the exhibitors still complained that the film would have done better if it had contained a love story.

Following *Chang*, Lasky asked Cooper and Schoedsack to apply their natural drama technique to a fiction film. Agreeing, the duo went with Rose to Africa, where they shot scenes of hippos, baboons, and the native Fuzzy-Wuzzy tribe for Paramount's *The Four Feathers* (1929). Upon completion, they returned to California to film dramatic sequences with a cast of actors that included Richard Arlen, Clive Brook, William Powell, Noah Beery, and a young actress who had recently appeared in Erich Von Stroheim's film *The Wedding March* (1928) named Fay Wray. When Cooper and Schoedsack finished editing the picture, David O. Selznick, the Paramount producer assigned to the film, ordered that some new scenes shot by Paramount staff director Lothar Mendes be added to the film. Although Cooper and Schoedsack both felt that the new scenes "dumbed down" the picture, they enjoyed their association with Selznick. By now, sound had arrived and was beginning to take hold. Shot as a silent picture, *The Four Feathers* was augmented with music and a sound effects track and released on June 2, 1929.

Jesse Lasky immediately offered to fund another natural drama. Schoedsack accepted the offer, but Cooper did not. Cooper was a partner in a company that invested in several start–up airlines (civil aviation was then in its infancy, but growing rapidly). In 1929, Cooper was appointed to the board of directors of two of those airlines—Pan Am Airways and Western Air Express. Discouraged with Hollywood after his dealings with Paramount over *The Four Feathers*, Cooper accepted the appointments and moved to New York. Schoedsack and Rose went to the Dutch East Indies to film *Rango* (1931), the story of a young boy who befriends a baby orangutan. After many adventures together, the orangutan eventually sacrifices himself to save the boy when the child is attacked by a tiger.

Back in Manhattan, Cooper found himself bored with business. To exercise his restless imagination, he began thinking up a new and exciting story, one that would ultimately combine his interests in apes, exploration, airplanes, and cinema into the idea that would become his masterpiece.

■ ■ ■

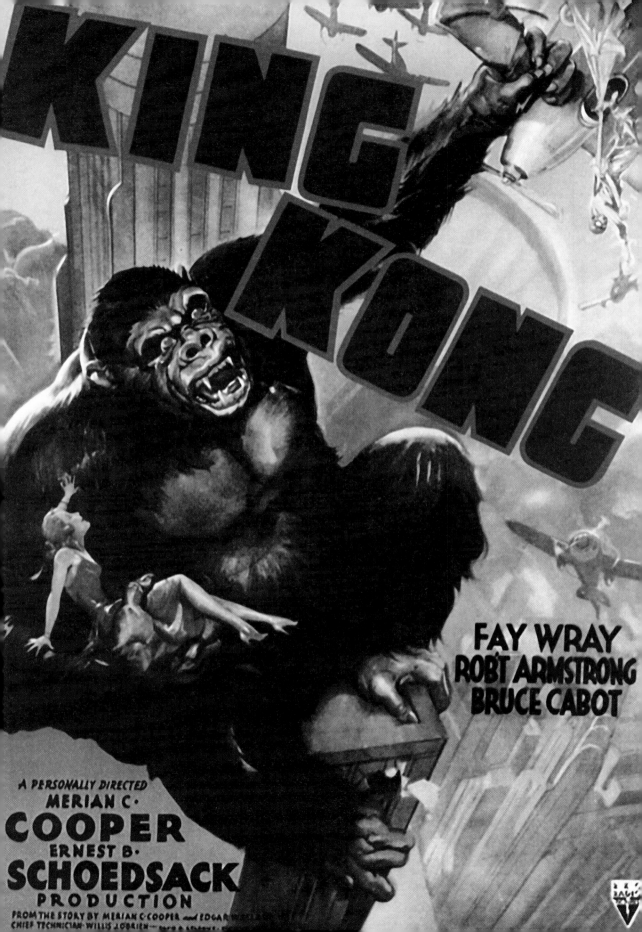

CHAPTER 2

"IT WAS BEAUTY KILLED THE BEAST"

The Making of *King Kong*

1932. Across the Hudson River from Manhattan, the tramp steamer *SS Venture* prepares to set sail. In the ship's wardroom, Carl Denham, the acclaimed director of "outdoor" pictures who has hired the *Venture* to take him to a secret location in the South Seas to film his latest movie, is fretting because he needs an actress to appear in the film. Exhibitors have complained that his previous pictures would have grossed twice as much if they had included a love interest, and the ambitious Denham is determined to give them what they want. Meanwhile, Captain Englehorn, the *Venture*'s skipper, is concerned because his insurance company has found out about the large amount of weapons and explosives Denham has brought aboard the ship and is sending a fire marshal to investigate. Englehorn warns Denham that if the marshal discovers the cache of gas bombs that Denham

One of the release posters for the original 1933 *King Kong*.

has brought aboard—one of which the director claims is strong enough to "knock out an elephant"—they'll find themselves involved in a legal case that will keep them in port for months. Needing to reach his destination before the monsoon season starts, Denham declares that they must give the fire marshal the slip and leave port the first thing in the morning. This means that Denham needs to find his actress tonight. Because of the mysterious nature of the trip and Denham's reputation for recklessness, none of the talent representatives in town will help him. When even his agent friend Weston refuses to help him, the defiant and determined Denham vows to find a girl himself, even if he has to marry one.

Denham goes to Times Square, where he searches for a suitable candidate among the down and out, but his search proves to be a bust. Discouraged, he stops at a fruit stand, where he sees a desperate young woman attempt to steal an apple. When the fruit stand's owner catches the young woman and threatens to call the police, Denham intervenes and pays the man off. Faint from hunger, the young woman falls into Denham's arms. As Denham catches her, he sees that she is extraordinarily beautiful and just the kind of girl he has been looking for. Denham takes the young woman to a one-armed lunchroom and buys her something to eat. Learning that she is an unemployed actress named Ann Darrow, he offers her the role in his picture. Although she wants the job, Ann hesitates because she is unsure of Denham's intentions. Denham assures her that he is strictly on the level and intends "no funny business." Assured, Ann asks what she needs to do. "Trust me and keep your chin up," Denham replies. They seal the deal with a handshake.

The next morning, the *Venture* sets sail. An excited Ann comes up on deck and stands behind hard-boiled first mate Jack Driscoll as he supervises the departure. Gesturing to a crewmember, Driscoll accidentally knocks Ann in the chin. He apologizes, but makes it clear he's not happy about having a woman aboard the ship. The tug whistle sounds and the journey begins. As the voyage progresses, Jack finds himself becoming increasingly attracted to Ann, but covers his feelings by continuing to expound on his negative view of women. One day, Jack confronts Denham and demands to know where they're going and what kind of danger they can expect to encounter when they get there. When Denham accuses Jack of having gone soft, Jack says he's not afraid for himself, but for Ann. Hearing this, Denham smiles and tells Jack that this is the theme of his picture. "The Beast was a tough guy too—he could lick the world. But when he saw Beauty, she got him. He went soft. He forgot his wisdom and the little fellows licked him."

When the *Venture* reaches the Indian Ocean, Denham tells Jack and Englehorn that they are headed for a small, uncharted island that Denham located with the help of a map given to him by the skipper of a Norwegian barque. According to the map, the island's most distinctive features are a giant mountain shaped like a skull and a large man-made wall that cuts the beach off from the rest of the island. Denham believes that the island is the home of Kong, a name Englehorn recognizes as that of an ancient native god of some sort. Denham confirms this and says it is his intention to find whatever this

Kong is and photograph it. "What if it doesn't like having its picture taken?" Driscoll asks. "Well," Denham replies. "Now you know why I brought along those gas bombs." That afternoon, Denham makes a screen test of Ann in which he directs her to scream for her life. Becoming hysterical, Ann does. The blood-curdling sound disturbs Driscoll. "What does he think she's really going to see?" he asks Englehorn, who has no answer.

A short time later, the *Venture* arrives at the island. A landing party consisting of Denham, Ann, Jack, Englehorn, and some sailors go ashore, where they discover a native village that appears to be deserted. Following the sound of drums, they make their way to the Great Wall, where they witness a strange ceremony already in progress. Native men dressed in ape skins are dancing around a young girl who is being dressed in flowers. As they do, they chant the name "Kong!" The girl is clearly being offered as a sacrifice to the native god. Suddenly, the Native Chief spots the intruders and stops the ceremony. Confronting the explorers, the Chief accuses them of spoiling the ceremony. Catching sight of Ann, the Chief thinks she would make a splendid gift for Kong and offers to trade six of his women for her. On Denham's instructions, Englehorn refuses the offer and the landing party makes a tense but casual retreat back to the ship.

CAST AND CREW: *King Kong* (1933)

Ann Darrow: Fay Wray; Carl Denham: Robert Armstrong; Jack Driscoll: Bruce Cabot; Capt. Englehorn: Frank Reicher; Charles Weston: Sam Hardy; Native Chief: Noble Johnson; Witch King: Steve Clemente; Second Mate: James Flavin; Charlie: Victor Wong; Fruit Vendor: Paul Porcasi; Dock Watchman: Russ Powell; Hotel Victim: Sandra Shaw; Sacrifice Victim: Etta McDaniel; Flight Commander: Merian C. Cooper; Chief Observer: Ernest B. Schoedsack; SS *Venture* Crew: Ethan Laidlaw, Blackie Whiteford, Dick Curtis, Charles Sullivan, Harry Tendbrook, Gil Perkins; Theater Patron: Vera Lewis; Theater Patron: Leroy Mason; Reporter: Frank Mills; Reporter: Lynton Brent; Engineer: Reginald Barlow; Police Captain: George MacQuarrie; Navy Pilots: Barney Capehart, Bob Galloway, Eric Wood, Dusty Mitchell, Russ Rogers; Stunts: Aline Goodwin, Pauline Wagner, Lee Kinney, Lillian Jones, Marcella Allen, Cherie May, Al McDonald, Gil Perkins, Bud Mason, Charles Sullivan, Bob McKee, Mike Lally, Bob Williams, Mike Graves, Duke Green, James Casey, Dorothy Cutis, Frank Cullen, Joe Dill, Charles Watt, Harry Wagner, Mike Lally, James Casey, Tex Higginson, Sam Cummings, Edith Haskins, Billy Jones, Chic Collins, Johnny St. Claire, Jack Holbrook, Betty Collins, Loretta Rush, Bobby Rose, Frances Mills, Harvey Perry

Produced and Directed by: Merian C. Cooper and Ernest B. Schoedsack; Executive Producer: David O. Selznick; Production Assistants: Archie F. Marshek, Walter Daniels

Screenplay by: James A. Creelman and Ruth Rose; From an idea conceived by: Merian C. Cooper and Edgar Wallace; Chief Technician: Willis H. O'Brien; Art Technicians: Mario Larrinaga, Byron L. Crabbe; Technical Staff: E. B. Gibson, Marcel Delgado, Fred Reefe, Orville Goldner, Carroll L. Shepphird, W. G. White, John Cerisoli; Technical Artists: Juan Larrinaga, Victor Delgado, Zachary Hoag; Music by: Max Steiner; Directors of Photography: Eddie Linden, Kenneth Peach (uncredited), J. O. Taylor, Vernon Walker; Camera Operators: Edward Henderson, Felix Schoedsack, Lee Davis

Camera Assistants: Bert Willis, William Reinhold, William Clothier, Clifford Stein; Optical Photography: Linwood G. Dunn, Cecil Love, and William Ulm; Rear-Screen Process: Sidney Saunders; Dunning process Supervisors: C. Dodge Dunning, Carroll H. Dunning; Williams Matte Supervision: Frank Williams; Film Editor: Ted Cheesman; Sound Effects: Murray Spivack; Sound Effects Assistant: Walter Elliott; Sound Recordist: Earl A. Wolcott; Sound Rerecording Mixer: Clem Portman; Supervising Art Director: Van Nest Polglase; Art Directors: Carroll Clark, Al Herman; Set Decorators: Thomas Little, Ray Moyer; Painter: Peter Stitch; Costumes: Walter Plunkett; Chief Makeup Supervision: Mel Berns; Property Master: George Gabe; Special Effects: Harry Redmond Jr.; Camera Aircraft Pilots: Duke Krantz and George Weiss; Titles: Pacific Title Company; Released by: RKO; Running time: 100 Minutes.

The Eighth Wonder of the World.

That night, Jack tells Ann how worried he was for her. Ann teases Jack about showing concern for a woman, which prompts him to realize that he does indeed love her. Ann admits that she feels the same way and they embrace. Just then, Jack is called to the bridge. As Ann lingers for a moment, lost in her happiness, she is suddenly grabbed from behind by a group of natives, who take her to their canoe and row her back to the island. A short time later, Denham sees a procession of torches moving through the native village, accompanied by the sound of drums. Meanwhile, Jack goes in search of Ann and finds that she is missing. When a native necklace is discovered on one of the decks, Jack realizes that Ann has been kidnapped and sounds the alarm.

Back in the village, the natives stage a spectacular torch-lit ceremony during which they escort Ann through a giant gate located in the middle of the Great Wall and tie her to a sacrificial altar on the other side. After they close the gate, the Chief strikes a huge gong positioned atop the wall. Suddenly, a terrifying roar comes from the jungle. Trees are shoved aside and Kong—a giant, 18-foot-tall gorilla—emerges from the foliage. Seeing him, Ann lets out a terrified scream. Kong roars, beats his chest, and then picks up Ann from the altar. Just then a rescue party from the *Venture* arrives. Jack reaches the gate just in time to see Kong carry Ann off into the jungle. Pulling open the gates, a search party led by Jack and Denham and carrying a healthy supply of gas bombs heads into the jungle in search of Ann.

Morning finds the search party tracking Kong through a primeval landscape in which they are amazed to discover that prehistoric dinosaurs still live. As an angry *Stegosaurus* charges toward them, Denham fells the creature with a gas bomb and then finishes it off with a shot to the head. A short time later, as the men are attempting to cross a fog-enshrouded swamp on a hastily assembled raft, they are attacked by a *Brontosaurus* that overturns the raft and bites down on several of the sailors. As the gas bombs fall into the water and are lost, the survivors swim to shore and run up the banks of the swamp. The *Brontosaurus* comes after them and traps one unlucky sailor up a tree. As the sailor tries to fend off the creature, the *Brontosaurus* seizes the screaming man in his jaws and silences him forever.

A few miles away, Kong carries Ann across a log that bridges a deep ravine and enters a peaceful clearing. Hearing the sounds of the search party behind him, he deposits Ann in the top of a dead tree and then heads back to investigate. Meanwhile, the search party, still running from the *Brontosaurus*, approaches the ravine. Denham gets caught on a branch, but the rest of the party run across the log. Suddenly, Kong appears on the far side of the ravine. Looking for cover, Jack grabs a vine and climbs down to a small cave along the ravine wall. The rest of the sailors are trapped on the log as a furious Kong picks it up and begins twisting it. One by one, the sailors fall off the log and plummet to their deaths on the floor of the ravine. Kong is unable to dislodge the last man, so he picks up the entire log and hurls it into the chasm. Kong then turns his attention to Jack, whom he sees hiding in the cave below. Reaching down, Kong tries to grab Jack, who fends him off with a knife.

Back in the clearing, Ann is startled by the sight of an approaching *Tyrannosaurus* rex. Alerted by Ann's screams, Kong abandons Jack and rushes back to the clearing. There he confronts the *Tyrannosaurus* rex and the two engage in a thunderous battle, during which the tree Ann is sitting in gets knocked over and pins her to the ground. The *Tyrannosaurus* almost gets the best of Kong, but then Kong turns the tables by grabbing the giant lizard's mouth and snapping its jaw. After planting his foot on the T-rex and beating his chest in triumph, Kong lifts the tree off Ann, picks her up, and carries her deeper into the jungle.

Meanwhile, Jack climbs back to the top of the ravine as Denham appears on the other side. After telling Denham to go back and get more gas bombs, Jack continues on after Ann. Denham returns to the Great Wall and tells Englehorn what has happened. Another search party is organized and plans are made to start out again first thing in the morning.

With Jack following close behind, Kong brings Ann to his lair—a cave located high atop Skull Mountain at the highest point on the island. There Kong saves Ann from a serpent-like *Elasmosaurus*, which wraps itself around Kong's neck and attempts to strangle him; Kong is able to free himself and beat the creature to death on a rock. Kong then carries Ann out onto a ledge that overlooks the entire island. After surveying his domain, Kong begins examining his new prize. Intrigued by Ann's clothing, Kong tears off pieces of her dress and sniffs them. Meanwhile, back in the cave, Jack dislodges a rock as he attempts to climb up to the cliff. Hearing the noise, Kong puts Ann down and goes inside to investigate. While he is gone, a *Pteranodon* swoops down from the sky and grabs Ann in its talons. Hearing her screams, Kong races back out onto the ledge and grabs the giant reptile before it is able to fly off. As Kong and the *Pteranodon* struggle, Jack finally reaches Ann. The couple slip past the battling monsters and start climbing down the high cliff using a vine. Finally defeating the *Pteranodon* by snapping its neck, Kong sees Ann and Jack trying to escape. Furious, he grabs the vine and starts pulling them back up toward him. With no other choice, they let go and plunge hundred of feet down into a river below. Letting out an angry roar, Kong goes after them.

Jack and Ann race back to the Great Wall with Kong in hot pursuit. Arriving at the wall, Kong breaks though the gates and tears up the village looking for Ann. He finally finds her on the beach, huddled with the crew of the *Venture*. As Kong advances, Denham rushes forward and hurls a gas bomb at him. The bomb explodes and Kong is quickly overcome by the anesthetic fumes. As the giant ape passes out on the beach, Denham decides to take him back to New York City, and put him on show. Convinced he's going to make millions, Denham imagines the ape's name up in lights: "Kong, the Eighth Wonder of the World."

Several months later, the show featuring "Carl Denham's Monster" sells out its opening night on Broadway. Denham has convinced Jack and Ann, who are now engaged, to make an appearance as Kong is unveiled to the public for the first time. The audience is startled by the sight of the giant beast, who has been chained to a platform in the center of the stage. All goes well until a group of photographers begin taking pictures. Convinced the flashbulbs are hurting Ann, Kong begins to pull at his chains. Terrified, the audience flees in fear as Kong breaks free, jumps down from the platform, and begins searching for Ann.

Panic breaks out as Kong smashes through the back door of the theater and spots Ann and Jack entering a hotel across the street. Hearing a woman scream from one of the hotel's windows high above him, Kong mistakes her for Ann and climbs up the wall of the building. Spotting a woman fast asleep in one of the hotel rooms, Kong reaches in the window and grabs her. When he realizes that terrified woman is not Ann, Kong drops her and continues his climb. Several floors higher, he finally spots the real Ann as Jack tries to comfort her in her hotel room. As Kong reaches in the window, Jack tries to stop him, but Kong knocks him out cold. Kong grabs Ann and carries her up to the roof of the hotel. Jack recovers, and together he and Denham run to the hotel roof in time to see Kong carry Ann off. A few blocks away, Kong is startled by a passing elevated train and angrily destroys a portion of the trestle as another train approaches. Unable to stop, the train falls into the gap. Terrified passengers flee as Kong demolishes the train and then departs by climbing up another building.

At a nearby police station, Jack and Denham monitor radio reports tracking Kong's progress as he makes his way toward the highest point on Manhattan Island — the Empire State Building. When they receive word that Kong is actually climbing the building, they fear that all is lost until Driscoll suggests that they call in airplanes to shoot Kong down. A short time later, a squadron of navy fighter planes takes flight and approaches Kong as he reaches the top of the Empire State Building. As soon as Kong puts Ann down on a ledge, the planes swoop down and begin shooting at him. At first Kong is simply puzzled by the bullets, but he soon begins to experience pain. Fighting back, Kong swats at the planes and manages to knock one of them out of the sky, but the others continue to attack and Kong soon begins to weaken. Picking Ann up, a dying Kong caresses her one last time, and then gently lays her back down on the ledge. As one of the planes swoops down and delivers a final blast of gunfire, Kong loses his grip and falls. Jack arrives and grabs Ann in a tight embrace as they hear Kong hit the ground far below.

A short time later, Denham approaches the fallen Kong lying in the middle of Fifth Avenue. "Well, Denham," a passing cop remarks. "The airplanes got him." A rueful Denham shakes his head. "Oh, no. It wasn't the airplanes. It was Beauty killed the Beast."

THE BIRTH OF KONG

In interviews given at the time of *King Kong*'s release and in all years thereafter, Merian Cooper claimed that the *Kong* story came to him fully formed. In these interviews, Cooper alternately explained that his inspiration came from either a book about the newly discovered dragons of Komodo or the sight of an airplane flying past the top of a New York skyscraper. The evidence suggests, however, that, as with most creative work, the concept actually developed in phases, each with its own particular inspiration and influences.

As previously noted, Cooper had been fascinated with gorillas ever since he read Paul du Chiallu's book, but the creative chain of events that eventually led to *Kong* began in earnest in Africa during the filming of *The Four Feathers*. In the course of the production, Cooper became intrigued by a tribe of baboons that lived near the location, and he began studying their lifestyle, behavior, and social interactions. In 1929, while living in New York, Cooper wrote an 85,000-word monograph recording his observations. Although the monograph was lost—his maid accidentally tossed it in the trash—Cooper began thinking about apes while he was writing the piece and he began pondering the possibility of doing a film about his favorite ape of all—the gorilla. His first thought was to produce a natural drama focusing on a group of two or three gorillas.

As Cooper was mulling over this notion, he read a book called *The Dragon Lizards of Komodo*, by W. Douglas Burden, an explorer and naturalist attached

Kong places Ann in the crook of a tree in the second scene shot for the *King Kong* test reel.

to the American Museum of Natural History and The New York Zoological Society and who was one of Cooper's closest friends. In 1926, Burden had led an expedition to the island of Komodo in the Dutch East Indies. A remote, volcanic island, Komodo was the home of the famed Komodo dragons, a species of large, vicious lizards thought to have been extinct since prehistoric times until the living specimens were discovered by a Dutch scientist named P. A. Ouwens in 1912. Burden had captured two of the ten-foot-long, 250 pound carnivores and brought them back to the United States, where they were exhibited to large crowds at the Bronx Zoo.

Cooper was intrigued by Burden's description of the dragons and began imagining exciting scenes in which his gorillas would fight them. He planned to realize these scenes by filming the gorillas in their natural habitat (most likely in the Congo) and the dragons on Komodo and then intercutting the two, with some sort of artificial stand-ins used for joint shots. As Cooper worked on his idea throughout 1929–1930, he decided it would be dramatically more potent to focus on a single gorilla rather than a group. True to the popular conception of the time, Cooper characterized his ape as a ferocious, rampaging menace. Determined to appease the exhibitors by including a love story, Cooper decided to include a woman in the tale as well, a notion sparked by the fact that Burden's wife had accompanied him on his trip. Inspired by the incident in du Chiallu's book in which an ape carried off a woman, as well as by a strong taste for melodrama, Cooper decided that at some point in the story the gorilla would do the same with the woman from the expedition. When Burden told Cooper that the dragons he brought back to New York were unable to survive in captivity and died soon after they arrived, Cooper thought that his simian protagonist should meet the same fate. Combining all of these ideas into one, Cooper wrote a treatment about an expedition that travels to a remote island upon which resides a ferocious gorilla that engages in fights with large prehistoric lizards and abducts a female member of the expedition. After the explorers rescue the woman, they capture the gorilla and bring him back to New York City to be put on display. Burden's dragons had simply fallen into poor health and expired, but Cooper, ever the showman, wanted to find a more spectacular way of killing his protagonist and decided that the gorilla would escape from captivity and wreak some sort of havoc before finally being killed. In interviews given years later, Cooper indicated that he planned to film the New York scenes with real gorillas as well.

In some of these same interviews, Cooper also claimed that he had already decided at this point to make his gorilla a giant, although he never explained where such an unusual idea came from. He also claimed that he intended to use special effects to increase the ape's size, but given that two of the techniques he mentions wanting to use (rear-screen projection and traveling mattes) were not considered viable at the time he was allegedly planning the film, it seems highly unlikely that this was the case. It is more plausible to think that the idea of making Kong a giant came later.

Cooper first pitched his concept to Paramount, but Jesse L. Lasky wasn't interested. He thought that it would be too expensive to send a film crew to both

Africa and Komodo, especially in those first days of the Great Depression. Cooper next met with David O. Selznick, who had left Paramount and was in New York trying to raise the money to start his own independent production company. Selznick liked Cooper's concept, but with no studio or financing of his own, he was unable to help. Disappointed, Cooper put the project on hold while he continued with his aviation work. A short time later, Selznick was offered a job as vice president in charge of production at RKO–Radio Pictures. Unable to secure sufficient backing for his own company, Selznick accepted the offer.

ENTER RKO RKO was founded in 1928 when Joseph P. Kennedy merged two of his companies—FBO Pictures, a production and distribution company, and the Keith-Orpheum theater chain—and then formed a partnership with David Sarnoff—whose Radio Corporation of America had developed a new motion picture sound system called RCA Photophone—to produce, distribute, and exhibit talking pictures. The new company's name was Radio-Keith-Orpheum and its films were released under the brand name Radio Pictures (its logo featured a giant radio tower atop a spinning globe). Taking over the old FBO studios on the corner of Gower Street and Melrose Avenue in Hollywood, RKO had barely gotten started when the Great Depression hit and threw the company's finances into turmoil. The fledgling studio hoped the returns from its first slate of pictures would save the day. Unfortunately, most of those pictures lacked distinction and failed to make much of an impact at the box office. In 1931, the struggling company merged with the equally struggling Pathé Pictures. When the company was placed into receivership by the Irving Trust Company, RKO president B. B. Kahane hired David O. Selznick to get the studio back on track both creatively and financially. Selznick had a huge task ahead of him and he needed help. In 1931, Selznick asked Cooper to come to work for him at RKO as his executive assistant. Cooper's job would be to evaluate all of the studio's projects to determine their creative and financial viability and then decide which ones should be salvaged and which ones should be shelved. To make the offer more attractive, Selznick promised Cooper that he would be allowed to produce his own films as well. Cooper accepted the position and soon found himself back in California, living at the Chateau Elysee apartments on Franklin Avenue.

Upon arriving at RKO, Cooper immediately began developing a film adaptation of *The Most Dangerous Game*, Richard Connell's 1930 short story about Count Zaroff, a mad big-game hunter who hunts humans for sport. To direct the picture, he hired his former partner, Ernest Schoedsack. Following *Rango* (1931), Schoedsack had gone to India to film scenes for Paramount's proposed version of Francis Yeats-Brown's *The Lives of A Bengal Lancer*, which the studio wanted to make in the same way as *The Four Feathers* (1929)—by combining location material with studio footage using actors. The Indian portion of the filming went smoothly enough, but the studio shoot was continuously postponed (and would not actually be completed until 1935). Frustrated, Schoedsack asked to be released from his contract and went to work for Cooper at RKO. Concerned that a silent film director like Schoedsack would be unable to handle dialogue scenes, the studio assigned a codirector—actor and director Irving Pichel—to the film as well. The cast included Joel McCrea, Leslie Banks, Robert Armstrong, and *Four Feathers* veteran Fay Wray. A huge jungle set was constructed on Stage 11 at the RKO-Pathè lot in Culver City. As soon as *Game* was safely launched, Cooper began reviewing all of the studio's other projects.

One of the first projects on Cooper's list was *Creation*—a big-budget fantasy about a group of travelers shipwrecked on an island populated by living dinosaurs. Cooper was not very impressed by the film—he felt that the story lacked drama and that the dinosaurs lacked character and were nothing more than "just big beasts running around." He also felt that there was no central figure to focus on, no distinctive main menace. Cooper was, however, impressed with the film's remarkable special effects, which were being created by an equally remarkable man—a hard-drinking Irishman who enjoyed prizefights and horseracing and whose nickname was "O'Bie."

WILLIS O'BRIEN Willis Harold O'Brien was born on March 2, 1886 in Oakland, California. The fourth of six children of a district attorney and his poet wife, the young Willis was a talented artist and a restless youth. He ran away from home at the age of thirteen and spent the next four years in the Pacific Northwest working at a series of odd jobs, including fur trapper and wilderness guide. On one occasion, he acted as a guide for a group of scientists from University of Southern California who wanted to go to the Crater Lake area in search of dinosaur bones. As a result of this experience, O'Brien developed a lifelong interest in dinosaurs and other prehistoric creatures. At the age of seventeen, O'Brien returned home to the Bay Area, where he worked as a draftsman in an architectural firm, a sports cartoonist for the *San Francisco Daily News*, a professional boxer, a railroad brakeman, and a surveyor. In 1913, he went to work for a decorating company. Finding himself with some time to kill one afternoon, O'Brien made a clay model of a boxer. One of his coworkers made a second model and the two men used their creations to stage a mock fight. While watching the models move, O'Brien was struck by the idea that it might be possible to animate a three-dimensional figure for a film.

The motion picture image is an illusion created by photographing a series of individual still pictures of a single moving subject one right after another in rapid succession on a single strip of film. Each still picture captures an incremental piece of the subject's overall movement. When the still pictures are projected onto a screen in rapid succession at the same rate of speed at which they were photographed, the human eye blends all of the images into one to create an impression of continuous action. Early motion picture pioneers found that if they photographed a succession of two-dimensional drawings of the same subject in all of the different poses required to form a single motion, then when the film was projected, it would look like the drawing had come to life and was moving around the screen. This discovery led to the creation of the motion picture cartoon, and O'Brien thought the same principle might be able to be successfully applied to three–dimensional figures as well.

To find out, O'Brien decided to shoot a test film of a dinosaur fighting a caveman. To begin, he built clay figures over articulated (jointed) wooden skeletons. He then set up a little studio on the roof of the Bank of Italy Building in downtown San Francisco, and, with the help of a newsreel photographer friend, photographed the figures in incremental movements at a rate of sixteen frames of film per second (the standard rate at which silent films were photographed and projected). When the test was done, O'Brien showed it to a local film distributor. Impressed, the distributor gave O'Brien $5,000 to turn the test into a fully realized short film. Starting over, O'Brien recreated his figures, this time using metal skeletons. To help the figures retain their shape, the clay was covered with a sheet of rubber. Working in a makeshift studio in the basement of the Imperial Theater on Market Street, O'Brien produced a short film called *The Dinosaur and the Missing Link* (1915). The film was picked up by the Edison Company for distribution. Impressed, Edison officials hired O'Brien to create a series of dinosaur and prehistory-themed shorts using his technique, which he alternately called "dimensional animation" or "animation-in-depth," but which became popularly known as *stop-motion animation*.

In 1918, O'Brien married Hazel Collette. The couple had two sons, but the marriage was an unhappy one from the start. O'Brien's response to his difficult home life was to throw himself intensely into his work. In 1918, O'Brien met Major Herbert M. Dawley, a sculptor from New Jersey who specialized in making dinosaur figures that he then photographed in dramatic poses. Interested in making a film, Dawley enlisted O'Brien's help. The finished short, called *The Ghost of Slumber Mountain* (1919), was distributed by the World Film Corporation and was a big success. Next, O'Brien was hired by the Rothacker Film Manufacturing Company, a company that specialized in making advertising and cartoon shorts. The company's head, Watterson A. Rothacker, wanted to move into features and obtained the rights to Arthur Conan Doyle's 1912 novel *The Lost World*, which told the story of a modern-day journey to a remote Amazonian plateau where living dinosaurs still roam. Rothacker pitched the project to First National Pictures, which agreed to finance the production. *The Lost World* was a more ambitious project than any that O'Brien had yet attempted. To help him make the dinosaur models for the film, O'Brien hired Marcel Delgado, a young grocery store clerk who had come to the United States from Mexico when he was a young boy. O'Brien met Delgado in an art class at the Otis Institute and, impressed with both his talent and his work, offered him a job. Delgado was wary at first, but a visit to O'Brien's studio won him over and he accepted the position, thus beginning a lifelong affiliation with "O'Bie."

The Lost World was released in 1925 and became a worldwide hit. O'Brien spent some time developing several follow-up projects, including a fantasy film called *Atlantis* and an animated version of *Frankenstein*, but neither project came to fruition. O'Brien and his wife separated in 1930. Shortly thereafter, Harry O. Hoyt, director of *The Lost World*, pitched RKO his idea for *Creation*. William LeBaron, Selznick's predecessor, approved the project. Shortly after, O'Brien joined the production, bringing Delgado with him. They had been working on the film for almost a year when Cooper arrived at RKO. With only a few tests and one complete sequence—in which a *Triceratops* chases a sailor, catches him, and then gores him to death—in the can, a quarter of its budget already spent and no end in sight, *Creation* was clearly an out-of-control production.

While Cooper didn't think much of *Creation*, he was fascinated by stop-motion animation. He spent hours discussing the process with O'Brien and began to wonder if it might be possible to use it to bring his gorilla story to the screen in an economical manner. Using animation, the film could be made completely in the studio, with no need for lengthy and costly location trips. Knowing that *Creation* was doomed and eager to interest Cooper in using his services on another picture, O'Brien painted (in collaboration with *Creation* staff artist Byron Crabbe) a portrait of an explorer and a woman being attacked by a gorilla. To increase the dramatic impact of the painting, O'Brien made the gorilla appear a little bit larger than life—about ten feet tall. It is this painting that tends to support the idea that Cooper had not yet decided to "giganticize" his gorilla, because, if he had, then O'Brien certainly would have made the creature much bigger in the painting. It is more likely that it was O'Brien's painting that inspired Cooper to consider increasing the size of his ape from normal to something more, a notion most likely reinforced by the prospect of having the great ape battle the giant dinosaurs from *Creation* rather than the comparatively puny dragons from Komodo (this idea was not only full of tremendous dramatic and visual possibilities, it was also economically appealing, since the dinosaur models had already been built and paid for). Inspired, Cooper began reworking his original story to focus on the adventures of a twenty-foot-tall ape that (in memos to Selznick) he was now referring to as a "Giant Terror Gorilla." Increasing the size of the creature increased the possibilities for mayhem it could create in New York City at the climax of the movie, so Cooper began envisioning scenes in which the Giant Terror Gorilla would run amok in Manhattan, overthrowing cars, stepping on people, and so forth. Knowing all this excitement would require an equally exciting capper, Cooper began looking for a spectacular way to end his story. Whether he got it from the sight of an airplane flying past the top of a tall skyscraper or not, the idea that came to him was to have the Giant Terror Gorilla climb to the top of a tall building and battle a squadron of airplanes before it was finally gunned down. Going to his usual extremes, Cooper decided that the ape should climb not just any tall building, but the tallest building in the world—a title that had just been claimed by the newly opened Empire State Building.

In a memo to Selznick written in December 1931, Cooper proposed canceling *Creation*, retaining O'Brien and his crew, and using them to produce the Giant Terror Gorilla story instead. At this point, Cooper planned to use animation only for full body shots of Kong and planned to use an actor wearing an ape mask and gloves to film the closer shots. Selznick liked Cooper's idea, but the RKO board did not. B.B. Kahane in particular hated it—he thought the idea was far too weird and that the film would be much too expensive to make, especially in those financially precarious times. Down, but not out, Selznick thought he

could persuade the board to approve a test and instructed Cooper to put together a presentation.

Even before Selznick made his pitch, Cooper and O'Brien had already been brainstorming and had come up with a number of scenes they wanted to incorporate into the story. Cooper selected two of these scenes and fleshed them out for the test. In the first, the Giant Terror Gorilla would confront a group of sailors in a jungle as they crossed a log that bridged the two sides of a deep chasm. The giant ape would lift the log and shake it, sending the sailors plunging to the bottom of the gorge, where they would be eaten by an assortment of giant spiders and lizards. In the second scene, the Giant Terror Gorilla would confront a ferocious *Tyrannosaurus* rex that has been menacing the abducted woman. The two prehistoric creatures would engage in a titanic battle from which the oversized ape would emerge the victor. Cooper had O'Brien create four detailed drawings depicting what these proposed scenes would look like on screen, to which Cooper then attached an estimated budget for $10,000 and a

Painting by Willis O'Brien and Byron L. Crabbe of a ten-foot-tall gorilla threatening a hunter and a damsel in distress, done to convince Merian C. Cooper that his gorilla story could be made in a studio using O'Brien's stop motion animation techniques. It is likely that this is the picture that first inspired Cooper to consider making his Terror Gorilla larger than life.

schedule. Selznick presented the proposal to the RKO board, which approved it.

To prepare for the test, Delgado, under O'Brien's supervision, constructed a model of the Giant Terror Gorilla to be used in the test alongside several dinosaur models left over from *Creation*. O'Brien also supervised the construction of two elaborate miniature sets on Stage 3 at RKO's Hollywood lot and readied the optical effects processes that would used in the test. In February 1932, O'Brien set to work animating the miniature scenes (which were referred to by the production as "technical scenes") under Cooper's direction. In late May, Cooper also began directing the live-action portions of the test on the jungle set of *The Most Dangerous Game*, which had begun filming a few weeks earlier. The set included many elements that would prove useful to Cooper, including the bank of a swamp and a chasm spanned by a fallen log.

To people the scenes, Cooper borrowed Robert Armstrong and Fay Wray from the cast of *Game*. Armstrong would play the leader of the expedition and Wray would play the part of the girl the Giant Terror Gorilla carries off. To play the part of a young sailor who survives the giant ape's attack at the log and sets

Concept painting depicting Kong's escape from captivity in Madison Square Garden as indicated in Edgar Wallace's original screenplay. In the final film, the site of Kong's exhibition was moved to a Broadway theater.

out to rescue the kidnapped girl, Cooper originally intended to use *Game* star Joel McCrea, but, put off by McCrea's reluctance to do any sort of vigorous action or stunt work, Cooper instead chose a more agreeable bit-part player that Selznick had recently put under contract named Bruce Cabot. The original plan had been for Cooper to shoot the jungle scene at night while Schoedsack filmed *Game* during the day, but the enthusiastic Cooper began moving onto the set earlier and earlier, which began to irritate Schoedsack. Irritating him even more was the fact that Cooper kept taking Wray and Armstrong away to film special effects tests and shots during the time they were supposed to be shooting *Game*. Cooper and Schoedsack engaged in several shouting matches over these issues, but eventually Cooper finished up and was able to leave his friend in peace.

When shooting of both the full-scale and miniature aspects of the tests were finished, Cooper edited the material together, added in an additional scene cribbed from *Creation* of a *Triceratops* chasing and killing a man, and then finished the piece with some temporary music and sound effects. In late June, Cooper showed the completed test to the RKO board, along with twelve additional concept drawings prepared by O'Brien and staff artists Mario Larrinaga, a former set painter originally from Mexico, and Byron L. Crabbe, a veteran set designer, to illustrate other exciting scenes they were planning for the movie. Although several members of the board, including B. B. Kahane, still didn't like the project and attempted to squelch it, the rest loved the test and voted to approve the project, which was tentatively titled *The Beast*. To avoid any claims of plagiarism from the similarly themed *The Lost World*, RKO bought the rights of the novel from the estate of Arthur Conan Doyle and the rights to the movie from Warner Bros. (which had acquired them when it merged with First National) and the Rothacker Film Manufacturing Company.

Merian Cooper's dream was about to become a reality. Now all he needed was a name for the Giant Terror Gorilla. At the time of the film's release, the story was floated that Cooper adopted the word for gorilla used by an unidentified African (or, in some tellings, East Indian) tribe to name his ape, but *The Dragon Lizards of Komodo* author Douglas Burden—among others—recalled years later that Cooper had simply made the word up. Since it was well known that Cooper was fond of short, one-syllable titles for his films (such as *Grass* and *Chang*) and equally well known that he liked hard-sounding words that began with the letter K, it seems probable that all he did was shorten the name of one of the places he had originally intended to film his gorilla epic and replace the letter "c" with a "k" (something he may have been inspired to do by a 1929 silent adventure film called *The King of the Kongo*). However he came up with the word, Cooper finally christened his creation "Kong."

WRITING THE SCRIPT Hoping for the best, Cooper had assigned Edgar Wallace, the best-selling British mystery and adventure writer, to begin working on a full-length screenplay before the test was even finished. RKO had recently hired Wallace to write original screenplays for the studio. Cooper wanted Wallace because he admired his work and because he knew that having Wallace's name on the film would increase its commercial appeal. Wallace loved the film's concept, so Cooper made a deal for him to write both a screenplay and a novel of the story. Ever the showman, Cooper planned to publish the novel before the movie was released, so the film could be advertised as being "based on the novel by Edgar Wallace." Before beginning, Wallace consulted with Cooper and O'Brien. O'Brien's significant contributions to the evolving storyline cannot be underestimated—he devised many ideas that were incorporated into the final script (including the scene in which Kong slowly plucks off Ann's dress). A legendarily fast writer (he would often write an entire novel in a weekend), Wallace began the script on January 1, 1932, and finished a first draft—titled *The Beast*—on January 5, 1932.

Wallace's script begins aboard a tramp steamer. Danby Denham, a big-game hunter in the tradition of Frank "Bring 'Em Back Alive" Buck, is sailing back from Africa where he has collected an assortment of wild animals he plans to exhibit in a traveling show back in America. Denham is unhappy with the run-of-the-mill animals he has captured and expresses a desire to find some sort of amazing creature that no one has ever seen before. This prompts Englehorn, the ship's captain, to tell Denham about a sea serpent he once saw off the coast of the remote Vapour Island. Intrigued by Englehorn's story, Denham decides to visit the island. Meanwhile, a group of convicts escape from the hold of a prison ship. Taking a young woman named Shirley (alternately referred to as Zena) hostage, the convicts escape in a lifeboat and row toward the very same Vapour Island. Before they reach the shore, a *Brontosaurus* rises from the sea and sinks the lifeboat. Stranded on the island, the convicts have to fight off a variety of dinosaurs and other prehistoric animals. One of the prisoners tries to rape Shirley, but before he is able to, an eighteen-foot-tall gorilla named Kong emerges from the jungle. The convicts fight with Kong, who makes quick work of most of them. Kong then seizes Shirley and carries her off into the jungle. The surviving convicts go after her. Kong confronts the men as they are crossing a log bridge. Kong picks up the log and twists it, causing most of the men to fall into the chasm below, where they are eaten by giant spiders and lizards. Kong then battles a *Tyrannosaurus* rex that is menacing Shirley and defeats the fearsome creature by snapping his jaw. Kong then takes Shirley to his mountaintop lair, where he plucks at her clothes and then makes a nest for her. He then falls asleep in the entrance to the cave, preventing her escape. The next morning, Shirley wakes and washes her face while Kong imitates her. Two of the surviving convicts—John, who has fallen in love with Shirley, and another fellow named Tricks—rescue Shirley and escape with her back to the beach. Kong chases after them and arrives just as Denham is coming ashore. Seeing Kong, an amazed Denham uses a trichloride gas bomb to knock him out and then takes the giant ape back to New York City, where he is caged and put on display in Madison Square Garden (thought to be a more impressive place to present a giant ape than the zoo) along with the rest of Denham's menagerie. While this is happening, Shirley is trapped in a tiger cage by a jealous female animal trainer. Hearing her screams, Kong breaks out of his cage, battles the tigers and then escapes from the Garden, causing much panic and havoc in the streets. John takes Shirley to her hotel room. Kong follows and, after mistaking another woman for Shirley and dropping her to her death, recaptures Shirley and carries her to the top of the Empire State Building. As an electrical storm rages, Kong battles a squadron of fighter planes sent up to kill him before he is finally struck by lightening and falls to his death.

Cooper thought that Wallace's script was a promising enough start, but felt that it still needed a lot of work. Wallace had just begun revisions when he died of pneumonia complicated by diabetes on February 10, 1932. To replace Wallace, Cooper chose RKO contract writer James A. Creelman, who was already working for him on the script for *The Most Dangerous Game*. Cooper worked as closely with Creelman on the next several drafts as he had with Wallace on the first. As the screenplay, now called *The Eighth Wonder*, was reworked, the convicts were eliminated and Denham (now called Carl) and his expedition became the main focus of the story. In an autobiographical switch, Denham's profession was changed from big-game hunter to movie director specializing in natural dramas. The purpose of Denham's trip now became to investigate the mysterious legend of Kong, a native god that supposedly lives on an uncharted island in the Indian Ocean. Denham learns of Kong and the island from an old friend, the skipper of a Norwegian barque. Following the dictum that all legends have a basis in fact, Denham is determined to find the island, which is now unnamed (though it is commonly referred to by fans as Skull Island, Kong's home is never actually called that in the film, although it certainly does contain a place called Skull Mountain), discover the creature that lies at the heart of the Kong legend, and make a movie about it. Shirley is now an actress Denham brings along with him to give the film love interest so that it will gross more at the box office (Cooper's response to the exhibitors' reaction to *Grass* and *Chang*) and her name was changed to Ann Darrow. Convict John became the ship's first mate Jack Driscoll. The location of Kong's escape was changed from Madison Square Garden to Yankee Stadium and finally, because Cooper and O'Brien felt Kong would look more imposing in an enclosed area, to a Broadway theater. Cutesy moments such as the scene in which Kong imitates Shirley as she washes her face were eliminated in order to toughen Kong's character. Cooper wanted Kong to be a fearsome beast on the assumption that the more monstrous the ape was, the more awesome and tragic his fall would be. "I want the fiercest, most brutal, monstrous damned thing that has ever been seen," Cooper was quoted as saying. "I'll have women crying over him before I'm through and the more brutal he is, the more they'll cry at the end." To enhance this idea, the "beauty and the beast" theme suggested in the story was developed much further in subsequent drafts than it was in Wallace's. It was at this point that the film's famous closing line was added. When a police officer remarks that the airplanes got Kong, Denham shakes his head ruefully and replies, "It wasn't the airplanes. It was Beauty killed the Beast."

For part of the time that he was working on *The Eighth Wonder*, Creelman was also writing the screenplay for *The Most Dangerous Game*. At one point, *Game*'s approaching start-date required Creelman to devote all of his time to finishing that script. RKO staff writer Horace McCoy (who would later write the novel *They Shoot Horses, Don't They?*) was brought in to work with Cooper on *The Eighth Wonder*. It was during McCoy's tenure that Cooper decided that prehistoric island should be populated by a tribe of primitive natives. The natives would live behind a giant wall that sealed them off from the rest of the island and would sacrifice young maidens to Kong, who they worshipped like a god. Although these new ideas added a powerful mythic element to the story that it previously lacked, Creelman hated them, feeling that they added even more far-out concepts to a story that already contained too many of them. Despite his reservations, Creelman did his best to make the new ideas work when he returned to the project full-time. As the writing progressed, Cooper had to resist pressure from Selznick and other RKO executives to introduce Kong early in the story. They felt that the audience would get bored waiting for Kong to appear, but Cooper felt that a slow, suspenseful buildup would make the giant ape's eventual entrance all the more exciting.

Cooper was pleased with the way the storyline was developing, but he was unhappy with Creelman's final draft, which he felt was slow-paced, too full of flowery dialogue and description, and too bogged down with heavy-handed exposition scenes. This was not the fast-paced, snappy adventure story Cooper had in mind, so he decided to bring in Ruth Rose to liven things up. Although Rose was a writer, she had never before written a screenplay. This didn't bother Cooper—he felt Rose was qualified for the job because she knew him, understood his style, and, because of her expeditionary experience, could bring a flavor of reality to the script that Cooper felt it presently lacked. Accepting the assignment, Rose streamlined the plot and eliminated all unnecessary lags in the action. For example, she eliminated Creelman's lengthy explanation of how Kong is brought to New York by simply cutting from Kong's island to

The creators of *King Kong* pose with Fay Wray and some of the natives. From left to right: Merian C. Cooper, Willis O'Brien, Wray, and Ernest B. Schoedsack.

Broadway. She enhanced the autobiographical aspects of the script by peppering it with details from actual Cooper-Schoedsack adventures and revising the main characters to more directly reflect their creators—the enthusiastic-to-the-point-of-recklessness Carl Denham was based on Cooper, the gruff-on-the-outside, tender-on-the-inside Jack Driscoll on Ernest Schoedsack, and struggling actress Ann Darrow on Rose herself. Mrs. Schoedsack also rewrote the dialogue to make it simpler and snappier. Finally, she added an opening section to the screenplay showing how Denham discovers Ann and hires her for the job. Rose based this sequence both on the complaints Cooper and Schoedsack received from exhibitors about the lack of romance in their previous pictures and on the real-life experience of Native American actor and vaudeville performer Esteban (Steve) Clemente, a friend of both Cooper and the Schoedsacks. On one occasion, Clemente needed a girl for a knife-throwing act, but no talent agent would help him because the job was thought to be too dangerous. Clemente had no luck filling the position until he met a beautiful, destitute woman outside a coffee shop and offered her a job.

Cooper was thrilled with Rose's final draft. After adding one final touch himself—the "ancient Arabian proverb" that opens the film ("And the Prophet said: And lo! The Beast looked upon the face of Beauty. And stayed its hand from killing. And from that day, it was as one dead.")—Cooper approved the script for production. It was now called *Kong*.

After a five-year separation, Cooper decided that he and Schoedsack would codirect the picture, as they had their "natural dramas." Initially they intended to direct each scene together, but quickly found that, in their years apart, they had developed very different styles of working. Schoedsack liked to move at a brisk pace, but Cooper was just the opposite. Slow and meticulous in setting up a shot, he did take after take until he was satisfied that everything was as perfect as he could make it. Each man became irritated with the other, so they decided that it would be best if they worked separately. Schoedsack would direct the live-action sequences and Cooper would helm the miniature scenes and any special effects–related work.

PREPRODUCTION

As with all movies involving special effects, *King Kong* was going to be expensive. At a time when the average budget for an A-level feature was $200,000, the initial budget for Kong was set at $500,000. Since this was a huge investment for the financially strapped RKO, the board was understandably nervous, but Selznick defended the high cost because he believed in the film and in its box office potential. He did, however, impress upon Cooper the need to keep a tight hold on spending in order to prevent *Kong* from becoming a runaway production like *Creation*. Cooper cleverly augmented the budget by reusing props and sets from other films (rumor had it that one of Cooper's main reasons for wanting to make *The Most Dangerous Game* was because he saw it as a way of charging the costs of the elaborate jungle set he would need for *Kong* to another production).

As with the test, the majority of the live-action scenes were scheduled to be filmed on the soundstages and on the backlot of RKO-Pathè. Location work would be done at San Pedro Harbor and at the Shrine Auditorium in downtown Los Angles. A second unit trip to New York City was also planned. The miniature scenes would continue to be filmed on Stage 3 at RKO's Hollywood lot. Work on the miniature scenes began in midsummer, as soon as the project was approved and the live-action sequences were scheduled to begin filming in August 1932.

As the project's start date neared, Cooper began assembling the people he would need to help him make his movie. In the grand old days of the studio system, each company maintained a roster of talent in all areas who would be assigned to each production by the department supervisors. Top producers could handpick their teams, which Cooper certainly did.

Willis O'Brien was, of course, on board from the beginning. He was given the title of chief technician and put in charge of assembling his own team. Because of the intensive amount of focused labor required over what was expected to be a lengthy shooting schedule, O'Brien had assembled his own self-contained, special effects unit for *Creation*. Although such a practice is standard these days, at a time when creative work was parceled out to a series of departments and job assignments were rigidly controlled by department heads, it was quite unusual. O'Brien brought most of his *Creation* team with him when he began work on *Kong*. In addition to Delgado, Larrinaga, and Crabbe, O'Brien's crew included assistant animators E. B. Gibson and Fred Reefe; technical coordinator Carroll Shepphird; staff artist Ernest Smythe; miniature set builders W. G. White and Orville Goldner, a former puppeteer. Although each member of the team had a specific job, because of the collaborative nature of the work, there was a lot of overlap.

Archie Marshek and Walter Daniels were brought onto the project as "production assistants," although that title does not reflect the true nature of their responsibilities. In the modern era, production assistants are entry-level workers who run errands, answer phones, and make copies. Marshek, a former film editor, was Cooper's right-hand man and acted as a liaison between the production and the optical effects company. Today, he would probably be credited as an associate producer. Walter Daniels was the unit business manager and assisted Schoedsack on the set. Today, he would most likely be referred to as a unit production manager or a first assistant director.

Eddie Linden was assigned to the film as director of photography. With the help of a team of assistants, Linden supervised the lighting on both the miniature and full-scale scenes. Kenneth Peach, Sr., was his uncredited alternate. Vernon Walker, a specialist in effects photography, shot most of the optical and process shots. J. O. Taylor photographed some of the live-action material directed by Cooper at the end of production, including the full-scale portions of the elevated-train sequence.

Working under RKO Art Department head Van Nest Polglase, art director Carroll Clark was in charge of reconfiguring the elaborate jungle set he had designed for *The Most Dangerous Game* to suit the needs of *Kong*. The jungle set had been designed in modular sections that could be rearranged to form a variety of settings, which allowed Clark to create a seemingly endless jungle within the relatively tight confines of a Hollywood soundstage. He simply continued the reconfiguration process to create an all-new jungle for *Kong*. Art Director Al Herman was responsible for designing the rest of the sets, including the Great Wall, the native village, the ship interiors and exteriors, and the Empire State Building. Thomas Little was in charge of decorating the finished sets and George Gabe supplied all of the necessary props. On-set practical and mechanical special effects were handled by Harry Redmond, Jr. Renowned Hollywood costume designer Walter Plunkett and several of his associates created the costumes.

CASTING   One of the most legendary stories concerning the casting of *Kong* is how Cooper approached Fay Wray and told her that she was going to have the "tallest, darkest leading man in Hollywood." Wray thought he was referring to Clark Gable, but, when he showed her a picture of a giant ape climbing up the side of the Empire State Building, she realized that he was talking about someone a little taller and a little darker.

The daughter of an expatriate American rancher and a former schoolteacher, Vina Fay Wray was born in the remote Canadian town of Cardston in 1907, the fourth of six children. Her family moved to Arizona when she was three and then, after her parents separated, Fay was sent with a family friend to live in Southern California. Her mother and siblings followed a year later. The family friend was a photographer who arranged for Fay to get a few bit parts in movies at the local studios. At the age of sizteen, she became a contract player at the Hal Roach Studios and then moved to Universal Pictures, where she appeared in Westerns. In 1926, director Erich Von Stroheim selected Wray to play the lead in his landmark film *The Wedding March*. A contract with Paramount followed, during which Wray appeared in many films, including *The Four Feathers*, the film that introduced her to Cooper and Schoedsack. In 1928, Wray married Academy Award-winning screenwriter and novelist John Monk Saunders (*Wings*, *The Dawn Patrol*), with whom she had a daughter. When her Paramount contract ended, Cooper cast Wray in *The Most Dangerous Game*. After the RKO board approved the Kong test, Cooper went looking for a blonde actress to play the role (Cooper wanted a blonde so that the girl would stand out in contract to Kong's dark pelt) first offered the role of the kidnapped girl to his fiancée, actress Dorothy Jordan, but she declined because she wasn't interested in co-starring with a big animal. He then considered Ginger Rogers and Jean Harlow, but ultimately decided to offer the role to Wray. In her autobiography, *On the Other Hand*, Wray reports that she was taken more by Cooper's enthusiasm than she was by the film itself. That enthusiasm proved sufficient, however, and she accepted the part, covering her naturally dark hair with a blonde wig.

The part of Carl Denham was awarded to veteran character actor Robert Armstrong. Armstrong was born on November 20, 1890, in Saginaw, Michigan. After serving in the infantry in World War I, he enrolled in law school at the

TOP: Vina Fay Wray as Ann Darrow.

BOTTOM: The stars of *King Kong*. From left to right: Frank Reicher as Captain Englehorn, Fay Wray, Bruce Cabot as Jack Driscoll, and Robert Armstrong as Carl Denham.

University of Washington in Seattle, but dropped out so that he could go on tour with a vaudeville troupe. He ended up on Broadway, where for many years he was a celebrated leading man. In 1926, he signed a contract with Pathé and began appearing in silent films, mostly as a supporting player. He joined RKO's stock company when that company bought out Pathé, although he appeared in pictures for other studios as well. In 1932, he played a supporting role as Fay Wray's doomed alcoholic brother in *The Most Dangerous Game*. During the shooting, Armstrong became good friends with both Cooper and the Schoedsacks and when the time came to cast Denham, Armstrong was the natural choice.

Jacques De Bujac, the man chosen to play Jack Driscoll, was born on April 20, 1904, in Carlsbad, New Mexico. After graduating college, De Bujac embarked on an eclectic career path. In a period of approximately eight years, he worked as a dinosaur bone collector on an archaeological dig, a sailor, a sparring partner, oil field worker, civil engineer, surveyor, stockbroker, and nightclub manager. After meeting De Bujac at a party, David O. Selznick signed him as an RKO contract player and changed his name to Bruce Cabot. Cabot first met Cooper when he auditioned for the role of Count Zaroff in *The Most Dangerous Game*. Although he had done a few brief bits prior to *Kong*, Jack Driscoll was Cabot's first starring role. Even so, Cabot quit during the making of the test when some stuntmen convinced him that he was only a stunt double for Joel McCrea, although Cooper quickly talked him into returning.

The steadfast Captain Englehorn was played by the versatile Frank Reicher. Born in Germany on December 2, 1875, Reicher performed on stage in Berlin and London before coming to the United States in 1899, where he appeared regularly on Broadway. Reicher began appearing in silent films in the teens and then became a director, making dozens of films, including a well-regarded ver-

The natives of Kong's island, with Noble Johnson (center) as the Chief and Etta McDaniel (kneeling) as the intended bride of Kong.

sion of Jack London's *The Sea Wolf*. He returned to acting at the end of the silent era, although after the arrival of sound, he would occasionally direct German-language versions of American films for distribution in foreign markets, which is the way studios used to export their product overseas in the days before dubbing.

Two more members of the Cooper-Schoedsack inner circle were cast as the leaders of the Skull Island tribe. The aforementioned Steve Clemente was given the role of the Skull Island tribe's rather insistent Witch Doctor and Noble Johnson played the Native Chief. Johnson was born in 1881 in Missouri. A founder of the Lincoln Motion Picture Company, a company devoted to making "race" pictures for black audiences, Johnson often portrayed menacing sidekicks in studio films such as *The Thief of Bagdad*, *The Mummy*, and *The Most Dangerous Game*.

Popular character actor Victor Wong was cast as Charlie, the ship's cook, and veteran Sam Hardy portrayed Weston, the theatrical agent who refuses to help Denham find a girl. The ill-fated crew of the *Venture* was made up of veteran bit players and stuntmen, including James Flavin, Victor Long, Dick Curtis, Shorty English, Charles Sullivan, Harry Tenbrook, Blackie Whiteford, and Gil Perkins. The woman Kong mistakes for Ann and drops to her death was played by Sandra Shaw (who would later marry Gary Cooper). Etta McDaniel was hired to play the role of the young native woman originally intended to be Kong's bride. Perhaps the two most famous bit parts in *King Kong* were played by the film's codirectors. Figuring that "we might as well kill the son of a bitch ourselves," Cooper played the pilot of the plane that finishes off Kong, and Schoedsack played the gunner who actually does the deed.

MAKING MONSTERS

Merian Cooper may have created Kong, but Marcel Delgado is the man who actually made him.

When the RKO board approved the production of a test reel, the first thing Cooper did was order the construction of a model of his Giant Terror Gorilla. In their initial discussions, Cooper and O'Brien, thinking that it would be hard for an audience to feel much sympathy for a pure beast, thought it might be a good idea to give Kong some human features. Delgado set to work and created a creature that has been described as being a cross between an ape and a hairy man. When Cooper saw the result, he rejected it as being silly-looking and ordered Delgado to try again. The second attempt, which was more ape-like but still had some human qualities, was also rejected as not being fearsome enough. At this point, Cooper decided that Kong should be pure gorilla after all. After Cooper contacted the American Museum of Natural History in New York to obtain a precise description of an adult male gorilla, Delgado created a final version that met with Cooper's approval.

To fashion Kong, Delgado began by sculpting a clay model that depicted what he wanted the final model to look like. Next, he created an armature—a jointed metal skeleton that could be moved into different positions as the scene dictated. Based on a design by O'Brien, Delgado created an eighteen-inch-tall armature for Kong out of high-tempered dural aluminum. He began with two blocks, one each for the hip and shoulder. The two blocks were connected with a spine that was hinged so that it could be moved backwards and forwards and from side to side. Ball-jointed arms and legs were then attached to the shoulder and hip blocks. Kong's hands and feet were made from smaller aluminum blocks fitted with jointed fingers and toes made from steel. A mold was made from a wooden carving of Kong's skull, which was then cast from aluminum and attached to the rest of the body with a jointed neck. When the armature was finished, Delgado wrapped it with layers of cotton sheeting to build up the body and then cut pieces from a sheet of foam rubber, which he glued on top of the cotton to define Kong's muscles. Delgado based Kong's shape on that of a real gorilla, but gave him a streamlined torso—real gorillas have a rather pronounced belly and rear end, which Delgado eliminated because he thought they could make Kong appear awkward or comical. Delgado then wrapped the body with sheet latex to create the outer skin.

Next, holes were drilled into the aluminum skull and threaded with thin, bendable wires. Lips, eyebrows, and a nose made from rubber were then attached to these wires. When the features were moved into different positions, the wires would hold them in place, which allowed the animators to create Kong's facial expressions. Eyeballs made of glass were set into sockets in the skull. Delgado painted liquid latex over the skull and features to create Kong's face, which was then detailed with bits of cotton that were also painted with liquid latex. Finally, Delgado glued strips of pruned rabbit fur to Kong's body to create his pelt, which was then smoothed down with glycerin. Delgado

didn't want to use rabbit fur because he knew it would retain the impression of the animators' fingerprints, but he was overruled. When the first rushes of Kong were screened, Delgado's worst fears were confirmed when the animators' fingerprints could be seen rippling across Kong's pelt. Schoedsack was reported as saying that when he saw this, he thought the whole project was sunk. But then, as the oft-repeated story goes, an RKO executive watching the test approvingly cried out: "Look! Kong is angry—his fur is bristling!" A minus had been turned into a plus and the day was saved.

The model based on Delgado's third design was used in the initial test sequence and met with overwhelming approval. During filming, Kong's rubber skin dried out quickly under the hot studio lights and had to be frequently replaced. This was a time-consuming process, so when the full-length production was green-lit, Delgado created a second Kong with slightly longer arms to be used in rotation with the original to prevent any long delays in filming. Whenever the skin on the heads was replaced, Delgado had to rebuild the faces from scratch. As a result, Kong's appearance changes subtly throughout the film. Both models were built on a scale of one-inch-equals-one-foot to simulate a gorilla that was eighteen feet tall. These models were used in the jungle sequences, but when the New York sequences were filmed, Cooper felt that they looked too small in comparison to the miniature buildings, so he ordered Delgado to build an additional two-foot-tall model that would make Kong appear to be a more imposing twenty-four-foot-tall as he ran amok in Manhattan (there is some evidence to suggest that the large model was used in the sacrifice scene and in some shots in the cave and cliff Scenes as well). A stickler for accuracy and consistency, O'Brien protested the change, but Cooper dismissed his concerns. He felt Kong should appear to be whatever size looked best for the scene. While this may not have been technically correct, it proved dramatically right and, for Cooper, that's all that mattered. The twenty-four-inch Kong had a rounder head, longer arms, and smoother and darker fur than the other two models and looks distinctly different than the other two onscreen. A fourth Kong model—which was made of lead and fur and was only a few inches long—was created for the long shot in which Kong tumbles down the side of the Empire State Building at the end of the film.

THE BIG HEAD   To film close-ups of Kong chomping on Skull Island natives and Manhattan Island New Yorkers, a full-size bust—encompassing Kong's head, shoulders, and top of the chest—was constructed on the RKO lot. With E. B. Gibson in charge of construction, the basic frame of the bust was made from wood and cloth and equipped with metal levers and hinges; an air compressor designed by Fred Reefe was used to open Kong's mouth and manipulate his facial features. Twelve-inch eyeballs were installed in the Big Head's eye sockets and fangs ten inches long were placed in the mouth. Marcel Delgado made the giant's face and chest from rubber and covered the rest of the structure with pruned bearskin. The finished product was placed on a flatcar so it could be moved from set to set. During filming, three crew members were placed inside the bust to operate the mechanisms. The scale of the bust did not

ABOVE: The Big Head under construction.

OPPOSITE: The two eighteen-inch-tall Kong models created by Marcel Delgado.

match that of any of the other models—fully realized, the Big Head Kong would have been somewhere between thirty and forty feet tall.

THE BIG HAND   Gibson, Reefe, and Delgado also created two full-scale versions of Kong's right arm and hand for the film. Both were built from steel, fleshed out with sponge rubber, and covered in rubber and bearskin. The first hand was nonarticulated and used for the scene in which Kong reaches for Jack while he is trapped in the cave. Mounted on a crane, it was rolled in and out of shots by grips. The second hand had articulated fingers and was mounted on a lever so that it could be raised or lowered. This version was used to hold and lift Fay Wray in the many shots in which Kong takes Ann in hand.

THE BIG LEG   A nonarticulated leg was created in the same manner as the Big Hands and used for the shots in which Kong stomps on the natives who get in his way. The Big Leg was mounted on a crane so that it could be lifted up and lowered down onto the actors playing Kong's victims.

THE DINOSAURS   The dinosaur models were constructed in the same fashion as the Kong models. Delgado based his designs on the images from the famed dinosaur murals at the American Museum of Natural History in New York City painted by Charles R. Knight. He also received advice and input from the museum's vertebrate paleontologist Dr. Barnum Brown, with whom O'Brien had been consulting since his Edison days.

With the exception of the armature used for the original Kong model, all of the armatures were manufactured in the RKO machine shop. As with Kong, all of the models were built up using cotton and foam rubber and then covered in sheet latex, which was then detailed using cotton and liquid latex. To simulate breathing in some of the reptiles, football bladders were placed inside the models and a specially designed pump used to inflate and deflate the bladders in small increments during the animation process. All of the dinosaurs were built on the one-inch-equals-one-foot scale and ranged from eighteen inches to three feet in length. The creatures were all depicted as being much larger than they probably were in real life, but the filmmakers were far more interested in dramatic impact than they were in scientific accuracy.

Aside from Kongs, the film's various creatures included:

The Stegosaurus Two different models were used in the film, both originally built for *Creation*. For both, the dorsal plates were made from wood, attached to the armature, and covered in liquid latex.

The Triceratops There were three *Triceratops* models—one of a mature cow and two of its offspring. Like the *Stegosaurus*, all three were originally made for *Creation*.

The Brontosaurus There were three different incarnations of the *Brontosaurus* used in the film. The first was a three-foot-long articulated model. The second was a large articulated model of the creature's head and neck that could be used for more detailed animation. The third was a mechanical model mounted on wheels that could be rolled in and out of a studio tank

ABOVE: Marcel Delgado (right) at work on the full-scale portion of the Pteranodon.

OPPOSITE: A wooden sailor carved by John Cerasoli faces off against one of the eighteen-inch Kong models in a test shot from the log sequence.

for use in water scenes. (In recent years, scientists have renamed the *Brontosaurus*. It is now known as *Apatosaurus*. However, since it was referred to as a *Brontosaurus* by the film's makers, so shall we refer to it here.)

The Tyrannosaurus rex Like the *Stegosaurus* and the *Triceratops*, Kong's most fearsome opponent was also built for *Creation*. The creature's upright stance was based on the famous skeleton in the American Museum of Natural History in New York that was reconfigured in the 1980s after scientists decided that the creature really leaned forward and ran parallel to the ground, using its giant tail (which in all likelihood did not wiggle) as a counterbalance. (There has been much debate over the years as to whether the creature Kong battles in the film is a *Tyrannosaurus* or its smaller, lighter cousin the *Allosaurus*. The script refers to the creature simply as "The Meat Eater." Cooper referred to it as an *Allosaurus* and, like that fearsome lizard, the creature in Kong has three fingers. However, O'Brien and Delgado always referred to the monster as a *Tyrannosaurus*. Since most fans do also, we will too.)

The Arsinoitherium Like the *Stegosaurus* dorsal plates, the two horns on the *Arsinoitherium*'s snout were made of wood, attached to the armature and covered with liquid latex.

The Styracosaurus This dinosaur resembled a *Triceratops* with long, tapered spikes extending out from the back.

The Elasmosaurus This is the "snake with legs" that Kong wrestles when he first enters his lair. Like Kong's fingers, this creature's legs were made from jointed steel.

The Pteranodon This is the flying dinosaur that plucks Ann from the ledge overlooking Skull Island. A full-scale replica of the creature's legs and claws were built for the shots of Fay Wray struggling in its grip, and an extremely tiny model was built for the shots in which the creature is seen flying in the distance.

The Giant Vulture This is the creature seen snacking on the T-rex's carcass as Jack slips past in search of Ann.

The Giant Spiders, Lizards, and Octopus-like Creature These are the creatures from the pit that devour the members of the search party after Kong knocks them off the log.

The Birds A series of miniature birds were created and animated to flit in and out among the treetops and mountain peaks of Skull Island.

Because prolonged exposure to the hot studio lights played such havoc with the creatures' rubber skin, sculptor John Cerasoli carved wooden replicas of each model. The replicas were painted to match the originals and were used as stand-ins during test shoots and lineups.

WOODEN ACTORS Cerasoli also carved a six-inch wooden model of Fay Wray for use in long shots in which Kong carries Ann. Six-inch models of Jack Driscoll, various sailors, natives, and Manhattanites were also created. All of the wooden figures had joints that locked into place so that they could be posed in a variety of positions.

OTHER MODELS Both a floating and a nonfloating miniature model of Englehorn's ship—which was renamed the SS *Venture* at some point after the script was finished—were constructed for the film, along with several miniature subway cars and a series of model fighter planes in various sizes.

OPTICAL EFFECTS

One of the biggest challenges facing the *Kong* team was to integrate the live-action footage with the miniature work in ways that would convince an audience that an eighteen-inch-tall puppet was actually an eighteen-foot-tall gorilla performing alongside full-scale people in full-scale settings. If the team could pull this off, then *Kong* would have the potential to be a monster-sized hit. If not, then it could be nothing but a gargantuan failure.

Since the birth of the cinema, artists and technicians had been experimenting with methods to successfully combine separately filmed images into one. There were two primary reasons they sought to accomplish this. One was practical—to place actors in settings that were too distant, too dangerous, or otherwise impractical. The second was fantastic—to create the illusion that a magical, supernatural, or otherwise physically impossible feat had been photographed and put on screen. Initially, one of the few ways filmmakers could manage such a feat was to intercut footage of the actors with footage of the desired setting or effect. This is the technique Willis O'Brien used in his early dinosaur films. Another approach was *double exposure*. To create a superimposition, a background scene was photographed on a piece of raw (unexposed) negative. The negative was then rewound and reused to photograph a foreground subject (usually an actor or a prop of some sort). When the negative was developed and printed, the end result was a composite image in which the foreground image appeared over the background. The main drawback to this approach was that the foreground subject always appeared somewhat transparent in the final composite. While this was a suitable method for creating some effects such a ghosts and dream images, its overall potential was understandably limited.

As film technique advanced, *split-screen matting* was developed. Split-screen (aka *stationary matte*) is a process that places separately photographed images alongside one another in the same frame, usually in side-by-side or top-and-bottom combinations. The word "matte" means mask. In photography, a matte is an opaque object placed in front of a camera lens that prevents light from striking and thus exposing a certain portion of the raw negative. Early mattes were made from cardboard or paper. Later, they were painted onto clear pieces of glass and placed in a holder on the front of the camera. When the process was first originated, a matte was placed in front of the camera lens and the first portion of the composite was photographed. The film was then rewound and a second matte that covered the part of frame that had already been exposed was placed in front of the lens. The next portion of the composite—which might be filmed in a completely different location from the first portion or else consist of a painting, a miniature, or a special effect of some sort—would then be photographed onto the virgin part of the raw negative. Care was taken to align the two images along some sort of natural edge—the end of a wall, a horizon line, and so on—where the join wouldn't be noticed. When the film was developed, the two images would appear together in the same frame, blended inconspicuously along the matte line. That line was often straight, which made it easier to align but also easier to spot. On occasion, however, a more random line was employed, making the split much harder to spot. This was called a *soft-edged matte*. When creating a split-screen matte, the edges of both mattes had to be carefully matched to make sure that there wasn't a gap between them—which would cause a black line to appear in the final composite—or that there was no overlap between them—which would cause a white line to appear in the final composite. Although O'Brien used split screen matting to effectively combine actors with dinosaurs in *The Lost World*, the process did have some significant limitations, the primary one being that no movement across the join was possible. This meant that characters and objects were confined to their portion of the composite, which limited the ways in which shots could be composed, intra-frame action could be staged, and characters could interact. While Cooper and O'Brien planned to use all three of these techniques to create *Kong*'s illusions, they also wanted to go further. One of their main interests was to find ways that would allow characters to appear in front of or behind one another in the same frame, which they felt would go a long way in convincing an audience that the miniature and full-scale action was all happening at the same time and in the same place.

To create shots in which the actors appeared in front of the animated monsters, the filmmakers had two basic approaches available to them. The first was *rear-screen projection*, a process in which a previously filmed background scene is projected from behind onto a translucent screen that allowed the image to appear on both sides. Actors perform in front of the screen as the camera photographs them and the background image together in the same frame, merging the two. The benefit of the rear-screen process to a film like *Kong* was obvious—animated miniatures could be projected onto a large screen behind the actors, making them appear to be enormous in size. Unfortunately, although the concept had been around since the early days of cinema, it had proven enormously difficult to perfect. To begin with, the background projector had to register the film—hold each frame in place in front of the projection beam—in a rock-steady manner in order to prevent the background image from jumping around behind the actors. Traditional projectors had registration mechanisms that held the film relatively loosely. While this was sufficient for theatrical projection, it produced an image that was much too shaky to use in rear-projection. After years of experimentation, the problem was finally solved by installing the registration mechanism from a film camera—which uses a set of retractable pins to hold the film solidly in the aperture during exposure—into the rear-screen projector. A second problem was that the shutter in the camera and the shutter in the projector had to be synchronized precisely or else the background image would flicker, ruining the illusion. This problem was solved by interlocking the motors in the camera and the projector so that they both opened and closed their shutters at the same time. The main challenge in perfecting the process, however, was to develop an acceptable screen on which to rear project the image. The first rear screens were made out of glass, were limited in size, and broke easily. Their biggest flaw, however, was that they were incapable or reproducing a full range of tones – that is they couldn't generate dark blacks or bright whites. As a result, rear-projected images that utilized a glass screen tended to be gray, flat, and dull. They were also prone to "hot spots"—intensely bright image at the center of the screen—and "fall off"—a dimming of the image at the edges. The result looked terrible and, since no one had been able to come up with a screen that corrected these flaws, Cooper and O'Brien did not feel that rear screen was a viable option.

Their second option was to employ a *traveling-matte* process. Unlike a split-screen matte, in which the join between the composite images is static, a traveling-matte blends the foreground and background images along a moving line that adjusts itself frame by frame according to the movement of the foreground silhouette. In the early 1930s, there were two ways to create a traveling matte. The first was the Dunning process. Created by seventeen-year-old C. Dodge Dunning in 1925, this complex technique (aka The Dunning-Pomeroy process) was the primary method used in the early 1930s. To understand how the process worked, it is first necessary to understand how a black-and-white film image is generated.

Motion picture film is essentially a strip of cellulose coated with an emulsion made up of silver particles suspended in gelatin. When light reflected from the subject being photographed strikes the silver particles, they are activated. When the camera negative is developed, the activated areas turn white or gray, depending on the intensity of the light that struck the negative in that spot (the more intense the light, the whiter the spot). The unactivated areas turn black. When a positive print is made from this negative, the white areas turn black, the gray areas remain gray, and the blacks become clear. When the film is projected, the dark areas on the print block the projector beam, creating a black or a gray shadow on the screen. The clear areas allow the projector beam to pass through and illuminate the screen, thus creating the white portion of the black, gray, and white image.

At the start of the Dunning process, a background scene called a "plate" would be photographed. The negative was then developed and a positive print made from it. The silver particles that made up the gray and black areas of the print were then bleached away and replaced with an orange dye. The clear areas of the print remained clear. When the time came to photograph the foreground image, the orange print was placed into the camera in front of a fresh roll of negative called a duplicate negative or "dupe." This process was called *bi-packing*. The foreground action was then filmed in front of a large white screen. The screen was lit with blue light and the foreground subject was lit with orange light. When the foreground subject was photographed, the light reflected from it passed through the orange-dyed print and struck an image of it on the dupe. At the same time, the orange portions of the dyed print blocked the blue light coming from any area of the backing not blocked by the foreground subject, although it did pass through the clear areas. As a result, a negative image of the background plate on the dyed print was imprinted on the dupe, surrounding the image of the foreground subject. The end result was a composite in which the foreground subject and the background plate had been seamlessly merged. While the Dunning process was workable, it had a significant number of drawbacks. The main one was that the orange light coming from the foreground image sometimes had difficulty penetrating the darker areas of the dyed print. This caused transparent "holes" to appear in the foreground image on the final print. Also, since the process was all done in-camera, it was impossible to precisely coordinate the action of the foreground with that in the background. Filmmakers dealt with this problem by running a print of the background action on a Moviola (a portable editing machine) while they were filming the foreground action and signaling the actors to move at the appropriate moments by ringing a small bell. While this system worked, it was obviously not ideal. Because two images were combined in the camera, it was also impossible to determine whether or not all of the elements of the composite were properly aligned until after the film was processed. If they weren't, there was no recourse except to discard the shot and start all over again. Finally, because the process required the use of two different types of colored light, it wasn't suitable for outdoor or large-scale shots. For those scenes and others requiring white light, the team had to use another traveling-matte technique called the Williams Double Matting process.

The Williams system was invented in 1916 by visual effects pioneer Frank D. Williams, who refined the process several times in the ensuing years. As with the Dunning process, a background plate was photographed first. Next, the foreground subject was illuminated with white light and photographed in front of a white screen illuminated with blue light. The negative image was then printed onto a strip of high contrast black-and-white film, which eliminated all of the grays and pictorial details and turned the image areas either pure black or pure white. The end result was a strip of film containing a black silhouette of the foreground subject against a stark white background. This was called a *holdout matte*. A reverse print of the holdout matte was then made on another piece of high contrast black-and-white film, resulting in a second strip of a film containing a white silhouette of the foreground subject against a black background. This was called a *cover matte*. Once the mattes had been completed, a positive print of the background plate was bi-packed with the holdout matte and printed onto a duplicate negative. The holdout matte blocked the printing light and prevented an area in the exact shape of the foreground subject from being exposed on the dupe, thus creating a "hole" in the background. The duplicate negative was rewound and a print of the foreground subject was then bi-packed with the cover matte and printed onto the dupe. The cover matte blocked the backing but allowed the foreground image through to be exposed onto the dupe. If all went well, the foreground subject fit precisely into the "hole" in the background plate in the same way a final piece fits into a jigsaw puzzle.

The Williams system produced better, more consistent composites than the Dunning process, could be used in a wider variety of situations, and eliminated the transparent holes in the foreground images that plagued the Dunning process. Despite these advantages, it too had some serious pitfalls. As with the Dunning process, the composite could not be checked until it came back from the lab. Another potential pitfall was matte misalignment. When the foreground and background images were composited onto a duplicate negative, there needed to be a fine line no thicker than a human hair between the two images. In order to achieve an exact fit, the mattes had to be extremely precise. This precision was hard to achieve because matte building is an imprecise science at best. To create a sufficiently dense mask, the mattes sometimes had to be overexposed. This caused them to "spread"—to be bigger than they should have been. If a holdout matte was too big, it left a noticeable black outline around the foreground image in the final print. On other occasions, mattes had to be copied multiple times in order to make them sufficiently dark, which caused their edges to soften and led to an overlap between the mattes. If this happened, the cover matte would cut the edges off of the foreground subject, giving it a chopped-off look in the final composite. If the mattes were almost the right size, but the line between the images was just a little too thick, then a sliver of the foreground image and the background plate were double exposed together in the same spot, causing a white halo to appear around the foreground image. This effect was called "fringing." The Williams system's biggest drawback, however, was that the composites were not done in the camera, but were instead assembled on a device known as an *optical printer*. A combination projector and camera, the optical printer allowed previously filmed images to be manipulated in a variety of ways and then rephotographed onto dupe negatives, giving filmmakers the capability to create a range of optical effects, including fades and dissolves. Although optical printers had been in use for a while, they were usually handmade devices that were clumsy, inefficient, and produced inconsistent results, which made many special effects technicians and cinematographers hesitant to use them. The fact that *Kong*'s success was so dependant on the success of the composites made O'Brien and Cooper especially wary.

With no standout choice available to them as the start of filming approached, O'Brien and Cooper decided to proceed with the Dunning process and hope for the best. However, just as work began on the log scene, a technological breakthrough was announced that would turn out to be of enormous benefit to the production. Dispensing with glass, Sidney Saunders, the head of RKO's paint department, had constructed a new kind of rear-projection screen by stretching a sheet of acetate across a large wooden frame and then painting it with a layer of cellulose. At 16 x 20 ft., Saunder's screen was bigger than previous rear screens had been and generated a much better image, reproducing a full range of tones from the deepest black to the brightest white. Because the acetate was flexible, it could also be adjusted to minimize both hot spots and fall off. Suddenly, rear-screen projection had become a viable option after all. Impressed by some of Saunders's tests, Cooper and O'Brien immediately began using the process on *Kong*. In fact, they used it in the second scene they shot—Kong's fight with the *Tyrannosaurus* rex.

As good as the rear-screen process now was, the limited size of the screen meant it couldn't be used for every composite shot. For those that required a wider view than the rear screen could provide, the production would still need to employ a traveling-matte process. As the main shoot began, the producers were still planning to use the Dunning process throughout, but that would change when another technological innovation was announced. Vernon Walker's assistant Linwood G. Dunn had designed and engineered a new and much-improved optical printer that was a huge leap forward from previous machines of its kind. It was more precise, more reliable, and had a wider range of capabilities than any other printer in operation at that time. Most significantly for *Kong*, because Dunn's machine was capable of generating sharper mattes and aligning them more precisely, it was possible to get a much better result from the Williams system. In fact, Dunn's initial composites were so impressive on the first Williams scene that he produced (Kong pushing open the gate at the Great Wall) that the production abandoned the Dunning process and began using the Williams system exclusively. The rest of the film industry soon followed suit and within a few years the Dunning process had become obsolete. Dunn's success also enabled him to talk an initially wary O'Brien into abandoning his time-consuming, trial-and-error approach to optical effects and to make more use of the optical printer. From then on, Dunn and his associate William Ulm created most of the film's optical effects—including split screens, traveling mattes, and dissolves—in the lab. Because the optical printer allowed each element of an effect to be processed individually, if a problem occurred, only the offending element needed to be redone, rather than the entire composite. This eliminated the need to do so many retakes, protected the original negative, and increased the rate of effects production considerably. Dunn's invention revolutionized the industry. In-camera opticals became a thing of the past and most visual effects from then on were produced on the optical printer.

For shots in which the full-scale actors were required to appear alongside or behind the animated figures, Cooper and O'Brien planned to employ a variation of the rear-screen projection concept called miniature projection that O'Brien had been developing since 1928. In this process, a tiny screen—made of rubber because the cellulose used on the large-scale rear screen was too grainy to be used with small-scale images—was positioned inside a miniature set. A projector was positioned behind the set, interlocked with the production camera and equipped with a *stepper motor* (a motor that allowed a strip of film to be projected one frame at a time). Previously filmed footage of full-size actors would then be projected onto the screen and photographed on a frame-by-frame basis along with the animation. Because the image was projected from behind, the animated figures could pass in front of it without disruption, increasing the illusion that all of the figures, large and small, were existing and interacting in the same space. Several screens could be used to introduce a number of full-scale elements into a single miniature scene. O'Brien had done some preliminary test shots with the process while he was working on *Creation*, and refined the process further for *Kong*. He received a patent for his invention in 1933 and used it in all of his future work.

Another visual effect technique the production planned to employ was *glass painting*, a method of augmenting existing sets and locations that had been around since the early days of the cinema. To begin this process, a minimal portion of a set was built on a soundstage or a location. An artist would then paint the rest of the set on a large piece of glass, leaving a transparent hole in the painting where the set was supposed to appear. When the time came for the scene to be filmed, the painting would be placed between the camera and the set and precisely aligned so that the set would be visible through the hole. If photographed correctly, the set and the painting would be combined into a single image. A variation on this idea was the *foreground miniature*, in which a model would be placed between the camera and the set, aligned and photographed in the same way that the glass painting was. Both were ideal and economic ways to place actors in enhanced or fantastic settings. Finally, the team planned to use a technique called *rotoscoping*—a process in which a cartoon image is painted over the actions of a real figure.

ABOVE: A present-day photo of the Culver Studios, formerly RKO-Pathé, where the live action scenes for *King Kong* were filmed.

OPPOSITE: Filming the first scene in the native village on the RKO-Pathé backlot.

PRINCIPAL PHOTOGRAPHY

The filming of the live-action portions of *Kong* occurred in several stages over an eight-month period.

MAY–JUNE 1932 The first live-action scenes shot for *Kong* were those done for the test reel in late May and early June 1932. As previously mentioned, these scenes were all directed by Merian Cooper and filmed on *The*

Most Dangerous Game jungle set constructed on Stage 11 at RKO-Pathé Studios. Because the jungle set was due to be struck soon after the completion of *Game*, Cooper filmed all of the other jungles scenes at this time as well, even though many of them would not appear in the test. Because Ruth Rose had not yet begun her rewrite of the script, Cooper worked from the most recent James Creelman draft, which included some scenes that would later be dropped. Since the final dialogue had not been approved, many of the lines in these scenes were improvised.

The test reel began with the scene in which Denham and Jack lead the search party into the jungle and discover Kong's footprint in the mud. The next two scenes—in which the members of the search party build a raft to float across the swamp and in which they later run out of the swamp to escape the *Brontosaurus*—were filmed on a section of the *Game* jungle set that had been nicknamed Fog Hollow. The next scene was shot in an area called the ledge set. Here Cooper filmed shots of the search party as it watches a fight between Kong and the *Triceratopses*, as well as shots of the men scattering as one of the *Triceratopses* begins chasing them. A brief scene was also filmed in which one of the sailors gets separated from the group. This bit was meant to lead into the sequence from *Creation* in which one of the *Triceratopses* chases a man and

gores him to death. Since the actor in the *Creation* scene was wearing striped trousers, the Kong actor had to wear them as well so that the shots would match. (The character was actually called the Striped-Trousers Sailor in the shooting script.)

Next on the schedule was the log scene, which began with a shot of the search party spotting Kong as he carries Ann across the log. As the sailors watch Kong go, the *Arsinoitherium* charges out from the jungle behind them. Denham hides in the bushes as Jack and the rest of the men escape by running out onto the log, at which point Kong returns. Jack grabs a vine and climbs down to a cave in the cliff wall, but the rest of the search party, their retreat blocked by the *Arsinoitherium*, are trapped on the log as Kong upends it and begins dislodging them. They fall down into the pit below, where they are devoured by giant spiders, giant lizards, and an octopus-like creature. One of the giant spiders tries to climb up a vine to get Jack, but he cuts the vine and sends it crashing back down into the pit. After disposing of the last sailor, Kong tries to pluck Jack from the cave, but Jack keeps him at bay by stabbing him with a knife. Ann's screams distract Kong and he departs. Jack climbs back up to the top of the cliff as Denham comes out of hiding. They agree that Denham will return to the Great Wall to get more gas bombs, while Jack will continue to follow Kong and attempt to rescue Ann. The side views of the scene were filmed on miniature sets, but the views looking across the ravine— including the shots in which Jack climbs down a vine to the cave and those in which Kong shakes the men off the log—were filmed on a full-scale log in the full-scale set in front of a blue backing so that the eighteen-inch Kong could be added in later. The log was turned by offscreen grips and lifted by offscreen ropes, while the sailors tumbled off into nets just below the frame line. For the close shots of Kong trying to grab Jack, the nonarticulated Big Hand was used. Grips moved it quickly in and out of the shot as Cabot stabbed at it with a knife. The scene in which Jack climbs up and talks to Denham was also filmed on the full-scale ravine, as were the shots of Denham starting back to the wall.

Some of Ann's reactions to Kong's battle with the *Tyrannosaurus* were also filmed on the jungle set, as were shots of Jack following Kong's trail at the end of the sequence. These were the last shots to appear in the test. The final shots filmed on Stage 11 were those of Jack and Ann running back toward the wall after they have escaped from Kong.

JULY 1932 After the RKO board gave Cooper the green light, art director Al Herman and his crew began preparing the native village set, where the bulk of the nonjungle island scenes would be filmed. Knowing that this portion of the film would be shot first, Cooper instructed Ruth Rose to begin her script rewrite with these scenes.

Meanwhile, Schoedsack and cinematographer Edwin Linden took a small second unit crew to New York City, where they filmed some establishing shots of the Harbor. Following this, the unit went to the U.S. Naval Air Station at Floyd Bennett Field in Brooklyn to film shots of the fighter planes taking off to begin their battle with Kong. Since Manhattan was not visible from the airfield, a glass painting of the skyline was incorporated into one of these shots in order to let the audience know where the planes were headed. Following the take-offs, the unit filmed the long shots of the fighter planes flying in formation as they approached the Empire State Building. Next Linden and Shoedsack went aloft in a Curtiss-Wright Travel Air camera plane to film closer shots of the planes in flight and performing various maneuvers that would later be intercut with the miniature footage of Kong atop the building. Most of these in-flight shots were filmed over Bennett Field and were initially hard to capture because the planes flew so quickly past the camera that they couldn't be photographed. Schoedsack had to teach the pilots how to slow down and stagger their flight paths so that they could stay in camera range long enough for him to get the shots. The unit finished up in New York by going up into the Empire State Building itself and filming views of the city that could be projected behind Kong in some of the miniature shots. Schoedsack also filmed a view looking straight down from the top of the building to be used for a shot of Kong falling to the street below. Schoedsack persuaded the owners of the Empire State Building to provide him with the architectural plans for the mooring mast at the top of the building that Al Herman could use to construct a mock-up on a soundstage back at RKO.

AUGUST 1932 Principle photography on the full production of *Kong* officially began in August 1932 on a stretch of beach in San Pedro, just south of Los Angeles, with the filming of the landing party's arrival on the island. Outrigger canoes used in King Vidor's South Seas epic *Bird of Paradise* (1932) were brought to the location to serve as transportation for the natives. The live-action portions of the scene in which Denham fells Kong with a gas bomb were also filmed at this time.

The main unit then moved to the RKO-Pathè backlot in Culver City to film all of the scenes involving the native village and the Great Wall. The seventy-five-foot tall wall was fashioned from the remains of a set representing the interior of the Roman Council House built for Cecil B. DeMille's passion play *The King of Kings* (1927). As was common in the silent era, interior sets without ceilings were often constructed outside so that natural light could be used to illuminate scenes. The wall had a twenty-foot-wide opening in the center. In *The King of Kings*, the opening was filled with a curtain that was ripped in two when Jesus died. For *Kong*, the curtain was replaced by two large wooden doors that were held in place by a massive restraining bolt. A large gong was placed on top of the wall and the surface of the structure was detailed with vines and pseudo-primitive carvings. The original set also contained a majestic set of steps and a series of columns that allegedly held up the council house's non-existent roof. To prepare for *Kong*, the columns were chopped off at the base and grass huts from a Polynesian village set built elsewhere on the backlot for *Bird of Paradise* (1932) were placed in front of the wall to create the native village.

The first scenes shot on the set were the landing party's arrival in the village, their discovery by the natives, the haggling over Ann, and the search party's

A terrified Ann is sacrificed to Kong

anxious retreat. The sacrifice scene—in which Ann is led through the gate, then tied to an altar, and left for Kong—was filmed next. This was the biggest and most spectacular scene of the live-action shoot. Hundreds of extras were assembled for the nighttime shoot; 350 lights were required to illuminate it; and the Culver City Fire Department was on hand to make sure that the native torches didn't burn down the lot.

The centerpiece of the sequence is a breathtaking moving shot that begins with a long view of the gates being opened and then swoops down into the set to follow Ann as she is led up the steps, through the gate, and tied to an altar on the other side. To achieve this shot, the camera was mounted on a high crane that was rolled forward and lowered down as the action progressed. Intercut with a reverse-angle moving shot of Ann being led by the natives and other details of the ceremony, the shot brilliantly portrays Ann's nightmarish conveyance from the world of the real into the world of Kong.

In a respite from all of the spectacle, a brief daytime interlude in which Denham returns from the jungle and tells Englehorn about the search party's encounter with Kong was filmed, followed by the scene in which Jack and Ann return and Denham conceives his half-mad idea to capture Kong. Hundreds of extras were again on hand for the filming of the scene in which Kong breaks through the wall and rampages through the village in search of Ann. The script originally called for Kong to reach though the half-open gates and throttle a few sailors before knocking the gates down on top of them. For practical and safety reasons, the scene was rewritten so that all Kong would have to do was push open the gates instead. To film the scene, off-screen tractors pulled open the doors as the extras playing natives and sailors leaned into them and pretended to try to keep Kong out. The giant ape himself was added into the scene later. Schoedsack also shot scenes of natives running to and from the gate, as well as the individual vignettes of the havoc and mayhem that ensue as Kong advances toward the beach.

As Schoedsack worked on the village scenes, Cooper worked on the soundstages, filming two scenes for the New York sequence. In the first, Kong reaches into a hotel window and grabs hold of a woman talking on the telephone that he mistakes for Ann. In the second, a group of men playing poker get quite a shock when Kong appears in their window. These scenes were filmed using the Big Hand and the Big Head, but Cooper didn't like the way the Big Head looked in the finished shots—he didn't think it looked like Kong was really hanging off the side of a building.

When these scenes were finished, production wrapped for several weeks in order to give Herman time to finish the interior sets and Rose time to complete her script revisions. In the freelance world of modern Hollywood—in which actors are contracted to a single project for a specified amount of time and schedule overruns can cost millions in overtime and penalties—it would be impossible to stop and start production in this manner. However, in the heyday of the studio system, the talent worked for the studio, not for any one production; when not working on *Kong*, the actors were reassigned to another picture and recalled when necessary.

SEPTEMBER-OCTOBER 1932 Schoedsack's unit returned to RKO-Pathè in September to shoot the bulk of the live-action sequences. They began with all of the scenes set aboard the *Venture*, including the opening in which Denham vows to get a girl for his picture even if he has to marry one; the love scenes between Ann and Jack; the scene in which Ann is kidnapped; and the screen test scene, in which Fay Wray screams for the first time in the film. To film these scenes, sets representing the outside decks and the inside cabins of the *Venture* were constructed on the soundstages. To simulate the bobbing of the ocean for daytime scenes shot on the faux exteriors, a painted backdrop of the horizon was positioned behind the actors and moved up and down by stagehands as the scenes were shot. Fog was generated for the scenes depicting the *Venture*'s arrival at Skull Island and a full complement of extras was on hand for the scene in which the men search the ship looking for the missing Ann.

Next up were the New York scenes, including Denham's search for a suitable girl; the "apple stealing" scene in which Denham first meets Ann; and the scene set in the one-armed lunchroom in which Ann tells her story and Denham offers her a job. The live-action portions of the hotel rooftop scene, as well as the scene in which Jack and Denham confer with the police and Jack gets the idea to send airplanes after Kong, were also filmed at this time.

From an acting perspective, *Kong* was not particularly challenging for most of the performers involved. With the exception of Bruce Cabot, the principal cast were all stage, screen, and vaudeville veterans who had with many years of experience. They executed their roles with professional energy and enthusiasm without much concern for attaining depth or complexity, which the film's script obviously didn't require.

In fact Fay Wray's biggest challenges during the production of *Kong* were personal rather than professional. Currently in the middle of a difficult marriage to John Monk Saunders that was complicated by his drinking, drug use, infidelity, and abuse, she did her best to focus on the job at hand and project the innocence and sincerity the role of Ann called for. On set, Wray's biggest challenge was performing with a Kong that wasn't there, which required her to utilize her great imagination and trust the directors when they told her she was doing what was needed.

Bruce Cabot was extremely inexperienced when he made *Kong* and he knew it. He later described the experience as standing in the right place, doing what he was told, and collecting a paycheck. Frank Reicher (Captain Englehorn) took Cabot under his wing and taught him how to perform for the camera. The final results were raw but effective and Cabot remained ever grateful for the experience.

Robert Armstrong's biggest problem at the beginning of the project was that he didn't know what role he was playing. When Armstrong was first hired, the script was unfinished and the role of Denham was only fuzzily defined as being a big-game hunter in the Frank Buck mode (which explains the rather elaborate safari suit Denham wears in the jungle scenes). In addition, the dialogue was incomplete, so Armstrong was unable to get a feel for the man he was

Fay Wray and Bruce Cabot pose for a publicity still on the set of the SS *Venture*.

supposed to be playing. Fortunately, most of what the test required him to do was physical, so all he had to do was follow Cooper's directions and do his best to muddle through. When the script was finally finished and Armstrong learned that he was playing a motion picture director of natural dramas, he decided to model his performance on Cooper and adopted not only the director's passionate enthusiasm, but also his constant fiddling with an ever-present, if rarely lit, pipe.

For all of the actors, the most difficult part of *Kong* was the on-again, off-again nature of the engagement. Fay Wray once remarked that she only worked on the film for ten weeks, but that those ten weeks were spread out over ten months. There was so much time between filming periods that some of the actors were able to make entire movies in the time they had off from *Kong*. Cabot, for example, made a film called *Road House* and Wray made two horror films for Warner Bros.—*Dr. X* (1932), with Humphrey Bogart, and *Mystery of the Wax Museum* (1933), with Lionel Atwill. Both films came out around the same time as *Kong*, a coincidence that caused the critics and the movie-going public to brand Wray a "scream queen."

This time lag had other consequences as well. From the time he made the original test in May to the beginning of principal photography in September, Cabot put on a considerable amount of weight, a change that is quite noticeable in the finished film (the fleshed-out first mate of the *Venture* turns into something of a skinny beanpole as soon as he passes through the Great Wall and enters the jungles of Skull Island). Unfortunately, the actors were only paid when they worked, which means that they earned very little relative to the amount of time they were on call for the project. Fay Wray, for example, made only $10,000 for almost a year of stop-and-go work.

Following the interior scenes, Schoedsack's unit returned to San Pedro and spent a day aboard a real tramp steamer to shoot the scene in which Jack accidentally hits Ann on the chin as the *Venture* leaves port. A high angle that included the ocean and a tugboat in the shot was chosen to provide "atmosphere" and to establish that the characters really were aboard a ship at sea. Reverse angles of the scene had already been shot on the shipboard sets back at RKO-Pathe. On this same day, Schoedsack also filmed several shots of real sailors working on the deck of the ship to give the departure scene additional authenticity and atmosphere.

The Shrine Auditorium located in downtown Los Angeles was rented for one day and used to film the interior shots of the "Broadway Theater" where Kong is presented for the first time. The audience and the hall were real. Kong wasn't there, of course. He was placed on stage later via optical effects. The backstage scenes with Denham, Jack, and Ann, as well as the scenes with Denham and the reporters, were also filmed that day.

Throughout the fall, Cooper would occasionally borrow the actors for special effects sequences, although most of those were actually filmed in a special shoot toward the end of the year. For most of the cast and crew of *Kong*, working with Merian C. Cooper proved to be a memorable experience. As has been noted, Cooper was an enormously passionate man, with a temperament that

Fay Wray and Bruce Cabot atop art director Al Herman's replica of the Empire State Building's mooring mast.

would occasionally lead him to erupt in volcanically angry outbursts (Cooper once dealt with a stalled car by pushing it off a cliff) that seriously intimidated the people around him. He was also a notorious perfectionist who would insist that things be done again and again and again until he was satisfied. At the same time, he also possessed an enormous amount of infectious enthusiasm that spread to the members of his team and inspired them to go above and beyond, especially when he asked them (as he frequently did) to attempt things that at first seemed impossible. All involved recognized and appreciated his genuine talent (Cooper was described by many as being a "visionary" and a "genius") and his all-encompassing commitment to the project. They also appreciated his commitment to them. Cooper was known to be an extremely generous and loyal man. He was generous with praise, gifts, and support, worked with the same family of collaborators for decades, and most of his friendships lasted for life.

The cast also enjoyed working with Ernest Schoedsack. They appreciated the trust he showed in them and the freedom he gave them in which to play their roles. The crew appreciated his enormous technical abilities, especially when it came to matters of photography. Schoedsack had a striking sense of composition, moved his camera in an exciting and dynamic manner, and made highly effective use of a wide range of atmospheric effects, most especially fog. He liked to work quickly and often completed most scenes in a single take. Possessing a dry, wry sense of humor, Schoedsack was as reserved and under-stated as his partner was effusive. Soft-spoken and easygoing, Schoedsack lost his temper only once on the set, on an occasion when Bruce Cabot reported for work drunk. When the inebriated actor refused to settle down, Schoedsack lost his temper and slapped him. Schoedsack later confessed that he felt terrible about the incident, even though Cabot himself felt he fully deserved it.

Principal photography wrapped toward the end of October with the scene in which Jack rescues Ann from the top of the Empire State Building (which was filmed on Al Herman's Art Deco mock-up). Schoedsack also filmed Robert Armstrong delivering his "It was Beauty killed the Beast" line from mock-up as he and two actors playing police officers looked down 102 imaginary floors to where the fallen Kong was supposedly laying in the middle of Fifth Avenue. With these scenes, Schoedsack had completed his work on the picture. In November, RKO sent him on an expedition to Syria to film "outdoor" scenes for a film called *Arabia*, a project that would never be completed.

DECEMBER 1932–JANUARY 1933 In mid-December 1932, a year after his initial pitch to Selznick, Cooper brought many of the actors back to film the balance of the optical effects shots, many of which were rear-screen projection shots. The rear-screen shots were extremely difficult to set up. First, the technical problems inherent in the process—shutter synchronization, hot spots, and fall off— had to be worked out. Then the shot had to be carefully lit so that the foreground subject was sufficiently illuminated without allowing any light to spill onto the screen, which would wash out the background image. Finally, all of the pictorial elements in the foreground—the movement, action, lighting patterns, camera angles, and relationships between characters and objects—needed to be matched to those in the background so that both would look like they were shot in the same place at the same time. If they weren't, then the final composite would seem disjointed—eyelines and actions wouldn't match and the illusion would be spoiled. All of this could be extremely time consuming—during the filming of the *Tyrannosaurus* fight, Fay Wray was once forced to spend twenty-two hours sitting in the top of a fake tree to film Ann's reactions to the battle. She was sore for days afterwards. In addition to the physical discomfort, such scenes also presented an acting challenge. The performers were so close to the screen that all they could see was a large blurry image, so they were forced to react to creatures and events they couldn't really make out.

Many of the famous scenes of Fay Wray struggling in Kong's hand were done with the rear-screen process. At the beginning of each shot, Wray stood in the hand while a grip wrapped the articulated fingers around her waist. The hand was then raised, lifting Wray about ten feet off the stage floor. For some of the scenes, a fan was turned on her to make her hair blow. As Wray struggled, the fingers in the hand would come loose. She would hold on until the last possible moment and then call out to the crew, who would immediately lower her back to the floor. She once remarked that the terrified look on her face in many of these shots was not a feigned reaction to Kong, but an honest expression of her fear that she actually might fall. Vernon Walker photographed the

Fay Wray in the Big Hand, with New York City rear-projected behind her.

rear-screen work, with O'Brien often on hand to ensure that the miniature and full-scale action matched.

The foreground portions of many of the Williams scenes were also shot during this period. As with the rear-screen shots, all of the foreground elements needed to be aligned with those in the background. As difficult as this was to do for the rear-screen shots, it was even harder to do for the Williams shots because the background plate wasn't visible the way it was in the rear-screen process. If the animated background plate had already been completed, then a clip played on a Moviola was used as a guide. While this helped, it was not ideal because you could not see the two elements put together as you could in rear screen. If the background plate hadn't been shot yet, then the alignments had

The completed Big Head—ready for action.

to be accomplished by carefully measuring the positions and angles of the miniature elements and then scaling them up to accommodate the full-scale action. Either way, the whole process was something of a shot in the dark. There was simply no way to tell for sure if a composite was right until it came back from the optical lab, which could often take a week or more. If the shot didn't work, then it either had to be lived with, redone, or discarded. Walker photographed all of these shots as well, with O'Brien and Frank Williams himself on the set to supervise.

During the December shoot, Cooper and cinematographer J. O. Taylor also filmed a retake of the scene in which Kong reaches into a hotel window and pulls out a woman he mistakes for Ann. In the original version of the scene, the woman was talking on the phone to her boyfriend. In the revised version of the scene, she is sleeping soundly in her bed when Kong attacks. Cooper also directed the scene in which Kong plucks Ann from her hotel room.

Cooper used stunt doubles to film underwater shots of Jack and Ann splashing down into a studio tank after the fall from Kong's cliff. The stuntwomen who doubled for Fay Wray in the course of the picture were Cherie May, Lee Kinney, Pauline Wagner, Marcella Allen, Lillian Jones, and Aline Goodwin. Gil Perkins and Al McDonald filled in for Bruce Cabot. The real Cabot and Wray were featured in shots showing Ann and Jack emerging from the depths and swimming away. Cooper then filmed the studio portions of the sequence in which Jack and Ann are swept downriver and go over a waterfall. Once again, stunt doubles were intercut with real actors. A second unit was sent to the Sierra Mountains to film an actual waterfall. The resulting footage was cut or matted into the final scenes.

A small piece of *The Most Dangerous Game* jungle set was reconstructed so that Cooper could shoot a brief scene of Armstrong getting snagged on a tree branch in order to explain his lagging behind during the jungle chase and so avoid being killed along with the other members of the search party when Kong flips them off the log. This replaced a small scene filmed during the test shoot in which Denham ducked into some bushes to get out of harm's way, which, it was decided, made Denham look cowardly.

Cooper's last scene was the same as Schoedsack's. As previously mentioned, Denham had originally delivered his classic closing line from a perch atop the Empire State Building, but Cooper later decided that he wanted to end the film with a shot of Kong lying dead in the street. On January 20, 1933, Cooper had Armstrong return to deliver his line while standing in front of a group of extras playing a New York crowd. All involved were filmed gazing at a nonexistent Kong, who would be added in later via an optical effect.

THE MINIATURE SCENES

The miniature work on *Kong* began in December 1931 when O'Brien's unit began shooting a series of tests to determine how Kong should move. To devise his walk, they studied films of gorillas and other apes, although it was ultimately decided to have Kong walk upright like a man rather than on all fours

A present day photo of Paramount Studios, formerly RKO-Hollywood, where the miniature scenes for King Kong were filmed. Note the RKO globe atop the walls.

like a real gorilla because it was felt he would look more imposing that way. The team also experimented with Kong's facial expressions to determine which ones were the most effective, watched films of elephants to determine how the dinosaurs should move, and shot tests to determine which optical effects techniques would be most appropriate for each scene.

Production on the two scenes that were featured in the test reel—Kong's fight with the *Tyrannosaurus* rex and the log scene—began in late February

ABOVE: Concept painting of the scene in which a curious Kong removes Ann's clothes.

BELOW: Conceptual art by Willis O'Brien depicting Kong's Manhattan rampage.

1932 and wrapped in May. As soon as the RKO board green-lit the rest of the film, O'Brien and his team began work on the other miniature sequences. As with the live-action, the miniature scenes were not shot in continuity. The shooting schedule was determined in large part by the optical effects processes that were going to be used to finish each shot. Animated shots meant to be used as rear-projection background plates were filmed first so that they would be ready by the time the live-action portions of the scene were scheduled to be filmed. Shots that incorporated miniature projection had to be filmed toward the end of the schedule, after the live-action elements had been completed.

The production of all of the miniature scenes followed the same basic process. First, Cooper and O'Brien broke down every scene into a series of shots, each of which was then transformed into an elaborate black-and-white concept drawing by O'Brien, Larrinaga, or Crabbe. (On occasion, the trio was assisted by Ernest Smythe, an artist who had once created movie posters for Universal Pictures.) Each concept drawing depicted every aspect of the intended shot, including the pictorial composition, the primary action, and the look of the set and the lighting. On O'Brien's instruction, the artists patterned their drawings on the work of the nineteenth-century French illustrator Gustave Dorè, whose dramatic images for the works of Dante and other literary classics featured a distinctive series of lush forests and twisted landscapes illuminated with dramatic shafts of light. The artists then broke down each concept drawing into a series of continuity sketches that detailed the specific actions and the progression of movement that each character needed to make throughout the shot. The forerunners of today's storyboards, the concept drawings and continuity sketches were all created with extensive input from Cooper and O'Brien.

Once the drawings were completed, O'Brien and his team would determine which technical processes and optical effects techniques would be required to bring each shot to life. It was then up to technical director Carroll Shepphird to create a precise plan to guide the execution of the shots. This plan would include architectural drawings and construction details for the miniature set that was to be used in the shot. It would also map out the exact placement of the camera, models, and lights; identify the precise type of lens and camera speed that were to be used; and indicate whatever special techniques, elements, or equipment that were required to shoot the scene.

After Shepphird completed his technical plans, the miniature set that was to be used for the scene would be constructed. W. G. White constructed the wooden framework for each set on bases made from two-inch slabs of pine into which White drilled a series of holes that would later be used to anchor the models. Once White had finished building the framework, Orville Goldner would detail it. For the jungle sets, miniature rocks were made from painted plaster and clay. Miniature trees were made from wooden dowels that were covered in clay, then wrapped in toilet paper, shellacked, and, finally, painted. Leaves for the trees were made from thin pieces of copper (so they would remain rigid and wouldn't blow around during filming), although some of the sets contained real plants as well (which caused problems when the plants

Kong carries a wooden Ann Darrow up the miniature Skull Mountain set during the filming of Kong's ascent to his lair, a scene that was later cut from the final film.

occasionally bloomed in the middle of shots). For the city sets, buildings and other structures were made from wood, metal, and plaster and vehicles were made from metal and wood. For any scene requiring miniature projection, tiny screens were built into the sets and projectors were placed behind them. Finally, Larrinaga and Crabbe would paint the backgrounds and scenic elements on large sheets of glass that were then placed at the rear of the sets. To create an even greater sense of depth and distance, several glass paintings at a time were often placed at the rear of the set, one behind the other.

All of the miniature sets were constructed on Stage 3 at RKO's Hollywood lot and were built on the same one-inch-equals-one-foot scale as the models (although the scale was sometimes adjusted to make Kong look bigger). To make the sets look bigger than they actually were, O'Brien's team often employed forced perspective—a set construction technique in which foreground elements are placed closer to the camera than they should be in order to make them look larger than they really are, or in which background objects are built smaller than they should be, in order to make them look farther away than they really are.

Once a miniature set had been completed, cinematographer Eddie Linden would light it. Every aspect of the miniature set construction and detail was designed to reproduce the look of the concept drawing exactly; the same was true for the lighting. If Linden could not replicate a lighting pattern indicated in one of the concept drawings by practical means, then Larrinaga or Crabbe would paint shafts of light onto the glass backings in the correct position to complete the effect. Because of the slow speed of early film stocks and early lenses, a great deal of light was required to illuminate the miniature sets in order to achieve both a satisfactory image and an acceptable depth of field. The lamps would be changed before every take to prevent them from blowing out in the middle of a shot. Before filming could begin, every element of the shot – from the camera to the sets to the models to the lights — had to be precisely aligned. This was a tedious task that could take hours, and sometimes days, to complete. Numerous still and motion picture tests were taken to facilitate the process. Only after every detail had been checked and every adjustment made would the animation process begin.

ANIMATION At the start of a shot, the models would be placed in the sets in their starting positions. If a model was standing, it would be held in place with clamps attached to its feet and anchored through the holes that had been drilled in the set's pine base. If a model was supposed to be leaping through the air or had to maintain awkward positions, it would be supported by rods, wires, or other devices devised by Fred Reefe or Orville Goldner. A single frame of film was exposed and then the models were moved into their next positions. If the scene included miniature projection, that footage would be advanced one frame at a time as well. It took twenty-four separate frames (and therefore twenty-four separate movements) to complete one second of sound film. Once a shot was begun, the animators worked straight through until the shot was finished. This was done to prevent any changes from occurring during a lengthy break (such as the scenery shifting, a model drooping, a light bulb losing its intensity, and so forth) that, although imperceptible to the casual eye, could show up on screen as a radical shift or jump. O'Brien did most of the animation himself, although Gibson and sometimes Goldner and Reefe assisted with more complicated, multiple character shots. As production went on, Gibson and Goldner animated some scenes on their own (Gibson animated Kong's climb up the Empire State Building, and Goldner animated many of the birds seen flying through the jungle sets).

When the work on each shot was completed, Cooper would then review it. A notorious perfectionist, he would often want changes made that would require the shot to be completely redone. While this could be frustrating for O'Brien and his team, ultimately they all shared Cooper's goal of making every shot as good as it could be. After the changes had been made and approved, the shot was handed over to the optical department for finishing or to the rear-projection unit so it could be used for process work.

CREATING KONG Kong's performance in the film was a collaboration between Merian Cooper and Willis O'Brien. In the course of devising the script, the concept drawings, and the continuity sketches, the two men defined Kong's personality and planned out all of his moves. As filming progressed, each man contributed additional bits of business and behavior that fleshed out the characterization even more. People who worked on the film claimed to have recognized aspects of both Cooper and O'Brien in the giant ape. The collaboration did not always go smoothly. Both men were feisty, opinionated, and stubborn. They fought loudly and often. One issue of constant contention was O'Brien's penchant for introducing offbeat or humorous touches into scenes that made Kong more sympathetic, which clashed with Cooper's desire to pres-

Willis O'Brien animates Kong's fight
with the Elasmosaurus.

ent Kong as a fearsome beast. Things occasionally got so tense that O'Brien would walk off the film (although he would always return). In spite of their differences, the two men respected one another's abilities and so continued to persevere.

The final miniature shot—the image of the dead Kong lying across Fifth Avenue that closes the film—was filmed at the end of January 1933. From beginning to end, the miniature scenes took fifty-five weeks to complete.

A SPECIAL EFFECTS OVERVIEW

Much has been written about the special effects work in *King Kong* over the years—some of it accurate and some of it not so accurate (when the film first appeared, one national magazine reported that Kong had been played by a man in an ape suit. Another told its readers that Kong was a giant robot built from wood and metal and operated by six men hidden inside him). Since all of the members of the miniature and optical effects teams have passed away, it is impossible to verify exactly how every effects shot in the film was created, but sufficient evidence remains to indicate how most of them were put together.

The very first special effect shot in *Kong* is the very first shot of the film— one of a tugboat chugging past a glass painting of the Manhattan skyline. The September 6, 1932, revision of the screenplay identifies the long view of the *Venture* at sea as the film's next effect shot, indicating that it was shot using a miniature ship that was most likely photographed in the waters off San Pedro during the August 1932 location shoot. Rear-screen projection was used for a shot of Ann and Jack at the rail of the ship with a shot of the ocean appearing behind them during their first extended conversation.

THE ARRIVAL AT KONG'S ISLAND To open the arrival sequence, a twelve-foot-long, nonfloating model of the *Venture*, complete with a crew of wooden sailors, was constructed and filmed on a soundstage filled with artificial fog.

For the first look at the island after the fog has lifted, the beach and ocean at San Pedro was combined with a glass painting of the village, the Great Wall, and Skull Mountain. Rotoscoped seagulls were matted into the shot, most likely using the Williams system. The finished composite was used as a rear-projection plate for a scene that was filmed in front of a mock-up of a portion of the ship's deck. The shot of the landing party rowing to the beach was also created using a glass painting and matted-in seagulls.

The nighttime view of the torch-lit native village seen through the window of the *Venture*'s bridge was created in the same manner and used as a rear-projection plate for a scene filmed in front of a mock-up of the bridge's window (a brief glitch in the rear-projected film can be seen toward the end of the sequence).

THE SACRIFICE SCENE The first effect shot in this sequence is the one in which the natives look down on Ann has she struggles to free herself from

The miniature Kong faces the real
Fay Wray in a composite shot.

the altar. The Great Wall that appears in this shot was a miniature. The natives were photographed standing atop an RKO-Pathè soundstage and matted into the shot via a split-screen. Fay Wray was filmed on the altar in front of a blue screen and matted into the shot using the Williams system.

For Kong's entrance, Fay Wray was again filmed on the altar in front of a blue screen and composited with a background plate of Kong emerging from the jungle. Cooper had the plate of Kong reshot sixteen times because he didn't think the animation was smooth enough, but in the end he decided to use the first take. The close-up of Kong's face when he first sees Ann was shot using the Big Head. When the time came for Kong to seize Ann, Fay Wray dropped down between the altar and the blue screen, after which Kong picked up the wooden doll on the background plate.

The long view of Kong looking up at the natives after he picks up Ann is a continuation of the earlier split screen shot and Jack's first look at Kong as he carries Ann off into the jungle is fully animated.

THE STEGOSAURUS CHARGE Two *Stegosaurus* models were built to portray two different creatures in *Creation*, but in *Kong* they traded off playing the same beast. The first model was used for a shot in which the *Stegosaurus* enters and exits the set on the rear plane, re-enters on a closer plane, and then rushes toward the camera. The finished composite served as a rear-projection background plate for the scene in which the *Stegosaurus* charges the search party before Denham fells it with a gas bomb. The gas bomb explosion was filmed separately against a black backing and matted into the plate. During the filming of this scene, the rear screen was partially obscured by set dressing at the sides of the frame, which added more depth and detail to the shot.

The second *Stegosaurus* model was used for the tracking shot in which the search party walks the length of the fallen creature as it experiences its final death throes. To film this scene, Armstrong, Cabot, and the rest of the crew walked in place on a treadmill in front of a rear-projection screen. The tracking camera movement had been animated into the original plate.

THE BRONTOSAURUS ATTACK

The raft seen floating across the swamp at the beginning of the scene was a miniature manned by a wooden crew. All of the shots of the *Brontosaurus* in the swamp—including the one when it first rises up out of the water—were filmed using the mechanical model. The model's neck was operated by a series of levers that allowed it to lift up out of the water, grab miniature sailors in its mouth, and fling them around. For the shot in which the Bronto rises up alongside the raft, the actors were positioned on a dry-docked platform in front of a Dunning screen and composited with the mechanical model on the backing plate. Studio grips tipped the raft at a crucial moment to make it look like the *Brontosaurus* had overturned it.

Once the *Brontosaurus* moves onto dry land, the mechanical model was replaced by the three-foot-long, articulated model animated by Willis O'Brien, which is first seen in the shots in which the *Brontosaurus* chases the surviving members of the search party through the shallows. The shot in which the sailor gets separated from the group and runs through the frame with the long-necked creature close at heels was filmed with the actor in front of a blue screen and composited with the animated model on a backing plate using the Dunning process (in an example of the Dunning process's transparency effect, the *Brontosaurus*'s neck can be seen faintly through the foreground tree to the left of the frame). In the wide shot in which the survivors run out of the swamp and into the jungle, animated models take the place of the live actors as the sailors run up the bank and pass behind a foreground bush. When they emerge from the bush, the sailors are now played by live actors placed into the scene via miniature projection; however, the sailor that climbs the tree is an animated figure.

For the close shots of the sailor being menaced in the tree, an animated shot of the large *Brontosaurus* head was rear-projected onto a screen behind the live actor hugging a prop tree. All of the elements in the long shot of the *Brontosaurus* snatching the sailor from the tree and snacking on him are animated.

THE TRICERATOPS FIGHT

As has been previously noted, following the *Brontosaurus* attack, the search party was originally supposed to witness a scene in which Kong is chased into an asphalt pit by a trio of *Triceratopses*, one of which gets stuck in the tarlike muck and begins to sink. Reaching a dry mound in the center of the pit, Kong tears up pieces of asphalt and throws them at his remaining pursuers, breaking the horn off one of them, which allows Kong to approach the beast and kill it. The surviving *Triceratops* then retreats, runs into the search party, and begins chasing them as Kong moves on

TOP: Kong attacks one of the Stegosaurus models in this publicity still.

BOTTOM: A composite publicity still for the Brontosaurus scene.

with Ann. This action was originally supposed to lead into the scene from *Creation* in which the *Triceratops* chases the sailor wearing striped trousers and gores him to death. The *Creation* clip featured both a side view and an over-the-shoulder shot of the model *Triceratops* chasing a live man, both generated through miniature projection (O'Brien's first use of the process). Although work on the asphalt pit sequence was begun, it was later abandoned when Cooper decided to cut the scene. The *Creation* clip was dropped as well.

THE LOG SCENE   As previously mentioned, this was the first scene shot for the test reel and was inserted—with a few changes—directly into the final film. The shot of Kong walking across the log holding Ann utilized Delgado's original eighteen-inch Kong model holding the wooden Ann. Kong actually walked across a flat ramp located just behind the log that was drilled with holes to allow Kong's feet to be properly clamped into place.

The Arsinoitherium that was later cut makes an appearance (on the right) alongside an unusually large flower in this composite publicity still from the log sequence.

The shot of the search party approaching the ravine was a Dunning shot. The men were filmed in front of a blue screen and the ravine and log were miniatures on a background plate. As previously mentioned, in the test reel, as the search party approached the ravine, the *Arsinoitherium* charged out of the jungle and chased the men out onto the log (thus explaining why the men just don't run back the other way when Kong appears). Later on, Cooper decided to reshoot the scene and replace the *Arsinoitherium* with the *Styractosaurus*.

The shot in which Kong puts Ann in the tree and then heads back to investigate the commotion at the ravine was a Dunning shot—the tree was filmed in front of a blue screen and Kong was on the background plate. Although Ann was portrayed by the wooden doll in the first part of the scene, it is the real Fay Wray that Kong deposits in the tree's crook. This marvelous bit of slight of hand was apparently accomplished by having Wray emerge from behind the blue screen and drop into a seat built into the treetop just as the animated Kong opens his hand.

For the wide shot of the search party running across the log, the full-scale men were matted onto the miniature log using the Dunning process. The shot of Kong rushing back toward the ravine was fully animated, but all of the shots featuring the miniature Kong and the full-scale men were Dunning shots. The men were filmed on a full-scale log in the full-scale ravine set in front of a blue backing and were then composited with plates of the eighteen-inch Kong filmed on a miniature set. The transparent "holes" the Dunning process sometimes created in foreground figures are especially evident in these shots.

THE PIT This scene was filmed using wooden sailors on a miniature ravine set. As every *Kong* fan knows, when the sailors fell to the bottom of the ravine, they were originally supposed to be eaten by a variety of giant animated spiders, lizards, and an octopus-like creature. As legend has it, a preview audience was so horrified by the scene that it was cut before general release. Evidence

Conceptual art from the notorious "spider" scene.

Kong battles the *Tyrannosaurus* rex.

suggests, however, that the sequence was actually removed much earlier—most likely following a rough cut screening at the studio. Cooper was quoted as saying that he removed the scene because it "stopped the show"—implying that it shocked the audience so much that they couldn't continue watching the movie—but it is just as likely that the scene was removed because it slowed the film's pacing and took the audience's attention off the main plotline. Cooper replaced the so-called "spider" scene with simple shots of miniature sailors falling to the bottom of the ravine and bouncing in the air as their screams are suddenly cut off, which, it could be argued, is even more disturbing than seeing them being munched into oblivion. The miniature sailors' limbs were loosely jointed and weighted so that they would flail about on impact. For years, rumors have circulated that the spider scene has been discovered intact in a print of the film found in one foreign country or another, but all of these rumors have turned out to be false. In all likelihood the footage was destroyed, a common practice in those days for discarded material.

KONG VS. JACK Bruce Cabot filmed his portions of this scene on the full-scale ravine set. For the low angle shot in which Jack looks up at Kong raging on the cliff above him, the view of Cabot was composited with the miniature Kong via a split screen. For all of the other shots featuring Kong and Jack together, Cabot was miniature-projected into the miniature ravine set and animated along with Kong and the pit creature that crawls up the vine. In the test reel, the pit creature was a giant spider, but after the spiders were cut, the scene was reshot using a nonspecified lizard. After Jack cuts the vine and the lizard falls, O'Brien animated a clever camera tilt to bring Kong back into the frame.

THE TYRANNOSAURUS BATTLE As with the log scene, this scene was shot for the test reel and then incorporated into the final film. The scene originally began with Ann being distracted by a giant snake, which keeps her from noticing the *Tyrannosaurus* as it enters the clearing behind her. For this scene, Wray was positioned in the prop tree in front of the Saunders screen while a clip of the *Tyrannosaurus* entering the clearing was rear projected behind her. At the appropriate moment, she turns, sees the *Tyrannosaurus* and lets out a scream that summons Kong back from the ravine.

Once Kong and the *Tyrannosaurus* begin to fight, all of the wide shots in which the real Ann watches the fight were filmed by placing Wray in the prop tree in front of the blue screen and backing them with animated plates via the Dunning process. Several noncomposite wide shots were filmed using the six-inch wooden Ann doll in a miniature tree (in these shots, Ann's tree is positioned to the left of the frame, whereas in the Dunning shots, the tree is in the center of the frame). All of the closer shots of Ann watching the fight were rear-screen shots. The rather unsimian fighting style that Kong uses in this scene was the result of the research O'Brien and Gibson did for the scene by attending boxing and wrestling matches. For the shots in which Kong flips the *Tyrannosaurus* over his shoulder, the dinosaur model was held in mid air by a series of propping poles.

O'Brien employed some impressive slight-of-hand work to create the moment in which Kong falls back into Ann's tree and knocks it over. The animated Kong puppet was backed up toward the camera and cleverly aligned in a wide Dunning shot with the prop tree to make it look like he was colliding with it. A cut was then made to a closer shot of Wray in the prop tree reacting as the image on the rear-projection plate whipped from Kong to a shot of the sky to make it look like the tree was falling (even though it never actually moved). The scene returns to a long shot as the prop tree fell over, pinning Ann—played here by a stuntwoman—beneath it. As the tree hits the ground, the background plate, featuring Kong and the *Tyrannosaurus,* freezes for a very brief second.

After Kong kills the *Tyrannosaurus,* O'Brien included one of his marvelous trademark "touches" in the moment when Kong playfully wiggles the dead creature's broken jaw. The long shot of Kong beating his chest in triumph over the dead *Tyrannosaurus* features the wooden Ann puppet. The close-up of Kong looming over Ann features the Big Head and is matched with a zoom in on a screaming Fay Wray that was made on the optical printer—one of the first optical zooms ever to appear in a film.

For the close-up of Kong lifting the log off of Ann, the Big Hand performed with Wray in front of the rear screen while a plate of a straining miniature Kong was projected in the background. The shot in which Kong lifts Ann off the jungle floor made very clever use of miniature projection. Wray was filmed on a full-scale set being lifted by the Big Hand and then miniature-projected behind an over-the-shoulder shot of the Kong model to make it look like the model was lifting her. Adding to the shot's effectiveness, the Kong model was filmed just a bit out of focus, which is the way the image would have appeared if the camera had been shooting over the shoulder of an actual twenty-foot tall ape. All of the elements in the shot of Kong leaving the clearing while carrying Ann were animated.

The two shots of Jack making his way past the carcass of the *Tyrannosaurus* are rear-screen shots. For the first, Cabot crossed in front of the screen and exited the frame as a flock of giant vulture models take flight. A few seconds later, the wooden Driscoll model entered the frame on the background plate. For a second, closer shot, Cabot was once again filmed in front of the rear screen as an animated shot featuring the remaining giant vulture feasting on the *Tyrannosaurus,* blood trickling from the dead lizard's broken jaw, appeared behind him. The final effects shot of the sequence—Kong pulling down a vine as he carries Ann deeper into the jungle—contained a split screen matte that placed a real river in the foreground of the miniature set.

KONG APPROACHES SKULL MOUNTAIN At the beginning of this shot, the animated Kong carries the wooden Ann into the frame. After a pause to look at the mountain in the distance, Kong continues down a hill and out of the shot. The real waterfall filmed in the High Sierras was split-screened into the lower left corner of the shot and a mountain pathway filmed in Nicholas Canyon was split-screened into the right side of the shot. A stunt double stood in for Bruce Cabot as he follows after Kong. This same shot was reused later in the story, as Cabot's double carries Wray's double away from the river after Jack and Ann have made their escape from Kong.

A closer shot of Kong beginning his ascent up the side of Skull Mountain was split-screened with a closer shot of the real waterfall. A later scene, in which a furious Kong climbs down the mountain in pursuit of Ann and Jack, was a continuation of this setup.

THE CAVE SCENE Kong's arrival at the entrance to his lair features miniature birds flying off past some foreground glass paintings. After Kong enters the cave, the animated Jack appears in the lower right corner of the frame.

The interior of Kong's cave was a combination of a miniature set and several glass backgrounds. The steam rising from the volcanic vents was filmed separately and superimposed onto the shot. The bubbling lava was also filmed separately and split-screened into the foreground. The pool of water in the center of the cave was real and inserted into the shot using miniature projection, as was Wray when Kong places her on the ledge and the *Elasmosaurus* slithers up to threaten her.

Jack enters the scene as Kong battles the *Elasmosaurus* via miniature projection and later observes the fight from a wider angle through a split screen. Kong's fight with the *Elasmosaurus* required a lot of support to keep the four-legged snake airborne as he wraps himself around Kong's neck.

THE CLIFF SCENE The cliff scene was filmed on a miniature set with an elaborate glass backing that showed the jungle, the Great Wall, and the ocean (complete with the SS *Venture*) in the distance. A miniature projection screen was incorporated into the cliff set. It appears just to the right of a rock that has been strategically placed in the center of the set. Whenever Ann is seen on the right hand side of the rock, she is played by the real Fay Wray in miniature projection. Whenever Ann crawls behind the rock and emerges on the left side, she is played by the six-inch wooden miniature.

Perhaps the most notorious scene in *Kong* is the one in which Kong pulls off Ann's clothes and sniffs them. Over the years, critics, scholars, and audiences have interpreted the scene as having a deliberately erotic intent, but O'Brien—who dreamed up the scene—saw it in much more innocent terms. To O'Brien, Kong saw Ann as a beautiful object and his removal of her clothes was akin to plucking the petals off a flower. Merian Cooper saw the scene as a playful, comic one. To film the scene, Fay Wray was placed in the Big Hand and photographed against a full-scale section of cliff wall. Fishing line was attached to pre-scored pieces of Wray's costume. At appropriate moments during the filming, crewmembers yanked the filament and pulled off the costume pieces. The finished shots were then miniature-projected behind the Kong model on the miniature set. Kong was angled so that his right arm was hidden behind his body, making it look like the full-scale arm on the miniature projection screen was really his. Kong's left arm was then animated to reach up and pull as the dress pieces came off. At one point, a miniature dress piece was placed in the model's hand. Kong was then animated to lift the piece up to his nose and sniff it.

THE BATTLE WITH THE PTERANODON After a noise from within the cave prompts Kong to put Ann down and go back inside to investigate, the tiny *Pteranodon* model enters the scene far off in the distance, flapping in behind a miniature-projected shot of the real Fay Wray on the miniature set as she starts to crawl toward the edge of the cliff. After a cutaway to Kong inside the cave, the scene returns to the cliff as the animated Ann approaches the edge. At this point, the full-size *Pteranodon* model enters the frame and grabs the Ann doll. The close-ups of Ann in the *Pteranodon*'s claws was filmed using a stuntwoman in the full-scale talons on a full-scale portion of the set placed in front of the rear screen. The glass shot of the horizon was filmed and rear projected onto the screen.

The subsequent scene—in which Kong grabs the *Pteranodon* and attempts to bite it to death while the creature furiously flaps his wings and pecks at him—was one of the most complicated scenes in the picture and took seven weeks to complete. Keeping the *Pteranodon* aloft during the battle was especially difficult and was accomplished using a series of support rods and wires, some of which are visible in certain frames of the finished film. Further complicating

The miniature Kong peels away a rear-projected Fay Wray's clothes as she is gripped by the Big Hand.

matters, the wooden figures of Jack and Ann had to be animated while crawling beneath the battling creatures as they head toward the cliff to escape.

In Ruth Rose's final draft of the script, Jack and Ann escape from Kong's lair by jumping into the pool located in the center of Kong's cave, after which they are sucked into a raging torrent and then carried over a waterfall that cascades down the face of Skull Mountain. Before the scene was shot, the pool dive was eliminated and it was decided that Jack and Ann would climb down the face of the mountain on a vine instead. Kong tries to pull them up, at which point they let go and drop down into a river, which carries them to the waterfall.

The full-scale portion of Jack and Ann's climb down the vine was filmed on the cliff mock-up using two stunt doubles that unfortunately look nothing like Wray or Cabot (Cabot's double had blonde hair and is visibly balding). The vine was winched up for the shots in which Kong is supposedly pulling on it and intercut with animated shots of the miniature Kong lifting a miniature couple up on a miniature vine. At the appropriate moment, the stunt doubles let go and

Publicity still showing the twenty-four-inch Kong model battling the Pteranodon as the real Fay Wray screams.

Concept painting showing Kong as he breaks through the Great Wall.

fell into a net just out of camera range. Jack and Ann's actual fall was filmed by dropping two wooden models down a miniature cliff into a tank.

KONG'S RAMPAGE THROUGH THE VILLAGE
The shots in which Kong approaches the Great Wall and begins pushing on the gate were all done with miniatures, although some miniature-projected people can be seen occasionally through the grills at the bottom of the gates. The shot of Kong pushing open the gates was filmed on a miniature set and then matted into a full-scale shot of the doors opening (the shot that was filmed using tractors to pull open the door) using the Williams system. The long shot of Kong emerging from the opening in the wall was filmed on the miniature wall set and then composited, again using the Williams system, with a shot of fleeing extras filmed on the backlot.

The scene in which Kong smashes up the native hut and then throws it onto some of the villagers was animated on a miniature set. When the time came for Kong to throw the hut, the debris was animated up and out of the frame. The finished shot was then rear-projected onto the Saunders screen. As soon as the miniature debris left the backing frame, full-scale debris was dropped down onto a group of fleeing extras positioned in front of the screen. A later shot in which Kong drops a tree onto some more natives was done the same way. The shot in which a little native boy is whisked out of Kong's path was also a rear-screen composite.

The scene in which Kong smashes the native scaffold was complex. Full-scale natives were filmed throwing spears on a full-scale set. These shots were then placed into a miniature set via miniature projection and animated along with Kong and a flight of miniature spears. To complete the shot, natives run-

TOP: Kong appears onstage at the Shrine Auditorium via a split-screen matte.

BOTTOM: The twenty-four inch Kong chomps on a miniature Manhattanite.

ning by in the foreground were filmed against blue screen and matted in via the Williams system. The close-up of Kong chomping on the hapless native was done with the Big Head. The later scene in which Kong pulls the natives out of the hut and steps on them was all done using miniatures except for the close-ups of Kong stomping the natives into the mud, which were done on a full-scale set using real actors and the Big Leg.

The scene in which Denham knocks out Kong with a gas bomb was filmed on a miniature beach set. As in the *Stegosaurus* scene, the flash of the gas bomb was matted into the background plate. The composite was then used as a plate for a Dunning shot featuring the *Venture* crew and some running natives. The reverse shots of Denham, Jack, Ann, and the rest of the *Venture* crew standing near the boats were filmed on the beach at San Pedro and combined with a glass shot of the *Venture* on the sea behind them. The completed shot was miniature-projected behind a slightly out-of-focus, miniature Kong.

THE BROADWAY THEATER   The sign advertising "King Kong: The Eighth Wonder of the World" that opens the sequence was a glass painting. The camera then tilts down to reveal a real crowd in front of an exterior theater façade. Inside the theater, a shot of a real audience filmed inside the Shrine Auditorium appears to be split-screened with a miniature curtain, which is then raised via animation to reveal the chained Kong, who is placed on the real Shrine stage via another split screen. The close-up shot of Kong grunting at the crowd was filmed using the Big Head.

The side views of Kong becoming agitated were filmed on the miniature stage and then rear-projected behind the actors playing the reporters in the wings. To film the shot of Kong jumping off his platform, the actors playing reporters were filmed running off into the real wings of the Shrine Auditorium and then rear projected behind the miniature Kong as he drops down into the frame.

PANIC IN THE STREETS   For the scene in which Kong breaks out into the street, a shot of a panicked crowd running out of an alley was miniature-projected behind the animated Kong as he knocks down two miniature stage doors made of copper.

Jack and Ann rush into a full-scale mock-up of the entrance to Ann's hotel as a full-scale car crashes into the wall next to them. Spying them, a rear-projected miniature Kong approaches a miniature version of the hotel entrance as full-scale extras run past in the foreground. The miniature Kong then picks up a miniature New Yorker, but the close-up in which Kong munches on the unlucky Manhattanite was filmed using the Big Head and a full-scale extra. The scene in which Kong rips the marquee off the hotel and drops it on the fleeing extras was filmed in the same manner as the shots in which Kong threw the hut and tree in the native village.

THE HOTEL   Kong's climb up the front of the hotel was all done in miniature. His appearance in the Sleeping Woman's hotel window was also filmed in miniature and matted into the full-scale scene via the Williams system (this shot replaced the live-action shots originally filmed with the Big Head, which Cooper found unconvincing). Kong's reach into the Sleeping Woman's window was filmed using the Big Hand (which now sported a faux-chrome manacle on its wrist) on the full-scale set. The shot of the Big Hand holding the Sleeping Woman over the crowd was a rear-projection shot with a real crowd on the background plate. The shot in which the Sleeping Woman falls to her death was filmed against a blue screen and composited with a real crowd scene via a Williams matte. Kong's recapture of Ann was filmed using the exact same methods. Bruce Cabot filmed the scene in which Jack tries to stop Kong from taking Ann, except for the shot in which Kong knocks him over. For that, the balding stuntman once again took his place.

Once Kong reaches the roof of the hotel, all of the shots of Ann in his hand were filmed using the wooden model. Any shots of Ann after Kong puts her down feature Fay Wray in miniature projection. As originally scripted, a group of policemen were supposed to confront Kong on the roof of the hotel and begin shooting at him. To escape, Kong was supposed to make a spectacular leap from the top of the hotel to the top of the building across the street, after which Jack, Denham and the police would chase him across the rooftops of Manhattan as he headed for the Empire State Building. When the scene proved too complicated to execute, the policemen were eliminated and Kong simply climbed down the back wall of the hotel. Shots of Jack and Denham watching him go were filmed against a rear-screen shot of the miniature buildings that Kong was originally supposed to jump across.

A damaged test shot from Kong's escape across the rooftops of Manhattan, a sequence that was dropped before it was filmed.

Kong tears down the Sixth Avenue El.

THE ELEVATED SUBWAY SCENE After the rooftop chase was dropped, the plan was to have Kong disappear and to then have Jack, Denham, and the police search the city for him to no avail until they finally spotted him climbing up the Empire State Building. After screening a rough cut of the film, Cooper decided to replace the search with a more exciting scene in which Kong destroys an elevated subway track and causes a train to derail.

A miniature street and elevated train trestle were constructed for the wide shots in which Kong enters the scene and single-handedly tears down the trestle while still holding the wooden Ann doll. Animated people run past in the background while real people matted in via the Williams system run by in the foreground. A full-scale apartment building full of screaming onlookers was composited into the shot on the same matte as the foreground runners.

The bit that occurs after Kong has decimated the trestle contains one of the wonderfully creative touches typical of O'Brien—as Kong is pulling himself up to get a look at the oncoming train, he wiggles his dangling foot like a young child eagerly anticipating a present. For the Kong's-eye-view shot of the oncoming train, a miniature subway car was filmed against an exquisite glass painting of the city skyline. For the shot of Kong rising up in the gap in the track as seen from the perspective of the elevated train's driver, the camera itself was animated moving toward Kong and then later composited with a mock-up of the subway cab via the Williams system. Images of Kong were matted into the derailed train's window using the Williams system. At the end of the scene, animated figures can be seen jumping out of the train and running away as Kong climbs up the side of the live-action building.

CLIMBING THE EMPIRE STATE BUILDING The smoothness of the animation in the long shot of Kong climbing up the side of the Empire State Building as the biplanes approach has provoked much speculation over the years that Kong was portrayed in the scene by a man in an ape suit. While several people have come forward over the years to claim that they played Kong, this is simply not true—although Cooper had originally considered doing so, no actors in ape suits were used to make the movie. Others have claimed that the ape seen in this shot was rotoscoped over footage of an actor and then matted onto a shot of the Empire State Building. While this is certainly a more plausible explanation, it is also not the case. The figure seen in the film was in fact an animated figure (close scrutiny of the scene reveals the jittery motion typical of stop-motion animation).

E. B. Gibson animated Kong as he climbed up a row of wooden dowels in front of a blue screen. Kong was then matted into a shot of the real Empire State Building using the Dunning process. Kong's ever-changing size reaches its biggest extreme in this shot, where he appears to be somewhere between three and four stories tall.

KONG'S LAST STAND The scenes atop the Empire State Building were filmed on a miniature set featuring a small-scale replica of the building's spire. The spire was set against a photo-realistic view of the city painted on three large panes of glass. The original plan was to film Kong against a miniature projection screen featuring the background plates of the actual city filmed by Schoedsack and Linden from atop the real Empire State Building, but the initial test shots looked terrible, so the glass backings were employed instead. The shots in which Kong holds Ann in his hand were filmed using the wooden miniature. Otherwise, Fay Wray plays Ann throughout the scene via miniature projection.

The airplanes were a mix of the real planes shot by Schoedsack and the miniature planes animated by O'Brien and his team. The planes were built in several sizes, with the smaller ones placed in the backgrounds of the shots to create a forced perspective impression that they were farther away than they actually were. The planes were hung from wires that ran over the miniature set and

One of the most famous publicity stills in movie history—King Kong's last stand atop the Empire State Building. This composite photo was created using one of the eighteen-inch models, even though the twenty-four-inch model was used in the actual scene.

moved incrementally along at the same time as Kong himself was being animated. For the pilot point-of-view shots of the planes swooping down on Kong as they fire their guns at him, the camera was animated moving down a long ramp toward Kong. The plane that Kong cripples was filmed in front of a blue screen and matted onto a miniature portion of the building. The scale of the plane and the building didn't match and, as a result, the plane looks like it is several stories tall. The side views of the pilot and gunner played by Cooper and Schoedsack were filmed in front of a rear-projection screen, with aerial shots of Manhattan playing behind them. For the head-on shots of the pilots firing their guns, Cooper and Schoedsack were replaced by two other actors. Rear-screen projection with a Manhattan plate was also used for the final shot of Fay Wray in the Big Hand as the dying Kong picks Ann up for the very last time.

There is perhaps no better example of Willis O'Brien's artistry than the moment in which the dying Kong sees his own blood for the first time. The confused and bewildered look on the great ape's face is utterly real and absolutely heartbreaking. That O'Brien was able to create such a powerful and affecting moment using nothing more than a two-foot-tall puppet makes his accomplishment even more incredible than it already is.

KONG FALLS   The original plan was to film a shot of the miniature Kong falling away from the camera to the ground far below. As written in the script, this would have been the last time Kong is seen in the film. One of the Kong models was filmed against a blue screen and matted via the Dunning process into the shot Schoedsack took in New York that looked straight down from the top of the building. Unfortunately, a Dunning "hole" appeared in the final composite and so the shot was scrapped.

To replace it, the fourth, very small Kong model was dropped down a mock-up of the Empire State Building. To give the model the proper weight and heft on screen, the decision was made to run the camera at a very high speed (when film shot at a high rate of frames per second is projected at normal speed, the action in the scene actually slows down. This is because it takes a lot longer for the film used to record the moment to pass through the camera). During the first take, the film jammed in the camera, but during the second take everything went fine.

FADE OUT   As mentioned previously, Cooper decided at the last minute to move Denham's closing line from the top of the Empire State Building to the street below. It is likely that Cooper did this because the fall away shot of Kong was scrapped and Cooper wanted to provide a dramatic fade-out for his creation. To create the shot, Armstrong was filmed in front of a crowd of extras and then miniature-projected behind the inert, slightly out-of-focus, miniature Kong.

POSTPRODUCTION

EDITING   The film was assembled by RKO staff editor Ted Cheesman. As with every other aspect of the film, Cooper closely supervised the process.

Having already left for Arabia, Schoedsack was not involved. The first complete cut of the film was approximately 125 minutes long. Upon viewing it, Cooper felt that it was far too long and that the pacing lagged in too many places. His goal was to produce a film that built steadily toward the introduction of its fantastic main character and thereafter move at a fast, action-packed pace that didn't leave the audience a moment to catch its breath. With this goal in mind, Cooper and Cheesman reedited the film to remove all of the slow spots. They shortened many of the scenes by removing any element—scenes, dialogue, bits of business—that did not contribute to the direct advancement of the story. To this end, Cooper cut huge sections from the first half of the jungle sequence, including the asphalt pit scene, the *Creation* clip, the charge of the *Styracosaurus*, and the giant snake that threatens Ann just before the T-rex appears. As spectacular as these scenes were, Cooper felt that they tended to divert the audience's attention from the search for Ann. Cooper and Cheesman also cut out Kong's climbs up and down Skull Mountain, the waterfall scene, and the scene in which Kong startles the guys playing poker in the New York hotel. The final cut of the film was finished by February 1933 and was 100 minutes long.

SOUND EFFECTS Murray Spivak, the head of RKO's sound department, created the sound effects for the film. At the time, motion picture sound was in its infancy. When the process had been introduced a few years earlier, all of the dialogue, sound effects, and music had to be recorded at the same time on a single track while a scene was being filmed and it was not possible to go back and add in any additional sounds afterwards. By 1932, three separate tracks were being used—one for dialogue, one for music, and one for effects—and sound engineers now had the means to rerecord the sound, mixing the three tracks together onto a single master that was then attached to the film. This made it possible to add sound, music, and dialogue to a scene after filming was completed. This ability would prove to be a vital one for Spivak, because all of Kong's animated scenes had been filmed without sound, meaning that he had to add in every sound for every scene after the fact. Spivak also had the daunting task of creating convincing "voices" for a menagerie of extinct or wholly imaginary creatures. The nine-month project was an extremely ambitious one – nothing like this had ever been done before, especially on such a grand scale.

To create Kong's roar, Spivak went to the Selig Zoo—a facility that raised and trained animals to appear in motion pictures—and recorded the growls of lions and tigers. He spliced the growls together and then played them backwards at a really slow speed (which lowered their tone an octave, making the growls sound like they were coming out of much bigger animals) as he rerecorded them. Spivak then cut together all of the high points to create one long, dissonant roar. For moments in which Kong carried on at length, Spivak had to cut together several sets of highlights. He then added a sound tail—a gradual fade—to the end of the roars so that they would not just abruptly cut off when Kong was done.

For Kong's distinctive love grunts, Spivak recorded himself grunting into a megaphone and then re-recorded the results at slow speed. To create the sound

One of the monstrous spiders from the pit.

of Kong's footsteps, Spivak wrapped plungers in foam rubber and stomped them across a box filled with gravel. Kong's chest beats proved to be one of Spivak's biggest challenges. He began by beating on a kettledrum with a padded drumstick. That didn't sound right, so he next tried beating the drumstick on the bottom of a cane chair. Neither approach had a sufficiently fleshy sound, so Spivak next tried striking his assistant Walter Elliott on the chest with the drumstick while a microphone was held up to Elliott's back. This approach worked and the resulting sound was the one they ended up using.

On the advice of a vertebrate paleontologist from the Los Angeles County Museum of Natural History, Spivak decided to have the dinosaurs hiss and croak rather than roar. To create the hissing sounds, Spivak recorded the noises from a compressed air machine. He did the croaking himself. For the T-rex, Spivak mixed in a backward recording of a panther growl. Spivak used an elephant's roar for the *Triceratopses* (before they were cut, of course) and some bird squawks for the *Pteranodon*. Bellows were employed to create the sound of the creatures' heavy breathing. All of the sounds were re-recorded at a slow speed to create a lower tone. For the human sounds, Spivak did all of the screaming for the sailors as they fell into the pit during the log scene. The only character Spivak didn't scream for was Ann. For some of the most famous sounds in movie history, Fay Wray did all of her own screaming, which she recorded in a single afternoon session.

MUSIC *Kong*'s musical score was the work of legendary film composer Max Steiner. Born in Vienna, Austria-Hungary, on May 10, 1888, Steiner was a musical prodigy. As a child, he studied under Gustav Mahler and Johannes Brahms and he finished a four-year course of study at the Imperial Academy of Music in a single year when he was only fifteen. At sixteen he wrote an operetta and at eighteen moved to London, where he worked as a composer and concert pianist and eventually become the conductor of the London Opera House Orchestra. When World War I broke out, Steiner was deported from England for being an enemy alien. In 1914, he came to the United States, where he worked as a pianist in vaudeville theaters before becoming a conductor of silent film scores for the William Fox chain of movie theaters. He worked on Broadway orchestrating and conducting for both the *Ziegfeld Follies* and the *George White Scandals* before going to work for RKO in 1929.

Along with Erich Wolfgang Korngold and Franz Waxman, Steiner became one of the premiere composers of Hollywood's Golden Era. Aside from his enormous talent, Steiner made two significant contributions to film scoring. Inspired by Wagner, he began the practice of using leitmotifs—specific musical themes—for the major characters in a film, mixing them together and elaborating on them as the film progressed. He also introduced the practice of precisely matching the music to the onscreen action—a technique exemplified in *Kong* when the native chief strides forward toward the landing party, when Kong slams the *Elasmosaurus* in the rock in the Cave scene, or when Kong pounds on the decimated subway car (because this technique was widely used in cartoons, it was known as "Mickey-Mousing").

When the time came to score *Kong*, RKO president B. B. Kahane didn't want to spend any money on original music. He still thought the movie didn't stand a chance at the box office and didn't want to increase the already large budget any further. Instead, he ordered Steiner to reuse music that had already been recorded for other films, a not-uncommon practice at the time, especially for lower budget films. Cooper disagreed with this directive—he felt Kong required a big, original score. Unable to persuade Kahane to change his mind, Cooper decided to pay the additional $50,000 out of his own pocket (although the studio did later reimburse him). It took Steiner eight weeks to write all of the music for the film, which he and Murray Spivak then recorded using a forty-six-piece orchestra. Both in the composition phase and when it came time to mix the music in with the rest of the soundtrack, Steiner and Spivak worked closely together to coordinate the placement of music and sound effects so that they would complement rather than compete with one another. In the end, Steiner had produced one of the landmark scores in Hollywood history.

THE BOTTOM LINE RKO finalized the cost of the film at $672,254.75, which included approximately $430,000 in direct production expenses, the money spent on *Creation*, and some additional overhead expenses.

A NEW TITLE During the postproduction process, Selznick asked Cooper to come up with another title for the film. He felt that *Kong* sounded too much like *Grass* and *Chang* and was concerned that audiences would think it was another natural drama or else that it was a film about a Chinese general. Cooper thought this was a ridiculous concern because he knew that once the public saw the poster for the film showing a giant ape holding a woman in one hand and an airplane in the other while perched atop the Empire State Building, they would have a pretty good idea of what the film was about, but he agreed to come up with another title. To do so, Cooper returned to one of his original inspirations. There was a passage in Douglas Burden's book in which one of the locals was referred to as being "The king of Komodo." Both Cooper and Selznick like the alliteration and the implication and so Cooper's giant gorilla story was rechristened one last time as *King Kong*. A glass shot incorporating the new title was incorporated into the opening shot of the New York sequence.

RELEASE

In early March 1933, the completed film was screened for the exhibitors who would be showing the film in their theaters when it opened nationwide in April, after playing premiere engagements in New York and Los Angeles in March. The reaction was overwhelmingly positive and all predictions were that the picture was going to be a smash. At this point, the RKO board members who opposed the film finally came around. B. B. Kahane (who, as it turned out, loved the movie) ordered the RKO publicity department to mount a huge promotional campaign.

That campaign actually began in December 1932 with the publication of the novelization of the film's story by Grosset & Dunlop. The original plan had been for Edgar Wallace to write the novel after he finished the screenplay, but following Wallace's death, Cooper hired Delos W. Lovelace to do the job instead.

The drumbeat continued on February 10, 1933, when RKO sponsored a thirty-minute radio program on NBC advertising the movie. The program included sound and dialogue clips from the movie and earned high ratings. Ads were placed in magazines showing a drawing of Kong atop the Empire State Building and featuring the tag line: "The picture destined to startle the world." *Mystery* magazine began serializing the story, promoting it as "The last and greatest creation of Edgar Wallace." A trailer was prepared that showed no scenes from the movie, but only a giant, menacing shadow. A series of posters and lobby cards were prepared that featured the illustrations Byron Crabbe and Mario Larrinaga had prepared for the test-reel presentation the previous year, as well as some newly created artwork in the same vein.

THE OPENING *King Kong* opened in New York City on Thursday, March 2, 1933, at the city's two largest theaters: the 6,200 seat Radio City Music Hall and its sister theater across the street, the 3.700 seat RKO-Roxy. As was the custom in those days, the film was preceded at the Music Hall by a lavish stage show called *Jungle Rhythms*. On opening day, crowds were lined up around the block. Ten shows a day were scheduled and the film sold out every one for the first four days of its run, setting an all time attendance record for an indoor attraction. With ticket prices ranging from $0.35 to $0.75, the film grossed $89,931 in those four days—a spectacular amount, especially in the darkest days of the Great Depression (times were so bad that Franklin Roosevelt delivered his "We have nothing to fear but fear itself…" at his inauguration just two days after *Kong* premiered and declared a nationwide bank holiday the following Monday to prevent a run on the country's banks).

The film had its official world premiere on March 23, 1933, at Grauman's Chinese Theater in Hollywood. The Big Head was placed in the theater's forecourt and the cast and crew attended the screening. When Fay Wray first saw the film, she was distracted by all of her screaming, which she thought was excessive. As in New York, the screening was preceded by a seventeen-act stage show, the centerpiece of which was a performance by a troupe of African-American dancers called *The Dance of the Sacred Ape*. The film opened nationwide on April 10, 1933, and began its overseas run when it opened in London on Easter Sunday to sold out houses.

REVIEWS AND ANALYSIS The reviews were overwhelmingly positive:

"A spectacular picture, a sensational thriller, *King Kong* had its premiere last night at Grauman's Chinese Theater, and an intrigued and stimulated audience went home afterward to enjoy a first class nightmare. It's really a dandy pipe dream and every device of the trick camera and miniature setting, not to say, perhaps, some fancy enlargement of the ape, has been used to lend it realism. The fight between Kong and the dinosaur is a magnificent bout. Some of the horrors, it must be said, are a little strong. You won't want to miss this show!" —Edwin Schallert, *Los Angeles Times*

"At both the Radio City Music Hall and the RKO Roxy…the main attraction is a fantastic film known as *King Kong*. The narrative is worked out in a decidedly compelling fashion…Miss Wray goes through her ordeal with great courage. Robert Armstrong gives a vigorous and compelling impersonation of Denham. Bruce Cabot, Frank Reicher, Sam Hardy, Noble Johnson, and James Flavin add to the interest of this strange tale. It is when the enormous ape…is brought to this city that the excitement reaches its highest pitch." —Mordaunt Hall, *New York Times*

"*King Kong* is the supreme product of the coordination of human imagination and human skill." —Relman Morin, *Los Angeles Record*

There are many reasons why *King Kong* can be considered a classic film. The first is the story itself. On the surface the tale of a giant gorilla that falls in love with a beautiful girl and runs amok in New York City is an absurd and perhaps even a ridiculous one, but in choosing to marry this improbable yarn to the timeless theme of Beauty and the Beast, Merian Cooper transformed what could have been unbearably silly into something entirely sublime. In the process, he created an exciting fairy tale that connects directly with the viewer's subconscious in that wonderfully primal way that all great myths, legends, and fairy tales invariably do. On top of this incredible foundation, Cooper sprinkled a plethora of exciting elements—a lost island, a native sacrifice, a primeval land of still-living dinosaurs, the mysterious connection between apes and humans, and battles between the incredibly big and the impossibly small—that provoke the same wonderfully elemental and primal fascination. Cooper's final stroke of genius was to take this entire amazing confection and set it down right smack in the heart of the modern world. The clash between the prehistoric beast-god and the forces of modern technology served to create a story that was as new and original as it was ancient and familiar. Plus, the story is a lot of fun. In creating *Kong*, Cooper's primary goal was to create the greatest adventure story of all time and at this he succeeded magnificently.

Adding to the strength of the story, the film itself is extremely well made. The script that Edgar Wallace, James A. Creelman, Horace McCoy, Ruth Rose, and Cooper himself fashioned from Cooper's story is a masterpiece of construction. Cooper was right to resist the RKO executives' entreaties to introduce Kong at the beginning of the film. The almost hour-long build-up that the great ape receives creates so much anticipation in the audience that when he finally appears, we are struck not only by the power of the character itself, but also by the power of all of the amazing and terrible things we have been conjuring up in our minds about him since Denham first mentions the name "Kong." Cleverly, the script also provides all of the exposition necessary for us to understand the story before Kong arrives, so that once he does, the film is free to move at a breakneck pace that keeps us on the edge of our seat, never giving us time to catch our breath or ponder the absurdity of what we are seeing. The script is written in a broad, melodramatic style and the characters and dialogue are elemental and direct. While this lack of subtlety might not be appropriate for a serious drama, it is perfect for the archetypal story being told here. Of course, some of its social attitudes are now quite dated, which adds to the film's charm if not always to its sensitivity.

Like the writing, the directing and acting are simple and to the point. In helming the film, Cooper and Schoedsack demonstrate a strong sense of pacing and composition. Although they worked separately, the duo exhibit a remarkable unity of style that infuses the film with energy, excitement, and an exhilarating sense of high adventure. The standout in the human cast is Robert Armstrong. On paper, Carl Denham is a difficult character to warm to—he's callous, egotistical, and extremely reckless—but by portraying the ambitious film director with an energetic, visionary, and at times even manic enthusiasm, Armstrong turns a borderline villain into a roguishly charming anti-hero. Fay Wray plays her part simply, emphasizing Ann's sweet innocence and plucky nature. In addition, Wray projects a luminous beauty that leaves no doubt as to why the lost island's terrible Beast falls for her. Although Cabot struggles a bit in the dialogue scenes, he comes into his own during the action sequences as the perfect embodiment of a red-blooded hero. As Englehorn, Frank Reicher projects a stalwart rectitude that acts as a reliable ground to Denham's more colorful flights of fancy. Johnson, Clemente, and Hardy offer solid support and Wong provides welcome, if occasionally unintelligible, comic relief.

The music is stunning. With his ominous main and lilting love themes, as well as his frantic, thunderous action cues, Max Steiner has created the perfect symphonic equivalent to the incredible fantasy and adventure being portrayed onscreen. The score is so integral to both the film and its effect on an audience that it practically becomes another character in the story. The same can be said for the sound work, which is as intense as it is innovative. The editing is brisk and the cinematography is highly atmospheric, perfectly capturing the despair of depression-era New York, the nightmarish spectacle of the sacrifice scene, and the eerie beauty of the mist-covered prehistoric tableaus. The sets for the shipboard scenes are somewhat perfunctory, but the jungle settings are consistently lush and exotic.

The visual effects are truly groundbreaking. Aside from their technical brilliance, Marcel Delgado's models all have tremendous personality. They are not just props in this film, they are actual characters. The miniature settings are the best of their kind ever made. Most stop-motion films make do with the most perfunctory of settings—a rock here, a tree there—but the *Kong* team went far beyond this to create a minutely detailed, multidimensional, and completely believable world for their characters to inhabit. The use of the technical processes is as creative as it is innovative and helped the Kong team blend full-scale and miniature work into a thoroughly convincing whole.

Finally, there is Willis O'Brien's animation. It is certainly not overstating matters to say that O'Brien was a genius. No stop-motion animator or computer-generated character creator before or since has ever used the technique with O'Bie's degree of skill and finesse. O'Brien did not just animate his models; he brought them to life – imbuing them with an incredible amount of charm, personality, humor, and quirkiness. His masterpiece is Kong himself.

O'Brien took a simple eighteen-inch (sometimes twenty-four-inch) puppet and created a character so real—so terrifying and tragic, furious and funny, tender and touching—that he not only stole the film, but captured the imaginations of generations of moviegoers. Despite the great advances in materials, resources, and technology that have occurred since 1933, O'Brien's accomplishment remains as amazing and unique today as it was 72 years ago. In the film's opening credits, Willis O'Brien is identified as a technician, but his accomplishments go far beyond the technical and enter the realm of art and, at times, even enchantment.

BOX OFFICE *King Kong's* tremendous New York success was repeated all over the country and, eventually, all over the world. The film made approximately $2 million during its initial release, a staggering amount for 1933 and enough to pull RKO out of receivership and post a profit for the first time since its founding five years before.

AWARDS Surprisingly, *Kong* did not receive a single Academy Award nomination. David O. Selznick attempted to nominate O'Brien and his team for a special award for visual effects, but the Academy declined to do so. (At the time, no awards of any kind were given for special effects. After 1940, special awards were given only when a specific film's effects were deemed especially worthy. Visual Effects finally became a regular Oscar category in 1995.) The only *Kong*-related award that was given out that year was won by Sidney Saunders with Fred Jackman, who received a special achievement award for their development of the translucent acetate/cellulose rear screen.

LEGACY

For the cast and crew, working on *King Kong* was a very happy experience. Many of them knew each other before the film and most remained friends for years afterward (Fay Wray, Robert Armstrong, and the Schoedsacks remained especially close). Although no one realized at the time that they were working on a project that would come to be regarded as a classic, all regarded the experience as one of the highlights of their careers.

Most of the *King Kong* team went on to work on the film's sequel, but Fay Wray's involvement in the project ended with the first film. For many years afterward, Wray had an ambivalent attitude about having appeared in *King Kong*. Although she had enjoyed the experience and was quite proud of the finished product, she found that her appearance in the film had typecast her as a "scream queen," and that the only roles she was then offered were in thrillers and horror movies, which, for a talented actress who yearned to play a variety of roles, was extremely discouraging. Wray also encountered difficulties in her personal life. Her marriage to John Monk Saunders ended in 1939 and the alcoholic writer committed suicide in 1940. In 1942, Wray married screenwriter Robert Riskin (*It Happened One Night, Mr. Smith Goes to Washington, Mr. Deeds Goes to Town*), after which she retired from the screen in order to raise their two children. In 1950, Riskin had a stroke, which left him severely incapacitated; Wray cared for him until he died in 1955. She returned to acting in 1953, taking roles in a series of undistinguished films, as well as on television and the stage. She retired again in 1965, but returned for one last role in the 1980 television movie *Gideon's Trumpet*, opposite Henry Fonda. Always a writer (she was once quoted as saying "I've always cared much more about writing than I do about acting."), Wray coauthored the 1941 play *Angela Is Twenty-Two* with Sinclair Lewis and in the 1980s wrote another play called *The Meadowlark*. She also wrote articles for newspapers and magazines, as well as an autobiography titled *On the Other*

A life-size Kong balloon was placed atop the Empire State Building in 1983 to celebrate the film's fiftieth anniversary.

Hand. In 1970, Wray married Dr. Sanford Rothenberg, who had been Robert Riskin's doctor. They remained married until his death in 1991. For years, Wray did not understand the extreme fascination people had for *Kong* and at times resented the relentless focus on what, to her, was only one of the almost 100 films she had appeared in (her personal favorite was *The Wedding March*). In later years, however, Wray came to see how important the film was to people and how beloved the character of Kong had become. The fans enthusiasm for *Kong* made her enthusiastic and she eventually came to embrace her role in the phenomenon. Fay Wray died on August 10, 2004. Two days later, the lights on the Empire State Building were dimmed for fifteen minutes in her honor.

David O. Selznick worked at MGM for several years as a staff producer. In 1936, he started his own company, Selznick International Pictures, where he produced many pictures including his magnum opus *Gone With the Wind* (1939). In the years after *GWTW*, Selznick produced a string of other films, including *Rebecca* (1940), *Duel in the Sun* (1946), and *A Farewell to Arms* (1957). He died in 1965.

Bruce Cabot became a strong and versatile character actor, playing mostly villains. He served in World War II as an army intelligence officer and then spent much of the rest of his career appearing in films with his close friend John Wayne. His final film was the 1971 James Bond adventure, *Diamonds Are Forever*. Bruce Cabot died of throat cancer in 1972.

Co-screenwriter James A. Creelman went on to write (with Melville Baker) the story for Cooper's *Last Days of Pompeii* and then wrote his final screenplay, *East of Java*, in 1935. On September 9, 1941, he committed suicide by leaping from the roof of a building in New York City. After working for a few years as a production manager, Orville Goldner left Hollywood and became a producer of educational films. In 1975, he co-wrote (with George Turner) *The Making of King Kong*. He died on February 28, 1985. Character actor Sam Hardy passed away in 1935, following complications from surgery and Sandra Shaw died in 2000.

The money generated by *King Kong* saved RKO, putting it on a firm financial footing that allowed it to produce films such as the great Fred Astaire–Ginger Rogers musicals, Orson Welles's *Citizen Kane*, Alfred Hitchcock's *Notorious,* and many others. In the spring of 1933, RKO sold the Pathè lot. The Great Wall appeared in several more films until it was finally redressed to look like the city of Atlanta and then burned to the ground in 1938 for Selznick's production of *Gone With the Wind*. Ownership of the film itself has changed several times over the years. In the 1960s, RKO sold most of their films, including *King Kong* to United Artists (although RKO retained remake, sequel, and merchandising rights). MGM acquired the film in 1981 when it bought United Artists, and Turner Entertainment acquired *Kong* when cable television mogul Ted Turner bought MGM/UA in 1986. Time Warner bought Turner's company in 1996 and *King Kong* along with it.

King Kong enjoyed several successful theatrical rereleases over a twenty-three year period; the first was in 1938. Since the film's debut five years earlier, the Motion Picture Producers Association had stepped up the enforcement of its Production Code, which spelled out very clearly what could and could not be shown in motion pictures. Heading the list was nudity and excessive violence. As a result, RKO was forced to edit out several scenes that did not pose a problem in 1933 but were now considered unacceptable. In the revised version of the film, the scene in which the *Brontosaurus* kills the sailors was trimmed and the scenes in which Kong peels off Ann's dress and smashes the natives on the scaffold were excised completely. The scene in which Kong snatches the unsuspecting woman from her hotel bed and drops her, as well as all of the scenes in which Kong bites or stomps on people were also cut. The film was rereleased again in 1942, 1946, and 1952, each time with terrific success (it did so well in 1952 that theater owners actually named it Picture of the Year). At the close of the 1952 run, *Variety* estimated that *Kong* had earned an incredible $4 million in cumulative domestic rentals. RKO rereleased the film in theaters one last time in 1956. By then Hollywood, facing increasing competition from television and foreign films, had begun to relax the strictures of the Production Code, so all of the scenes that had been cut in 1938 were restored, with the exception of the scene in which Kong peels off Ann's dress, which couldn't be found.

After the 1956 release concluded, the film was sold to television. During its debut week, New York's WOR Channel 9 showed the film seventeen times in a single week on their Million Dollar Movie program. The film was shown twice each night during the week and seven more times over the weekend and topped the ratings every time. From then, the film became a television mainstay. It played constantly on television, capturing legions of new fans with every showing.

By the mid-1960s, the character was more popular than ever before. In response to heavy demand, RKO began licensing a series of Kong-related products, including posters, games, models, and comic books. In 1969, a print of the film containing the "lost" scene in which Kong peels off Ann's dress was found in Philadelphia. The scenes were restored and the movie was rereleased to art houses by Janus Films in 1971.

By then, Kong himself had become a genuine pop-culture icon. The character was referenced constantly in jokes and cartoons (one extremely prescient *New Yorker* cartoon from 1972 featured a wag at a cocktail party atop the newly constructed World Trade Center commenting how impressed he is that the twin towers were "finished so quickly and without incident," as a very determined Kong makes his way up the building below him). Academics and film theoreticians began studying the film. Many found symbolic meanings and hidden subtext in the picture and identified Kong as everything from a symbol of oppressed workers striking back against their capitalist exploiters to a towering metaphor on race relations to a Freudian nightmare of the first order. All of these interpretations were rejected by an increasingly irritated Merian Cooper, who maintained to the end that Kong was simply a gorilla and the film nothing more than a simple adventure story. Kong had even become an effective commercial spokesman. One local New York insurance company used clips from Kong's Manhattan rampage in the original film to illustrate the need for citizens to protect against the unexpected hazards of city living. Kong also appeared in ads for window cleaners, bras, and even the American Express card.

In 1975, the American Film Institute named *King Kong* one of the fifty best American films ever made. To howls of protest, the film was temporarily withdrawn from theatrical and television distribution in 1976 to clear the way for the Dino De Laurentiis remake. It returned in 1977 stronger and more popular than ever before and its appearance on home video in the early 1980s only reinforced its popularity. For the film's fiftieth anniversary in 1983, a recreation of the Big Head was placed in the forecourt of Mann's Chinese Theater in Hollywood for a repremiere of the film. Many surviving members of the film's cast and crew, including Fay Wray, attended. In New York City, a forty-foot-tall inflatable Kong balloon was placed atop the Empire State Building to mark the anniversary. The winds played havoc with it and it didn't remain in place long, but for those lucky enough to catch a glimpse, it was good to see the old boy back where he belonged. The film's honors continued in 1991, when it was added to the National Film Registry of the Library of Congress. In 1998, the American Film Institute ranked *Kong* as number 43 on its list of the 100 Greatest American movies of all time.

Seventy-three years after its release, *King Kong* continues to enthrall. Over the years, many people have attempted to explain the hold the film has on the popular imagination in terms both esoteric (it's themes and content form an intimate connection with our collective mythic unconscious) and concrete (people like monster movies). Ultimately, however, I think that *Kong*'s grip can best be explained by the fact that it is a breathtaking work of pure cinema—a stellar example of the twentieth century's most powerful art form. As exciting

Mario Larrinaga's epic conceptual drawing of the film's final scene.

as it is, the story would not have the impact that it does had it been realized instead as a novel or a stage play or even as a comic book (it has been translated into all of these forms, with diminished results). It is only through the cinema's unique and alchemic mixture of image, movement, and sound that Merian C. Cooper's strange and fantastic tale can come roaring to life and fulfill its incredible potential to amaze, to terrify, and, ultimately, to move. At its core, *King Kong* is a supreme example of the power and the magic of the movies.

■ ■ ■

CHAPTER 3

"SOME BABY"

The Making of *The Son of Kong*

1933. A month after the death of King Kong, Carl Denham is hiding out in his New York City apartment, trying to avoid an army of process servers. The now-infamous director is being sued for all of the death, damage, and mayhem caused by Kong's Manhattan rampage and is now flat broke. Denham feels terribly guilty about what happened to Kong and now wishes he had just left the giant ape back on the island where he found him. Charlie, the cook from the SS *Venture*, arrives at Denham's rooming house with the message that Captain Englehorn wants to see him. To escape his apartment house undetected, Denham enlists the help of Mickey, a sympathetic process server who is grateful to Denham for keeping him employed for much of the past month. Mickey disguises Denham as his assistant and sneaks him out of the building.

An original release poster for *The Son of Kong*.

Denham makes his way to the Brooklyn docks, where the SS *Venture* is moored. He meets with Englehorn, who, as it turns out, is also being sued. To escape the hot water they both are in, Englehorn proposes that he and Denham throw together a skeleton crew, leave New York, and sail the *Venture* to the East Indies, where he is sure that they can make a living carrying freight. Denham is interested, especially when he learns that he is about to be indicted by a grand jury. Eager to be free of his troubles, Denham accepts Englehorn's offer and they soon set sail.

Several months later, Denham and Engelhorn end up in the port of Dakang in the Dutch East Indies. While waiting for some business, they attend a threadbare tent show run by Peterson, a former circus ringmaster whose drinking cost him his job. Peterson now presents a pathetic animal act in which several monkeys dress up in costume and play musical instruments. When the monkeys finish, Peterson introduces his daughter Helene, who sings a plaintive song called "Runaway Blues." Although her voice is a bit rough, Denham is charmed by Helene and thinks she has show business potential. Englehorn remains unimpressed.

That night, Peterson gets together with Helstrom, a disreputable, down-at-the-heels ship captain of whom Helene disapproves. As Helene sleeps, the two men get drunk and begin to argue. During the fight, Peterson accuses Helstrom of deliberately losing his ship so that he could collect on the insurance. Helstrom is enraged by the obviously acurate accusation and hits Peterson over the head with a bottle. As Peterson falls, he knocks over an oil lamp, which ignites a pile of straw and starts a fire. Panicking, Helstrom runs out. Helene wakes up, frees the monkeys and pulls her father out of the burning tent. Unfortunately, she is too late and he dies in her arms.

The following morning, Denham comes across Helene as she tries to recapture the monkeys by calling to them. "You'll never catch a monkey that way," Denham says. "Did you ever catch a monkey?" Helene asks. "Did I?" Denham replies. "Lady, you'd be surprised." Helene tells Denham what happened to her father. Moved, Denham does his best to console her and tells her (as he once did Ann Darrow) to "keep your chin up." Later, Helene encounters Helstrom. She confronts the reprobate and tells him that she knows he killed her father. Helstrom warns Helene that she better keep quiet, but she informs him that she plans to talk to the Dutch magistrate when he arrives in port sometime in the next few days.

Worried, Helstrom goes into a nearby bar, where he encounters Denham and Englehorn just as Denham is telling the skipper that they need to find some excitement. Denham and Helstrom know one another—it turns out that Helstrom is the Norwegian skipper who once gave Denham the map to Kong's island. Worried about the magistrate, Helstrom (without saying why) asks Denham and Englehorn to take him to another port, one out of Dutch jurisdiction. They decline, saying they would have to travel too far out of their way to do so. To persuade them, Helstrom makes up a story about a trove of treasure that he claims was left behind on Kong's island by the people who built the wall. Excited, Denham wants to go to the island to look for the treasure.

Englehorn agrees. Helstrom becomes their partner and will accompany them—right out of Dutch waters. Before they leave, Denham says goodbye to Helene and gives her some money for passage out of Dakang. She asks if she can go with him instead. He says no and they part.

The *Venture* once again sets sail for the land of Kong. During the journey, Helstrom spends a lot of time with Red, the ship's surly Communist bosun. Scheming to take over the ship, Helstrom begins sowing the seeds for a mutiny by telling Red about all the men who died on the *Venture*'s last trip to the island, implying that it was all Denham and Englehorn's fault. Playing on Red's fear, Helstrom makes it clear that if he were the ship's captain, he would never lead his crew into danger. Meanwhile, Charlie discovers Helene—who decided not to take Denham's no for an answer—hiding in the ship's hold. Denham is both annoyed and pleased to see her. Helstrom is not at all pleased and warns Helene to keep quiet. Meanwhile, it becomes clear that Denham and Helene are attracted to one another. When the *Venture* arrives at Kong's island, Helstrom leads a mutiny. The crew takes over the ship and sets Denham, Englehorn, and Helene adrift in a lifeboat. Not wanting to stay aboard with the mutineers, Charlie comes along, smuggling some guns into the boat along with him. After they go, Helstrom starts ordering the crew about. Through with captains, the crew tosses Helstrom overboard and Denham reluctantly rescues him.

The castaways row to shore. Denham assumes that the natives will be glad to see him because he got rid of Kong for them, but he is wrong. The Native Chief confronts Denham and makes it clear that he is furious because Denham

CAST AND CREW: *The Son of Kong*

Carl Denham: Robert Armstrong; Helene Peterson: Helen Mack; Englehorn: Frank Reicher; Helstrom: John Marston; Charlie: Victor Wong; Mr. Petersen: Clarence Wilson; Red: Ed Brady; Native Chief: Noble Johnson; Witch King: Steve Clemente; Mickey: Lee Kohlmar; Lady Reporter: Gertrude Short; Mrs. Hudson: Katherine Ward; Stunts: Cy Clegg, Jack Holbrook

Produced and Directed by: Ernest B. Schoedsack; Executive Producer: Merian C. Cooper; Associate Producer: Archie F. Marshek; Screenplay by: Ruth Rose; Chief Technician: Willis H. O'Brien; Art Technicians: Mario Larrinaga, Byron L. Crabbe; Technical Staff: E. B. Gibson, Marcel Delgado, Fred Reefe, Carroll L. Shepphird, W. G. White, John Cerisoli; Technical Artists: Juan Larrinaga, Victor Delgado, Zachary Hoag; Music by: Max Steiner; Directors of Photography: Eddie Linden, Kenneth Peach (uncredited), J. O. Taylor, Vernon Walker; Camera Operators: Bert Willis, Linwood Dunn; Cliff Stein; Eddie Pyle; Edward Henderson, Felix Schoedsack; Camera

Assistants: William Reinhold, Clarence Slifer, James Daly; Chief Electrician: S. H. Barton; Grips: Pete Bernard, Tom Clement; Still Photographer: Gaston Longet; Optical Photography: Linwood G. Dunn, Cecil Love, and William Ulm; Rear-Screen Process: Sidney Saunders; Dunning process Supervisors: C. Dodge Dunning, Carroll H. Dunning; Williams Matte Supervision: Frank Williams; Film Editor: Ted Cheesman; Assistant Editor: Herny Berman; Sound Effects: Murray Spivack; Sound Effects Assistant: Walter Elliott; Sound Recordist: Jim Speak, Bill Turner; Supervising Art Director: Van Nest Polglase; Art Director: Al Herman; Set Decorator: Thomas Little; Costumes: Walter Plunkett; Wardrobe: Maxine Lockwood, Homer Watson; Makeup: Mel Berns, Al Senator; Property Master: Gene Rossi; Special Effects: Harry Redmond Jr.; Production Manager: C. J. White; Assistant Directors: William Cody, Ivan Thomas; Assistant Director (Additional Scenes): Walter Daniels; Titles: Pacific Title Company; Released by: RKO; Running time: Seventy-one minutes led Kong inside the Great Wall, which led to the destruction of the village. The castaways retreat and row around the coast of the island looking for another place to land. They finally find a small inlet on the far side of the island that leads to a small canyon surrounded on three sides by sheer precipice. Denham and Helene look around for a way out of the canyon. They discover a set of steps carved into one of the cliffs. Climbing the steps, Denham and Helene come upon a quicksand pit with a twelve-foot-tall albino gorilla stuck in the middle of it. This is Kiko, the apparent son of Kong. Feeling sorry for Kiko, Denham knocks over a small tree. The tree falls across the quicksand pit, giving Kiko a handhold. The young ape pulls himself out of the pit and scampers away.

Englehorn, Charlie, and Helstrom catch up to Denham and Helene and together they all discover the ruins of an ancient temple carved into the side of Skull Mountain. The entrance to the temple is sealed. Denham wonders if the treasure is inside. Helstrom sarcastically replies that it would be wonderful if it were. Englehorn, Charlie, and Helstrom set out to find some food. They encounter a *Styracosaurus*, which chases them into a cave and eats their gun. Meanwhile, a giant cave bear attacks Denham and Helene. Kiko hears Helene's scream and comes to the rescue. Kiko fights the cave bear and eventually beats him off with a stick. During the battle, Kiko injures his finger. Helene urges Denham to help him. Using a piece of Helene's skirt as a bandage, Denham binds Kiko's wound. As he does, he apologizes for what he did to Kong. That night, Helene and Denham make a fire and keep watch for the others. Helene falls asleep. Denham tenderly watches over her while an unseen Kiko watches over him.

Cut to: The next morning. After the *Styracosaurus* leaves, Englehorn, Charlie, and Helstrom emerge from their cave. Meanwhile, Denham and Helene try to get into the temple. Kiko helps them by knocking down the wall of rocks that block the entrance. Inside, they discover a giant carved idol that holds an incredible cache of valuable jewels—the treasure of the island is real. Denham declares that they're rich, but Helene points out that it isn't going to do them much good as long as they are stranded on the island. Just then, a giant dragon enters the cave and threatens them. Kiko battles the dragon and eventually defeats it. Englehorn Charlie and Helstrom return and Denham shows them the treasure. No one is more surprised than Helstrom to see it. Then Helstrom catches sight of Kiko. Frightened, he runs back to the boat. Worried that Helstrom will take the boat, Englehorn, Charlie, and Helene go after him while Denham goes back to get the rest of the treasure. As Helstrom tries to take the boat, a giant sea serpent emerges from the water and eats him. Suddenly, a storm blows up and the island begins to quake. The ground opens up and the mountains collapse as the island begins to sink into the ocean. To escape, Englehorn, Charlie, and Helene jump into the lifeboat and row away.

Meanwhile, the temple begins to collapse. To escape, Kiko and Denham climb out through a hole in the roof. They emerge onto the top of Skull Mountain as the island continues to sink. Helene spots Denham and Kiko and directs Englehorn and Charlie to row toward them. Kiko's leg gets caught in a

his usual method of recording the cries and roars of real animals and then rerecording them in reverse at a slower speed in order to lower the tone. Kiko's chatter was created by manipulating the sounds of baby gorillas and his roar was produced from a mixture of tiger and elephant roars. One of Fay Wray's screams from *King Kong* was dubbed in for Helen Mack in the cave bear scene and Spivak once again threw his own voice into the mix on occasion.

MUSIC Max Steiner created an all-new score for the film, based primarily around the theme of the song Helen Mack sings in the tent show, the aptly titled "Runaway Blues." He also devised a theme for Kiko and reprised bits of the *King Kong* score at key moments.

The postproduction period had its own drama when, in September 1933, Cooper suffered a massive heart attack and almost died. Although he eventually recovered, the incident, along with O'Brien's tragedy a month later, cast a pall over the film's finishing stages.

Postproduction was completed in October 1933, at which point *Jamboree* was officially retitled *The Son of Kong*. The final cost of the film was $269,262.

RELEASE

ADVANCE PROMOTION Compared to its predecessor, *The Son of Kong* received little in the way of advance promotion. It didn't really need any—*King Kong* was still fresh in the public's mind (and still playing in many markets around the country) when *Son* was ready for release. The ads for the picture emphasized its lighter tone ("All of the thrills of *King Kong*, but none of the horrors. A treat for the children" proclaimed one newspaper advertisement.) In England, the film was advertised as "A serio-comic phantasy."

OPENING *The Son of Kong* was released on December 22, 1933—eight months and twenty days after the debut of his father.

REVIEWS AND ANALYSIS The reviews were generally lukewarm:

"The Prince of the celebrated House of Kong is a vaudeville buffoon alongside his old man. This sequel to last season's hair raiser is a low melodrama with a number of laughs...although the comical intent of the producers is open to argument." —B. R. Crister, *New York Times*

"This is the sequel to and wash-up of the *King Kong* theme, consisting of salvaged remnants of the original production and rating as fair entertainment. Some technical advantages which put *King Kong* over as a novelty smash were dished up for the sequel...but the punch is no longer there and, in this rehash, the same qualities that thrilled on the first trip are likely to impress now as being too much for anybody to swallow. Producers appear to have forseen a psychological change in probable audience reception of another dose of the goofy theme. Evidence of this is reflected in the attempt to ginger up the proceedings with hokum." —*Variety*

"*Son of Kong* is a much friendlier ape than his blood-thirsty parent. The mysterious Skull Island of the former picture is destroyed by a quake and flood before the eyes of the audience in a breath-taking sequence." —*Los Angeles Times*

If the reviewers' sentiments were unduly harsh, their assessments were pretty accurate, because, sadly, *The Son of Kong* doesn't even begin to approach the greatness of its classic parent. To begin with, the story just isn't as dynamic—it lacks a theme with the same power and resonance as the Beauty and the Beast premise of the original. It also lacks the original's mythic undertones, as well as its spectacularly conceived set pieces and terrific narrative drive—the buildup is fine, but once we get to the island, *The Son of Kong*'s story is rushed and choppy. The ending comes out of nowhere and is illogical (Since when do earthquakes cause storms?).

The special effects are also less impressive: The optical work is excellent, but the miniature sets lack the depth and finesse of those in the original picture and sadly anticipate the threadbare sets that became the hallmark of the low-budget animated films of the 1950s and 60s. The creature design is also problematic—the painstakingly assembled dinosaurs in the first *Kong* seemed like real animals. The fantasy beasts on display here lack reality and seem hastily thrown together. The animation is not nearly as smooth and accomplished as in the original film—there's a rushed quality to the animals' movements and there's a sameness to the battles (which all seem to begin with a monster rushing in out of nowhere and attacking people, who then either run away or wait for Kiko to save them) and the animation lacks the quirks and personality so evident in every frame of *King Kong*.

One of the film's biggest problems is the son of Kong himself, who is nowhere near as compelling a character as his father. Part of the reason for this is that Kiko is not really central to the story. The first film was about Kong. *Son*'s story is about Carl Denham and his search for treasure. Kiko doesn't play a major part in this search. Instead, he is simply along for the ride. (This is one of the reasons why the fight scenes lack excitement. In the first film, Kong's battles with the dinosaurs were a central part of the story. In *Son*, they interrupt the story. Whenever a battle breaks out, the search for the treasure gets put on hold, only to start up again as soon as the battle is over.) And the attempts to make Kiko appear cute don't help much. His mugging and cooing are only mildly amusing, and the lack of ferocity robs the character of an essential dimension.

In spite of all these flaws, however, the film has much to recommend it. To begin with, it is very entertaining – it contains a generous helping of humor and is quite exciting in spots. The effects, while not as polished as those in the original, are cleverly conceived and still astounding. Max Steiner's score is quite good, if highly different than that of the original.

The Son of Kong's greatest asset is the character of Carl Denham. Seriously shaken by the events of the previous film, the showman's characteristic bravado is gone, along with its attendant recklessness. In its place, Denham has developed a conscience and even a heart. As a result, the character is softer and easier to like. Robert Armstrong enhances these qualities with a terrifically charming performance that absolutely steals the film. Armstrong makes Denham funny, heroic, romantic, and even tender. It's a bravura turn that makes one wish he had been given more leading-man roles in his film career. He carries the film on his shoulders and does so wonderfully. The rest of the cast is equally good. Helen Mack delivers a spunky performance with a touch of world-weariness that is quite appealing. Frank Reicher is his usual steady self and brings an unexpected bit of humor to his role. John Marston takes an unusual approach to the role of Helstrom, making the character more pathetic than evil. Victor Wong in terrifically funny, if still hard to understand. Finally, Lee Kohlmar gives a delightfully comic performance as Mickey the process server, surely the only German-accented Irishman in Depression-era New York.

The story problems aside, Ruth Rose's script is well written—the characterizations are fuller and the dialogue much wittier than in the original film. It also contains some wonderfully bizarre touches—for example, the character of Red the bosun, whose Marxist diatribes come totally out of left field and are all the funnier for it. The directing is also extremely sharp. Schoedsack brings an amazing amount of energy and visual flair to the proceedings. Some examples: The clever opening shot of Kong's fearsome face that turns out to be just a poster on Denham's wall; the terrifically exciting scene in which a desperate Helene tries to pull her father out of the burning show tent, kicking chairs out of her way as she goes; the close-up on Denham's feet that widens into a full shot as he hurries to say good-bye to Helene; and the sequence in which the sailors whisper to each other when Helene is found to have stowed away aboard the *Venture*. These shots show what a clever, inventive director Schoedsack could be and makes one wonder why he didn't become a more important director in the aftermath of the Kong pictures. (A question that could be asked about all of the participants for that matter. In spite of how well done and popular the Kong pictures were, with the exception of Steiner, Cooper, and Linwood Dunn, none of the cast and crew went on to do major films, but instead spent the balance of their careers working in B pictures.) Finally, the ending of the film, despite the illogic of its conception, is undeniably powerful. It is almost impossible not to shed a tear as Kiko sacrifices himself for his new friend Denham. If the character has failed to make much of an impact before, at this point he achieves a tragic nobility that is truly affecting. The final shot of Kiko's bandaged hand sinking below the waves is a real kicker.

If *King Kong* is a classic cinematic myth, *The Son of Kong* is more akin to a fondly remembered bedtime story, but as that it succeeds just fine.

BOX OFFICE The film did very well when it first opened in the United States, although it didn't have the staying power of the original film. It was a smash hit overseas, especially in Asia, but its total earnings never came anywhere near its parent.

LEGACY

Merian C. Cooper resigned from RKO in May 1934. After producing two epic films—*She* and *The Last Days of Pompeii* (both 1935)—to settle his contract,

Cooper became part-owner of the Technicolor Company and formed Pioneer Pictures in order to use the three-strip process to make color films such as *La Cucaracha* (the first Technicolor short) and *Becky Sharp* (the first Technicolor feature). After David Selznick and Pioneer cofounder John Whitney formed Selznick International Pictures, Cooper joined that company as vice president. He resigned in 1937 and teamed up with director John Ford to form Argosy Pictures. When the United States entered World War II, Cooper joined the Army Air Corps and fought in China, New Guinea, and Europe. After the war, Cooper became a Brigadier General in the Air Force Reserve and produced such John Ford classics as *Fort Apache* (1948), *She Wore a Yellow Ribbon* (1949), and *The Quiet Man* (1952). After formally ended their partnership, the two teamed up one last time to make Ford's masterpiece *The Searchers* (1956). In the early 1950s, Cooper became a partner in Cinerama, a company that had developed a process that utilized three separate pieces of film running side by side in synchronization to create an enormous three-dimensional widescreen picture. Cooper produced and codirected *This Is Cinerama* (1952) to introduce the process. In 1952 Cooper received a special Academy Award for his "many innovations and contributions to the art of motion pictures." He died of cancer on April 21, 1973. To the end, he felt that *Chang* was his best picture.

After *The Son of Kong*, Ernest Schoedsack teamed up with Cooper, Rose, and O'Brien again for *The Last Days of Pompeii*. After that, the Cooper-Schoedsack partnership officially ended, although they remained friends and worked together occasionally in ensuing years. In 1937, Schoedsack directed two low-budget action films—*Trouble in Morocco* and *Outlaws of the Orient*—and in 1940 he directed *Dr. Cyclops* (1940), a horror film about a mad scientist who shrinks his victims to miniature size. During the war, Schoedsack joined the air force as a combat and aerial photographer. During a high altitude flight to test photographic equipment, he accidentally dropped his face mask and his eyes were severely damaged by the extremely cold temperatures. As a result, his vision was impaired to the point of near-blindness and remained so for the rest of his life. After an unhappy experience directing *Mighty Joe Young* (1949) for Cooper and Ford and a prologue for Cooper's *This Is Cinerama* (1952), Schoedsack retired from motion picture directing and devoted himself to sound recording. He died on December 23, 1979.

As for Mrs. Schoedsack, Ruth Rose wrote the screenplays for *The Last Days of Pompeii*, *She*, and *Mighty Joe Young*. She also gave birth to a son, Peter. Ruth Rose and Ernest Schoedsack remained married until her death on June 8, 1978.

Sadly, Willis O'Brien's string of tragedies continued. Toward the end of 1933, he began dating a woman named Hazel Rutherford. Soon after, Rutherford learned she had cancer and leaped to her death from the top of a hotel in downtown Los Angeles. Having survived her self-inflicted gunshot wounds, Hazel O'Brien died from complications of both tuberculosis and cancer in January 1935. In a more positive turn of events, O'Brien married Darlyne Prenett on November 17, 1934. The marriage turned out to be a happy one and they remained together for the rest of O'Brien's life. O'Brien's career also had its ups and downs. He supervised the special effects for *The Last Days of Pompeii*, but after that, several other proposed projects failed to come to fruition. During World War II, O'Brien produced miniature work for several military-training films. When the war ended, O'Brien had trouble finding work and was reduced to doing matte paintings in order to make a living. In 1949, he reteamed with Cooper and the Schoedsacks for *Mighty Joe Young*, for which he won an Oscar for Best Special Effects. After *Joe Young*, O'Brien produced animation effects for three low-budget features – *The Animal World* (1956), *The Black Scorpion* (1957), and *The Giant Behemoth* (1959). He also worked on producer Irwin Allen's remake of *The Lost World* (1960)—for which Allen substituted photographically enlarged lizards for O'Brien's animated dinosaurs—and spent his time developing a series of projects that, for one reason or another, never got off the ground. In the fall of 1962, O'Brien was hired to animate the final sequence of *It's a Mad, Mad, Mad, Mad World* (1963). On November 8, in the midst of preproduction, O'Brien suffered a heart attack and died at the age of 76.

After *The Son of Kong*, Robert Armstrong continued to work as a character actor in dozens of films, the most memorable of which was his semi-reprise of the Denham character when he played showman Max O'Hara in *Mighty Joe Young*. Armstrong retired in 1952 after suffering a serious heart attack and died on April 21, 1973, at age of eighty-two, just a few hours before Merian Cooper.

Helen Mack went on to appear in films such as *His Girl Friday* (1939). In 1941 she began appearing on radio in the series *Myrt and Marge* and later became a very successful radio producer and director. She died on August 13, 1986. Frank Reicher appeared in *The Life of Emile Zola* (1937), *Ninotchka* (1939), and *The Secret Life of Walter Mitty* (1947) and worked again with Ernest Schoedsack in *Dr. Cyclops* (1940). His last film was *Superman vs. the Mole Men*, starring George Reeves. He died on January 19, 1965 at the age of ninety. John Marston appeared in films such as *Manhattan Melodrama* (1934), *Angels with Dirty Faces* (1938), and *Union Pacific* (1939), mostly in small and uncredited parts. He died in 1962. Clarence Wilson appeared in *The Life of Emile Zola* (1937), *You Can't Take It with You* (1938), *Son of Frankenstein* (1939), and dozens of other films before his death in 1941. Ed Brady passed away in 1942, Lee Kohlmar in 1946, Steve Clemente in 1950, Victor Wong in 1972, and Noble Johnson in 1978.

Max Steiner worked at RKO until the late 1930s, when he moved to Warner Bros. In the course of his long career he amassed over 500 credits, was nominated for twenty Oscars, and won three for his work on *The Informer* (1935), *Now Voyager* (1942), and *Since You Went Away* (1944). He also composed the scores for two of the greatest American films of all time—*Casablanca* (1942) and *Gone With the Wind* (1939). He died on December 28, 1971. His *King Kong* music was reused in many RKO films over the years and he always referred to the score as one of his favorites.

After working with Cooper on *Last Days of Pompeii*, Archie Marshek became a film editor at Paramount. He retired in the early 1970s and died on March 29, 1992. Walter Daniels became a well-respected second unit director and production manager. He became RKO's studio manager in 1941 and remained there until he retired. He died in 1969. Following *The Son of Kong*, Eddie Linden photographed a long string of B pictures before moving in to television in the early 1950s. He died in 1956. *The Son of Kong* was J. O. Taylor's last feature film credit as a cinematographer, but he continued to work in special effects photography for years to come. Vernon Walker remained the head of RKO's Optical Effects Department until he died in 1948, working on over 300 films, including *Citizen Kane* (1941). Linwood Dunn succeeded Walker and later became the head of the studio's entire Special Effects Department. When RKO stopped producing movies in 1957, Dunn started his own company, Film Effects of Hollywood, where he worked until he retired in 1985. In his spare time, he developed one of the first zoom lenses, and a version of his optical printer that he sold commercially. He died on May 15, 1998.

Ted Cheesman edited many more films for RKO, including *She* and *Mighty Joe Young* for Cooper. He died on December 30, 1964. Murray Spivak continued his career as a motion picture sound recordist and editor. He worked on films such as *Flying Down to Rio* (1933), *Laura* (1944), *Spartacus* (1960), and *The Sound of Music* (1965). In 1966 Spivak worked for future *King Kong* producer Dino De Laurentiis on De Laurentiis's production of *The Bible* and in 1969 Spivak won an Oscar for his work on *Hello Dolly*. He died on May 8, 1994. Van Nest Polglase worked at RKO and then Columbia until retired in the late 1950s. He died in 1968. Carroll Clark worked at RKO until the late 1950s, then went to Disney to work on *Darby O'Gill and the Little People* (1959), *Mary Poppins* (1964), and other productions. He died in 1968. Al Herman continued to design sets for *The Hunchback of Notre Dame* (1939), *They Live By Night* (1949), and many other films. He retired in the late 1950s and died in 1973. Walter Plunkett designed the costumes for David O. Selznick's production of *Gone With the Wind* (1939) and then moved to MGM, where he worked for many years designing costumes for films such as *Singing in the Rain* (1950), *An American in Paris* (1951), *Seven Brides for Seven Brothers* (1954), and *How the West Was Won* (1962). He died in 1982.

As for O'Bie's team: Marcel Delgado worked with his friend Willis O'Brien again on *The Last Days of Pompeii, Mighty Joe Young* and *It's a Mad, Mad, Mad, Mad World*. In between, he continued to create miniatures and special effects for films such as *War of the Worlds* (1953), *20,000 Leagues Under the Sea* (1954), and his last project: *Fantastic Voyage* (1966). He died on November 26, 1976. Mario Larrinaga worked on many RKO films as a matte artist and special effects technician, including *She, Gunga Din* (1938), and *Citizen Kane* (1941). He died on December 15, 1979. Byron L. Crabbe worked on the special effects settings for *The Last Days of Pompeii* before dying suddenly in 1935. Ernest Smythe, W. G. White, and John Cerisoli continued their work for the RKO Art and Special Effects Departments. Carroll Shepphird continued to work in visual effects both at RKO and later at MGM, where he became head of the Visual Effects Department. He died on March 1, 1984. E. B. Gibson and Fred Reefe continued working as grips on various RKO productions. In the 1950s, Reefe moved to Warner Bros. to work on that studio's Western television shows. He retired in 1962 and died on February 17, 1971.

In 1948, RKO was bought by Howard Hughes, whose eccentric management destabilized the company and caused it to flounder. In 1955, Hughes sold RKO to General Teleradio, a division of the Ohio-based General Tire and Rubber Company, which was interested in obtaining the company's film library so it would have something to show on its television stations. In 1957, the renamed RKO-General stopped making movies and from then on concentrated solely on its broadcasting operations. The Hollywood lot was sold to television producer Desilu and then acquired by Paramount Pictures when it bought Desilu in 1966. In 1989, General Tire left the broadcasting business and sold what was left of RKO to actress Dina Merrill and her husband, Ted Hartley, who have since attempted to revive the company as an active production entity, with limited success.

And what of Kong/Kiko himself? O'Brien took one of the eighteen-inch Kiko models home with him after filming on *The Son of Kong* was complete and kept it there for many years. Somewhere along the line, O'Brien loaned the model to a friend named Phil Kelison, who, in turn, lent it to Movieworld, a memorabilia museum in Burbank, California. When Movieworld closed in the early 1970s, Kelison retrieved the model and gave it to Bob Burns, an editor and gorilla-suit performer well known for collecting and caring for science fiction and horror film props. By the time Burns acquired the model, the foam and rubber elements were in such a serious state of decomposition that they were beginning to eat away at the armature itself. To save the armature, Burns had the foam and rubber steamed off. The armature itself is now in Burns's private collection. A hand from the twenty-four-inch King Kong model is in the collection of the Los Angeles County Museum of Natural History. *King Kong* 2005 director Peter Jackson owns a hand from the second eighteen-inch model, as well as the tiny Kong model used to film Kong's fall from the Empire State Building and the articulated *Brontosaurus* model. For years, the *Stegosaurus* and the mechanical *Brontosaurus* models were in the personal collection of *Famous Monsters of Filmland* publisher Forrest J. Ackerman. The fate of the other models remains uncertain. Some are probably owned by private collectors, but given the tendency of the old time studios to regularly cannibalize and reuse props from their films over and over again, it is likely that many of them were broken down and reused several times over before finally being discarded (O'Brien himself used the giant spiders in *The Black Scorpion*). The fate of the Big Head and the Big Hand are also uncertain.

The Son of Kong has not enjoyed the longevity of the original *King Kong*. After it concluded its initial run, it was never given a major rerelease. It was sold to television in 1956 and appeared occasionally as a late-night or Saturday-morning feature, but never became the staple that *Kong* did. Today it is something of a forgotten film—while many have heard the title, few have actually seen the movie. When it does play, however, it is certainly worth watching, both as a companion piece to its epic parent and as a welcome treat on its own.

■ ■ ■

CHAPTER 4

KING KONG GOES TO JAPAN

The Making of

King Kong Versus Godzilla and *King Kong Escapes*

By the early 1960s, it had been almost thirty years since a new King Kong film had appeared in theaters. All that was about to change, however, thanks to a down-on-his-luck animator and a 165-foot-tall radioactive lizard with a (literally) scorching case of bad breath.

Poster for a 1977 re-release of *King Kong Versus Godzilla*.

KING KONG VERSUS GODZILLA (KINGUKONGU TAI GOJIRA)

1963. Mysterious warm currents in the Bering Sea are causing large icebergs to break up and drift southward toward Japan. *The Seahawk*, a United Nations submarine, is sent to investigate. Meanwhile, the Tokyo-based Pacific Pharmaceutical Company has developed a new, nonaddictive sleeping agent based on the juice of an exotic red berry found on Faro, an isolated island located sixty-two miles south of the Solomon Islands. Unfortunately, Pacific Pharmaceutical cannot mass-produce the sleeping agent because the Faro Islanders refuse to let them have any more berries, which the natives claim they need to placate their god—a giant monster that allegedly lives on the island. Further frustrating Mr. Tako, the head of Pacific Pharmaceutical, is the fact that the ratings for the company-sponsored scientific television program are declining. To increase them, Tako wants to find some sort of big gimmick that he can build a publicity campaign around. The tales of Faro's giant monster arouse Tako's interest, so he orders two of his subordinates—Osumu Sakuri and Kinsaburo Furue—to go to Faro Island to get more berries and find the monster. Before he leaves for Faro, Osumu has dinner with his sister, Fumiko, and her boyfriend, Kazuo Fujita, who is himself about to leave on a business trip to Hokkaido. Kazuo's company has developed a new thin wire that is as strong as steel.

The *Seahawk* arrives in the Bering Sea and discovers a weird light coming from one of the icebergs. The *Seahawk* collides with the iceberg, which begins to break up. As a rescue helicopter approaches, the pilots see Godzilla, a giant prehistoric lizard with scorching radioactive breath, breaking out of the iceberg. Once free, Godzilla heads for Japan. Reaching the outer islands, it attacks a refinery. Army tanks attempt to destroy Godzilla, but their firepower has no effect on the giant creature.

Meanwhile, Osumu and Kinsaburo sail to Faro Island, where they are captured by hostile islanders and taken to the natives' village, where they come upon a large scaffold designed to prevent something large from entering the village from the island's interior. Osumu and Kinsaburo also observe the natives crushing scores of the precious red berries into juice, which is then stored in large jars kept in an isolated hut on the edge of the village. The angry native chief demands that Osumu and Kinsaburo leave the island immediately, but Osumu wins them over with an offer of cigarettes. A storm whips up, during which Osumu and Kinsaburo hear what sounds like the roar of a giant beast coming from the island's interior.

The next day, the two men hike into the interior of Faro Island in search of the monster. They hear another loud roar and get caught in an avalanche, during which Kinsaburo is superficially injured. They return to the native village and send a young boy to get some of the berry juice to ease Kinsaburo's pain. While the boy is in the storage hut, a giant octopus emerges from the sea and envelops the building. The natives rush to the rescue, but are unable to drive off the giant creature. Suddenly, the loud roar is heard again, this time coming from behind the scaffold. Kong, a giant ape approximately 150 feet tall, smashes through the scaffold and enters the village. Seeing the giant octopus, Kong throws boulders at it, eventually driving it off. Afterward, Kong drinks some of the berry juice, which causes him to pass out. As the natives do a dance of worship around the fallen Kong, Osumu and Kinsaburo decide to capture Kong. Kong is lashed to a large raft and towed back to Japan by a Pacific Pharmaceutical ship. Mr. Tako arrives to take charge of the project as word arrives from the Japanese government that it will not allow Kong to be brought to Japan. Busy dealing with Godzilla, the government doesn't want another giant monster on its hands.

Back in Tokyo, Fumiko gets word that Kazuo's plane has crashed. Learning that there are survivors in Hokkaido, she immediately departs for that distant city.

Soon after she leaves, Kazuo—who, as it turns out, missed the plane—arrives at Fumiko's apartment. He learns that Fumiko has gone to Hokkaido just as news arrives that Godzilla is headed there as well. Fearing for Fumiko's safety, Kazuo immediately goes after her. Godzilla attacks Fumiko's train, destroying it. She escapes and tumbles down into a riverbed. After running a roadblock and pushing past a stream of frightened passengers, Kazuo locates Fumiko and they return to Tokyo.

Back at sea, Kong wakes up. He begins thrashing around, which upsets the raft and almost sinks the Pacific Pharmaceutical ship. The raft is blown up, but Kong survives and swims toward Japan. Coming ashore, he encounters Godzilla and the two creatures engage in a brief skirmish. Kong throws rocks at Godzilla, who responds by blasting Kong with his radioactive breath. Burned and confused, Kong retreats.

As Godzilla continues his advance toward Tokyo, the army attempts to stop him by driving him into a pit and blowing him up, but the plan fails and Godzilla keeps going. When scientists notice that Godzilla is weakened by electrical current, government officials order the military to erect a string of high-tension wires around Tokyo.

Arriving in Tokyo, Godzilla attempts to break through the wires, but the electricity repels him and he retreats to Mount Fuji. Soon after, Kong arrives on the outskirts of the city. The electrical wires have no effect on him. In fact, the electrical current actually makes Kong stronger. Millions flee as Kong bites through the wires and enters the city. Kazuo and Fumiko try to flee, but get separated when they attempt to board an evacuation train. Kazuo is left behind as the doors close and the train pulls out of the station. Kong attacks the train and picks up the car Fumiko is riding in. She falls out of the car and Kong catches her. Infatuated with Fumiko, Kong tosses aside the train car and carries her to the top of Tokyo's Capitol Building. The armed forces surround the tower. Soon after, Osumu and Kinsaburo arrive. Talking to the general in charge, Osumu suggests using the red berry juice to knock out Kong. Gallons of the juice are loaded into missile warheads, which are then launched at Kong. The warheads explode in the sky above Kong, dousing him in narcotic berry spray. Kong

King Kong Goes to Japan:

The Making of

King Kong Versus Godzilla

and

King Kong Escapes

———

119

passes out, and Kazuo rescues Fumiko from his grasp. Government officials then decide to transport Kong to Mount Fuji and pit him against Godzilla. Their hope is that the two monsters will destroy one another.

Using Kazuo's superstrong wire, Kong is attached to a series of inflatable balloons. Helicopters are then used to airlift him to Mount Fuji and drop him on top of the dormant volcano. Skidding down the side of the mountain, Kong slams into Godzilla and knocks him over. The fight is on.

Godzilla immediately gains the upper hand—the giant lizard knocks Kong down with its tail and buries him in boulders. The situation looks grim, but then an electrical storm whips up. Kong is struck by lightning and revives. With electrical current shooting out of his hands, he grapples with Godzilla and the two monsters battle their way across the countryside until they reach the ocean. Locked in a mutual death grip, both creatures fall off a cliff and plunge into the sea. An earthquake strikes as they disappear beneath the waves. A few minutes later, Kong surfaces. There is no sign of Godzilla, who has apparently been buried in the quake. Kong swims off toward the horizon, presumably headed for Faro Island.

KONG GOES EAST The Japanese King Kong films of the 1960s are usually considered the low point of the great ape's cinematic career. Cheaply made and featuring tacky special effects that rejected stop-motion animation in favor of men in poorly made monster suits, they are considered an affront to everything Willis O'Brien stood for. In light of this, it is ironic that O'Bie himself was the man who was (indirectly) responsible for initiating them.

In the late 1950s, O'Brien was experiencing another one of his periodic career slumps. Looking for a way to improve his fortunes, he began thinking about ways to bring King Kong back to the screen. Short of an out-and-out remake, O'Brien thought that the most exploitable approach would be to team Kong with another famous monster and have the two of them do battle. He knew just the monster he wanted to use. *Frankenstein* had always been one of O'Bie's favorite novels and he had long dreamed of using stop-motion animation to bring the Monster to life. O'Brien had actually done some preliminary work on a stop-motion adaptation of the novel at First National Pictures in the late 1920s, but the project was canceled before it entered production. The phenomenal success of Universal's 1931 version of *Frankenstein* starring a live-action Boris Karloff as the Monster put an end to O'Brien's plans, but the notion of doing a Kong team-up revived his interest in the subject. In 1961, O'Brien wrote a treatment for a story that combined Mary Shelley's famous creation with his own.

King Kong Versus Frankenstein focused on Dr. Frankenstein's great grandson, who assembles a giant monster made from the bodies of dead humans in his secret African lab. After Dr. Frankenstein brings the creature to life, it kills him and escapes. As the Monster goes on a murderous rampage, several American promoters decide to capture the creature and put it on display. As they depart for Africa, another expedition sets sail for Skull Island, intending to do the same thing with King Kong. Both giant creatures are captured and brought to

San Francisco, where they are put on show in a stadium. During the show, the monsters break loose and engage in a titanic battle that spills out into the streets and levels a good part of the city in a duel to the death.

Figuring that the story would be more effective if Kong fought another beast, O'Brien then revised the concept and replaced Frankenstein's multipart human monster with a creature assembled from the pieces of dead animals. He named the creature Ginko and changed the title of his story to *King Kong Versus Ginko*. After finishing the treatment, O'Brien created several dramatic pieces of concept art depicting the highlights of his story and then set out to secure RKO's permission to use the character of Kong. To do so, he needed to meet with a man named Daniel T. O'Shea.

By 1961, RKO-General was no longer an active motion picture studio. Although the company had sold its film library to United Artists, it retained the remake, sequel, and merchandising rights to all of its old properties, so anyone seeking to use them had to obtain a license from the company to do so. To broker these properties, RKO-General had retained the New York–based O'Shea, a retired attorney who had worked in RKO's legal department back in the 1930s. O'Shea, who received a commission on the deals he brokered, was empowered to negotiate deals, but not to confirm them or to sign contracts. That power rested with Thomas O'Neil, the president of General Tire, RKO-General's parent company.

O'Shea liked O'Brien's concept and recommended that he pitch the idea to John Beck, producer of the Ava Gardner vehicle *One Touch of Venus* (1948) and the James Stewart classic *Harvey* (1950). Beck liked O'Brien's concept and the two made a handshake deal to proceed with the project. Beck then hired sci-fi screenwriter George Worthing Yates (*Earth Versus the Flying Saucers* [1956], *The Amazing Colossal Man* [1957]) to turn O'Brien's story into a screenplay called *King Kong Versus Prometheus*. Beck then pitched the project to a num-

King Kong Goes to Japan:

The Making of

King Kong Versus Godzilla

and

King Kong Escapes

———

121

CAST AND CREW: *King Kong Versus Godzilla*

Osamu Sakurai: Tadao Takashima; Kazuo Fujita: Kenji Sahara; Fumiko Sakurai: Mie Hama; Kinsaburo Furue: Yu Fujiki; Mr. Tako: Ichirô Arishima; General Shinzo: Jun Tazaki; Prime Minister Shigezawa: Akihiko Hirata; Tamiye: Akiko Wakabayashi; Dancing Girl: Akemi Negishi; Faro Island Chief: Yoshio Kosugi; Witch Doctor: Ikio Sawamura; Scientist: Harold Conway; Submarine Captain: Osman Yusuf; Kingukongu: Shoichi Hirose; Gojira: Haruo Nakajima, Katsumi Tezuka; Stunt Choreographer: Haruo Nakajima. *English Version*: Eric Carter: Michael Keith; Yutaka Omura: James Yagi; Dr. Arnold Johnson: Harry Holcombe; Newscaster: Byron Morrow; Narrator: Les Tremayne

Directed by: Ishirô Honda, Produced by: Tomoyuki Tanaka and John Beck; Screenplay by Shinichi Sekizawa; Music by: Akira Ifukube; Director of Photography: Hajime Koizumi; Art Directors: Teruaki Abe, Takeo Kita; Film Editor: Reiko Kaneko; Sound Editors: Sadamasa Nishimoto, Hisashi Shimonaga; Assistant Directors: Koji Kajita, Koji Hashimoto; Special Effects: Eiji Tsuburaya; Special Effects Crew: Teruyoshi Nakano, Teizo Toshimitsu, Akira Watanabe, Fuminori Ohashi; Miniature Effects Photography: Teisho Arikawa, Koichi Kawakita, Kuichiro Kishida; Optical Effects: Yukio Manoda, Hiroshi Mukoyama, Sokei Tomioka, Taka Yuki. Released by: Toho Company, Ltd.; Running time: Ninety-eight minutes. *English Version*: Directed by: Thomas Montgomery; Produced by: John Beck; Screenplay by Bruce Howard, Paul Mason; Editorial supervision: Peter Zinner; Sound Editor: William L. Stevenson; Music Supervisor: Peter Zinner; Released by: Universal; Running time: Ninety-one minutes.

ber of studios, but couldn't find a buyer. Eventually, O'Brien and Beck lost touch and the project fell by the wayside, or so O'Brien thought. In actuality, Beck continued to pitch the project, this time to foreign companies. One of those companies was a well-known maker of giant-monster movies—Japan's Toho Studios.

THE HOUSE OF GODZILLA   In 1953, Warner Bros. released *The Beast from 20,000 Fathoms*. Based on a story by Ray Bradbury and featuring stop-motion animation effects by O'Brien protégé Ray Harryhausen, the film told the story of a giant prehistoric lizard that is awakened from hibernation by an atomic bomb test in the Arctic. The creature makes its way to New York City, where it comes ashore and destroys many well-known landmarks before it is finally killed off. The film was extremely successful and kicked off a cycle of giant, atomic radiation-created monster movies, including *Them!* (1954), *It Came from Beneath the Sea* (1955), *Tarantula* (1955), *Attack of the Crab Monsters* (1956), and *The Deadly Mantis* (1957).

Inspired by the success of *Beast*, Toho staff producer Tomoyuki Tanaka decided to do his own version, set in Japan and playing off the current concerns over atomic testing in the Bikini Atoll. Tanaka hired science fiction writer Shigeru Kayama to write a script about a prehistoric monster that is awakened by an atomic bomb test. After making its first appearance on a remote Japanese island, the 165-foot tall, fire-breathing creature makes its way to Tokyo, where it lays waste to the city before being destroyed by an "ultimate weapon" that removes all oxygen from the ocean. Tanaka brought in Ishiro Honda, a director best known for making small-scale dramas, to direct the film. Honda also worked on the script with Kayama and cowriter Takeo Murata. Eiji Tsuburaya, the head of Toho's special effects department, was put in charge of creating the film's effects.

The film's budget was too low to afford stop-motion animation, so the decision was made to take the more cost-effective approach of using a man in a monster suit to play the creature. Several designs were considered before one for a monster that looked like a cross between a *Tyrannosaurus* rex and a *Stegosaurus* was chosen. The creature was supposed to be either a prehistoric dinosaur or an atomic mutation, but given its look and the fact that it breathed fire, it was actually more of a dragon than anything else. Effects designer Fuminori Ohashi helped to construct a dramatically detailed, 200-pound rubber suit that was worn by actor/stuntman Harou Nakajima. As the start of filming approached, the dragon still did not have a name. As a joke, the film's crew began calling it Gojira, a word that means half-gorilla, half-whale and was the nickname of an overweight man who worked in Toho's publicity department. The name stuck. During production, the man-in-the-suit was supplemented by the use of an articulated Gojira head for fire-breathing close-ups and a miniature puppet to film long shots. Animation was used to create a glow on Gojira's dorsal plates when it used its radioactive breath and rear-screen projection and traveling-matte processes were used to combine shots of Gojira with footage of frightened humans. Finished at a cost of approximately

$900,000, *Gojira* (1954) was the most expensive Japanese film ever made at that time.

Despite its rip-off origin, the film was surprisingly effective. Photographed in stark black-and-white and featuring a powerful score by Akira Ifukube, the film was moody, dark, and deadly serious. Given a chilling roar made by rubbing a leather glove on the strings of a contrabass, Gojira itself was quite terrifying. The suit was convincing, the miniatures well photographed, and the optical effects competently handled. Honda patterned the scenes of destruction after newsreel footage of Hiroshima, and, while claims that the story had been conceived as a cautionary tale about the abuse of atomic power were exaggerated, the allegorical aspects of the finished film were hard to miss. The film was a smash hit in Japan and the following year was sold to an American distributor—Joseph E. Levine's Embassy Pictures.

Thinking that U.S. audiences would not accept a purely Japanese film, Levine decided to shoot some additional scenes (directed by Terry Morse) using American actor Raymond Burr that were then spliced into the dubbed picture. Levine also changed the name of the dragon from Gojira to Godzilla (legend has it that "Godzilla" was a mispronunciation of the word "Gojira," but that story may be apocryphal) and the title of the film to *Godzilla: King of the Monsters*. Released as an exploitation picture in 1955, the film did very well.

Toho followed up *Gojira* the following year with a sequel: *Gojira No Gyakushu* (*Gojira's Counterattack*). Directed by Matoyoshi Oda, the new film featured a second giant dragon (since the original had been killed off) with a slightly different appearance than the first (this one had pointy bat ears and fangs). Gojira II (played by *Gojira's* Haruo Nakajima) is found living on an island with another revived prehistoric creature named Angiras. Both creatures end up fighting in the streets of Osaka, leveling the city in the process. At the end of the film, Gojira II kills Angiras, but ends up buried beneath tons of ice. Although it lacked the punch of the original film, the sequel was still serious minded, effective, and successful. Warner Bros. acquired the film for U.S. distribution in 1959. After the film was dubbed into English, the Japanese music track was replaced with music from the Warner Bros. films *Kronos* (1957) and *The Deerslayer* (1957), a narration track was added, and the film was retitled *Gigantis: The Fire Monster*.

The success of the two Gojira films prompted Toho to produce a series of Kaiju (giant monster) movies that included *Rodan* (1956) and *Mothra* (1961). By the early 1960s, Toho was thinking about bringing Gojira back and Beck's *King Kong Versus Prometheus* project seemed like an ideal way to do so. The Japanese loved Kong. The original film was so popular when it first opened in the country that an unauthorized silent remake called *Wasei KinguKongu* (which literally means *Japanese King Kong*) was produced in 1933 starring actor Isamu Yamaguchi in a Kong suit. This film was followed in 1938 by an equally unauthorized sequel called *Edo Ni Arawareta KinguKongu* (*King Kong Appears in Edo*), which featured Ryanosuke Kabayama in a Kong suit made by Fuminori Ohashi. In 1959, Toho's biggest rival, the Toei Studios, produced a film called *The Monster Gorilla*, about a giant horned gorilla that fights a giant

King Kong Goes to Japan:

The Making of

King Kong Versus Godzilla

and

King Kong Escapes

———

123

gorilla robot. It is alleged that Toho itself had once approached RKO about doing an official remake of Kong but was rebuffed. (Although RKO was willing to license the Kong character for sequels, for years the company refused to consider proposals for direct remakes of the original film.)

Tanaka told Beck he would be interested in his project if he could replace Prometheus/Ginko/the Monster with Gojira. Beck agreed, so Tanaka bought the script and made a deal for Beck to coproduce the film. Beck and Tanaka then met with O'Shea and licensed the rights to the Kong character from RKO-General for $25,000 plus a percentage of the profits. Beck did not tell O'Brien about the deal. In fact, O'Brien did not hear anything at all about the project until shortly before his death in November 1962. When he did he was, by all accounts, heartbroken. Merian Cooper, on the other hand, was furious. Insisting that he had only licensed the rights to his creation to RKO for two films rather than sold them outright, Cooper felt that the rights to Kong and any further use of the character belonged to him and not RKO. Upon learning of Beck's production, Cooper initiated a legal battle with his former studio that would not be settled until 1980, when a judge in the United States District Court of Los Angeles ruled that, while the rights to *King Kong* and *The Son of Kong* belonged to RKO, the rights to the character did indeed belong to Cooper (and, by then, his estate). In 1962, however, all of that was far in the future and there was nothing Cooper could do to keep RKO or Beck from going ahead.

WRITING THE SCRIPT   Tanaka brought in veteran screenwriter Shinichi Sekizawa to rewrite Yates's script. The primary alteration, of course, was the replacement of Prometheus with Gojira—or actually, Gojira II—who enters the new film by breaking out of the ice in which it was entombed at the end of *Gojira No Gyakushu*. The location of the story was switched to Japan and the nationality of the main characters was changed from American to Japanese, although some American characters were included. The set-up for the King Kong storyline pretty much remained the same, but the idea that promoters would try to capture Gojira and put him on display was dropped. Instead, Gojira would journey to Japan simply because it was the giant lizard's ancestral home. Rather than have both monsters accidentally break loose and begin battling, Japanese officials would now deliberately pit them against one another in the hope that Kong would defeat Gojira (Kong was considered the hero of the story and Gojira — as it was in its first two films — the villain). For years, a rumor circulated that the film actually had two endings—an American version in which Kong won and a Japanese ending in which Gojira won. That rumor was false—Kong was intended to be the victor from the very inception of the project.

To even the odds between the two opponents, some changes had to be made to Kong's basic character. The official height of the giant gorilla was increased from 18 or 25 ft. to approximately 150 feet so that he would make a better match for the 165-foot tall Gojira (although, as was common in Kaiju films, the actual size of the creatures would vary wildly from scene to scene, with both monsters often represented as being 200 to 400 feet tall). Although many key concepts were reprised from the original *King Kong*—i.e. Kong's island home, a tribe of natives that worship him, the Great Wall (although in the finished film it is really more of a Great Scaffold), Kong's fascination with a human girl, his wrecking of a train, and his climbing of a landmark building (which, in this case, was smaller than he was)—some changes were made to Kong's backstory. Rather than be discovered on Skull Island by a movie director, he would now be found on Faro Island by a Japanese pharmaceutical company. Kong was also given a superpower of sorts (the Japanese were fond of inserting science fiction touches into their Kaiju films)—the ability to grow stronger by absorbing electricity. Gojira was given a corresponding Achilles' Heel—electricity would now make it weaker (a handicap it did not possess in previous films).

Finally, Sekizawa introduced a great deal of humor into the piece (much of it generated by Mr. Tako, the head of Pacific Pharmaceutical). This was a big change from the serious tone of the original *King Kong* and of the first two Gojira films and was done to make the film more suitable for younger viewers, who made up a sizeable portion of Toho's audience. The script's final title was *KinguKongu Tai Gojira* (*King Kong Versus Gojira*).

PREPRODUCTION As the script was being written, Tanaka and Beck brought original *Gojira* director Ishiro Honda back to direct. Hajime Koizumi was engaged to photograph the film—the first Gojira or Kong film to be shot in color— and Eiji Tsuburaya was once again assigned to create the film's special effects. Although it is alleged that some consideration had been given to producing the film using stop-motion animation, ultimately the film's effects were produced in the standard Toho Kaiju fashion—using men in suits acting on miniature sets. Art directors Teruabi Abe and Takeo Kita designed the full-scale and miniature sets, all of which were erected on the Toho soundstages and backlot.

Toho contract players Tadeo Takashima (Osumu), Kenji Sahara (Kazuo), Yu Fujiki (Kinsaburo), and Mie Hama (Fumiko) were hired to head the cast. Popular comedic actor Ichiro Arishima was engaged to play Mr. Tako. A group of Japan-based Americans were brought in to play the crew of the *Seahawk* in the submarine scenes.

Effects designer Akiro Watanabe created an all-new Gojira suit for the film. This time Gojira's head was slimmed down; it lost its fangs, ears and a few toes; and its eyes were enlarged. Watanabe was allegedly instructed to make some of these changes in order to make Gojira appear less frightening to children. Two men were cast to play the part—veteran Gojira Haruo Nakajima and new-comer Katsumi Tezuka. A veteran stuntman, Nakajima also choreographed the fights between Gojira and Kong.

For Kong, Fuminori Ohashi (who had also created the gorilla suit for *Edo Ni Arawareta KinguKongu*) created a fur-covered rubber suit and mask that was worn by actor/stuntman Shoichi Hirose. As talented as Watanabe was at creating giant dragons, he was much less skilled at creating apes and his Kong has been derided over the years as being one of the most ridiculous-looking gorilla costumes ever created. The baggy body suit with mangy-looking fur was bad enough (and looked even worse when it was wet), but it was the poorly

King Kong Goes to Japan:

The Making of

King Kong Versus Godzilla

and

King Kong Escapes

————

125

sculpted, expressionless mask with sunken, lifeless eyes that really torpedoed it. Kong not only doesn't look like an ape, but he doesn't look like any other creature on the face of the earth either. In order to help Hirose appear more gorilla-like, the suit was given crude arm extensions (actually just long sticks attached to the suit's gloves) that bent the arms in unnatural directions and made the suit look even more awkward than it normally did. There was speculation that Watanabe deliberately made Kong look silly so that he wouldn't frighten young children and so that audiences would root for him instead of Gojira.

PRODUCTION Production began in early 1962. The live-action scenes were filmed on the Toho soundstages and in a variety of locations in and around Tokyo. The Kazuo/Fumiko scenes are played straight, but in an attempt to increase the film's level of comedy, Honda directed the scenes involving Osumu, Kinsaburo, and especially Mr. Tako in an overly broad manner. An elaborate native village set was built on a Toho soundstage and was used to stage the tribe's ritual chanting, singing, and dancing in honor of Kong, as well as to stage the full-scale portions of the giant octopus fight. In a sincere but racially insensitive attempt to portray the people of Kong's island as they had been in the original film, the Japanese actors playing the natives were painted with black body makeup and given modest afro wigs to wear on their heads.

The miniature scenes were all filmed at Toho. Assisted by Tsuburaya, Honda directed the battle scenes between Kong and Gojira in a fairly straightforward manner, although some of the moves both creatures employed during their fights sometimes made them seem more like professional wrestlers than prehistoric beasts. As was typical in Japanese productions, all of the actors performed in their native languages. The scenes in which the English-speaking actors appear were subtitled for the film's Japanese release.

SPECIAL EFFECTS In addition to men in suits performing on miniature sets, Tsuburaya employed several other effects techniques to realize the miniature scenes. An articulated Kong head (one that could blink its eyes, open its mouth, and even extend a tongue) was used for close-up shots of Kong drinking berry juice and biting through electrical wires. While it was not a tremendous improvement over the regular mask, it looked at least something like an actual ape).

The giant octopus was portrayed by four different live octopi (one of which Tsuburaya took home and had for dinner once the filming was over). A plastic-and-rubber version was also created for the shot in which the octopus grabs Kong around the head. Stop-motion animation was also used for some shots of the octopus grabbing a native with one of its tentacles. Willis O'Brien's beloved technique was also used for two long-distance shots of Kong rampaging through Tokyo, and for a shot during the climactic fight in which Godzilla leaps up and kicks Kong in the chest. The miniature Kong puppet featured in these scenes was also used (without animation) to film part of the sequence in which Kong is airlifted to Mount Fuji. The scene in which Kong awakens as he approaches the dormant volcano incorporates all three versions of Kong—man in a suit, articulated head, and miniature puppet. An inert giant Kong hand was also used for several shots in which Kong holds Mie Hama, who is replaced in some long shots by a semi-articulated doll. To combine the miniature footage with the full-scale actions, Tsuburaya employed several optical effect techniques, including split screen and rear-screen projection. He also made used of a color film adaptation of the Williams Double-Matte system called *blue screen.*

As with shots produced by the Williams system, a blue screen shot is begun by separately photographing a foreground subject and a background plate. The foreground subject is photographed against an evenly lit, pure blue backing. Before filming, all traces of blue are eliminated from the foreground subject, which is then lit with white or amber light. Steps are also taken to prevent blue light from the screen from reflecting onto the foreground subject. Once the foreground subject has been photographed, the shot is sent to the optical effects lab, where it is printed onto three separate strips of black-and-white film. Each

King Kong Goes to Japan:

The Making of

King Kong Versus Godzilla

and

King Kong Escapes

———

127

Kong battles Godzilla in this composite publicity still.

time the shot is printed, a different filter— blue, red, or green—is used. In the end, three separate black-and-white copies of the shot—one recording all of the blue information in the shot, one recording the red information, and one recording the green—are produced. Once completed, these records—called positive color separations—are temporarily set aside. A holdout matte is then produced by printing the original camera negative onto high-contrast black-and-white film through a blue filter. Because of the filter, all of the blue areas in the original image (including the screen) are removed and appear as white in the final print. All of the other colored areas in the original image are reproduced as a dark gray or black. The holdout matte is then reverse-printed to create a cover matte.

Once the mattes have been completed, the background plate is placed into an optical printer along with the holdout matte and printed onto a dupe negative. As with the Williams system, the black sections of the holdout matte prevent an area in the exact shape of the foreground image from being exposed on the dupe. The dupe is then rewound so that the foreground image can be printed on it. Before this can be done, the blue background must be removed from the foreground image. This is where the positive color separations come in. Rather than using the original negative to reprint the foreground image, the red and green separations are placed into the optical printer one at a time, along with the cover matte, and printed onto the dupe negative through the appropriate color filter, a process that inserts the foreground image into the "hole" in the background plate one layer at a time. The blue separation is left out, which eliminates the blue screen from the foreground image. Unfortunately, it also creates another problem, because all of the non-blue material in the Blue separation must somehow be reinserted into the foreground image or else the final picture will be incomplete. There are several ways to accomplish this, all of them complex and all requiring a great deal of skill and know-how.

As with the Williams system, matte lines, image cut off, and fringing are big problems with the use of blue screen. Color adds an additional complication into the mix, because if the mattes are improperly made, then light from the backing screen creeps through the cover matte and turns the fringing halo in the final composite a bright and noticeable blue. It takes a great deal of time, expertise, and money to create effective blue screen shots, which were all resources that Tsuburaya's team unfortunately lacked. As a result, most of the composite work in *KinguKongu Tai Gojira* is extremely poor.

POSTPRODUCTION When production wrapped, the film was assembled by editor Reiko Kaneko. The ninety-eight-minute final cut was released in Japan in August 1962 and was a tremendous success. In fact, *KinguKongu Tai Gojira* was then and remains the highest grossing Gojira film in the series' long history.

After the Japanese launch, John Beck made a deal with Universal Pictures to release the film in the United States and then went to work preparing a new version of the film for American audiences. To this end, he hired television writers Bruce Howard (*My Favorite Martian*) and Paul Mason (*Ben Casey*) to translate the Japanese dialogue into English. In their script, Gojira was once again renamed Godzilla.

Television director Thomas Montgomery (*Gilligan's Island, My Mother the Car*) supervised a group of American actors as they performed the new English-language dialogue, which was then cut into the film's soundtrack in place of the original Japanese dialogue (the American submarine crew's voices were also replaced, since the original performances were deemed wooden). Montgomery also directed some additional scenes Howard and Mason had written that were designed to clarify the plot for American audiences. These scenes starred Michael Keith as Eric Carter, a newscaster who sets up the story for American viewers, confers with his Japanese colleague Yutaka Omura (played by Japanese-American actor James Yagi), and later interviews a Dr. Arnold Johnson (played by Harold Holcombe), who explains the origins of both Kong and Godzilla and details their long history of mutual animosity. These scenes were then edited into the original film by Peter Zinner (who would go on to better things when he worked on *The Godfather* and *The Godfather Part II*). To make room for them, some of the original Japanese scenes—mostly ones involving Mr. Tako and Pacific Pharmaceuticals—were pared down or eliminated. The U.S. version of the film ran ninety-one minutes—seven minutes shorter than the Japanese release. In a final touch, most of the original score, composed for the film by Akira Ifukube, was removed and replaced by music from Universal's 1954 monster film *The Creature from the Black Lagoon*. John Beck received a presentation credit and an "English Version produced by" credit on the American prints.

In the run up to the film's release, Universal's promotional department prepared some posters and lobby cards to advertise the film. Unimpressed with the look of Toho's Kong, the studio pasted images of Marcel Delgado's twenty-four-inch Kong model over some of the stills.

REVIEWS *King Kong Versus Godzilla* was released in the United States in June 1963. The U.S. reviews were mixed. Most of the complimentary notices evaluated the film strictly as exploitation or kiddie fare:

"A funny monster picture? That's what Universal has in *King Kong Versus Godzilla*. Audiences which patronize this kind of picture will eat it up. It should be a big success via the multiple booking, exploitation route." —James Powers, *The Hollywood Reporter*

"Exploitation-minded exhibitors should have a field day with this Japanese import. While the story is preposterous and loaded with stilted dialogue...the special effects are unusual and merit considerable praise." —*Box Office*

"Sublime stuff. Richly comic, briskly paced, oddly touching, and thoroughly irresistible. Outrageous of course, and deplorably acted and atrociously dubbed to boot. But what matters most is the sheer invention of its exemplary trick work." —John Cutts, *Films & Filming*

Others were less charitable:

"To the list of the century's great preliminary bouts—Dempsey–Firpo,

King Kong Goes to Japan:

The Making of

King Kong Versus Godzilla

and

King Kong Escapes

————

129

Sullivan–Paar, Nixon–Kennedy, Patterson–Liston, Steve Reeves–Gordon Scott—add the main event, *King Kong Versus Godzilla*. From the mysterious East comes this monstrosity to end all monstrosities, the epic clash between the 30-year old, breast-beating, Hollywood-born-and-bred gorilla with the overactive pituitary and the seven-year old, pea-brained, flame-throated, tail-wagging cross between a stegosaurus and a Tyrannosaurus rex who fights out of Tokyo, Japan. Onward and upward with the arts."—"Tube,"— *Variety*

"*King Kong Versus Godzilla* should be an explicit enough title for anyone. Viewers who attend the ridiculous melodrama unveiled at neighborhood theaters should know exactly what to expect, and get what they deserve. The one real surprise of this cheap reprise of earlier Hollywood and Japanese horror films is the ineptitude of its fakery. When the pair of prehistoric monsters finally get together for their battle royal, the effect is nothing more than a couple of dressed-up stuntmen throwing cardboard rocks at each other."—Eugene Archer, *New York Times*

It is hard to evaluate the Japanese Kaiju films in the same way that one evaluates a regular film, because they tend to exist in a very unique world (or worlds) of their own. That said, however, *KinguKongu Tai Gojira/King Kong Versus Godzilla* is still a pretty bad movie. The concept, as in all "meet-up" films, is a gimmick and the rest of the film's elements are not strong enough to overcome the inherently phony premise. The script is weak and unfocused, and the tone of the piece is all over the place—it's hard to take the action and battle scenes seriously when they are surrounded by broadly played (and not very funny) comedy scenes. The acting is good enough within context, but the special effects work is just awful. The Gojira costume is passable, but the Kong suit is an unqualified disaster. The miniature sets and vehicles are impressively designed and constructed, but, as in most Kaiju films, they are terribly photographed and completely unconvincing. The scale is all over the place—never more so than in the scene in which Kong pulls Fumiko from the train when Kong holds the train in one hand and Mie Hama in the other and both are the same size—and the optical work is terribly shoddy. The American version is choppy and ham-fisted and creates considerable confusion as to Godzilla's place in the world (the Americans act like it has just been discovered, while to the Japanese it seems like old news). With that all said, the film is still reasonably entertaining as long as your expectations aren't too high. No matter how badly done, it is still fun to watch two giant monsters throwing one another around and smashing miniature sets to pieces. In addition, the film demonstrates a great deal of undeniable respect and affection for the character of Kong that shines through in spite of the character's less-than-stellar onscreen appearance. The Japanese clearly love Kong and that love is evident in spite of the lousy production values.

BOX OFFICE The film played around the United States on a series of exploitation double-bills with other horror and monster movies and as a kiddie matinee attraction. While it was not a blockbuster, it was very successful.

LEGACY Following *King Kong Versus Godzilla*, John Beck went on to produce *The Singing Nun* (1966) starring Debbie Reynolds and *The Private Navy of Sgt. O'Farrell*, starring Bob Hope. He died in July 1993.

In 1965, a portion of Willis O'Brien's original concept for *King Kong Versus Frankenstein* was used as the basis for another Toho Kaiju film called *Furankenshtain Tai Chitei Kaiju Baragon* (*Frankenstein Versus the Giant Monster Baragon*), which was released in the United States as *Frankenstein Conquers the World*. The film begins at the end of World War II, with Nazi scientists bringing the heart of the Frankenstein Monster to Japan just as the Hiroshima bomb hits. Irradiated by the atomic blast, the heart grows into a 20-foot-tall boy who looks as much like the Universal Frankenstein monster as copyright laws would allow. Eventually, the Monster battles a giant reptile called Baragon and much destruction ensues. The film spawned a sequel: *Furankenshtain No Kaiju: Sanda Tai Gaira* (*The Giant Monster Frankenstein: Sanda Versus Gaira*), in which the giant Monster battles his evil twin. The film was released in the United States as *War of the Gargantuas*, with all of the Frankenstein references removed. O'Brien received no credit on either film.

Toho produced twelve more Gojira movies before ending the series in 1974. The films became increasingly juvenile as they went along. Gojira became a heroic figure, and the plots started to feature more science fiction, fantasy, and comedy. The quality of the effects also declined significantly and the Gojira suit itself became more cartoonish and less convincing. Most of the films were released in the United States (some directly to television) in atrociously dubbed and choppily edited versions. Toho revived the Gojira series in 1984 and has continued it in various incarnations ever since. In 1998, Tri-Star Pictures produced a big-budget American remake of the original *Gojira* called *Godzilla*, starring Matthew Broderick and Jean Reno and directed by Roland Emmerich (*Independence Day*). The film was universally panned by the critics and was a major disappointment at the box office.

KING KONG ESCAPES (KINGUKONGU NO GYAKUSHU)

1967 (?): The United Nations submarine *Explorer* is traveling through the Java Sea in search of oil. The *Explorer* is commanded by Carl Nelson, whose hobby is researching Kong—a legendary giant gorilla alleged to exist on Mondo Island. In his spare time, Nelson has also drawn up plans for a giant Kong robot that he someday plans to build. Realizing that the *Explorer* is going to pass by Mondo Island, Nelson and his first officer and fellow Kong enthusiast, Lieutenant-Commander Jiro Nomura, would like to stop at the island to investigate the legend, but their mission doesn't allow them the time.

What Nelson doesn't know is that his plans for the giant Kong robot have been stolen by the nefarious Dr. Who—a criminal mastermind with a secret base in the North Pole. Dr. Who has been hired by an unnamed foreign government to obtain large quantities of Element X, a radioactive substance that will allow the unnamed foreign government to achieve worldwide nuclear domi-

King Kong Goes to Japan:

The Making of

King Kong Versus Godzilla

and

King Kong Escapes

———

151

nance. It exists beneath the surface of the North Pole, but only a creature with Kong's size and strength is able to dig it out fast enough and in sufficient quantities. Dr. Who has used Nelson's plans to construct his own Kong robot—called Mechani-Kong—that is the same size and has the same strength as the real Kong. Dr. Who demonstrates his creation's abilities to Madame Piranha—an agent of the unnamed foreign government who is supervising him. Dr. Who orders Mechani-Kong to climb down into a fissure in the earth, where it begins to dig out ore containing Element X. Unfortunately, Element X's magnetic mass destroys the robot's circuits and it shuts down. Madam Piranha is disappointed and is on the verge of pulling Dr. Who's funding, but he convinces her to give him additional time so that he can repair Mechani-Kong and make another attempt to mine Element X.

Meanwhile, the *Explorer* is damaged in an underwater landslide and has to stop in a bay off Mondo Island to make repairs. Nelson and Nomura decided to take advantage of the downtime to explore the island. Accompanied by the *Explorer*'s nurse (and Nomura's girlfriend) Lieutenant Susan Watson, they board the *Explorer*'s hovercraft and fly to the island. There they encounter a mysterious old hermit who warns them that they are trespassing on Kong's home. Nelson and Nomura leave Susan with the hovercraft as they set out to investigate. As Susan waits, a giant dinosaur appears and threatens her. Her screams awaken a giant creature living in a nearby cave. As the dinosaur moves in for the kill, Kong—a sixty-foot-tall gorilla—emerges from the cave and lets out a roar. Spying Susan, Kong is entranced by her beauty. He picks her up and caresses her gently. He then places her safely in a tree and squares off against the dinosaur. The two engage in a titanic battle that ends with Kong pounding the lizard into submission. Kong then retrieves Susan from the tree. She asks him to put her down and he complies. When Nomura and Nelson escort Susan to the hovercraft, Kong tries to follow, but the dinosaur revives and bites him in the leg. As Nelson, Nomura, and Watson fly off, Kong kills the dinosaur once and for all by snapping its jaw. Pursuing Susan, Kong follows the hovercraft into the water. After saving the hovercraft from a giant snake, Kong reaches the *Explorer* and starts rocking it back and forth in an attempt to get Susan to

CAST AND CREW: *King Kong Escapes*

Commander Carl Nelson: Rhodes Reason; Lieutenant Susan Watson: Linda Miller; Lieutenant-Commander Jiro Nomura: Akira Takarada; Dr. Who: Eisei Amamoto; Madame Piranha (Madame X): Mie Hama; Hermit: Ikio Sawamura; Kingukongu: Haruo Nakajima; Mekanikongu: Hiroshi Sekita; English version: Voice of Dr. Who: Paul Frees; Female voices: Julie Bennett

Directed by: Ishirô Honda; Screenplay by: Kaoru Mabuchi; Produced by: Tomoyuki Tanaka, Arthur Rankin; Music by: Akira Ifukube; Director of Photography: Hajime Koizumi; Lighting:

Toshio Takashima; Film Editor: Ryohei Fujii; Production Designer: Takeo Kita; Assistant Director: Ken Sano; Sound Recordists: Shoichi Yoshizawa; Sound Effects: Sadamasa Nishimoto; Special Effects Supervisor: Eiji Tsuburaya; Special Effects Crew: Teisho Arikawa, Yasuyuki Inoue, Fumio Nakadai, Teruyoshi Nakano; Miniature Photography: Kuichiro Kishida, Yoichi Manoda, Hiroshi Mukoyama, Sokei Tomioka; Released by Toho Company, Ltd. Running time: 104 minutes. English version: Produced and directed by: Arthur Rankin; Screenplay by: William J. Keenan; Released by: Universal Pictures; Running time: 96 minutes.

come out. Susan finally emerges and calms Kong down. Kong returns to shore and watches forlornly as the now-repaired sub sails away.

Nelson travels to New York and announces Kong's discovery at U.N. head-quarters. Nelson is ordered to return to Mondo and study Kong, an assignment he enthusiastically accepts. Meanwhile, Dr. Who decides to speed up his plans by capturing the real Kong and then using him to mine Element X. Dr. Who and his henchmen travel to Mondo Island and use ether bombs to knock out Kong. After shooting the hermit, Dr. Who orders Kong loaded onto a ship and returned to the North Pole. When the *Explorer* returns to Mondo, Nelson discovers that Kong has been taken.

Dr. Who uses a pulsating light to hypnotize Kong in order to get him to go into the mine and begin digging out the ore that contains Element X. Dr. Who's plan works for a while, but eventually Kong stops responding and attempts to escape. Dr. Who prevents him from doing so by locking him in the mine, but the doctor realizes he is going to have to find a better way to control Kong. Knowing that

King Kong Goes to Japan:

The Making of

King Kong Versus Godzilla

and

King Kong Escapes

———

155

Poster for *King Kong Escapes*.

Nelson, Nomura, and Watson are able to influence Kong, Dr. Who kidnaps them. Utilizing torture, seduction, and bribery, Dr. Who tries to force the trio to help him, but they resist and refuse to help. Meanwhile, Kong gets fed up, claws his way to the surface of the North Pole, and runs away. Dr. Who sends the now-repaired Mechani-Kong after him, but Kong eludes the robot by jumping into the water and swimming away. Since Mechani-Kong can't swim, he is forced to give up the chase. At this point, Madame Piranha tells Dr. Who that her government is going to cancel his contract. Determined to prevent this, Dr. Who decides to go after Kong and use Mechani-Kong to recapture him.

Kong swims to Japan and comes ashore near Tokyo. Dr. Who follows in his ship. Seeking to avoid an international incident that will reflect badly on her unnamed country, Madame Piranha has a change of heart and frees Nelson, Nomura, and Watson, who escape from the ship as it enters Tokyo Bay. Dr. Who discovers Madame Piranha's treachery and detains her.

Meanwhile, an agitated Kong enters Tokyo and appears ready to rip the city to pieces. As millions flee, the Japanese army deploys its tanks to confront him. Nelson, Nomura, and Watson arrive on the scene and convince the authorities not to hurt Kong. Susan runs out to greet Kong, who picks her up. Susan's presence calms Kong. She is about to convince him to leave the city peacefully when Mechani-Kong suddenly appears. Kong puts Susan down and faces off against the robotic monstrosity. Operating Mechani-Kong by remote control from his ship, Dr. Who tries to hypnotize Kong by activating a pulsating light on the top of robot's head, but Nomura shoots it out. Free from hypnosis, Kong goes on the offensive and the battle begins. The two monsters smash each other around a bit before Mechani-Kong grabs Susan and climbs up the Tokyo Tower. Kong follows in hot pursuit. Mechani-Kong drops Susan, but Kong catches her. Delivering Susan to safety, Kong goes after Mechani-Kong with a vengeance. Nomura retrieves Susan as Kong and his robotic doppelgänger battle it out atop the tower. Back on Dr. Who's ship, Madame Piranha tries to help by destroying Mechani-Kong's controls. Dr. Who responds by shooting her dead. Back on the tower, Mechani-Kong shorts out and falls to the ground, where it is smashed to pieces. Kong roars in triumph as the city cheers.

The next morning, Kong, Nelson, Nomura, and Watson go after Dr. Who as the villain tries to escape by sailing away on his ship. Leaping into the bay, Kong catches up with Dr. Who's ship and begins pounding on it. As Kong rocks the ship back and forth, Dr. Who is pinned to a wall by a heavy console and dies. The ship sinks and Kong begins swimming out to sea. Susan calls after him, begging him to return, but Nelson tells her to let him go. "I think he's had enough of what we call 'civilization.'"

THE PERILS OF KONG Following the tremendous success of *Kingu-Kongu Tai Gojira*, Toho was eager to produce an entire series of Kong films. To this end, Tomoyuki Tanaka commissioned a new script called *KinguKongu Tai Ebirah (King Kong Versus Ebirah)*, in which Kong battles a giant condor, Mothra (Toho's Kaiju moth), and finally a giant shrimp, Ebirah. All of the monster props and costumes were built for the film, including a new Kong suit and a miniature set representing Kong's island home. Tanaka then approached Daniel O'Shea to negotiate the rights, but RKO-General wouldn't grant Toho permission to make a series. Disappointed, Toho asked for permission to make a single film, so that it could at least recoup the cost of its new Kong suit and sets. RKO-General was willing to allow Toho to make a one-off, but it did not like Tanaka's proposed script. At that point, RKO-General turned to Arthur Rankin.

Rankin started his career as a graphic designer and art director in the early days of live television and then began producing television commercials in the 1950s. In the early 1960s, he teamed with ad man Jules Bass to form a production company called Videocraft International, which they eventually renamed Rankin/Bass Productions. In 1964, the duo produced the classic Christmas special *Rudolph the Red-Nosed Reindeer* using a variation on the stop-motion animation process that they called Animagic. Soon after, ABC made a deal with the company to produce a series for children using traditional cel animation. Casting around for a subject, Rankin thought back to a film he had loved since childhood and began negotiating with Daniel O'Shea for the rights to turn King Kong into a Saturday-morning cartoon show. Debuting in fall 1966, *The King Kong Show* focused on Kong—here re-imagined as a friendly resident of Mondo Island—and his pal, young Bobby Bond, who lived on Mondo Island with his father, research scientist Professor Bond, and his sister, Susan. In the course of the series, Kong, Bobby, and the Bonds had numerous adventures, many which involved being menaced by a recurring villain—an evil scientist named Dr. Who. The show was extremely popular and its catchy theme song became a hit record.

Rankin/Bass's deal with RKO included an option to produce a full-length feature version of the show. Fully intending to exercise that option, Rankin had commissioned a script from television writer William J. Keenan that pitted Kong against an equally giant robot version of himself called Mechani-Kong, a creation of Dr. Who's that had already appeared in an episode of the TV show. The Rankin/Bass script was submitted to RKO-General for approval around the same time that Toho submitted its script for *KinguKongu Tai Ebirah*. The executives at RKO-General liked the Rankin/Bass script much better than they liked Toho's and made Toho an offer. RKO-General would grant Toho permission to make another King Kong film, but it had to use the Rankin/Bass script. To protect their most valuable property, the RKO-General executives—which had been extremely pleased by the way *The King Kong Show* had turned out—also wanted Arthur Rankin to act as its representative and supervise the production. Toho agreed and worked out an agreement to license the character for $50,000 plus a percentage of the profits. The deal included a provision that allowed RKO-General to acquire the U.S. distribution rights to the finished film for a fixed fee if it was happy with the final product.

WRITING THE SCRIPT In transforming the animated show into a live-action feature, the Bond family was dropped and Kong was given a new set of human friends: United Nations submarine commander and Kong buff Carl Nelson, his first officer Lieutenant-Commander Jiro Nomura, and the ship's

King Kong Goes to Japan:

The Making of

King Kong Versus Godzilla

and

King Kong Escapes

———

155

nurse, Lieutenant Susan Watson. True to form, Kong falls for the blonde Lt. Watson and willingly follows her commands. Dr. Who was given vaguely communist affiliations through his association with Madame Piranha (who appears to be an agent of Red China). Since the film was not intended as a sequel either to the original *Kong* or to *KinguKongu Tai Gojira*, the story begins with Kong not yet discovered by the world. The natives and the wall were dropped and replaced by a single hermit who lives on the island along with Kong. In a nod to the original film, Kong was given a fight scene with a giant Tyrannosaurus-like dinosaur that Kong kills by snapping its jaw. Since Kong wouldn't be Kong if he didn't climb a tall building, a scene was also added in which Kong and Mechani-Kong battle it out atop the Eiffel Tower–like Tokyo Tower. William Keenan's final script was translated into Japanese by Toho staff writer Takeshi Kimura and titled *KinguKongu No Gyakushu* (*King Kong's Counterattack*).

PREPRODUCTION   As preproduction commenced, Rankin traveled to Japan to prepare the film with Tanaka. Ishiro Honda signed on to direct and *KinguKongu Tai Gojira* veteran Hajime Koizumi was hired as the film's director of photography. *Kingu Kongu Tai Gojira* art director Takeo Kita also returned to design the production and Eiji Tsuburaya once again supervised the film's special effects. The film's budget was considerably larger than before, which allowed the filmmakers to give the production a bigger and more polished look than its predecessor.

Arthur Rankin brought over television actor Rhodes Reason from the United States to star in the film as Commander Carl Nelson (Reason once said in an interview that he accepted the job mostly because he always wanted to see Japan). *KinguKongu Tai Gojira* costar Mie Hama, who had just appeared opposite Sean Connery in the James Bond adventure *You Only Live Twice*, returned to play Madame Piranha and famed Japanese character actor Eisei (Hideo) Amamoto was cast as the evil Dr. Who. To round out the cast, Toho regular Akira Takarada was assigned the role of Jiro Nomura and Linda Miller, an American model living in Japan, was cast as Susan.

Although the new Kong suit constructed for *KinguKongu Tai Ebirah* was a modest improvement over the one used in *KinguKongu Tai Gojira*, it was still pretty shoddy. The suit was baggy and ill proportioned and had a visible zipper that ran straight up the back. There was a tremendous amount of padding in the shoulders but almost none in the legs, giving Kong a shape something like an inverted pyramid. The flimsy arm extensions were reused and, as a result, Kong's forearms tended again to flap around in the long shots. The mask was a bigger improvement—the face was somewhat more ape-like and the big, round eyes were much more visible. However, it was still crude-looking, stiff, and inexpressive. More successful was the suit constructed for Mechani-Kong. Made primarily from plastic that was then painted to look like metal, it had a sleek look that worked perfectly within the film's fantasy context. Tanaka persuaded Gojira-performer Haruo Nakajima to play Kong in the film and choreograph the fight scenes. Toho considered Nakajima's casting to be a considerable coup and made a big announcement about it in the press. Another veteran Kaiju suit performer, Hiroshi Sekita, was given the role of Mechani-Kong. In addition to Kong and Mechani-Kong, a rubber dinosaur suit was also constructed, as were a vast array of miniature sets and vehicles, including tanks, helicopters, a submarine, and a ship.

King Kong Goes to Japan:

The Making of

King Kong Versus Godzilla

and

King Kong Escapes

———

137

PRODUCTION Production on *KinguKongu No Gyakushu* began in the latter part of 1966. The full-scale scenes were shot at Toho and in various locations in and around Tokyo, including a wilderness area that stood in for Mondo Island. Honda directed the film in a more consistent and less comedic style than he had *KinguKongu Tai Gojira*. This is not to say that the film wasn't funny, but this time the laughs came from the inherent silliness of the material rather than any overt overacting by the performers. Once again, all of the actors performed in their native languages.

Giant monsters destroy Tokyo in this composite publicity still from *King Kong Escapes*.

The miniature work was better than that in *KinguKongu Tai Gojira*. The sets were more elaborate and the sequences were more ambitious. Honda and Tsuburaya brought a great deal of visual flair to the miniature shots, employing some extremely unusual angles and choreographing some highly clever and intricate byplay between the various elements. Many of these scenes featured flying miniatures that flew, which required a great deal of delicate wire-work to realize.

SPECIAL EFFECTS   As on *KinguKongu Tai Gojira*, a separate, articulated Kong head was created for the close-up shots. This one could blink its eyes and move its upper lip. Two big Kong hands were also constructed—one to hold Linda Miller and a second with a single articulated finger that was used to caress her in one of the scenes set on Mondo Island. Full-scale mock-ups of both sides of Kong's head were also constructed for scenes in which Dr. Who's henchman attach an earpiece to the giant ape. Miniature puppets of Kong and Mechani-Kong were used in some of the long shots of the Tokyo Tower fight, although they were manipulated with rods and wires rather than with stop-motion animation.

The blue screen process was again employed to merge the miniature footage with the full-scale scenes. There was a great deal more blue screen work than there was in *KinguKongu Tai Gojira*, and the quality was much improved. Rear-screen projection, split-screen, and rotoscoping were also employed in a few shots.

POSTPRODUCTION   Ryohei Fujii edited the film into a 104-minute final cut. *KinguKongu No Gyakushu* was released in Japan in July 1967, and, like its predecessor, was an immediate hit.

To prepare the film for its American release, Arthur Rankin assembled a group of American actors to dub the film's Japanese dialogue into English. William J. Keenan prepared a new dialogue script (in which Madame Piranha's name was changed to Madame X). Paul Frees voiced Dr. Who, and Linda Miller's lines were rerecorded by veteran voice-over performer Julie Bennett. Rankin also reedited some portions of the film, removing approximately eight minutes of footage and received a producer/director credit on the ninety-six-minute final cut. Rankin screened the finished product for Daniel O'Shea. Pleased with the film, O'Shea purchased the U.S. distribution rights from Toho and sold them to Universal. Arthur Rankin was made a profit participant. Retitled *King Kong Escapes*, the film was released in United States in June 1968.

REVIEWS   As with *King Kong Versus Godzilla*, the film's best reviews came from those that regarded it strictly as a movie for children:

"It makes no difference what you call it—corny, contrite, or contrived—it still spells excitement for the young 'uns [that includes everyone up to 80] and success at the box office for the producer, and that, after all, is what film entertainment is all about. Watching the robot and the giant Kong battle one another is quite something to behold. It stands to reason that special effects are exceptionally handled—probably the film's main asset." —Nadine M. Edwards, *The Citizen News*

"The Japanese give King Kong a workout again in a color film that will have to look to the kids primarily for patronage. The Toho Production has little to offer the mature person. It is strictly a routine job filled with the kind of stuff that easily excites youngsters. That it is loaded with action helps make it further appealing to the young ones." —Louis Pelegrine, *Film & Television Daily*

Others placed it in the "It's so bad, it's good" category:

"The visiting Americans with the funny purple process outlines and the untracked samurai in the monster suits are at it again, trampling the neon and paper-maché skyline of Tokyo down at the Toho tabletops. The special effects are standard Toho brand, quite unreal but with a Mattel charm all their own. Paul Frees comes up with the fine voices that persist in spite of obstinate lip movements. Good matinee fodder." —John Mahoney, *The Hollywood Reporter*

"A shoddy production in all aspects, including washed-out color, it's so gloriously awful it's fun—and pretty funny too. The dubbing job is the most hilarious since… *"What's Up Tiger Lily?"* The difference is, of course, that comedy wasn't intended here. As always with such productions, the real star is special effects man Eiji Tsuburaya. His miniatures wouldn't fool a 10-year-old, but no one in his field does more with less. Even when it's not the least convincing, his imaginative work has the quaint charm of Méliès." —Kevin Thomas, *Los Angeles Times*

But many reviewers had no patience for it at all:

"The Japanese, who show the greatest delicacy in arranging flowers and manufacturing transistor radios, are all thumbs when it comes to making monster movies like *King Kong Escapes*. The Toho moviemakers are quite good in building miniature sets, but much of the process photography—match the miniatures with the full-size shots —is just bad. Really unforgivable, however, it what has been done to King Kong himself. The great, dignified, 80-foot ape of the 1933 Hollywood classic has been turned into a spineless, groveling Uncle Tom in the community of prehistoric beasts." —Vincent Canby, *New York Times*

"Dull but exploitable update of King Kong character. *King Kong Escapes*, an English-lingo version from a Japanese production, is adequate filler material for exploitation dual or triple bills…Special effects footage is interesting. English-lingo voices are not billed and the dubbing job is just horrible. Performance and direction are below average. A theatrical bill of this and the original film could be successfully promoted." —"Murf," *Variety*

The reviewers' mixed reactions are understandable, because *King Kong Escapes* is one weird movie. Whatever its flaws, *KinguKongu Tai Gojira* was a straightforward monster movie. The genre of *KinguKongu No Gyakushu* is much harder to define—it's a wild combination of traditional monster movie, science fiction adventure, and a vintage 1960s James Bond film. Filled with giant apes, killer robots, flying submarines, a fanged and cape-wearing villain

King Kong Goes to Japan:

The Making of

King Kong Versus Godzilla

and

King Kong Escapes

———

159

who lives in a secret North Pole hideout, a dragon lady, and a rousing U.N. floor speech, the film has much more in common with comic books and Saturday morning adventure serials than it does with Merian C. Cooper's classic film. Seen from this perspective, *KinguKongu No Gyakushu* isn't really a King Kong movie at all. Instead, it's a crazy salad of a movie filled with bits and pieces of many genres and in which Kong is but a single ingredient. Given the film's indescribable concept, the script is reasonably well done. It does leave a lot of questions unanswered (for example, Carl Nelson and Dr. Who have clearly crossed paths before, although we never find out the circumstances. Also, it is never explained why Nelson is designing a Kong robot or why Dr. Who needs a giant ape to dig out Element X when he could just as easily use a commercially available mining machine. Finally, the time period of the story is unclear—it appears to be the 1960s, and yet the Explorer comes equipped with a flying dingy, which suggests a futuristic setting of some sort), although given the circumstances, that doesn't really seem to matter. The acting is good enough for this type of picture, with Amamoto and Hama as the standouts. The film is much better produced than its predecessor—it has a bigger look and the miniature work is much more elaborate (although still terribly photographed). The Kong suit is again a catastrophe, but the optical work is better, if still not up to Hollywood standards. The film's major flaw is its pacing, which is quite slow (the sequence in which Dr. Who tries to persuade Nelson, Nomura, and Watson to cooperate with him brings the film to a dead halt and Nomura's rescue of Miller from the Tokyo Tower goes on forever). The American reedit eliminates some of the Japanese version's pacing problems and is much better done than the U.S. version of *King Kong Versus Godzilla*. Like *KinguKongu Tai Gojira/King Kong Versus Godzilla*, *KinguKongu No Gyakushu/King Kong Escapes* isn't really a good movie, but it is a fun one to watch if you're in the mood to watch giant monsters knocking one another around miniature sets. And, as with the previous film, the love of the Kong character is palpable, even if the film that surrounds him borders at times on the inexplicable.

BOX OFFICE Like its predecessor, *King Kong Escapes* was released as a double-bill and kiddie show attraction and did extremely well for a film of this sort.

AFTERMATH The unused script for *KinguKongu Tai Ebirah* was rewritten for Gojira and produced using all of the props and costumes that had been created for the Kong version. *Gojira, Ebira, Mosura: Nankai No Daiketto* (*Gojira, Mothra, Ebirah: Big Duel in the South Seas*) was released in Japan in 1966 and to American television in 1968 as *Godzilla Versus the Sea Monster*. Over the years, Toho has attempted to make several more King Kong films, but none have ever came to fruition.

Tomoyuki Tanaka continued to produce Kaiju films well into the 1990s. He produced his last film, *Gojira Tai Desutoroia* (*Gojira Versus Desutoroia*) in 1995 and died in 1997 at the age of 87. Ishiro Honda directed his last Kaiju film, *Mekagojira No Gyakushu* (*MechiGojira's Counterattack*) in 1975. In his later years, he worked as a second unit director and creative consultant to his friend Akira Kurosawa on films such as *Kagemusha* (1980), *Ran* (1985), and *Yume* (1990). Honda died in 1993 at the age of eighty-two. Eiji Tsuburaya supervised the special effects on Toho films until his death at the age of sixty-nine in 1970.

Arthur Rankin and Rankin/Bass continued to produce animated films and television programs until well into the 1980s. Some of the company's best-known productions include: *Mad Monster Party* (1967)—an Animagic feature film tribute to classic movie monsters that featured a giant ape identified only as "It"; the classic Christmas television specials *Frosty The Snowman* (1969) and *Santa Claus Is Comin' to Town* (1970); and the animated feature film *The Last Unicorn* (1982). After a long period of inactivity, the company returned in 1999 with the animated feature *The King and I*.

Immediately following their theatrical runs, both *King Kong Versus Godzilla* and *King Kong Escapes* were sold to American television. Popular with children and adults that appreciated their kitschy appeal, they became Saturday afternoon staples throughout the 1970s. *King Kong Versus Godzilla* appeared on VHS in America in the 1980s and on DVD in the 1990s. *King Kong Escapes* remained unreleased on home video in the United States until 2005, when it was finally released on DVD. Both films remain popular in Japan, although they are no longer as visible in the United States.

■ ■ ■

King Kong Goes to Japan:

The Making of

King Kong Versus Godzilla

and

King Kong Escapes

———

141

The most exciting original motion picture event of all time.

King Kong

For Christmas

76/212

"KING KONG"

CHAPTER 5

"HERE'S TO THE BIG ONE"

The Making of Dino De Laurentiis's *King Kong*

1976. A mysterious young man stows away aboard the oil exploration ship *Petrox Explorer* as it prepares to set sail from Surabaya, Indonesia, on a classified journey to a top-secret destination. Soon after leaving port, the ship runs into a terrible storm, during which the radio operator receives a mayday call, but is unable to determine its origin. The next day, Fred Wilson, the Petrox Oil Company executive in charge of the expedition, meets with the crew and informs them that they are traveling to an uncharted island far out in the Indian Ocean that has heretofore remained undiscovered because it is covered by a massive fog bank that never dissipates. Theorizing that the fog is generated by petroleum vapors seeping up through the ground, geologist Roy Bagley suspects that the island contains huge untapped reserves of oil. Having risked his career to

Advance poster for *King Kong* (1976).

persuade the Petrox board to finance this expensive expedition, the greedy Wilson is convinced they are headed for the ultimate payoff. As Fred talks, the mysterious stowaway slips into the meeting and offers an alternative theory— he thinks that the vapor may be generated by massive amounts of animal respiration. The stowaway introduces himself as Jack Prescott, a primate paleontologist from Princeton University. Prescott has uncovered evidence that suggests that there may be some sort of giant anthropoid living on the island. Determined to prove his theory, he slipped aboard the *Explorer* in order to hitch a ride to the island. Convinced Jack is a spy for a rival oil company, Fred has him locked up.

Before the situation can be resolved, a life raft is spotted floating on the ocean. The raft contains a beautiful young woman who introduces herself as Dwan, a would-be actress who was sailing to Hong Kong aboard the yacht of a producer who promised to put her in a movie there. Dwan was hoping that her role in the movie would make her a star, but the yacht exploded during the storm, leaving her as its sole survivor. Dwan asks to be taken to Hong Kong, but is told that she will need to stay aboard for the duration of the trip. Meanwhile, Jack's story checks out, so Fred decides to have him work off his passage by acting as the expedition's official photographer. As the voyage continues, Jack and Dwan hit it off and develop a mutual attraction. The ship arrives at the island and Jack and Dwan join a landing party led by Fred. Exploring the island, the party comes across a giant, wooden wall and, soon after, a tribe of primitive natives. From a bluff overlooking the native village, the landing party watches as the tribe prepares one of its young maidens for an elaborate ritual to be held that night when the moon is full. As the tribe makes its preparations, the natives continually chant a single, mysterious word. "Kong…Kong…Kong." Roy and Fred spot a pool of oil in the center of the village, but before they can investigate, the natives discover them. Confronting the explorers, the Native Chief accuses them of contaminating the tribe's magic and demands that they hand over Dwan in order to make amends. When the crew refuses, the natives charge. Firing guns into the air, the crew beats a hasty retreat and returns to the ship.

That night, Fred makes plans to take over the island. His imperialistic attitude infuriates Jack, but Fred ignores him and wires New York that he is "bringing in the big one." Fed up, Jack prepares to leave the ship and go on a camera hunt in the island's interior. His plans are interrupted when a group of natives kidnap Dwan and take her back to the village. After dressing Dwan in a ritual gown and drugging her with a powerful elixir, the natives perform a spectacular ceremonial dance, after which Dwan is carried through a giant opening in the gate and tied to a ceremonial altar. Closing the gates, the natives rush to the top of the wall and sound an enormous horn. Something huge comes crashing through the woods, knocking down trees as it goes. A terrified Dwan looks up and finds herself facing Kong—an enormous forty-foot-tall gorilla. Letting out a terrifying roar, Kong picks Dwan up off the altar and carries her off into the jungle. As the tribe cheers, a rescue party from the ship arrives. Scaring off the natives with flares, the rescue party opens the gate and rushes to the altar, only to find that they are too late. Jack leads a search party into the jungle to search for Dwan.

The next morning, Dwan awakens in a glade and finds Kong looming over her, studying her intently. Frightened, Dwan tries to escape, but Kong grabs her and lifts her into the air for a closer look. Terrified, Dwan begins babbling. When Kong puts Dwan down, she makes a run for it. Kong chases her, but she falls into a mud puddle. Kong lifts Dwan out of the mud, carries her to a waterfall, and dunks her under the cascade to wash her off. He then uses the breath generated by his enormous lungs to blow her dry. Meanwhile, Fred discovers

CAST AND CREW: *King Kong* (1976)

Jack Prescott: Jeff Bridges; Fred Wilson: Charles Grodin; Dwan: Jessica Lange; Captain Ross: John Randolph; Roy Bagley: Rene Auberjonois; Boan: Julius Harris; Joe Perko: Jack O'Halloran; Sunfish: Dennis Fimple; Carnahan: Ed Lauter; Garcia: Jorge Moreno; Timmons: Mario Gallo; Chinese Cook: John Lone; Army General: Garry Walberg; City Official: John Agar; Ape-Masked Man: Keny Long; Petrox Chairman: Sid Conrad; Army Helicopter Pilot: George Whiteman; Air Force General: Wayne Heffley; Radar Operator: Ray Buktenica (uncredited); King Kong: Rick Baker, Will Shephard (uncredited); Stunt Coordinator: Bill Couch; Stunts: Lightning Bear, Steven Burnett, Lloyd Catlett, Loren Janes, J. David Jones, Gene LeBell, Julius LeFlore, Beth Nufer, Diane Peterson, Jesse Wayne, Sunny Woods

Directed by: John Guillermin; Produced by: Dino De Laurentiis; Screenplay by: Lorenzo Semple, Jr.; Based on a screenplay by: James A. Creelman and Ruth Rose; From an idea conceived by: Merian C. Cooper and Edgar Wallace; Executive Producers: Federico De Laurentiis and Christian Ferry; Director of Photography: Richard H. Kline, A.S.C.; In charge of production: Jack Grossberg; Music composed and conducted by: John Barry; Film Editor: Ralph E. Winters, A.C.E.; Production designed by: Mario Chiari and Dale Hennesy; second unit Director: William Kronick; Kong designed and engineered by: Carlo Rambaldi, Glen Robinson (uncredited); Kong suit and masks Designed by: Carlo Rambaldi, Rick Baker (uncredited); Supervisor of Photographic Effects: Frank Van Der Veer, A.S.C.; Photographic Effects Assistant: Barry Nolan; Assistant to the Producer: Frederic M. Sidewater;

Production Manager: Terry Carr; Unit Production Manager (Hawaii): Brian Frankish; Unit Production Manager (New York): George Goodman; Assistant Directors: David McGiffert, Kurt Neumann; Second Assistant Director: Pat Kehoe; Camera Operator: Al Bettcher; Assistant Camera: Robert Edesa; Gaffer:

Ed Carlin; Electrician: Michael Burke; Key Grip: Robert Sordal; second unit Director of Photography: Harold Wellman A.S.C. (uncredited); second unit Assistant Director: Nate Haggard; Kong constructed by: Carlo Rambaldi and Glen Robinson; Sculptor of Kong: Don Chandler; Hair Design for Kong: Michaeldino; Mechanical Coordinator for Kong: Eddie Surkian; Additional Photographic Effects: Harold Wellman, A.S.C.; Matte Artist: Lou Lichtenfield; Postproduction Supervisor: Phil Tucker; Assistant Film Editors: Margo Anderson, Robert Pergament; Sound Effects Editor: James J. Klinger; Art Directors: Archie J. Bacon David A. Constable, Robert Gundlach; Set Decorator: John Franco Jr.; Illustrators: Mentor Huebner, David Negron; Property Master: Jack Marino; Construction Coordinator: Gary Martin; Greensman: Ken Richey; Set Painters: Robert Clark, Curtis "Red" Hollingsworth; Miniature Coordinator: Aldo Puccini; Costume Designer: Moss Mabry; Gowns and native costumes designed by: Anthea Sylbert; Wardrobe: Arny Lipin, G. Fern Weber; Makeup Artist: Del Acevedo; Hair Stylist: Jo McCarthy; Special Effects Supervisor: Glen Robinson and Joe Day; Sound Mixer: Jack Solomon ; Sound Rerecording Mixer: William McCaughey; Sound Rerecording Mixer: Harry W. Tetrick; Score Mixer: Dan Wallin; Music Rerecordist: Aaron Rochin; Native Dance Choreographer: Claude Thompson; Script Supervisor: Doris Grau; Casting by: Joyce Selznick & Associates; Extra casting by: Sally Perle and Associates; Publicity Coordinator: Gordon Armstrong; Unit Publicist: Bruce Bahrenburg; Still Photographers: Dave Friedman, Elliott Marks; Production Coordinator: Lori Imbler; Production Secretary: Charlotte Dreiman; Messengers: Jeffrey Chernov, Michael Winter, Scott Thaler; Production Auditor: Robert F. Kocourek; Production Accountant: Meryle Selinger; Construction Accountant: Laurie Arnow-Epstein; Transportation Coordinator: Joe Sawyers; Financial Services: Frans J. Afman; Titles by: Pacific Title and Art Studio; Camera equipment provided by: Nikon; Miss Lange's jewelry by: Bulgari; Released in the United States and Canada by: Paramount Pictures; Running time: 135 minutes that the island's oil supply will require 10,000 more years of "aging" before it will be usable. The expedition is a bust. Fred is miserable, until it occurs to him that he has something better than oil—he has Kong. Realizing that the giant ape could be an incredible promotional tool, Fred begins making plans to capture Kong. Back in the jungle, the search party comes to the edge of a deep ravine bridged by a fallen tree. As the party starts across, Kong appears on the opposite side of the ravine. Frightened, the search party shoots at him. Enraged by the attack, Kong grabs the log and starts twisting it. Jack and crew member Boan dive for safety, but the other members of the party fall to their deaths. Kong tries to grab Jack until a scream from Dwan calls him away. Recovering, Jack tells Boan to get back to the wall and tell Fred what happened. Boan departs and Jack goes after Dwan. Meanwhile, Fred has a huge pit dug in front of the wall, which he lines with canisters of chloroform that have been air-dropped from Surabaya.

As night falls and a full moon rises, Kong brings Dwan to his lair in a giant volcanic crater nestled between two twin mountains. In an amorous mood, Kong begins caressing a terrified Dwan and peeling away her gown. Suddenly, Dwan is attacked by a giant snake. Coming to her rescue, Kong grabs the massive reptile and the two engage in a titanic battle. As they do, Jack appears and Dwan runs to him. Seeing this, a furious Kong tears the snake to pieces and goes after them. To escape, Jack and Dwan leap from a high cliff into a raging river and then make their way back to the wall. Kong arrives a few minutes later and begins pounding on the wall, shattering it to pieces. Fred dumps the chloroform as Kong smashes through the gates and falls into the pit, where he is soon overcome by the fumes. Kong is placed into the hold of a giant Petrox oil supertanker and shipped to New York, where Fred plans to feature him in a huge promotional spectacular in which Dwan will star. One night, as Jack and Dwan attempt to consummate their relationship, Kong goes berserk and begins destroying the hold. When the tanker's captain orders that Kong be drowned, Dwan tries to calm him, but ends up falling into the hold. Kong catches her and she spends a few minutes soothing him. Dwan then slips away as Kong falls asleep.

A few weeks later, fireworks explode over Manhattan as the Petrox spectacular gets under way in a park in Queens that has been dressed with a gaudy reproduction of the Great Wall. Deciding that he can't be part of Kong's exploitation, Jack quits the show. He asks Dwan to go with him, but the lure of stardom is too great. Dwan and Fred are flown into the park by helicopter. Fred emcees as Dwan is escorted to a replica of the altar and a giant Petrox gas pump is rolled onto the field through the gate in the wall. The gas pump is lifted away, revealing Kong to the world. Imprisoned inside a giant cage and wearing a ridiculous crown, the king has been brought low. Angling for a picture, photographers begin manhandling Dwan. Furious, Kong begins pulling at his chains. Jack whisks Dwan away as Kong smashes out of his cage, causing the crowd to panic and rush for the exits. As Kong stomps through the crowd, a terrified Fred Wilson runs smack into his leg. Recognizing his captor, a vengeful Kong stomps down on Fred with his foot, killing him. Kong then smashes his way out of the park and chases Jack and Dwan through the borough of Queens.

Trying to elude him, they board an elevated subway train, but, before they can get too far, Kong grabs the train and destroys it. Jack and Dwan escape as Kong picks up a woman he thinks is Dwan. Realizing his mistake, Kong tosses the poor woman aside and destroys the rest of the train.

Using the 59th Street Bridge to cross the East River into Manhattan, Jack and Dwan hide out in a deserted bar, where the sight of the twin towers of the World Trade Center triggers in Jack a memory of Kong's island lair. Calling the mayor's office, Jack offers to tell the city authorities where to capture Kong if they first promise not to harm him. The mayor agrees, so Jack tells him to let Kong through to the World Trade Center. Meanwhile, Kong eludes the armed forces that have been called out to capture him and wades across the river. He recaptures Dwan and carries her off to the Trade Center. A huge crowd floods the Center's plaza as Kong climbs up the South Tower. As Kong and Dwan arrive on the roof, they are attacked by a trio of Marines, who open fire on Kong with a flamethrower. Kong escapes by leaping from the South Tower to the North Tower and then hurls debris at the Marines until a piece of it hits their fuel tank, which explodes. Unfortunately, Kong's victory is short-lived. Three Air Force helicopters approach and begin firing at Kong, who is cut to pieces by their bullets. Hoping to stop the slaughter, Dwan begs Kong to hold her, but he protectively pushes her away. Kong smashes two of the helicopters, sending one of them crashing into the side of the building, but he is finally overwhelmed. Weakened by the bullets, Kong collapses. As Dwan reaches out to caress him, Kong rolls off the building and falls 110 stories to the plaza below.

Kong lies dying. A crying Dwan comes to him. He turns to look at her one last time and then dies. Jack tries to reach Dwan, but he can't push his way through the crowd. As the film ends, a sobbing Dwan is surrounded by photographers. She is finally a star.

THE REBIRTH OF KONG

By the mid-1970s, Kong's popularity was at an all-time high. Given how large the character was looming in the pop cultural zeitgeist, as well as the renewed interest in big-screen spectacle prompted by the success of so-called disaster movies such as *The Poseidon Adventure* (1972) and *The Towering Inferno* (1974), it was only a matter of time before someone in Hollywood got the idea to revive the king. As it turns out, several people got the idea at once, sparking a fight between giants even more spectacular than Kong's battle with the *Tyrannosaurus* rex. One of those giants was MCA-owned Universal Pictures, which was run by legendary Hollywood dealmaker and power broker Lew Wasserman. The other was a maverick independent producer newly arrived from Italy named Dino De Laurentiis.

THE STEPFATHER OF KONG Agostino De Laurentiis was born on August 8, 1919 in the small town of Torre Annunziata, located just outside Naples. Agostino fell in love with movies at an early age and dreamed of becoming an actor. At the age of fifteen, he quit school and went to work as a traveling salesman for his father's pasta manufacturing company. Answering an ad for the Centro Sperimentale, Rome's famous film school, Agostino enrolled in the fall of 1937 as an actor, but quickly found himself becoming more and more interested in producing. Following graduation, the young man worked as an actor, extra, stagehand, and assistant director before finally producing two short films for the FERT studios in Turin. After shortening his name to Dino, De Laurentiis began making feature films at the age of twenty-one, continuing in this capacity during and after World War II. In 1949, he produced *Riso Amaro* (*Bitter Rice*), a sexy film about rice pickers that went on to become an international box office sensation. That same year, Silvana Mangano, the voluptuous star of *Bitter Rice*, became De Laurentiis's second wife. The couple went on to have four children—Veronica, Rafaella, Federico, and Francesca. In the 1950s, De Laurentiis joined forces with Carlo Ponti and together the pair produced films by some of the key directors in the Italian cinema's extraordinary postwar renaissance, including Roberto Rossellini, Vittorio De Sica, and Federico Fellini. Although De Laurentiis's output consisted mainly of commercial programmers, he had artistic aspirations as well. In fact, De Laurentiis's production of Fellini's classic *La Strada* (1954) earned him an Oscar for Best Foreign Film of 1956.

The extraordinary worldwide success of *Bitter Rice* created in De Laurentiis a desire to move beyond the domestic Italian market and compete on the world stage. To do so, De Laurentiis began making big-budget films featuring using international superstars such as *Ulysses (1955*—starring Kirk Douglas and Anthony Quinn) and *War and Peace* (1956—starring Henry Fonda and Audrey Hepburn). A flamboyant, enthusiastic showman, De Laurentiis spent huge sums of money on his ambitious projects and achieved tremendous success. After splitting with Ponti, De Laurentiis opened his own studio—the Dino De Laurentiis Center for Cinematic Production, nicknamed Dinocittà ("Dino

Producer Dino De Laurentiis.

City")—and continued to produce big-budget epics such as *Barabbas* (1962), *The Bible* (1966), and *Waterloo* (1970).

To fund his increasingly opulent productions, De Laurentiis developed an innovative new way to finance motion pictures. At the time, independent producers would raise the money they needed to make their movies by selling the project to a single studio, which would then bankroll the production, distribute the final product worldwide, and keep a lion's share of the returns. De Laurentiis took a different approach. Whenever he wanted to make a film, he would pitch the project to individual distributors in every territory across the world. If they were interested, these distributors would sign contracts agreeing to pay De Laurentiis a predetermined amount of money in exchange for the right to exhibit the film in their area when it was completed. Ideally, the total amount of these guarantees would equal or exceed the amount De Laurentiis would need to make the film. De Laurentiis then took these guarantees to his bankers and use them as collateral to borrow the money he needed to produce the film. When the film was finished, De Laurentiis would use the money he collected from the distributors to repay the loan. This approach allowed De Laurentiis to retain a larger percentage of the returns, as well as creative control and ownership of his movies. At the time, De Laurentiis's method was considered quite daring, but over the years it became more and more accepted until it is now one of the standard methods of finance for independent films.

As successful as De Laurentiis was, by the early 1970s, changes in Italian politics and laws concerning motion picture finance began having more and more of a negative impact on him. Dinocittà closed and De Laurentiis decided to leave Italy and establish himself elsewhere. After having a positive experience producing *The Valachi Papers* (1972) on location in New York City, De Laurentiis decided to move to America. Opening an office in the Gulf & Western Building on Columbus Circle, he immediately optioned the rights to Peter Maas's book about a young police officer who exposed the rampant corruption in the New York City Police Department. Starring Al Pacino and directed by Sidney Lumet, *Serpico* (1973) went on to become both a critical and commercial smash. The successes of De Laurentiis's follow-up films *Death Wish (1974), Mandingo (1975)*, and *Three Days of the Condor* (1975) firmly established him as a major player in the American film industry, where he earned a reputation for being a strong producer with exceedingly commercial tastes, as well as an aggressive competitor and a shrewd dealmaker.

ONCE AND AGAIN There are two different versions of how the idea to remake *King Kong* came about. In several interviews given at the time of the film's release, future Walt Disney head Michael Eisner, then an executive at ABC, claimed that the idea to do a remake came from him. Eisner said that he got the idea in December 1974 while watching the original film on television, after which he claimed that he pitched the idea to his friend Barry Diller, the chairman and chief executive officer of Paramount Pictures, who then brought the idea to Dino De Laurentiis (Paramount was the distributor of most of De Laurentiis's American films). De Laurentiis, on the other hand, claimed that the idea came about following a meeting with Diller in which the studio chief expressed interest in making a monster movie of some sort. Shortly after this meeting, De Laurentiis was waking his daughter Francesca up for school when he noticed a *King Kong* poster hanging on her wall. Something clicked and De Laurentiis found himself becoming inspired.

However the idea came about, Frederic M. Sidewater, the executive vice president of the Dino De Laurentiis Corporation and De Laurentiis's self-described "Number 2," recalls De Laurentiis first mentioning the idea to him one winter morning in late 1974 or early 1975 as they walked to work from De Laurentiis's apartment on Central Park South. The two men began discussing the feasibility of doing a remake and quickly determined that, from a business point of view, it was an excellent proposition—given the popularity of the character and the film at that moment in time, even a perfunctory retread seemed likely to be a hit. However, De Laurentiis thought the idea had even greater potential. Sensing the moviegoing public's growing interest in fantasy and escapism after a decade of gritty, downbeat realism (an interest that would reach full flower in the summer of 1977 with the release of *Star Wars*), De Laurentiis felt that a color, widescreen retelling of the Kong story done on a grand scale could have worldwide appeal and could become a true international blockbuster. Plus, he loved the noble, tragic character of Kong (whom he referred to affectionately as "The Big Monkey") and his story—which the producer saw as being a monster movie, an adventure story, a fairy tale, a comedy, and, most of all, a love story all rolled into one—appealed to De Laurentiis's showman's instinct for blockbuster spectacle. De Laurentiis began to wax rhapsodic about the emotional impact he hoped his proposed film would have on an audience, which he summarized in one of his most widely repeated quotes from the period: "When Jaws dies, nobody cry, but when Kong dies, everybody cry."

De Laurentiis ran the idea past Charles Bludhorn, the president of Paramount's parent company Gulf & Western, who liked it and suggested that De Laurentiis find out if the rights were available. At that point, De Laurentiis called his friend Thomas O'Neil, the president of both General Tire and RKO-General, who told him that the rights were indeed available. (RKO-General had apparently relaxed its "no remakes" policy following the death of Merian C. Cooper in 1973.) De Laurentiis then formally pitched the project to Barry Diller, who agreed that Paramount would put up half of the film's proposed $12 million budget in return for the rights to distribute the film in the United States and Canada if De Laurentiis could obtain the rights. With their main distributor in place, De Laurentiis and Sidewater began formal negotiations with Daniel O'Shea, who informed them that any offer was going to have to include a percentage of the new film's gross receipts, a condition to which De Laurentiis was amenable. The talks went smoothly and ended with De Laurentiis offering to pay RKO-General $200,000 plus three percent of his gross profits (rising to ten percent after the film had recouped two and a half times its budget). O'Shea submitted De Laurentiis's offer to Thomas O'Neil, who approved it. On May 6, 1975, Dino De Laurentiis signed a contract with RKO-General granting him the rights to remake *King Kong*.

After finalizing the agreement with Paramount, De Laurentiis and Sidewater began meeting with their foreign distributors to pitch the project and secure the necessary guarantees. During these discussions, it was decided that the film would be released in December 1976. Things were progressing smoothly, when, much to De Laurentiis's surprise, Universal Pictures suddenly announced that it had also made a deal with RKO-General granting it the rights to remake *Kong*.

THE BATTLE WITH UNIVERSAL, PART I Early in 1975, at about the same time that De Laurentiis was having his initial inspiration, Universal had also become interested in doing a remake of *King Kong*. Michael Eisner took responsibility for the seeming coincidence of the De Laurentiis and MCA brainstorms. In the same interviews in which he said he had pitched the remake idea to Barry Diller, Eisner also claimed that he had discussed the idea with Sidney Sheinberg—chief operating office of MCA (Eisner explained that his rampant pitching was a result of his desire as a Kong fan to see a new movie made). If this is indeed what happened, Eisner's suggestion couldn't have come at a better moment. At the time, Universal was in the final stages of postproduction on *Jaws*. Early previews of the shark epic had gone extremely well and the film was expected to be a big hit when it was released that June. Anticipating that this success would generate a demand for more monster movies—especially ones featuring giant, marauding animals—the studio began searching for a suitable follow-up. *Kong* seemed like the perfect property.

Intent on producing a big-budget version of the story utilizing its patented Sensurround process, Universal assigned staff attorney Arnold Shane to begin negotiating with Daniel O'Shea. Shane began talking with O'Shea at approximately the same time that De Laurentiis and Sidewater did (O'Shea had informed each party that he was talking to the other, although he kept the identities of both confidential). While Universal agreed to pay the same amount of upfront cash that De Laurentiis did, it balked at sharing the gross. In a formal contract presented to O'Shea by Shane on April 15, 1975, Universal offered RKO-General $200,000 plus five percent of the net profits of its proposed film. According to Shane, while O'Shea didn't sign that contract (because he couldn't), he did tell Shane that they had a deal. Although O'Shea later insisted that he had never said any such thing, there was speculation at the time that he favored the Universal offer (allegedly because he was good friends with Hunt Stromberg, the father of Hunt Stromberg, Jr., the producer of Universal's intended *Kong*) and may have indicated his intention to recommend to Thomas O'Neil that RKO accept it over De Laurentiis's.

Whatever happened, Shane returned to Universal under the impression that his company had won the rights, which prompted Stromberg and his coproducer Joe Kerby to hire future Academy Award–winning screenwriter Bo Goldman (*One Flew Over the Cuckoo's Nest, Melvin and Howard*) to write a script. Meanwhile, O'Shea presented both proposals to O'Neil, who decided to accept De Laurentiis's offer. When Universal found out, it protested, claiming that, although it didn't have a signed written contract, O'Shea's alleged comment constituted a binding verbal contract. Seeking $25 million in damages, the company filed suit in Superior Court of Los Angeles in June 1975 against RKO-General for "breach of contract" and "fraud" and against De Laurentiis for "intentional interference with advantageous business relations" and "unfair competition." While De Laurentiis was certainly surprised by Universal's claim, he did not consider it valid, since he was the one with the signed contract. Confident that he was in the right, De Laurentiis pressed on with his plans.

WRITING THE SCRIPT   The first order of business was to get a screenplay. After moving his company to Beverly Hills in July 1975 (in order to be closer to the Hollywood studios he was now doing regular business with), De Laurentiis met with screenwriter Lorenzo Semple, Jr. A 1944 graduate of Yale University, Semple began his career in the 1950s as a short story writer and playwright and eventually began writing for television. In 1966, Semple created the *Batman* TV series. The huge success of that show prompted Twentieth Century Fox to hire him to write a feature film version of the show and Semple's movie career was launched. Semple went on to write films such as 1968's *Pretty Poison* (for which he won a Best Screenplay award from the New York Film Critics Circle), *Papillon* (1973), *The Parallax View* (1974) and *Three Days of the Condor* (1975), the latter of which brought Semple into professional contact with Dino De Laurentiis for the first time. De Laurentiis was extremely pleased with Semple's work on *Condor*, and the two became close friends. When the Kong project came up, it was a natural for De Laurentiis to give him a call. Semple thought the idea of remaking *Kong* sounded like great fun and immediately signed on.

When the two men first met to discuss the project, De Laurentiis already had two ideas solidly in mind—he wanted to set the climax of the film atop the twin towers of the newly completed World Trade Center, a change that automatically dictated setting the film in the present day rather than in the 1930s period of the original. Semple thought both were excellent ideas. As excited as both men were at the prospect of remaking *Kong*, they both realized that they were opening themselves to potential attack from critics, film buffs, and audiences for tampering with a classic. To prevent this, they decided that they would try to make their film as different from the original as possible so that there would be no way people would be able to directly compare the two. Semple now concedes that this reasoning was hopelessly naïve ("We were going to be attacked no matter what we did," he says now.). De Laurentiis also made it clear that he wanted to focus the film primarily around the love story between Kong and the girl and develop their relationship much more than it had been in the original film. He saw the film primarily as a Beauty and the Beast story and Semple agreed.

As Semple sat down to write, he realized that his biggest challenge was going to be figuring out a way to make the story play for a contemporary audience. As powerful as the original film was, Semple knew that many of the characters and much of the storytelling were fairly simplistic and primitive when viewed from a modern perspective and that he was going to have to develop new characters and story elements that would be believable and relevant in the 1970s. Semple also felt that there was an absurdity inherent in the premise of a giant ape that falls in love with a beautiful woman that a sophisticated and cynical 1976 audience might not accept as readily as their 1933 counterpart did. To prevent people from laughing at the film, Semple felt he had to acknowledge this absurdity in some way that did not undermine the overall story. His solution was to play the story straight, but infuse the script with a sly, ironic sense of humor that invited the audience to laugh with the concept's more bizarre aspects rather than at them. This approach was controversial and has caused some critics to label the script as camp, which is an unfair charge because camp implies a mocking attitude toward the material that Semple's script does not have. In fact, although the script does have fun with the material, it takes the story quite seriously, especially its more tragic aspects. (The bit most critics cite when making the camp charge is Dwan's dialogue in the glade sequence, in which she guesses Kong's astrological sign, identifies as insecurity his propensity to knock down trees, and calls him a "goddamn male chauvinist pig ape." What they tend to overlook is what the script and the film make perfectly clear—that Dwan is hysterical in this sequence and is supposed to be babbling nonsense.)

Having settled on the tone, Semple next tackled the story itself. He retained the basic plotline and set pieces from the original film, but updated and reworked many of the other elements. The first thing he had to do was figure out a reason an expedition would be going to Kong's island (which, as in the original film, goes unnamed, although this time there is a "Beach of the Skull" rather than a Skull Mountain) to begin with. With Natural Dramas and expedition films now a thing of the past, the motive for the trip in the original film no longer made sense. Inspired by the still-current energy crisis and a suggestion from his producer friend Jerry Bick to include a scene of Kong imprisoned in the hold of a giant supertanker, Semple decided that this time the expedition would be mounted by the Petrox Corporation, a giant petroleum company that suspects Kong's island harbors a huge, untapped oil reserve. Petrox would still discover the island by way of a map, but this time it would come not from the skipper of a Norwegian barque, but instead from the secret archives of the Vatican Library. To explain how an island could remain hidden and undiscovered in an era of satellite photos and aerial mapping, Semple came up with the clever idea of a perpetual fog bank (caused by petroleum vapors) that seep up through the ground, surround the island, and keep it hidden from the world. As requested, Semple developed the relationship between Kong and Dwan and made it the major focus of the story. In keeping with the erotic interpretation of the story that was popular at the time, the sexual undercurrents of the original film were brought to the surface and addressed head on. In the biggest departure from the original concept, Semple dropped the dinosaurs with which Kong shares his island. He did this for reasons both of plot (the elaboration of the love story between Kong and the girl didn't leave as much room for other action) and practicality (De Laurentiis didn't want to use stop-motion animation and the creation of believable dinosaurs in any other way at that time was pretty much impossible), although a giant snake was incorporated into the story. As in the original film, Kong would be captured and brought to New York—this time to serve as a mascot in a Petrox promotional campaign. He would make his escape not from a Broadway theater, but instead from a spectacular pageant in Shea Stadium.

Semple then addressed the characters. Given his status as a beloved cultural icon, Kong could no longer be portrayed as the fearsome monster that he was in the original film. Instead, Semple made Kong a totally sympathetic character—a noble beast with a sentimental heart that is exploited and ultimately destroyed by the greed of man. Kong was much less brutal and violent than he was in the original film (he no longer ate people or squished them into the mud) and was at times almost cuddly. While this may have, as some critics suggested, cost the film some of its thrills, given forty-two years of accumulated enthusiasm and goodwill toward Kong, at the time there was simply no other way to go—a 1970s audience never would have accepted a negative portrayal of the giant ape. The reckless Carl Denham became the villainous Fred S. Wilson, a greedy and unscrupulous Petrox executive in charge of the expedition. First mate Jack Driscoll became Joe Perko, the blue-collar foreman of a crew of oil drillers. The reserved Captain Englehorn became the earthy Captain Ross. Exposition, folklore, and comic relief were provided by the character of a male librarian on loan from the Vatican. And finally, unemployed actress Ann Darrow became a beautiful young photographer (modeled on Candice Bergen) traveling with the explorers to photograph their discoveries.

FINDING DIRECTION   While Semple was writing, De Laurentiis went in search of a director. His first choice was Roman Polanski, fresh from the success of *Chinatown* (1974), but the Polish-born director wasn't interested. De Laurentiis's next choice was a man he was already working with on another project.

Director John Guillermin.

John Guillermin was born in London on November 11, 1925. Although his parents were French, he grew up in England, attending the City of London School and Cambridge University. During World War II, Guillermin served as a pilot in the Royal Air Force. After the war, he moved to Paris and spent several years producing and directing documentaries. He returned to London in the late 1940s and went to work for J. Arthur Rank making "quota quickies" for the British home market. He began as a writer with 1948's *Melody in the Dark* and then made his move into directing with 1949's *High Jinks in Society* (which he also wrote and produced). He went on to helm a diverse series of films including *Torment* (1950), *I Was Monty's Double* (1958), *Tarzan's Greatest Adventure* (1959), and *The Day They Robbed the Bank of England* (1960). The success of the Peter Sellers comedy *Waltz of the Toreadors* (1962) brought Guillermin to the attention of American producers, and he spent most of the 1960s and early 1970s as a journeyman director in Hollywood making large-scale action films such as *The Blue Max* (1966), *The Bridge at Remagen* (1969), and *Skyjacked* (1972). Married to the Irish actress Maureen Connell, with whom he had two children, Guillermin was by all accounts an extremely complex and temperamental man. He was also an expert craftsman and a technical perfectionist. Described by *King Kong*'s director of photography Richard H. Kline as having "a great eye," Guillermin was as adept at directing intimate two character scenes as he was at handling large-scale action sequences. In 1974, Guillermin directed his most successful picture, the all-star disaster film *The Towering Inferno*, after which De Laurentiis hired him to direct another disaster movie about an oil supertanker trapped in a hurricane on the high seas. They ran into trouble with the script, however, and the film was shelved. At this point, De Laurentiis approached Guillermin about directing *King Kong*. Like Semple, Guillermin loved the idea. As a child he had seen and loved the original film and had long wanted to direct a larger-than-life fantasy. Attracted by the Beauty and the Beast theme, he signed on to the project in August 1975. Like Semple and De Laurentiis, Guillermin knew he was playing with fire by attempting to remake a beloved classic. He thought the only way to deal with the issue was to ignore it. "I didn't want to remake (*King Kong*), I wanted to *make* it," Guillermin told *American Cinematographer* at the time of the film's release. "For me, (the original film) didn't exist. Otherwise, I couldn't have made the bloody picture, you know." Guillermin screened the original picture once, then put it out of his mind and approached the new film as an entirely original project.

A fast writer, Semple completed a forty-page, double-spaced outline in a few weeks and delivered it in August 1975. Although De Laurentiis liked the outline, he had a few reservations. His primary concern was the Vatican library angle, which he felt was too esoteric. The library and the map were eliminated. Fred Wilson would now discover the island by obtaining top-secret photos taken by a U.S. spy satellite (which, in a post-Watergate touch, he would obtain by paying off a top Washington official hinted to be the President). As a result, the character of the Vatican Librarian was also dropped. The exposition and folklore he provided would now be delivered by a new leading man—an idealistic young associate professor of primate paleontology named Jack Prescott who, in search of the legendary Kong, stows away aboard the oil company's ship. Former leading man Joe Perko was reduced to a supporting character. The comic relief provided by the Vatican Librarian would now be provided by the character of Roy Bagley, an oil geologist who helps Fred plan his expedition. As for the girl—although De Laurentiis liked the character of the photographer, Semple himself decided it was too hackneyed and came up with the notion that Kong's inamorata should instead be a shipwrecked actress found adrift in the ocean. Initially, De Laurentiis didn't like the idea because he felt it was unbelievable, which is exactly why Semple did like it—he felt that a whimsical notion such as finding a beautiful girl in the middle of the ocean would serve as the perfect bridge from the reality of the film's beginning to the fantasy of the rest of the story. The two men went back and forth until their stalemate was finally broken by John Guillermin, who preferred Semple's approach.

Semple set to work and in a month's time wrote a 140-page first draft incorporating his shipwrecked actress, who he named Dwan (according to the script, Dwan was originally named Dawn until she decided to reverse the two middle letters to make it more memorable) and depicted as a logical 1970s counterpart of Ann Darrow. The innocent, young, unemployed actress seeking extra work on Long Island would now become a naïve, young, unemployed actress seeking work in Hong Kong exploitation films. The Candice Bergen character's photographic duties were given to Jack Prescott, now working as the expedition's official photographer in order to pay off his passage. De Laurentiis liked the new script and approved it. As Semple began rewriting the screenplay to bring it down to a more manageable 110 pages, preproduction officially began in October 1975. At this point, the plan was to prepare for seven or eight months and then begin shooting in spring 1976.

PREPRODUCTION

After setting up a subsidiary company called King Kong Productions to produce the film, De Laurentiis and Guillermin began assembling their production team. The film industry had changed quite a bit from the time of the original *King Kong*. Studios no longer maintained rosters of actors and technicians on payroll, so each time a new film was begun, a whole new crew had to be put together from a pool of freelancers.

De Laurentiis began by naming his son Federico, then twenty-one, as executive producer. A warm, charming, and exceedingly friendly young man, Federico had been working on his father's productions in various assistant capacities for several years and De Laurentiis was clearly grooming him for bigger things. To ensure that his interests were represented in production decisions, Guillermin brought in his *The Blue Max* producer Christian Ferry, to serve as co-executive producer. Ferry's primary duty was to serve as an intermediary between Guillermin and De Laurentiis and as a troubleshooter for the production. Fred Sidewater would manage the financial aspects of the production, as well as continue to run De Laurentiis's production company.

Veteran production manager Jack Grossberg, a native New Yorker who had worked on many of Woody Allen's films and who had a reputation for finding creative and effective ways of keeping the costs of big pictures under control, was hired as the film's production supervisor. Grossberg, who dealt primarily with contract and budget issues, brought in young production manager Terry Carr to draw up the shooting schedule, coordinate the various units, and run the day-to-day production. Carr also had to deal with the myriad permit, union, and insurance issues that the production faced on a daily basis. Grossberg hired Brian Frankish as a research assistant and later promoted him to location scout. Kurt Neumann came aboard as the first assistant director. When Neumann left the project halfway through the schedule, he was replaced by David McGiffert, who was promoted from location scout. Jeffrey Chernov, Michael Winter, and Scott Thaler were hired as production assistants.

To develop the look of the film, De Laurentiis brought his old friend, acclaimed production designer Mario Chiari (*White Nights, Barabbas*), over from Italy. Chiari's first assignment was to determine what Kong would look like. Since he intended to focus his story primarily on the love story between Dwan and Kong, De Laurentiis, like Cooper before him, initially wanted Kong to look as human as possible. With this in mind, Chiari and his team created a series of concept drawings that depicted Kong as a human/ape hybrid with the body proportions of a man and a face that resembled an *Australopithecus* more than it did a gorilla.

To photograph the film, De Laurentiis and Guillermin hired Richard H. Kline, who had worked for De Laurentiis the previous year on *Mandingo* (1975). A second-generation cinematographer, Kline began his career at the age of sixteen as a slate boy on the Gene Kelly/Rita Hayworth starrer *Cover Girl* (1944) and then worked his way up to camera assistant, camera operator and eventually cinematographer. In the process, he worked on over 300 films, including *The Lady from Shanghai, The Andromeda Strain, The Boston Strangler*, and *Hang 'Em High* and was nominated for an Academy Award for his work on *Camelot* (1967). In consultation with De Laurentiis and Guillermin, Kline decided to film the movie with anamorphic lenses to achieve a "big" widescreen look. He also decided to use low-key lighting to create a mysterious and suspenseful mood for the picture, as well as low contrast filters to give the film a slightly defused look that would both emphasize the fairy-tale aspects of the story as well as bridge the gap between the crispness of the original photography and the slightly degraded quality of the optical effects shots.

Knowing there was going to be more work than he could handle alone, Guillermin decided to form a second unit to handle some of the special effects sequences, background shots, and atmospheric footage. To direct the second unit, Guillermin hired William Kronick, a documentary filmmaker who had worked on several of David L. Wolper's award-winning television documentaries of the 1960s, helmed the popular George Plimpton specials in the 70s, and directed a second unit for Guillermin on *The Bridge at Remagen*. Guillermin immediately put Kronick to work shooting screen tests of the actresses who were auditioning for the part of Dwan. Cinematographer Harold

TOP: Executive Producer Federico De Laurentiis.

MIDDLE: In a contemporary photo, Assistant to the Producer Frederic M. Sidewater poses with one of the Kong statues given to theater owners at the time of the film's release.

BOTTOM: Director of Photography Richard H. Kline works with one of the Kong masks.

Wellman, who had worked on the original *King Kong* as a camera assistant and was an expert in miniature and special effects photography, was hired as the second unit director of photography. Academy Award winner Glen Robinson (*Earthquake, The Hindenberg*) was hired to engineer the film's elaborate physical and mechanical effects. Industry veteran Jack Solomon was engaged to record the sound and Moss Mabry was brought in to design the film's costumes.

To create the film's optical effects, the production first approached the legendary Hollywood special effects expert L. B. "Bill" Abbot, who had supervised the opticals for Guillermin on *The Towering Inferno*. Busy working on *Logan's Run*, Abbot was unavailable and recommended that the producers instead hire the man who did much of the optical processing on *Inferno*—Frank Van Der Veer. An expert in the use of the blue screen process, Van Der Veer had worked with Abbot for years in the special effects department at Twentieth Century–Fox. After that department closed in the late 1960s, Van Der Veer went to work at Warner Brothers and then started his own company, the Burbank-based Van Der Veer Photo Effects. To assist him, Van Der Veer brought along Barry Nolan. Nolan was a photographic engineer who had once worked for Lockheed. Fascinated by blue screen, he had done of lot of experimentation with it and devised some new approaches that he introduced to Van Der Veer. The two became friends and business associates and Nolan's expertise would prove to be vital to Kong's success.

Needing a place to shoot the film, the production leased office space and seven soundstages at the MGM Studios in Culver City, just a mile down the road from the Culver Studios, formerly RKO-Pathè, where much of the original *King Kong* had been shot. At this point, Universal reentered the picture.

THE BATTLE WITH UNIVERSAL, PART 2 In September 1975, the Superior Court of Los Angeles dismissed Universal's suit, calling its claim of having a verbal contract with RKO "tissue-paper thin." Not about to give up, Universal decided to take a different tact. Discovering that the copyright on Delos W. Lovelace's 1932 novelization had lapsed in 1960, Universal claimed that, while the film of *King Kong* was still under a copyright owned by RKO, the story, as depicted in the novel, was not. In late October, Universal filed a new lawsuit in Federal district court. Differentiating the "old material" of the novelization from the "new material" of the film's screenplay, Universal asked the court to issue a summary judgment affirming that the "old" material was now in the public domain and that therefore a film based solely on that material would not constitute an infringement of RKO's copyright. The court denied the request for an immediate decision, but did agree to consider the claim. Confident that it would prevail, Universal announced to the press that it was going to go ahead with its version of *King Kong*, which it said would now be based on the novel rather than the film. After instructing Bo Goldman to revise his script to conform to the novel, Universal hired veteran Joseph Sargent (*Colossus: The Forbin Project, The Taking of Pelham 1 2 3*) to direct and announced that shooting would begin in spring 1976. De Laurentiis responded by saying that he would begin casting in December and would start shooting in

April 1976. One question that remained in doubt was whether or not the title *King Kong* was covered by RKO's copyright. As part of their suit, Universal asked the court to determine if it could use the title, but in the meantime changed the name of its production to *The Legend of King Kong* just to be safe. Soon after, De Laurentiis announced that he was going to call his film *King Kong: The Legend Reborn*.

LOCATION SCOUTING AND PRODUCTION DESIGN Although most of the film was going to be shot on soundstages and on the studio backlot, two major locations—Kong's island and New York City—were also required. For Kong's island, locations as far flung as Malta, Bora Bora, and Catalina, California, were considered. Richard Kline, an avid surfer, suggested Hawaii—specifically the remote, breathtaking Na Pali coast on the island of Kauai, which had never before been used in a movie. In November 1975, Kline, Guillermin, Grossberg, and Chiari traveled to Kauai to survey the island and quickly selected it to serve as Kong's home. They then traveled to another island, Manhattan, where they selected several more locations, including the World Trade Center. During these trips, it became apparent that Guillermin and Chiari were not getting along. Guillermin didn't like Chiari's designs, and Chiari was having a hard time adjusting to Hollywood production methods. Eventually, American production designer Dale Hennesy, who won an Oscar for his work on *Fantastic Voyage* (1966), was brought in to take over the task of designing and building all of the sets. From then on, Chiari spent most of his time working on Kong's appearance. Realism was the prevailing design aesthetic in the films of the 1970s—even in fantasy films, the goal was to make settings and effects appear as true to life as possible. In order to give the film as different a look as possible from the original *Kong*, Hennesy followed this aesthetic in designing his sets. The lush fantasy environments of the original film were replaced by actual locations and realistic sets.

As preproduction continued, it became clear that *King Kong* was shaping up to the biggest production Hollywood had seen in quite some time. In the years following *Cleopatra* and other 1960s superproductions that had cost a great deal and lost even more, the film industry had tightened its belt. Most films made in the late 1960s and early 1970s were modest in both scale and ambition. De Laurentiis, on the other hand, was pulling out all the stops. The way *Kong* was produced reminded many of the crew of the way movies used to be made in Hollywood's Golden Age. *Kong* '76 was a much bigger and more elaborate production than the original film. Making it all the more remarkable was the fact that this *Kong* was an independent film produced by a single man, without resources—or the protection—of a major studio behind him.

On Sunday, November 30, 1975, De Laurentiis and Paramount took out an ad in the *New York Times* announcing their production. The ad featured a striking illustration by noted science fiction illustrator John Berkey of Kong straddling the twin towers of the World Trade Center holding Dwan in one hand and an airplane in another. The text of the ad read: "There still is only one King Kong. One year from today, Paramount Pictures and Dino De Laurentiis will

Color reproduction of the newspaper ad that announced Dino De Laurentiis's *King Kong*. This poster features John Berkey's initial version of an image that would become world famous by the time of the film's release.

bring you the most exciting, original, motion picture event of all time." The ad made a huge impact, but it also locked the film firmly into the December 1976 release date. This put a lot of pressure on the crew, which now had just thirteen months to complete an incredibly ambitious and complicated project that under normal circumstances should have taken no less than eighteen. Although many members of the production team thought it was going to be impossible to meet such a tight deadline, with deals having already been struck with distributors and theaters all over the world, it was now imperative that they do so.

CASTING Lorenzo Semple delivered his final draft of the script in December 1975 and casting began immediately afterward. Joyce Selznick (David O.'s niece) served as the film's casting director. De Laurentiis had an aversion to the high prices and demands of major stars, so from the beginning there was an emphasis on finding unknown and up-and-coming talent to fill the roles.

Several actors were considered for the part of Jack Prescott. Chris Sarandon, the star of De Laurentiis's recent production *Lipstick* (1976), was allegedly approached, but declined. The role was then offered to Jeff Bridges, twenty-six, the son of actor Lloyd Bridges and the brother of actor Beau Bridges. Bridges made his film debut at the age of one in *The Company She Keeps* (1950), went

Jeff Bridges as Jack Prescott.

on to appear in films such as *Fat City* (1972) and *Bad Company* (1972), and was nominated for an Academy Award for his work in both *The Last Picture Show* (1971) and *Thunderbolt and Lightfoot* (1974). The original *King Kong* was Bridges's favorite film when he was a child—whenever it was on, he would pretend to be sick so that he could stay home from school and watch it. Excited to "be part of this wonderful story that I had loved when I was a kid," he eagerly signed on.

Although names such as Peter Falk, George C. Scott, and Robert Mitchum were mentioned in the press, the part of Fred Wilson went to Charles Grodin, an experienced stage actor, writer, and director who had made distinctive supporting appearances in films such as *Rosemary's Baby* (1968) and *Catch-22* (1970). Grodin's performance as a man who leaves his new wife on their honeymoon for another woman while on his honeymoon in Elaine May's film of Neil Simon's *The Heartbreak Kid* won him widespread acclaim, but also branded him in the public's mind as a bit of a cad. Grodin came to De Laurentiis's attention when he won a Tony Award for his performance in the Broadway hit *Same Time, Next Year*. A fan of the original film and mindful of the negative image *The Heartbreak Kid* had given him, Grodin was reluctant to take the role of the man responsible for Kong's death, but the chance to appear in a film that had the potential to be seen by more people than any other in history won him over.

Robert Altman regular Rene Auberjonois was cast as Fred's sidekick, oil geologist Roy Bagley. Stage and screen veteran John Randolph was cast as Captain Ross. Character actor Ed Lauter, best known for villainous roles in *The Longest Yard* and *Family Plot* (Alfred Hitchcock's final film) was cast as

Charles Grodin as Fred Wilson.

TOP: Rene Auberjonois as Roy Bagley.

BOTTOM: John Randolph as Captain Ross, with Charles Grodin.

Carnahan, the *Petrox Explorer*'s first mate. Julius Harris, who had recently appeared in the James Bond film *Live and Let Die* (1974), was cast as oil driller Boan, the only member of the search party besides Jack to survive Kong's attack at the log. Former boxer Jack O'Halloran, who made a strong debut the year before in the Robert Mitchum–starrer *Farewell, My Lovely* (1975) was cast as Joe Perko. Jorge Moreno, Mario Gallo, and Dennis Fimple were cast as crewmembers Garcia, Timmons, and Sunfish, respectively. Television actor Ray Buktenica, then a regular on the TV series *Rhoda*, was cast as the *Explorer*'s radar operator, although he went unbilled in the final film. Future *The Last Emperor* star John Lone made his film debut in the role of the Chinese Cook and 1950s schlock sci-fi star John Agar was booked for a cameo appearance as the mayor of New York. The big question, of course, was: Who would play Dwan? Elaine Joyce was named as an early contender and stars such as Barbra Streisand, Valerie Perrine, and Cher were also mentioned in the press, but De Laurentiis—hoping to create a new star—was committed to finding an unknown. Dozens of young women were screen-tested with no success.

THE BATTLE WITH UNIVERSAL, PART III In the meantime, there was still Universal to contend with. On November 20, RKO filed a countersuit against Universal in Federal District Court claiming that *The Legend of King Kong* was an infringement on RKO's copyright. It asked the court to issue an injunction preventing Universal from continuing with "announcements, representations, and statements" about its proposed film. RKO also asked for $5 million in damages. On December 4, De Laurentiis filed his own suit against Universal, asking for $90 million in damages caused by "copyright infringement and unfair competition." He also sought an injunction against Universal to prevent it from making its film and from "interfering" with his production. In response, Universal decided to force the issue by announcing that it was moving up its start date and now planned to start shooting on January 5, 1976. Although De Laurentiis suspected that Universal was only bluffing—with its project only in its nascent stages, it didn't seem even remotely possible that the studio could begin production that soon—it would be a big problem if it weren't. Quite simply, it was highly unlikely that the marketplace would support two new versions of *Kong* at the same time, because, no matter how good both films were, there was only going to be so much audience interest in the subject to go around. Given how expensive both proposed films of *Kong* were going to be, each would need to make as much money as possible in order to be successful. Releasing the two films as the same time would dilute the audience pool, which had the potential to be financially ruinous for both sides. Realistically, there could only be one remake of *King Kong*. The question was—which remake would it be? Since no studio was going to throw good money after bad, the film that started shooting first was going to be the winner, because the second place production was sure to be cancelled.

With this in mind, De Laurentiis called the members of his production team together and asked them to determine what the earliest possible date was that they could start shooting. Everyone agreed that the major sets and special effects would not be ready for at least a few more months. They also knew that it would take that long to prepare the New York and Hawaii location shoots, both of which were going to be major expeditions. Production manager Terry Carr felt it would be possible to prepare the shipboard scenes to begin shooting by the middle of January and proposed a radical plan: the company would begin filming on January 15, 1976, shoot for three weeks in order to get some footage in the can, then shut down for another three weeks, during which time the crew would work around the clock to prepare the rest of the picture. De Laurentiis knew that moving production up in such a hasty manner would increase the budget significantly, but he was willing to risk it. Although it put enormous pressure on everyone involved, the production team agreed to Carr's plan. De Laurentiis and Universal were now in a race—one De Laurentiis was determined to win. The entire production team began working sixteen-hour days, seven days a week in order to get ready for the January start. This added millions of dollars to the budget that De Laurentiis didn't have, but he was determined to keep going, convinced that the money would come.

With the start of production rapidly approaching, it became imperative to find someone to play Dwan. With his plan to find an unknown not working out, De Laurentiis widened the search to include established (if not star) actresses. According to Fred Sidewater, De Laurentiis and Guillermin had just about decided to offer the part to Deborah Raffin when De Laurentiis received a call from Gulf & Western chairman Charles Bludhorn. Bludhorn, whose business interests included fashion as well as film, had encountered a young model at an event in New York who he thought had potential. Although De Laurentiis didn't think much would come of this recommendation, as a courtesy to his patron he agreed to screen test the model, whose name was Jessica Lange. Born in Minnesota in 1949, Lange's original ambition had been to be an artist. After attending the University of Minnesota for two years, she dropped out and moved to New York to study dance and then to Paris to train as a mime. This led to an interest in acting, which she returned to New York in 1973 to study. To support herself, she worked as a waitress and then signed with the Wilhelmina Agency as a model.

The production contacted Wilhelmina and arranged to have Lange and two other models flown out to Los Angeles. When De Laurentiis first met Lange, he wasn't impressed—she was pale, underweight, and wearing braces. William Kronick directed Lange's screen test—a performance of Dwan's stateroom monologue on the actual set in full costume and makeup. "I'd already filmed two girls, one worse than the other, when Jessica came on and rehearsed the scene," Kronick recalls. "She moved and performed in a quirky, refreshing manner that instantly told me she could bring color and life to the role." As impressed as he was with Lange, Kronick suspected that if De Laurentiis and Guillermin saw her test mixed in with a bunch of others, they might not take notice of her. Intuiting that Guillermin would react positively if he saw Lange in person, Kronick invited the director to come to the set and watch her rehearse. As Kronick had hoped, Guillermin was impressed and brought De Laurentiis to the stage to see Lange work. The producer was as impressed as

Guillermin and Kronick had been, but said he wanted to see what Lange looked like on film before making a final decision. Fortunately, she looked wonderful—one production associate described Lange's appearance in the test as "luminous." Jeffrey Chernov was with Guillermin when the test was screened and reports that the director became so excited that he literally ripped the leather cover off the back of the seat in front of him as he exclaimed, "I found my Fay Wray!" De Laurentiis agreed and offered Lange the part. He also

Jessica Lange as Dwan.

signed her to an exclusive seven-year contract. To prepare for her role, Lange had her braces removed and immediately began working with an acting coach.

As soon as De Laurentiis announced he would begin filming in January, Universal allegedly approached him about settling their respective lawsuits. There was some discussion about possibly teaming up to jointly produce a single film, but Universal made demands that De Laurentiis felt were outrageous. To begin with, Universal insisted that they use its script. They also wanted control of all of the merchandising and the sequel rights. De Laurentiis broke off talks and proceeded with both his plans and his lawsuit. Although De Laurentiis was confident that he would prevail, Barry Diller began pressing him to settle. Paramount was partners with Universal in Cinema International Corporation, a European film distribution company, and Barry Diller was reluctant to be party to a lawsuit against his partner. De Laurentiis refused—he felt that he was in the right and wanted to go to court to prove it. But then, just before Christmas and only a few weeks before De Laurentiis was about to start shooting, Diller gave him an ultimatum—if he didn't settle with Universal, then Paramount was going to pull out of the film. De Laurentiis was shocked and unhappy, but he also realized that, with no time left to find another distributor, he had no choice. Soon after, De Laurentiis and Universal began discussing settlement terms.

TOP: The USS *Melville* as the SS *Petrox Explorer*.

BOTTOM: A present day photo of Sony Pictures Studios, formerly MGM, where much of *King Kong* (1976) was filmed.

PRODUCTION BEGINS

January 5, 1976, came and went without *The Legend of King Kong* going before the cameras (although Universal—most likely to keep De Laurentiis on the defensive—claimed that it had, despite the fact that no sets had been built and no actors cast). On January 14, 1976, De Laurentiis held a press conference on the Paramount lot to announce the official start of his production and to introduce Jessica Lange. And then, on January 15, 1976, *King Kong: The Legend Reborn* began filming on the San Pedro docks. The first shot filmed was the first shot of the movie—an establishing view of the *Petrox Explorer* as it prepares to leave Surabaya. Scenes of Jack Prescott sneaking aboard and the ship setting sail were filmed the next night and the film was officially underway. De Laurentiis had won the battle. Whether or not he would win the war remained to be seen.

During the last week of January, the main unit shot scenes chronicling the *Explorer*'s journey to Kong's island in the channel between Los Angeles and Catalina Island. The ship used in these scenes was the USS *Melville*—a U.S. Navy research ship on loan to the University of California's Scripps Institute of Oceanography. Brian Frankish found the ship and Jack Grossberg rented it from Scripps for $250,000. To ready it for filming, Dale Hennesy repainted the hull and constructed false staterooms, cabins, and mess rooms onto the decks. To keep the horizon from bobbing up and down in each shot, Richard Kline used a special gyroscopic stabilizing device that kept the picture perfectly level. Jessica Lange's first sequence—a montage of Dwan's new life aboard the ship—was filmed during this voyage, as was the scene of her being rescued from the sea. To film this scene, Lange spent hours floating in a rubber raft in the freezing cold, drenched to the bone and wearing only a slinky black dress. Although Lange was unaware of it, there were sharks circling the raft the entire time.

The ship's approach to the mysterious fog bank that encircles Kong's island was filmed next. To generate the fog, Glen Robinson attached navy foggers to six custom-built wind machines powered by Volkswagen engines and mounted them on three tugboats. An expert sailor, John Guillermin used a radio to guide the boats in a pattern that laid down a five-hundred-foot-tall wall of fog that stretched out for three or four miles and socked in most of Catalina, which greatly annoyed the island's residents. At the end of the week, the second unit filmed long and aerial shots of the *Explorer* at sea, some of which were used under the film's opening credits. The second unit also filmed the long shot of the ship's approach to the fog bank, as well as a scene in which a Petrox cargo plane airdrops the canisters of chloroform that Fred Wilson will later use to capture Kong.

On January 28, 1976, De Laurentiis and Universal announced that they had come to terms. In return for a percentage (alternately reported as either 8% or 11%) of De Laurentiis's profits, certain merchandising rights and profits, and veto power over any proposed sequel, Universal agreed to cancel *The Legend of King Kong*, although it did retain the right to produce a Kong film sometime in the future, as long as production didn't start any sooner than eighteen months after the release of *King Kong: The Legend Reborn*. At the time, this stipulation had no practical payoff, because if De Laurentiis's film was a hit the market would be sated and if it was a flop there would be no interest in doing another Kong picture anytime soon. However, it would pay off twenty-nine years later when it allowed Universal to produce Peter Jackson's version of the

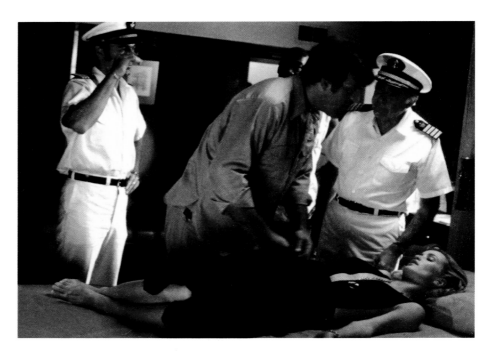

The stateroom scene. From left to right: Ed Lauter, Jack O'Halloran, John Randolph, and Jessica Lange.

story. Universal also agreed to drop De Laurentiis as a defendant in its lawsuit against RKO. (That suit would not be settled until the following September, when the court validated Universal's claim that the Lovelace novelization was indeed in the public domain, which meant that Universal was free to proceed with its project if it wanted to.) While De Laurentiis may not have been pleased with all of these terms, he was at least now free to make his own movie in his own way without competition. Moving on, he dropped *The Legend Reborn* and the film once again became known simply as *King Kong*.

During the first week of February, interior scenes set on the *Petrox Explorer* were filmed on the MGM soundstages. As the actors eased into their parts, they found themselves facing a series of creative challenges. For Jeff Bridges, the prime challenge was to play the straight man to the more comedic performances of Lange and Grodin and still make an impact with his character. To do this, he gave Jack a dry sense of humor that would allow him to get laughs along with the others while still enabling him to act as a realistic anchor to those around him. Bridges also had the most physical role in the picture. The script required Prescott to be in almost continuous motion—running, jumping, climbing. The energetic Bridges performed many of his own stunts, including the very difficult climb up the rope from pier to ship in the beginning of the film. He did not enjoy acting in front of a blue screen and found it difficult to react to a creature that wasn't there, a complaint echoed by most of the rest of the cast.

For Charles Grodin, the humorous aspects of his performance proved to be somewhat controversial. In the script, the role of Wilson was written as a straight villain. In a *New York Times* profile published at the time of the film's release, Grodin said that he chose to make Wilson more comedic because he thought it would be a way to keep the audience entertained for the first hour of the film while it was waiting for Kong to appear. Some crewmembers and studio executives were critical of this decision, feeling that Grodin was too broad, but the actor stuck to his guns and kept the character from going over the top by introducing elements of true menace at appropriate moments (such as the dyspeptic look Fred has when Jack calls him an environmental rapist and his chilling dismissal of Captain Ross's concerns about the search party).

Lange's biggest challenge was to find her legs as an actress amid a massive, often chaotic production and in the crosshairs of a relentless publicity machine, a situation even the most experienced actor might find overwhelming. Adding to the challenge was the fact that Lange herself—described by those who worked with her as fiercely intelligent, complex, and savvy—was nothing like the naïve, uncomplicated waif she was playing. After a rocky beginning in which she was encouraged to do a slightly awkward Marilyn Monroe impersonation, Lange quickly came into her own and succeeded in creating a memorable characterization. She succeeded so well, in fact, that many people who didn't know her mistook Lange for the "dumb blonde" she was playing, an assessment that hindered her post-*Kong* career for a while and that her later, double–Academy Award winning work thoroughly disproved. Bridges, for one, was a big fan of her performance: "Jessie...pulled that [role]

The landing party approaches Kong's island. This scene was filmed in the waters off Catalina Island in January 1976.

off spectacularly, considering how different she is in real life. At the time, people didn't realize what a good job she had done. Knowing her other work, you can see now what she put into it."

Rene Auberjonois gave one of the film's most delightful performances. By investing Roy Bagley with a bemused, eager-beaver attitude, and providing him with a series of clever and inventive comic bits of business, Auberjonois turned a flatly-written role designed only to provide exposition and act as a sounding board for Fred Wilson and turned it into one of the film's most charming and appealing characters.

Following the shipboard interior scenes, the main unit spent several nights north of Malibu at Zuma Beach shooting the scene in which Captain Ross gives Fred Wilson the idea to use Kong as an advertisement. They also attempted to film the scene in which the *Petrox Explorer* crew comes ashore to rescue Dwan after the natives have kidnapped her, but the surf was so choppy that the scene was postponed. With no other sets ready or locations prepared, production shut down following these scenes and remained shuttered until February 17, when filming resumed in Hawaii. During the layoff, the production focused on getting Kong in shape.

CREATING KONG When preproduction started in October 1975, one of the creative team's first tasks was to figure out how to bring Kong to life. The one method De Laurentiis knew that he didn't want to use was stop-motion animation. Besides not wanting to imitate the original film, De Laurentiis felt that stop-motion didn't look smooth enough and that it was too expensive and time-consuming to produce. After discussing the matter with Mario Chiari, Federico De Laurentiis, and John Guillermin, De Laurentiis decided that they would use a man in an ape suit—albeit one that was much more realistic looking and state-of-the-art than those used in the Japanese films—to realize Kong on screen. Knowing that they wanted their Kong to be able to express a wide range of emotions, the creative team decided that, rather than a mask, they would use appliance makeup to create his face. Appliance makeup, which was used in the *Planet of the Apes* films, was applied directly to an actor's face, allowing him to create a full range of expressions. Since they were dealing with a giant creature that had to interact with human performers, Guillermin felt that it was important to have a full-sized representation of Kong as well, so the decision was made to build a large Kong mannequin capable of making some limited head and arm movements for use in certain shots. The team also decided to create a separate pair of full-sized, articulated hands that could be used to pick up the girl and hold her when required.

Federico De Laurentiis immediately began searching for someone to create the Kong costume. When word of the remake first spread through Hollywood, a group of young animators had approached De Laurentiis to pitch their services. Told that the production was going to use an actor in costume, the animators recommended that the producers talk to a friend of theirs—a makeup man whose hobby was creating elaborate and realistic gorilla costumes named Rick Baker. Baker was born in New York in 1950 and grew up in Covina,

California, a suburb of Los Angeles. A talented artist, Baker became fascinated with monster movies at a very young age and began creating his own monster masks and makeups while still a preteen. Fascinated with apes, he made his first gorilla suit at age thirteen. A job at the Clokey animation studio (producers of the *Gumby* and *Davey and Goliath* series) introduced him to foam rubber, which would become a key ingredient in many of his future creations, as well as to the sculpting, mold-making, and casting techniques necessary to create effective masks and makeups. When Baker was eighteen, he wrote a letter to legendary makeup man Dick Smith (*The Godfather*), who invited Baker to his New York studio for a tour. Smith mentored Baker for the next several years and Baker later assisted Smith on *The Exorcist* (1973). Baker began his professional career at Cascade Pictures, a nonunion producer of commercials, and got started in features when he created the title character for *Octaman* (1971), which he followed with work on *It's Alive* (1973) and *Live and Let Die* (1973). Baker created his first cinematic ape suit in 1971 for John Landis's comedy *Schlock!* (released in 1973) and his first cinematic gorilla suit for 1972's *The Thing with Two Heads*, which was also the first time he acted in one of his own costumes onscreen. In 1974, Baker and fellow makeup artist Stan Winston collaborated to transform Cicely Tyson into a 100-year-old woman in the television movie *The Autobiography of Miss Jane Pittman*, for which both men won an Emmy Award.

After screening *Schlock!* and *The Thing with Two Heads*, Federico De Laurentiis gave Baker a call. Baker went to MGM to meet with Federico and Jack Grossberg and brought along some of his gorilla masks and sculptures to show what he could do. The first thing Baker did was talk them out of using appliance makeup to create Kong's face, arguing that the *Planet of the Apes* movies and TV show had wrung that idea dry. When Federico and Baker expressed concern that a mask would not convey the emotion they wanted,

Monster makers: A costumed Rick Baker (foreground) takes a break while Carlo Rambaldi (background) holds one of the Kong masks.

Baker assured them that he could incorporate mechanisms into the mask that would give it the proper expressiveness. Impressed, Federico and Grossberg invited Baker to work on *Kong*. Baker was interested, but had a previous commitment to do the makeup effects on a horror film called *Squirm*, which would prevent him from starting work for at least a month. At that point, time was not yet an issue and Federico and Grossberg were willing to wait, so Baker accepted the job.

To design and build the full-scale Kong mannequin and the articulated hands, De Laurentiis and Chiari decided to bring in Carlo Rambaldi. Born in Vigarano, Italy, in 1925, Rambaldi attended the Academy of Fine Arts of Bologna and went on to win many awards for his dramatic paintings and drawings. He entered the Italian film industry in the early 1960s as a prop maker and worked on many films with both Chiari and De Laurentiis, including *Barrabas* and *The Bible*. In 1968, he worked under special effects director Gerard Cogan on De Laurentiis's production of *Barbarella*. Cogan was a toy maker and special effects artist who had devised innovative ways of using cable-controlled mechanical devices to animate toys and props. On *Barbarella*, Cogan devised the vicious mechanical dolls that attack Jane Fonda. Rambaldi adopted Cogan's techniques, refined and improved upon them in subsequent projects, and earned a reputation as an expert creator of cable-controlled articulated props. His proudest achievement was a life-size wooden Pinocchio that he created for an Italian television special. Rambaldi was a great favorite of De Laurentiis's, who regarded him as a genius and used him whenever he could. *Kong* seemed like the perfect project for Rambaldi's talents, so Chiari called Rambaldi at his studio in Rome late one afternoon in October 1975 and invited him to come to America.

Upon arriving in the States, Rambaldi spent some time researching gorillas at the San Diego Zoo and then began working on plans for the Kong mannequin. At some point, however, the idea arose to build a mechanical Kong instead. It's not clear exactly where this idea came from (some suggest Rambaldi, others say it came from De Laurentiis), but at the time the remarkable mechanical shark that Joe Alves and Robert Mattey had created for *Jaws* was receiving a great deal of positive attention, so it made sense that the *Kong* people would consider doing something similar. After giving the matter some thought, Rambaldi told De Laurentiis that he was confident he could design a fully-functional mechanical Kong that could perform all of the actions required by the script, including walking and picking up the girl. While many in the production had strong doubts that Rambaldi could create something with the enormous range of capabilities he claimed his creation would have, De Laurentiis loved the idea and told Rambaldi to go ahead. Rambaldi began creating plans for his mechanical monster based on Chiari's ape-man concept.

Rick Baker finished his work on *Squirm* and reported for work at the end of November 1975. When he learned that Rambaldi had been hired as a special effects supervisor and that he planned to build a full-size Kong that was going to do most of the acting in the picture. Baker was incredulous. "I said, 'It's impossible. He [Rambaldi] can't do it. If NASA can't do it, he can't do it—especially on a short movie schedule.' But they assured me he (Rambaldi) was a genius who could pull it off." Baker was told that they still wanted him to build the Kong suit, but only as a back up. Because Rambaldi was now in charge of the entire Kong project, Baker was asked to work with him to make the suit. At first Baker wasn't interested, but after looking at Rambaldi's portfolio and seeing what a talented artist he was, Baker changed his mind. Both men had very different ideas as to how to go about making the suit, so the producers decided to give each of them six weeks to create a prototype. At the end of the six weeks, the prototypes would be compared and the best approach chosen.

Working out of his garage with an assistant (sculptor David Celetti), Baker got to work. The first thing he did was toss out Chiari's ape-man designs, which he thought were ridiculous. "I was going to save them from themselves," he says now with a laugh. Baker felt that Kong should be a gorilla and set out to make him one. Busy working on his plans for the Big Kong, Rambaldi was unable to meet the deadline and was granted an extension. Baker didn't find out about this until after he arrived at MGM on the day of the presentation and met Dino De Laurentiis for the first time. Baker felt it was unfair that Rambaldi had been given more time. Dissatisfied with many of the details of his suit, Baker wanted more time too, but his request was denied. With no other choice, Baker donned his suit, strutted out in front of De Laurentiis, Guillermin, Chiari, and other key members of the production team, and did his best giant ape impersonation. Because Baker had created a gorilla rather than the called-for ape-man, the initial reaction to his suit was extremely negative. Had Rambaldi's suit been finished, Baker feels he would have been dismissed on the spot, but, because it wasn't and because they had to get started on camera, miniature, and special effects tests, the decision was made to use Baker's suit to shoot the tests until Rambaldi could finish his suit. Because Baker had built his costume to fit himself, he ended up playing Kong in the tests. As time went on, the creative team, especially Guillermin, got used to the look of Baker's suit and the way he portrayed the giant ape.

In the meantime, Rambaldi went ahead and finished his designs for the mechanical Kong and the articulated hands. Glen Robinson, the film's special effects supervisor, was assigned to facilitate the construction of Rambaldi's creations. Examining Rambaldi's complex plans, Robinson—himself an experienced mechanical designer—felt that the designs were overly complicated and impractical and that there would be no way that he would be able to implement them or get the resulting constructs to work, especially in the limited amount of time he had to pull it all together. Knowing that De Laurentiis had complete faith in Rambaldi and that it would not be easy to persuade the producer that his star designer's ideas weren't working out, Robinson went ahead and submitted Rambaldi's plans to an aircraft construction company for a bid. Meanwhile, Robinson—who once ran a company that designed and built theme park attractions—quietly began preparing his own plans for a Kong and pair of hands that would be operated by hydraulics in the same way that amusement-park rides were. Robinson's Kong was less ambitious than Rambaldi's, but it was also much more practical and would take a lot less time to build. When the aircraft company estimated that it would take anywhere from eighteen months to three years to perfect and realize Rambaldi's plans, De Laurentiis was discouraged, but didn't want to give up on the idea. At this point, Robinson submitted his designs. With time running short, De Laurentiis put Robinson in charge of building the Big Kong and the Big Hands. Needless to say, Rambaldi was not happy about this turn of events and, although he continued to work on a design for Kong's exterior, there was considerable tension between Rambaldi and Robinson and their respective crews from that point on.

With Robinson now in charge of creating the Big Kong, Rambaldi finished his prototype Kong suit. When he finally presented it, the reaction was even more negative than the reaction to Baker's suit had been. Based on Chiari's original ape-man designs and, by most accounts, crudely fashioned, the suit did not look very good or work very well. A disappointed John Guillermin proclaimed it to be a "$200,000 disaster" and decided that he no longer liked the ape-man concept at all. He wanted to go instead with Baker's design, which he felt was more impressive and powerful looking in every way, and the rest of the team agreed. The ape-man concept was dropped and the decision was made to go ahead with a final suit that would be based on Baker's prototype – Kong was now going to be a gorilla, albeit it one with human qualities. Rambaldi's suit was put aside and no tests were ever shot with it. Rambaldi was no happier about all of this than he was about the Big Kong. Since his suit won the competition, Baker expected to be put in charge of making the final Kong costume, and so was surprised when De Laurentiis asked him to collaborate with Rambaldi on the final suit. Fed up, Baker decided to quit the project, but De Laurentiis asked him to reconsider. Attracted by what he saw as an opportunity to create the ultimate gorilla suit, he eventually agreed to stay on.

THE BIG KONG   Robinson began constructing the Big Kong on February 28, 1976, while the main unit was in Hawaii. The initial plan had been to build a thirty-foot-tall creature, but when it was determined that a larger hand would look better holding the girl, Kong's height was increased to forty-two feet. Both Rambaldi and Robinson's initial designs were based on the ape-man concept, which was still in place when construction began on the Big Kong's framework. Once the decision was made to go with a more gorilla-based design, the framework was modified, although some traces of the original concept remained (for instance, in the creature's too-long, too-slender legs). Work on the framework was guided by a four-foot-tall sculpture created by Don Chandler from Rambaldi's designs.

Like the armature created by Marcel Delgado forty-three years earlier, the Big Kong's basic skeleton was made out of dural aluminum. His many joints were equipped with hydraulic cylinders. Eddie Surkin assembled Kong's mechanical systems, which were operated from a control panel manned by six members of Robinson's team. The entire construct was assembled by cranes and supported by cranes and a scaffold. To fabricate Kong's exterior, patterns were made from Chandler's sculpture and then scaled up to giant size. Kong's various body parts were then sculpted according to those patterns. Molds were

FACING PAGE, CLOCKWISE FROM TOP: The Big Kong's aluminum skeleton is assembled in a work shed at MGM.

A portion of the Big Kong covered with fiberglass and resin.

The Big Kong—fully completed.

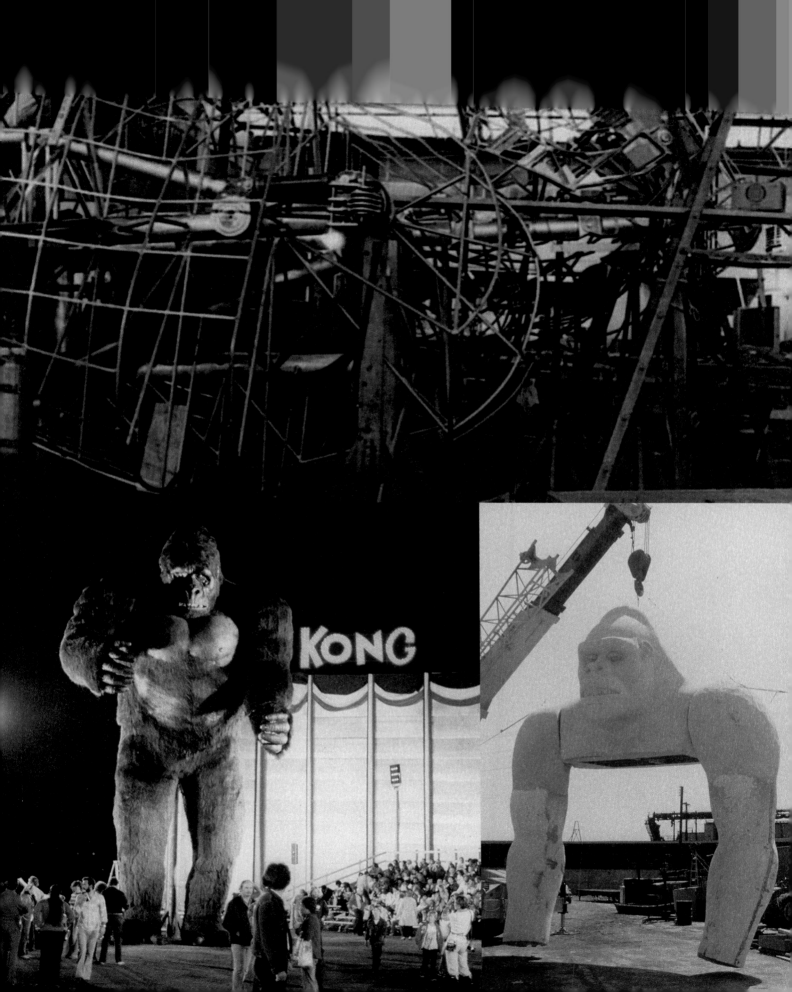

made of the sculptures, from which fiberglass and resin pieces were cast and then attached to the aluminum skeleton. Veteran Hollywood wig-maker Michael Dino was then brought in to create Kong's hide. To do so, Dino first imported 4,000 pounds of horsehair from Argentina and had it dyed a uniform color. The hair was woven into netting that was glued onto latex panels, which were then attached to Kong's fiberglass-and-resin exterior. The final construct weighed six and a half tons, contained 3,100 feet of hydraulic hose, and 4,500 feet of electrical wiring. The robot's chest was twenty feet wide and both of its arms were twenty feet long. It could turn its head, raise its arms, open its mouth, flex its chest, and move its fingers, eyes, and toes. It took four and a half months to build, at a cost of approximately $1.7 million.

Even with Robinson and his team moving as fast as possible, it quickly became clear that the Big Kong was going to take a lot longer to finish than originally anticipated. Although the initial plan to use the Big Kong for most of the filming had been scaled back considerably once it became clear that Robinson's simpler design would not have the elaborate capabilities that Rambaldi claimed his would have, the producers had hoped that the Big Kong would be ready in time to use in certain key shots in the film (for example, the original storyboards called for it to be used in the sacrifice scene when Kong picks Dwan up from the altar and on location at the World Trade Center) that would then be supplemented by shots of the man in the Kong suit. However, as construction dragged on, it became clear that the Big Kong wouldn't be ready until the very end of the shooting schedule and that most of Kong's scenes would have to be realized using the man in the Kong suit. Although at this point there wasn't much of a practical reason to continue building the Big Kong, there was a compelling promotional reason. Enjoying all of the favorable publicity his plan to use a giant robot was generating, De Laurentiis wanted the Big Kong finished. As long as it appeared in at least one scene in the movie, all of the publicity could be justified. The decision was made to feature the Big Kong in the Shea Stadium presentation scene—the one sequence in the film that required Kong to interact with a large number of people. Originally meant to be filmed in the middle of the production, the scene was pushed back to the end of the schedule to await the completion of De Laurentiis's "Big Monkey."

THE BIG HANDS Robinson's team began work on the Big Hands on the same day they began work on the Big Kong. Robinson had discarded Rambaldi's plan for marionette-like hands that would be manipulated by wires and replaced them with one for a pair of hydraulically driven limbs similar to his design for the Big Kong. This move exacerbated the tension between Robinson and Rambaldi and their teams. Communication was already difficult due to the language barrier and hard feelings over the Big Kong. This latest development caused relations between the Italians and the Americans to deteriorate to the point where any kind of true collaboration became almost impossible. The initial designs for the hands were scaled to fit a thirty-foot Kong. When the decision was made to increase Kong's size, the original hands were put aside and a new pair begun. (This was the truth behind an oft-repeated rumor that the allegedly inept and disorganized production had inadvertently created two

ABOVE: Members of Glen Robinson's team operate the Big Hands.

FACING PAGE: The Big Hands rehearse the crater scene. A stuntwoman sits in for Jessica Lange.

right hands for Kong.) The look of the hands had originally been based on Chiari's ape-man concept, with narrow, human-like palms and fingers that were long and pointy. Guillermin preferred the wide palms and stubby fingers of Baker's gorilla suit, so the hands were revamped accordingly.

In constructing armatures for the hands, Robinson duplicated the structure of the human hand and gave Kong's paws the same number of bones and joints. The armatures were made from dural aluminum and then attached to arms made from steel beams. After the right hand pressed too tightly around a frightened Jessica Lange during an initial run-through, bolts were placed in the knuckles of each finger to act as stops and to prevent them from closing completely and crushing the actress. To cover the armatures, full-scale sculptures of each hand were sculpted from clay. Molds were then taken from the sculptures and used to produce foam rubber pieces that were attached to the armatures and covered with the same Argentinean horsehair-mounted-on-latex that was used on the Big Kong. Each hand was then mounted on a crane so that it could be easily moved about. The right hand was the primary one used during production. The left hand was used only in the crater scene, where it served as a platform for Jessica Lange to sit on as the right hand peeled away her gown, and in the shot where Kong reaches up out of the chloroform-filled pit after he has broken through the Great Wall. Both hands were run from a control panel operated by a team of Robinson's men.

The creation of the Big Hands was not without incident. When the right hand was being sculpted, the heavy clay monstrosity started to tip over. Sculptor Tom Prosser ran over to brace it, but the hand fell on top of him and knocked him out cold. Rick Baker witnessed the incident and called Prosser "Kong's first victim." When the right hand was finished and was first being tested, the operators decided to have some fun by extending the middle finger in a particularly rude gesture. The crew laughed heartily until the hydraulics broke and the finger froze in that position.

THE KONG SUIT As Robinson was building the Big Kong and Big Hands, Baker joined Rambaldi in his workshop at MGM to start work on the Kong suit. The collaboration did not go smoothly—both men had definite ideas and strong wills and began clashing almost immediately.

Before construction could begin, a sculpture needed to be created that would show what the final product was supposed to look like. Since this sculpture would define Kong's onscreen appearance, both men naturally wanted to be the one to fashion it. To resolve the impasse, another contest was arranged. This time, Baker and Rambaldi would both sculpt a face for Kong. The creative team would pick the one they liked the best and the winner would sculpt the rest of the body. Baker created a free-form face, while Rambaldi sculpted one based on a photo Federico De Laurentiis had taken of a gorilla named Bum from the San Diego Zoo. On the appointed day, a blind judging was held and the creative team chose Baker's sculpture, a decision that again made Rambaldi extremely unhappy. Incorporating suggestions made by the various members of the creative team, Baker then did a final rendition of Kong's face and then modeled the rest of the body. Other sculptors did Kong's hands and feet. Molds were then made from all of these sculptures, which were then used to create a man-sized plaster statue of Kong. This statue looked quite different than the one Don Chandler had created for the Big Kong, which is why the final products don't look anything alike. Early on, Baker had argued that both versions of Kong should be based on the same statue, but he was overruled.

The next step was to create a padded "muscle" suit that the performer would wear under the outer fur to define Kong's shape. There were two possible approaches to fashioning the muscle suit. The first—called "building up"—was to cut pieces out of sheets of foam rubber and glue or sew them on to a lycra body stocking in layers in order to create the necessary contours. This was the approach Rambaldi wanted to take. The second approach—called "casting"—was to make molds of the various parts of the Kong statue and then use those molds to cast pieces of foam rubber that would then be attached to the lycra. This was the approach Baker wanted to take. Although it was more expensive and time-consuming, Baker felt it would allow for greater detail, as well as the ability to rapidly create multiple copies of the undersuit for backup or repair. Both men took their disagreement to De Laurentiis, who, as he would in most of their future disagreements, sided with Rambaldi.

Next they had to create Kong's chest. A mold was taken from the statue and a foam rubber piece was produced. Baker wanted to fill it with liquid to give it the heft and sway of a real chest. Rambaldi initially overruled him, but after Baker arranged a screening of *Murders in the Rue Morgue*, a film in which ace Hollywood gorilla suit creator and performer Charles Gemora had used a liquid-filled chest with impressive results, Rambaldi changed his mind. According to Baker, Rambaldi then went to De Laurentiis and pitched the idea as his own. Annoyed, Baker—who had already devised a method for filling the chest with liquid—decided to keep his ideas to himself and let Rambaldi figure things out on his own. After some experimentation, Rambaldi finally decided to place a dozen condoms filled with water into a net that would then be draped over the muscle suit. Because all of the weight rested on the under-

Rick Baker in the foam rubber undersuit.

Rick Baker in the complete Kong costume.

suit rather than the chest, this approach failed to create the desired impression.

Baker and Rambaldi next clashed over Kong's fur. Baker's initial preference was to ventilate the suit—hand tie individual shafts of synthetic hair one at a time to a piece of flexible fabric. Baker felt this was an ideal approach because it would also allow them to arrange Kong's hair in realistic, life-like patterns and because it would be lightweight, flexible, and relatively cool to wear. Rambaldi and Chiari rejected this idea because it was time-consuming and expensive. Baker then suggested having a batch of synthetic fur custom made instead. While this would also be expensive, Baker felt it would pay off in the long run because, in addition to being lightweight and flexible, it would allow them to make as much fur as they needed to cover multiple Kong suits as well as the Big Kong and Big Hands and still have everything match. This suggestion was also nixed. Instead, Rambaldi and Chiari decided to use real animal fur, which they felt would look more natural. Baker didn't like this idea at all. Besides an ethical aversion to using the skin of an actual animal, Baker argued that real fur would be hot and heavy to wear, wouldn't stretch, and wouldn't adapt properly to Kong's shape. Overruling him, Rambaldi and Chiari bought nine full bear hides from Bischoff's Taxidermy in Los Angeles and had studio tailors sew them together into a single suit. When the finished suit was draped over the padding, the hair—which was designed by nature to fit a completely different shape—stood straight up in the air, making Kong look like a big puffball. To fix the problem, Rambaldi clipped off the guide hairs—the long lustrous hairs on the top of a bear's coat—leaving behind only the fuzzy down beneath it. Making matters worse, the colors of the different furs didn't match and the seams where they were sewn together were quite visible. To hide the seams and blend the colors, Rambaldi sprayed the suit with an aerosol hair-coloring agent called Streaks 'N Tips. This process had to be repeated before every shot. The accumulated layers of color caused Kong's fur to change from dark black to brown from over the course of the filming.

Kong's hands also prompted several arguments. To begin with, Baker wanted the gloves to run all the way to the elbows. Besides allowing them to imitate the natural hair pattern of a gorilla (which breaks at the arm), Baker figured that this would be a good way to hide the join, since viewers tend naturally to look at the wrists. Rambaldi chose to place the join at the wrist. To give Kong proper gorilla-length arms, Baker wanted to incorporate working mechanical arm extensions into the suit. Rambaldi initially resisted but, after seeing how effective the use of arm extensions were in *Murders in the Rue Morgue*, he compromised and made a set of finger extensions that were worn on the fingers like rings. These extensions were strictly cosmetic and nonfunctional and were only used in shots in which Kong didn't have to actually use his hands. Thankfully, Kong's feet didn't create as much controversy—they were basically shoes fabricated out of slip rubber and covered with bear hair.

Baker was extremely disappointed in the final suit, which he felt wasn't at all convincing. He gives all of the credit for its passable appearance in the film to cinematographer Richard Kline. "Dick saved it…hid it all with his lighting. He made it look as good as it could possibly look."

THE MASKS The collaboration between Rambaldi and Baker went much more smoothly when it came to creating Kong's head. Baker began the process by creating a fiberglass core made from a mold of his own face. He then attached a fiberglass skullcap to the top of the core to allow it to fit snugly on the performer's head and prevent it from slipping around. Baker gave the finished core to Rambaldi, who, with his assistant Isadoro Raponi, attached a series of mechanisms to the core designed to push and pull Kong's face in the directions necessary to create his various expressions. These mechanisms were controlled by a series of thin bicycle-brake cables that were attached to the mechanisms and then run out of the back of Kong's head, where they were gathered into a bundle and then attached to a bank of control levers located out of camera range (often as far as thirty feet away). For wider shots in which the cables couldn't be seen emerging from the back of Kong's head, the bundle was snaked down inside the suit and threaded out one of the ankles. For all of their problems working together, Baker gives Rambaldi full marks for the creation of Kong's amazing facial expressions. Baker's original idea was to manipulate Kong's face using self-contained, jaw-operated mechanisms similar to the kind that British makeup legend Stuart Freeborn used in the ape masks he created for *2001: A Space Odyssey*, but Baker concedes that Rambaldi's mechanics were more effective and achieved some remarkable results. In the opinion of one production associate, Rambaldi's difficulties on the film arose from the fact that he was often operating outside of his area of expertise. Rambaldi was a talented artist and a creative designer of cable-controlled effects. Ape suits and giant robots were simply not his forte, but when he played to his strengths, as he did with the facial mechanisms, he shined.

While Rambaldi and Raponi were installing the mechanisms on the core, Baker supervised the creation of the outer skin. To do this, a mold was taken of the final sculpture of Kong's head and filled with liquid foam latex, which was then cured in a special oven and painted. The result was a foam rubber Kong face that Rambaldi and Raponi fit onto the core over the mechanics. Once this was done, Baker punched hair into the head one strand at a time and then installed Kong's teeth, which were made of wax. A small piece of black fabric was attached to the back of Kong's throat to hide the performer inside and the head was finished.

There were actually five Kong heads. Knowing that —because latex can only stretch so far without tearing—there would be limitations as to what a single mask could do, Baker suggested that they use multiple heads, each with a different range of expression. This idea was accepted, so Baker sculpted three different faces for Kong, each with a basic look that could then be accentuated by Rambaldi's mechanics. The first—called the generic head—had a neutral look that could be extended to create all normal expressions. This head had the most cables (eleven) and the most complicated mechanics. The second—called the angry head—began with a frown and could be extended to the beginning of a roar. The third—called the roar head—could be extended into a full roar with a wide-open mouth and fully exposed teeth. The later two heads had less cables and simpler mechanics. A fourth head was created for the waterfall

scene. This face had pursed lips and balloons installed in the cheeks that could be inflated and deflated as Kong "blow dries" Dwan. The latex was made thinner in the cheeks to facilitate the effect. There was also a "stunt" head that was sculpted with a fierce look and contained no mechanics. This mask was used for long shots and for action scenes in which it would be impractical to have Kong hooked up to a bunch of cables.

None of the masks had eyes—Kong's lids and pupils were actually those of the performer. To mask the performer's humanity, a pair of scleral contact lenses—clear, non-prescription lenses that fit under the upper and lower eyelids and covered the entire eyeball—with a gorilla pupil painted on each lens was used. Baker wanted to install a vacuform ring around the eyeholes that would allow the mask to fit snugly against the performer's skin, but the mechanics didn't leave room for them, so a small plastic ring was installed instead, but it never worked properly. As a result, in some scenes in the film there is a small but noticeable gap between the mask and the actor.

OPTICAL EFFECTS

As it was for the crew of the original film, the biggest challenge facing the team was to composite full-scale and miniature footage in a convincing manner. To accomplish this, John Guillermin originally wanted to use *front-screen projection.*

Front-screen is a process that involves filming a foreground subject in front of a large, highly reflective screen. A camera is aimed at the subject while a previously filmed background plate is beamed from a projector located near the camera into a one-way mirror positioned at a forty-five-degree angle in front of the camera lens. The mirror projects the background plate onto the screen, which then bounces it back into the lens of the camera at many times its original intensity, allowing the camera to photograph both the background image and foreground object together in the same frame. Under optimum conditions, the front-screen process can yield an almost perfect composite. To test the viability of the process, during the preproduction period, the *Kong* team constructed a fifty-foot-tall front projection screen and Richard Kline traveled to Hawaii to photograph VistaVision background plates. Unfortunately, the process didn't work quite as well as they had hoped. To begin with, there were serious contrast problems. The amount of light required to adequately illuminate the dark black Kong suit caused the background plates to wash out. In addition, because the front-projection screen could only bounce the background image back to the camera in a straight line, the process was really only suitable for head-on shots in which the camera directly faced the screen. Shooting at any sort of angle caused the background image to dim considerably. Since the film was going to require many angles shooting up at Kong or down over his shoulder to make him appear massive, this was clearly going to be a problem. Repositioning the large, inflexible rear-projection screen and the bulky camera to achieve these angles would be extremely time-consuming and logistically impractical.

FACING PAGE: One of the wonderfully expressive masks created by Rick Baker and Carlo Rambaldi.

Photographic effects supervisor Frank Van Der Veer (left) looks on as Rick Baker settles a disagreement with photographic effects assistant Barry Nolan (right).

At this point, Frank Van Der Veer suggested using the blue screen process, but Guillermin was reluctant to consider it because of how complicated it was to use and how hard it was to get good results. Van Der Veer understood Guillermin's concerns, but was convinced that the innovative processes and techniques he planned to employ would minimize problems and produce superior results. Guillermin finally agreed to shoot a few test shots. The results were impressive and the decision was made to proceed with the process.

As confident as Van Der Veer was that he would be able to produce successful composite images using blue screen, he also knew it wasn't going to be easy. To begin with, as with all composite processes, the foreground and background elements of a blue screen shot needed to be precisely aligned for the finished product to be successful. Before *Kong* '76, this alignment was usually accomplished through educated guesswork—all of the angles and placement of the elements in one part of a shot would be carefully measured and then reproduced as accurately as possible when the second part of the shot was filmed. Even with all of these careful calculations, it was still not possible to tell if the alignment was successful until the final composite was returned from the lab, which could often take a week or more. While this imprecise, time-consuming approach might have been acceptable for a film with just a few blue screen shots, it was not going to work for *Kong* '76—a film such as this was going to contain more blue screen shots than any other film in history, all of which needed to be as perfect as possible if the film was going to succeed. A new method of alignment was required—one that was faster, more accurate, and instantly verifiable. Barry Nolan solved the problem by developing a pioneering video compositing system. He did this by wiring a color video camera to the lens of a motion picture camera, which allowed the video camera to record the exact same image as the motion picture camera. The video camera was linked with a video recording and playback system equipped with Chroma Key (an electronic version of blue screen).

To create a shot, the background plate was (usually) filmed first, transferred to videotape, and placed in the system. When the foreground subject was later filmed against a blue screen, the image from the motion picture camera lens was transmitted through the video camera and into the video system. The Chroma Key system filtered out the blue and composited the foreground subject with a playback of the background plate. This allowed the production team to check the precision of the lineup instantaneously. Any necessary changes were made and then the scene was filmed and videotaped at the same time. Once the shot had been satisfactorily achieved, the foreground shot, the background plate, and the videotape were all sent to the lab at Van Der Veer Photo Effects, where the footage was matched to the tape and then processed. This system allowed the production to create excellent, precisely aligned composites in a reasonably quick amount of time.

Van Der Veer also knew that matte lines, image cut-off, and bright blue fringing were also going to be problems. To prevent them, blue screen had traditionally only been used with objects that had strong, thick, clearly defined contours that would produce strong, sharp-edged mattes. Hair, with its extremely thin, uneven edges, was considered a very poor subject for the process. Blonde hair, which is prone to picking up reflected light from the blue screen, was thought to be even more difficult, and blonde hair photographed with soft diffusion filters that blur the edges of the image was considered an impossibility. It only follows that a softly diffused film with a hairy gorilla and a blonde woman as its primary characters was going to be an enormous challenge. To meet it, Van Der Veer employed a variety of novel techniques. In conjunction with Richard Kline, Van Der Veer added gels to the lights used to illuminate the blue screen in order to turn it a very deep, pure, cobalt blue. Next, the foreground figures were lit with gels that produced a very deep, yellow light. The sharp contrast between the yellow light in the foreground and the deep blue in the background produced extremely well defined contours in the foreground figures and, thus, in the mattes. Next, Van Der Veer worked with his team to build their mattes with a minimum of regeneration and overexposure, which reduced the incidence of lines and overlap. Finally, to reduce the blue fringing, Van Der Veer used a technique developed by optical pioneer Petro Vlahos called the Color Difference System. In this approach, the original blue color separation is replaced by a synthetic blue separation, one that is created by combining the original green and blue separations. This was a very difficult and expensive technique to make work, but the Van Der Veer team pulled it off. When the three color separations—the red, green, and synthetic blue—were reprinted onto the dupe, all of the colors in the foreground image (except purple, which cannot be reproduced using this method) were recreated perfectly, while the color of the screen in the background turned from blue to a very dark gray-green—thus any fringing that did occur appeared in the final print as a nearly undetectable gray rather than an extremely noticeable blue. Creative use of these methods allowed Frank Van Der Veer and his team to create the most sophisticated and successful blue screen shots that had been done at that time.

In addition to blue screen, *Kong* '76 used another optical technique that had not been used in the original film: matte painting, a technique for augmenting existing sets and locations that combined glass painting with the split-screen process. To produce a matte-painting shot, the live-action portion of the scene was filmed first. A clip of the shot was then projected onto a large sheet of glass that had been painted white and traced. An artist then painted the rest of the image around the area where the live-action was supposed to appear, taking great care to match the elements of the real image with those of the painting. When the painting was completed, the white was scraped away from the live-action area and the resulting "hole" was then covered in black velvet. When the time came to composite the images, a positive print of the live-action was placed in the optical printer along with a cover matte and then projected onto a dupe negative. The dupe negative was then rewound and the painting—lit from behind—was photographed. The black velvet prevented any light from creeping through the live-action area and ruining the already exposed live-action.

Achieving a seamless join between live-action and painting was quite difficult and involved a great deal of aligning and testing. It was not unusual for a shot to be redone twenty or thirty times before it was right. Famed Hollywood matte painter Lou Lichtenfield did the paintings on *Kong*. He would begin by taking black-and-white photos of elements he intended to use in the painting (rocks, the wall, and so forth). He would then cut and paste the photos on the glass and then finish by putting down a color wash over them. In this way, he was able to make his images as realistic as possible, which is the reason they were so effective.

Apart from these new methods, *Kong '76* also used a few of the same optical techniques that had been used in the original *Kong*. The first was split-screen. While the concept and the results were essentially the same as they were in 1933, the *Kong '76* team used a slightly more sophisticated approach to produce its splits. First, the initial part of the composite image was filmed. As in matte painting, a clip from that shot was then inserted into an optical printer and projected onto a white board. A precise pencil drawing was made of the image with great care taken to mark the exact edge of the image. This drawing was then photographed. The resulting print consisted of a clear piece of film with a black drawing on it. The black drawing indicated the part of the frame occupied by the previously filmed material and the clear area showed where the new material would be inserted. A frame of this print was then placed into the viewfinder of the on-set camera and used to precisely align the edge of the previously shot image with that of the element about to be filmed. After the second portion of the shot was filmed, both images were composited onto a dupe negative on the optical printer.

The second optical technique shared by the two *Kong*s was miniature projection. However, while this was a key process in making the original *Kong*, in the new film it was used in only two brief shots.

PRINCIPAL PHOTOGRAPHY

The combined pressures of beating Universal and finishing the film by

Christmas threw the production into chaos. In the face of these pressures, the precise organization and methodical preparation that are the hallmarks of large-scale film production were tossed out the window and replaced by a seat-of-the-pants approach that was characterized by some crew members as being "exhilarating" and by others as "totally and completely insane." The original shooting schedule was scrapped. Scenes would now be shot when the sets were ready (and often before the paint on them had even dried), the locations became available, or the various pieces of Kong were working.

HAWAII Following the layoff, the cast and crew flew to Kauai over Valentine's Day weekend to shoot scenes of the Petrox team exploring Skull Island. Promoted to location manager, Brian Frankish had remained behind on Kauai after an initial scouting trip to prepare for the production's arrival, during which time he explored the island thoroughly and readied a place for the cast and crew to stay. With hotel space at a premium, Frankish took over the Hanalei Beach & Racquet Club in Princeville—an unfinished hotel whose owners had gone bankrupt. Frankish "opened" the place himself—establishing a lobby, bringing in locals to act as maids, and hiring a caterer to provide food. Although the unit was staying on the south shore of the island, the shoot took place on the north shore. There were no roads that led to that part of the island and the only way to reach it, short of hiking in on foot, was by helicopter. To facilitate travel, Frankish assembled a makeshift squadron of helicopters flown by pilots that were mostly Viet Nam vets. The trip to and from location took approximately ninety minutes each way. The first flights left at dawn and the return trip had to be started by 4 P.M. in order to get everyone safely back from the set before dark.

The first location on Kauai was Waimea Canyon, also known as "the Grand Canyon of Hawaii," where the scenes of the landing party making its way up from the beach were filmed. The second location was a ridge in Kalalau

Waimea—the Grand Canyon of Hawaii.

The landing party walks toward the giant arch on "Cathedral Beach."

Valley—a volcanic crater that received fifty feet of rain annually and was alleged to be the wettest spot on earth. There the scenes of Jack and the search party making its way along a lush green ridge and Jack making his way up a hill imprinted with Kong's footprints were filmed. Precipitation was not Kalalau's only oddity. During the filming, the crew discovered that the valley was inhabited by a motley group of dropouts and pot growers who emerged from the jungle and happily scrounged the crew's box lunches. The valley was also the sight of a near tragedy. One of the transport helicopters was balancing on a ridge using its rotors to maintain stability, when one of the rotors suddenly lost speed and the chopper kicked back. Richard Kline and camera assistant Robert Edessa had to jump out of the way to avoid being hit by the whirling blades. The third location was a spot in the jungle where high winds had blown over a bunch of trees, exposing their roots. Imagining that Kong himself could have knocked over the trees, the unit used the spot to film a scene in which the search party looks for Dwan after she has been taken from the wall.

The original plan had been to shoot all of the jungle scenes in Hawaii and all of the beach scenes in Zuma Beach, California. However, De Laurentiis was so pleased with the look of the initial Hawaiian rushes that he wanted the beach scenes filmed on Kauai as well. Honopu Beach—nicknamed "Cathedral Beach" because it was divided by an enormous rock through which the waves had worn an enormous, spectacular-looking arch—was chosen as the location for these scenes. To prepare for filming, two twenty-two-foot Chris Craft launches, three nineteen-foot zodiacs, and the six navy foggers were shipped to Kauai. When the crew arrived at Honopu by helicopter on the first morning of the shoot, they were surprised to find a honeymooning couple sleeping on the beach. Hoping to spend their first days of wedded bliss in peaceful seclusion, Dennis and Debbie Lofstedt had been dropped off in this remote location by Dennis's brother, a helicopter pilot. Their privacy ruined, the Lofstedts soon departed, leaving the crew to film scenes of the landing party's initial arrival on the island. These scenes were difficult to accomplish because the waves off Honopu often ran as high as twelve feet, making it hard to maneuver the landing and camera boats. Many of the crew got seasick filming these scenes and one of the camera boats almost capsized. Another try was also made to film the crew's nighttime arrival to rescue Dwan that had originally been attempted in Zuma, but the waves made it impossible. Other scenes shot in the location included those in which Fred Wilson directs the rescue mission by radio from his beach camp and supervises the arrival of the construction equipment that will be used to capture Kong. When it proved cost-prohibitive to bring an actual bulldozer required for this scene to the location, Jack Grossberg had the crew build a two-sided one out of wood. Because actor John Randolph did not make the trip to Hawaii, a double for Captain Ross was used in a few long shots.

The most difficult scene to film in Hawaii was the sequence in which the landing party travels through the fog bank on its way to the shore. To recreate the mist, the foggers were once again employed, although the unceasing trade winds made getting a consistent cloud a much bigger challenge than it was off Catalina. Once the fog was ready, the choppy waters made it almost impossible to align the camera boats with the launch containing the actors long enough to get a decent shot. Actor Rene Auberjonois recalls a time when the unit was trying to film a scene in which the launch was supposed to come out of the fog toward the camera boat. The run-throughs were done in the clear and went perfectly, but once the fog was laid down for the actual shot, neither pilot could see where they were going, causing the two boats to sail past each other in the fog. The passengers in each boat could hear the people in the other, but neither group could see the other, nor could the camera photograph anything. This went on for take after take, making Guillermin furious. Hours were wasted, the frustration level rose, people got sick, and tempers flared. Once the spectacular shot of the boat emerging from the fog to encounter the awesome Na Pali cliffs was finished, the shoot was called off. A few days later, the fog was laid down again; this time in the calmer waters of the sheltered Hanalei Bay, and the scenes that took place inside the fog were finally completed with (relative) ease. Shooting wrapped in Hawaii on March 10, and, following a celebratory luau, the unit returned to California.

THE SUPERTANKER From March 15–17, the company shot the scenes involving Kong's journey to America aboard the *Susanne Onstad*, an oil supertanker leased from the Onstad Shipping Company of Oslo, Norway, for

$125,000. This was the first time that any movie company had ever filmed on a supertanker. Before the crew could come aboard, the tanks had to be cleaned out and the ship degassed, lest a lit match or stray generator spark ignite any lingering oil fumes. This process took four days and had to be done one hundred miles out to sea. A false grill was placed on the ship's foredeck to make it look like an air vent had been cut in the hull to allow Kong, allegedly confined in the tank below, to breathe. The crew boarded the ship at San Pedro and spent four days sailing up and down the California coast approximately twenty miles out to sea. Wanting an exciting background for his shots, Guillermin continually ran the ship at full speed, leaving the support boats far behind. On one occasion, Guillermin pushed the ship so far that it ended up in Mexican waters, which was a problem because neither the ship nor the crew had the proper immigration papers that would allow them into Mexico.

ANOTHER SHUTDOWN   Following the work on the supertanker, the production shut down again. De Laurentiis had no other choice, because neither the main sets nor the various manifestations of Kong were ready and the main unit had run out of other scenes to shoot. Unlike the first shutdown, which was planned, this one had not been anticipated and so endangered the production, because it cost an enormous amount of money to keep an idle crew on payroll. If the hiatus went on too long, it was conceivable that things could reach the point where it would cost less money to shut down the production completely and write off the loss than it would to keep it going. As a result, there was a lot of pressure on Dale Hennesy to finish the next major set for the film—the Great Wall. The pressure became so intense that at one point Hennesy actually quit the film, although he soon returned. By the beginning of April, the wall was finished and shooting resumed.

THE WALL   The wall was constructed on MGM's Lot 2, a backlot facility across the road from the main studio that contained relics from Hollywood's Golden Age such as Esther Williams's swimming pool and Andy Hardy's hometown street. Mario Chiari had originally designed the wall to be a stone structure as in the original film. However, after Guillermin saw a series of photos of primitive native villages in New Guinea in a book called *The Gardens of War* that he liked, Dale Hennesy redesigned the wall as a primitive wooden structure.

To build the wall, telephone poles were sunk into the ground and secured with concrete. Eight thousand one hundred fifty-seven eucalyptus trees were then lashed to the poles to disguise them and to make the wall look like it was built from indigenous island trees. The poles were then connected with sheets of vacuform plastic that was shaped and painted to look like wooden panels. The final structure was 47 feet tall and 170 yards long. Two wooden ramps were built from the ground to the top of the wall and an artificial mountain was constructed next to it. The mountain was made of concrete poured over a wooden frame and painted. It looked good but was difficult to maneuver on. Led by construction coordinator Gary Martin, the construction crew worked in

TOP: Mario Chiari's original design for a Great Wall made of stone, drawn by production illustrator Mentor Huebner.

BOTTOM: Dale Hennesy's final design for a wooden wall, constructed on MGM's Lot 2.

two shifts six days a week for two months to complete the wall at a final cost of $800,000. Because of local noise ordinances, the company had to stop shooting every night by midnight. To accommodate this, the production went to a fifty-fifty schedule, spending half the night shooting at the wall and the other half shooting miniature scenes back on the soundstages.

The first scene shot at the wall was the one in which the landing party first encounters the natives, who offer to buy Dwan from them. Wearing a wooden

TOP: The landing party spots the natives. From left to right: Jeff Bridges, Jack O'Halloran, Ed Lauter, Rene Auberjonois, Charles Grodin, and Jorge Moreno.

BOTTOM: The sacrifice scene.

gorilla mask, actor Keny Long played a character called Ape-Masked Man, the assumed leader of the tribe. Next up was the actual sacrifice scene itself. To light the nighttime spectacle, Richard Kline used eighteen Brute arc lights mounted on nine, forty-foot forklifts. To simulate the flickering light from the native torches, light was bounced off sheets of gold Mylar mounted on wooden frames as crew members shook them to create a shimmering effect. To get high shots of the wall, a hydraulic construction crane was used to lift the camera crew more than 100 feet into the air. Three cameras were placed in a 6 x 4 ft. basket hung from the crane's telescoping arm, which could move the basket in every conceivable direction. Claude Thompson choreographed an elaborate native dance and over 300 extras were brought in to fill out the scene. All of the natives were dressed in gowns designed by Anthea Sylbert. The filming was not without incident. The nights were extremely cold and the scantily clad natives huddled around the on-set fires in between takes. Some toasted marsh-mallows, but others drank and used drugs. There were two overdoses and, in one instance, some extremely inebriated extras ran out onto the main street in front of the studio and threatened passing motorists with their spears. There was also a sniper threat and a bomb scare.

Following the dance, the construction crane was used to film the point-of-view shot of Kong coming through the jungle as he approaches the altar. Pre-rigged trees were pulled down on cue as the crane rolled through. The right Big Hand—the first of Kong's many incarnations to be completed—was used for the first time for the shot in which Kong picks Dwan up off the altar. Legendary Swedish film director Ingmar Bergman visited the set while this scene was being shot and watched as the Big Hand reached in, grabbed Jessica Lange, and whisked her twenty feet into the air.

THE GLADE SEQUENCE Following the scenes of the rescue team arriving in the village, the production moved onto the soundstages to film the glade sequence, in which Kong toys with Dwan until she falls into a mud puddle while trying to escape. Jessica Lange's costar in this scene was the right Big Hand. While preparing the scene, a wire in the Big Hand's wrist snapped, causing it to go suddenly limp. Luckily, the bolts in the fingers worked and the Big Hand neither dropped not crushed stuntwoman Sunny Woods, who was riding in the hand at the time. Later in the sequence, however, Lange did get a bruise on her back when the Big Hand pressed down too hard on her. Once all the bugs got worked out, the Big Hand performed well throughout the rest of the production, although its great size and weight did cause it to move slower than Guillermin would have liked, which caused problems with the timing of some of the shots.

BACK TO THE WALL Meanwhile, a giant pit was dug in front of the wall, after which the first unit returned to film scenes of the *Petrox Explorer* crew preparing to capture Kong while Captain Ross argues with Wilson about the safety of the search party. Night shooting resumed for the full-scale shots of the crew reacting to Kong smashing through the wall. The left Big Hand was

Crew members move the right Big Hand into position for the glade sequence.

used for the final shot in which Kong reaches up out of the chloroform before the fumes finally render him unconscious.

BUDGET WOES, PART I   Money was tight from the start. The race to beat Universal had pushed the initial $12 million budget to around $16 million, and the push to meet the Christmas deadline was driving it even higher. To help keep costs under control, a few separate scenes were combined, and a sequence in which a giant snake (the same one that Kong later fights in the crater scene) attacks the search party was eliminated entirely. To raise additional funds, De Laurentiis went back to his distributors and asked them all to increase the amount of their guarantees. To entice them to do so, he screened a cut of the all of the scenes filmed so far. Impressed by what they saw, all of the distributors agreed.

PEOPLE AND PERSONALITIES   For the crew, working on the picture was an intense experience. Eighteen-hour days and all-night shoots were common. Most of the scenes were incredibly complex and the rushed schedule left little time to adequately think, plan, or prepare. Photographic effects assistant Barry Nolan remembers Dino De Laurentiis telling him: "When this movie is over, you're either going to be famous or you're going to be dead," a sentiment that every member of the crew could identify with. For the actors, the chaotic production was a mixed bag. They never knew with any certainty when or where they would be called in and, like the cast of the original *Kong*, would often go for months on end without working at all. Unlike the cast of the original *Kong*, however, the *Kong* '76 actors were on salary for the entire eight-month shoot, whether they worked or not. For Rene Auberjonois, this was a perfectly acceptable set of circumstances. "At a time in my life when I had two young kids, that was just great!" The cast and crew dealt with the arduous conditions by forming a tight bond. They all liked and respected one another and everyone got along extremely well. As Brian Frankish comments: "Some pictures are family and some are war. *Kong* was family."

All involved credit Jack Grossberg with holding the production together and keeping the momentum going. His great skill at negotiating, organizing, and improvising brought order to the chaos and kept the picture on schedule even when no one knew what the schedule was. The team also appreciated the help of Federico De Laurentiis, whom Richard Kline remembers as being "a lovely person," and Jack O'Halloran describes as being "a super young man." While nepotism certainly played a part in his hiring, all involved agreed that Federico was a major asset to the project. He threw himself into every aspect of the production and made a great many creative and practical contributions, including, when necessary, lugging equipment on location. Rene Auberjonois recalls: "Federico was very much around that film. [He was] always very involved, ready to do, ready to help."

As for the head of the project, most everyone that worked on the film respected Dino De Laurentiis and admired his dedication. "Dino was the first one there in the morning and the last one there at night," Jeffrey Chernov

TOP: Kong grips Dwan in the glade sequence.

BOTTOM: Kong is captured! The left Big Hand reaches up out of the chloroform-filled pit.

recalls. De Laurentiis was intimately involved in every aspect of the production and no decision was made without his input and approval. In the words of one production associate: "This film was Dino's baby from start to finish." They also respected his resilience, his tenacity, and his refusal to allow problems or setbacks to deter or discourage him. Just about everyone who worked on the film describes De Laurentiis as being extremely nice and considerate and all attest to his unwavering support. "He would provide you with anything you needed as long as you convinced him it was necessary," Richard Kline recalls. "He was very resourceful and the best producer I ever worked with." Barry Nolan says that De Laurentiis was "always honest and straightforward. If he said he would do something he would do it and his word was his guarantee." Production manager Terry Carr felt that De Laurentiis was one of the last of the old-time independent producers—men like David O. Selznick and Samuel Goldwyn, who understood the entire process of making movies from beginning to end, who went out and raised the money for their productions, and who were willing to risk everything to bring their projects to fruition.

Opinion was more divided on John Guillermin. Most considered him a very good director—he got most shots in three or four takes and Lorenzo Semple was impressed with how hard this man with a reputation for making heavy action pictures worked to give the film the romantic, fairy-tale style they wanted it to have. Guillermin's personal style was something else. An eccentric man who was never without his trademark pipe and wool cap, Guillermin was prone to volatile outbursts, especially when he was under stress. Once while screening dailies, Guillermin saw something he didn't like and began kicking the back of the seat in front of him until it broke. Another time he allegedly threw a full drinking glass at the screen. While on location in Hawaii, the director shoved a crewmember he didn't think was moving fast enough and then picked up a table and threw it down in the sand. He got into a public shouting match with Federico De Laurentiis, after which Dino De Laurentiis was reported to have threatened to fire him if he didn't start treating people better. Following this incident, Guillermin reportedly reigned in his outbursts, although he continued to be quite moody and cantankerous.

For many, Guillermin's behavior was understandable, given the extraordinary pressure he was under. As the director of the film, the burden of finishing the film by Christmas fell squarely on his shoulders and the stress caused him to lose seventeen pounds during the course of the shoot. Jeff Bridges sums up the feeling of many involved in the production when he says, "There was a lot of pressure on John. He had to get what had to be gotten." First assistant director David McGiffert elaborates: "[John was]...the only one who had a solid handle on the film as a whole...there were a lot of people who thought they understood what had to be done, but he...[was the only one that]...really did." Quoted in an article in *American Film* magazine at the time of the film's release, Charles Grodin echoed this sentiment: "[John's]...really the star of this movie. He's got the rhythm and quality of the film in his mind constantly and holds it all together through all the delays." Able to dismiss his outbursts as simple bluster in the face of enormous stress, many people developed a gen-

John Guillermin and Dino De Laurentiis confer on the set as Federico De Laurentiis stands by.

uine affection for Guillermin. Jeff Bridges: "John's a real character...a real fascinating, eccentric guy. Sometimes the pressure got to him. It took so much time to get things right. I love the guy. He was great fun." Rene Auberjonois: "I found him amusing and liked him." Richard Kline: "[John's a] very good director [and]...a good guy. I like him a lot." Brian Frankish: "Guillermin was...a little tough to work with, but what the hell, he made a good movie."

The relationship between Guillermin and Dino De Laurentiis was reportedly a contentious one. Both men had very strong ideas about what they wanted the picture to be and when those ideas conflicted, things could get tense. At one point Guillermin allegedly barred Dino from the set, prompting De Laurentiis to swear to an associate that he would never work with Guillermin again.

NEW YORK   In June, the production traveled to New York City. The production offices were in the Sheraton Motor Inn on Twelfth Avenue. Most of the cast and crew stayed there as well. Jack Grossberg and New York location manager George Goodman had spent months negotiating with the New York unions for the use of the various locations needed for shooting, most significantly the World Trade Center. Talks with the Port Authority of New York and New Jersey, the owners of the Trade Center, had been difficult. There was a lot of contention over issues such as the size of the crowd that would be allowed on the plaza, who would pay for the security guards needed to watch them, and who would pay for the electricity required to light the buildings for the shooting. Things got so bad that at one point the production gave serious thought to switching to the Empire State Building, but eventually a deal satisfactory to all was worked out.

The first shots done in New York were high-angle shots of the military moving into position on the World Trade Center Plaza, which would later be used as background plates for the shots in which Kong climbs up the side of the building. To capture these shots, Richard Kline and his crew—all wearing safety harnesses—positioned themselves on the roof of the South Tower on a three-foot-wide plank that extended six feet straight out from the edge of the building, a quarter of a mile above the plaza. Kline recalls the experience as being "pretty hairy," especially when he found himself looking *down* onto the top of some clouds. It was hard to get an adequate exposure of the plaza from so far away, so Kline had to "push" the film (underexpose it while shooting and overexpose it during the developing process) in order to get an acceptable image. The camera then moved down to earth for shots of the military preparing to battle Kong. To portray the soldiers in these scenes, extras casting director Sally Perle recruited off-duty cops and firemen, military recruiters, and students from a local military school. Following this, scenes of Jeff Bridges riding a bicycle across the plaza, running into the South Tower lobby, and riding an elevator up to the observatory were filmed. The twin towers were so new when these scenes were filmed that spackle can be seen on the unpainted observatory walls as Bridges races past them. In light of the events of recent years, this may now be the most inadvertently poignant image in the film.

Filming then moved to Astoria, Queens, for scenes in which Dwan and Jack run through the streets to escape from Kong and then climb the stairs to an elevated subway station to catch a train. The aftermath of the scene in which Kong wrecks that train was also filmed, with Jack and Dwan climbing down from the tracks and commandeering an abandoned motorcycle. Before filming began, a mock-up of a wrecked subway car was placed in the street, which caused more than a few weary commuters to do a double take as they made their way home from work. The special effects smoke and fire used in these scenes prompted some local residents to call the fire department and the crew

Thirty thousand New Yorkers converge on the Styrofoam Kong in the plaza of the World Trade Center—June 1976.

got a New York welcome when some local thugs looted the food tables during the evening meal breaks.

In the second week of the New York trip, the crew returned to the World Trade Center to spend three nights filming Kong's death scene. The Kong used in this scene was not the mechanical robot, but an exact, nonmechanical duplicate. Fiberglass copies of Kong's body parts were produced from the same molds used to produce parts for the Big Kong and then attached to a Styrofoam core, which was then dressed with more latex panels covered in Argentinean horsehair. The completed model was cut up into ten sections and driven across the country in three large moving vans. After arriving in New York, it was reassembled at the foot of the South Tower and surrounded by three hundred square feet of imitation terrazzo made out of plaster meant to simulate the plaza's surface, supposedly smashed to pieces by the impact of Kong's fall. Because of the enormous size of the plaza, Richard Kline recalls that he had to use practically every available arc light and generator in New York to light it.

A huge crowd was required for the scene. A certain number of paid extras had been hired to encircle Kong and Lange, but the company could not afford to hire enough to fill the enormous plaza, so an ad was placed in the local newspapers inviting the public to attend the filming. The hope was that enough people would show up to sufficiently occupy the wide shots. On the first night of shooting, between 2,000–3,000 people showed up—a big number, but not enough to fill the plaza. The crowd was kept behind barricades at the edge of the plaza until the moment came for them to surge forward toward Kong. The circle of paid extras was supposed to act as a second barrier to keep the crowd from getting too close, but when action was called, the crowd pushed right past the paid extras and Lange and swarmed over Kong, grabbing anything they could to take as souvenirs. Kong lost large chunks of his hair, a fingertip, and even a bowling ball-sized eye in the frenzy. As one of the crewmembers suc-

Lange, Bridges, and the Styrofoam Kong between takes.

cinctly put it: "Kong got mugged." The plaza was cleared and the night finished with the close-ups of Dwan crying over Kong.

Despite the frenzy, the production was disappointed at the turnout and worried that there wouldn't be enough people the next night either, but the first night's shoot had received a great deal of coverage in the local press, which spiked interest enormously. The next night, 30,000 people turned out. This was many more people than anyone had anticipated and there were serious concerns about how manageable such a large crowd would be. Additional police were called in and even some of the extras dressed as soldiers and police were drafted to assist with crowd control. Thankfully, when the barriers were removed and the crowd surged onto the plaza, it came to a stop right in front of the ring of paid extras. Lange and the patched-up Kong were untouched and the crowd remained generally well behaved. Despite this, the Port Authority officials became concerned that the weight of so many people would cause the plaza to collapse and decided to shut down the filming. The producers tried to talk them out of it, but the Port Authority was resolute. The crew moved off to a nearby side street to shoot a scene of Jack riding his bike through the deserted city and the third night of filming was canceled.

Dwan screams for Jack in the final scene of the film.

The next three nights were spent shooting on and below the Fifty-Ninth Street Bridge for the scenes in which the army commanders the bridge, Jack and Dwan dash across it, and helicopters fly above it searching for Kong. The filming tied up the bridge for hours, which did not endear the company to the scores of irate motorists trying to cross it. A brief shot of Jeff Bridges walking into a park beneath the bridge was also filmed. It would later be inserted into the presentation scene to establish where the event was supposed to be taking place.

Second unit director William Kronick spent the New York trip shooting background plates at different locations around the city. He also filmed some aerial shots of the World Trade Center that would be used behind Jessica Lange in the scene where Kong leaps from one tower to another; some additional shots of the massive World Trade Center crowd; and scenes tracking Kong's progress as he makes his way down Fifth Avenue after recapturing Dwan. Kronick recalls spending an entire evening in the oppressive summer heat setting up the shot in which Kong's shadow passes over a priest on the steps of Saint Patrick's Cathedral, which required blocking off Fifth Avenue for blocks on either side of the cathedral, lighting the cathedral itself, turning out the lights in all of the surrounding buildings (to simulate a blackout), and rehearsing a riderless horse and carriage. Just when Kronick got everything ready, it started to rain, forcing him to cancel the shoot, to come back the next night, and do it all over again.

The main unit quietly returned to the World Trade Center on Sunday, June 27, to film the shots of Jack pushing through the crowd to get to Dwan and the penultimate shot of the film in which the camera pulls up and away from Dwan as she stands crying in front of the fallen Kong. Executive producer Christian Ferry had negotiated the return with the Port Authority by promising that the shoot would not be publicized, that it would attract no crowds, and that only paid extras would be used. The company finished up in New York the following night shooting the scene in Hanover Square in which Dwan asks Jack to buy her a drink and then headed back to Los Angeles. The second unit remained behind to film the spectacular July 4, 1976 Bicentennial fireworks display in New York Harbor, shots of which were used at the beginning of the Presentation scene.

THE RETURN TO LOS ANGELES   Upon returning to the West Coast, the production spent an evening in Santa Monica shooting the rescue-party beach landing for a third time. This time they got it. The company then moved to the Biltmore Hotel in downtown Los Angeles for the scene in which Jack quits the show. Back at MGM, the full-scale portions of Dwan's encounter with Kong aboard the supertanker were filmed by having Lange interact with Big Kong's legs and the right Big Hand.

Following this, the full-scale portions of the log scene were filmed on an enormous wall-to-wall set that was constructed on Stage 29. The log itself was sixty feet long and made of foam and fiberglass built over an aluminum core. It was placed on a hydraulically operated roller that rocked it back and forth. When it came time for the Petrox crewmembers to tumble off the log, the actors were placed in harnesses that were attached to wires and then rolled off onto a platform just under the log. For the actual falls, stuntmen dropped into a well beneath the set.

Lange and Bridges filmed the beginning of their leap off the cliff to escape Kong on the concrete mountain built alongside the Great Wall. Stunt performers Bill Couch and Sunny Woods did the actual jump from the top of the wall, the back of which had been redressed to look like a mountain. They landed as expected on an air bag placed at the foot of the wall, but then bounced off and fell into the space between the bag and the wall. At first everyone thought they had been killed, but luckily they were all right.

For the shot of Jack Prescott hiding in a *Petrox Explorer* lifeboat during a

LEFT: Preparing to shoot the log scene on Stage 29 at MGM. RIGHT: First mate Carnahan (Ed Lauter) looks on in horror as Joe Perko (Jack O'Halloran) falls to his death.

The waterfall scene.

storm, a mock-up of the ship's exterior was placed on a hydraulic rocker system built in a tank on Stage 14. Lightning machines flashed as nine custom-made dump tanks drenched the set with thousands of gallons of water. For the interior portions of this scene, Captain Ross's dining room was built on another hydraulic rocker located on Stage 15 and moved back and forth as Charles Grodin and John Randolph played the scene.

On August 2, the full-scale portions of the waterfall scene were filmed using the Big Hand. The technicians were worried that Kong's latex skin would split when it got wet, but fortunately it didn't. An underwater shot of Dwan's dive into the waterfall's pool was filmed in a backlot tank. The Big Hand was then moved to the full-scale Sutton Place Bar set to film the scene in which Kong recaptures Dwan. The set was built on risers to allow the crane-mounted arm to enter at ground level.

BUDGET WOES, PART II   As production wore on, the budget continued to rise. Having gotten all he could from his distributors, De Laurentiis eventually began borrowing directly from his European bankers. Although they had faith in De Laurentiis, the bankers became seriously concerned that he might not be able to finish the film. In spite of these doubts, De Laurentiis persevered, mainly, because, as the production wore on, he became more and more convinced that his film had a chance to not only be an enormous hit, but indeed had the potential to beat *Jaws* and become the highest grossing movie of all time. Charles Bludhorn joined him in this view and the two of them began sounding a drumbeat in person and in the press that made such an outcome seem all but inevitable.

THE PRESENTATION SCENE From August 11–20, the main unit filmed the last big sequence of the production—the presentation scene. As originally written, this was to be a spectacular scene in which Fred puts on a huge, gaudy extravaganza at Shea Stadium, featuring marching bands, rock groups, and a ballet routine performed in front of thousands of spectators. At the height of the extravaganza, a giant Petrox gas pump is wheeled up to Dwan in centerfield. The gas pump is lifted away, revealing Kong inside a giant iron cage festooned with flowers. Photographers begin manhandling Dwan and Kong smashes out of his cage to save her. Mayhem ensues as Jack rescues Dwan and they escape. Kong trashes the stadium, chews on a few guards, and then scales the stadium wall to escape. Although De Laurentiis liked the scene, he felt that it would be much too expensive to mount and wanted to find an alternative, but Guillermin wanted to do the scene as written, so the production began looking around for a stadium. Shea itself was out because it would have been impractical to move the Big Kong all the way across the country to film the scene. Anaheim Stadium and the Rose Bowl were also considered, but in the end, the costs were just too prohibitive. Semple then came up with several alternatives, including a scene in which Kong escapes from the Bronx Zoo, freeing all of the other animals in the process; a scene in which Kong escapes from a barge as he is being delivered to a pier in Brooklyn; and scenes in which Kong escapes from Madison Square Garden, the Brooklyn Academy of Music, and Central Park, respectively. By this point, however, money was so tight that De Laurentiis decided to take the most economical route possible and reuse the Great Wall to shoot a scaled-down version of the original Shea Stadium scene — now set in a mythical Queens park along the East River — on Lot 2. Dale

The crew readies the Big Kong for the presentation scene.

Hennesy refurbished the wall by covering it with big panels of Mylar, draping the structure with red-white-and-blue bunting, and erecting several rows of bleachers in front of it. The centerpiece of the presentation scene was, of course, the Big Kong, which, after months of work, had finally been completed. To prepare for the scene, Robinson's team broke Kong down into pieces, transported him to Lot 2, and then reconstructed him on a large trolley designed to move along down a long track into the center of the arena.

Once again, a large crowd was required to fill the bleachers. As in New York, the production planned to use some paid extras but couldn't afford enough to fill the entire park. To get the numbers they needed, Jack Grossberg ran an ad in the *Los Angeles Times* inviting people to attend Kong's screen debut. The ad contained a coupon people could use to order tickets, all of which were given away in a matter of days. On the first night, approximately 3,000 people showed up to appear in the scene in which Dwan and Fred arrive in the park by helicopter. Before the helicopter could land, a generator blew and the lights went out. The helicopter had to circle for fifteen minutes until the lights came back on, causing Jessica to get airsick. Although the Big Kong wasn't being used that night, the producers knew that crowd would want to see him, so when the shooting was over, lights were trained onto the wall and the giant gates were pulled open to reveal the giant robot. Unfortunately, Kong's eyes were crossed and a wire in his neck had snapped, causing his head to plop forward onto his chest. Realizing how bad he looked, De Laurentiis immediately ordered the lights shut off and the gates closed.

On the second night, the public wasn't invited and the production used paid extras to film the scenes of the crowd panicking and running out of the park, jostling Jack and Dwan as they try to escape. On the third night, the public came back for the Big Kong's unveiling. For this scene, an aluminum cage was erected around Kong and a giant Petrox crown placed on his head. The entire structure was then covered with a giant Petrox gas pump made from muslin draped over an aluminum frame. After the gas pump was rolled into the park, the cover was hooked to a helicopter and lifted off as four cameras rolled. On the first attempt, the cover snagged, but on the second try it came right off, revealing the Big Kong, which was in full working order—his eyes were rolling and his fingers and toes were wiggling as he lifted his head and opened his mouth to roar. Kong looked magnificent and the crowd applauded. It was a

The Big Kong looks on as the production team parties. From left to right: Richard Kline, Jessica Lange, Barry Nolan, Frank Van Der Veer, John Guillermin, an unidentified crew member, and gaffer Ed Carlin.

wonderful moment. Unfortunately, it didn't last long, because at the conclusion of the first shot, one of Kong's hydraulic lines sprung a leak and hydraulic fluid came spraying out of his crotch. John Guillermin was the first to notice. "He's peeing oil," the frustrated director cried.

The following night, the giant robot was used again for a shot of Kong dropping pieces of his shattered cage. Unfortunately, the aluminum pieces were too heavy and put a great strain on Kong's hydraulic systems. After a few minutes, his arm broke and his jaw went slack. A few nights later, the Big Kong was moved off the platform and placed in the middle of the arena for a shot of the crowd rushing past Kong as he raised his arms. On the final night of work on the sequence, Kong's right leg was disconnected from his body and mounted on a crane for the shots of Kong stomping on Fred Wilson. These shots were Charles Grodin's last work on the film, which—Grodin wryly wrote years later—he was certain was just a coincidence.

In the end, the Big Kong was a major disappointment—working no better than the partially articulated mannequin the producers originally planned to use. Unable to move quickly or smoothly enough to appear realistic, the mechanical monster was ultimately featured in just six shots in the finished film. While it actually looks quite impressive in the initial shots of Kong being revealed, it is static and unimpressive in the rest. Making matters worse, it did not match up with Rick Baker in the ape suit in either appearance or movement, making the substitution painfully obvious. While pieces of the Big Kong were used in other scenes, the complete construct was used again only for publicity stills.

WRAPPING UP   The last major full-scale sequence shot for the film was the one in which Kong wrecks the elevated-subway train. A mock-up subway car was built on a gimbal and hoisted up on one end as Jeff Bridges and Jessica Lange fought their way out of the other. This was Bridges's last work on the film. After he was done, the Big Hand was rolled in to pick up the actress playing the poor woman that Kong mistakes for Dwan. Although Lange would continue to film blue screen shots with the Big Hand well into September, principal photography was now officially over. The cost of the production had reached $19 million and was continuing to rise. A wrap party was held on Monday, August 30, 1976, on Stage 27 at MGM. To prepare for the party, the Big Kong's head and torso was placed on the stage in front of the blue screen and draped with a sash containing a simple message to the cast and crew: "Thanks, Kong."

THE MINIATURE SCENES

As the start of production on the "miniature" scenes approached, a decision had to be made as to who would actually play Kong. When Rick Baker first met with Federico De Laurentiis and Jack Grossberg, he told them that he could play the part as well as build the suit, but at the time the producers wanted to hire a skilled mime to portray the ape. An actor and acting teacher with extensive training in playing animals named Hampton Fancher (who would later

Rick Baker as King Kong.

cowrite the script for 1982's *Blade Runner*) applied for the job. He did a persuasive impersonation of a gorilla and so was hired. Soon after, however, Mario Chiari got the idea that Kong should be played by an African-American man. His racially insensitive reasoning was that African Americans had muscular physiques and so could play the part without padding. A casting call went out to various agencies representing black talent, creating a tidal wave of controversy. The call was immediately rescinded, but the production still received hundreds of applications from actors both black and white. Fancher was assigned the task of auditioning the hopefuls and eventually chose Albert Popwell, an actor most famous for his role as the "punk" to whom Clint Eastwood delivers his "Do you feel lucky?" speech in the original *Dirty Harry* (1971). Rambaldi's test suit was built to fit Popwell, who wore it during its disastrous debut. But when Guillermin saw the way Baker played Kong in the test footage, he decided that he wanted Baker to play the part after all.

Although Baker knew he could handle the role, he also knew that—given the physical strain that playing Kong was going to entail—he would need a backup. Baker envisioned a tag-team approach to playing Kong in which he would begin a scene and act until he was too exhausted to go on, at which point the backup performer would then step in and finish the scene. In order to fit into the Kong suit and masks and be the proper size to match the scale of the miniature sets, the backup performer needed to be the same basic size and shape as Baker. Neither Fancher nor Popwell were, so they were let go. Returning to the list of applicants, Federico De Laurentiis found someone who fit the bill. Will Shephard was an actor and writer who had performed off-Broadway and in experimental theater. He was in California looking for movie work when his

Concept drawing for the log scene.

agent got a call from the De Laurentiis organization asking if she had anyone who could do animal movements. Since Shephard had extensive formal training in this area, his agent sent him over. Shephard met with Baker and showed him some of his movements. Soon after, Shephard got a call from Jack Grossberg asking him if he wanted to be Kong. He did. A second ape suit was made for Shephard, whom William Kronick, in a wry reference to the pretender to the Tsar's throne in *Boris Gudonov*, nicknamed "The False Dimitri."

STORYBOARDS As on the original film, the production of all of the miniature scenes on *King Kong* '76 began with a series of concept drawings created by Mario Chiari and his production illustrators, Mentor Huebner and David Negron, that depicted the major action and feel of each scene. During preproduction, John Guillermin sat down with Huebner and broke down all of the scenes into a series of illustrations—one for each shot—called a storyboard. Later, Guillermin reviewed the storyboards with Kline, Chiari, Rambaldi, Hennesy, and Van Der Veer in order to determine just what sets, effects, optical processes, and Kong pieces would be needed to bring each shot to life. Bound together in a big book, the storyboards were distributed to all of the key production personnel. They guided every department's work on the project and were duplicated exactly in the finished film.

MINIATURE SETS Next, the miniature sets were constructed. For most of the scenes, Dale Hennesy had to create exact miniature duplicates of his full-scale sets. The island and jungles sets were all built 1-to-7 scale, which allowed an approximately six-foot-tall Kong to appear to be forty-two-feet tall on screen. As Merian Cooper did before him, Guillermin realized that even at this great size Kong would be dwarfed by the towering skyscrapers of Manhattan, so the New York miniatures were built in 1-to-10 scale to allow Kong to appear to be fifty-five feet-tall in those scenes. Most of the miniature sets were built on raised platforms to give the cameras room to be properly positioned to shoot up at Kong in order to make him look properly massive. Miniature coordinator Aldo Puccini (grandson of the famous composer) supervised a crew that worked long hours in two soundstages at the Culver Studios, fabricating the miniature trees, rocks, cars, and buildings that adorned the sets.

PHOTOGRAPHY Once of the biggest challenges director of photography Richard Kline faced in photographing the miniature scenes was matching the lighting of the full-scale sets with that of the miniature sets. In the January 1977 issue of *American Cinematographer*, Kline described his dilemma. Citing the 1-to-7 scale Hennesy used to proportion the sets, Kline said that if he used a big lamp to create a shaft of light twenty feet wide on the full-sized set, then on the miniature set he would need to use a smaller lamp to create a shaft of light only three feet wide in order for the two to match. Matching filters and lenses required similar calculations. Second unit director of photography Harold Wellman's expertise in shooting miniatures came in handy when shooting these scenes, because he knew all of the proper camera speeds, light levels, and lens

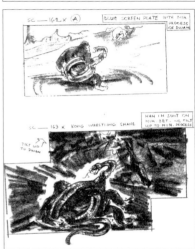

TOP: One of the storyboards for the film's climax atop the World Trade Center. The storyboard indicates both the miniature element that needs to be filmed (bottom) and the final composite (top).

BOTTOM: Storyboard for the snake battle.

sizes required to make the miniature Kong appear full-size. Lighting Kong was also a problem, given that his black fur absorbed all of the light thrown on him. To prevent the giant ape from becoming nothing more than a big black blob on the screen, Kline used a great deal of rim light to define his contours. Shooting up at Kong to make him look massive also caused some problems, because doing so often revealed the tops of the sets or the rafters of the soundstages. To prevent this, Kline placed teasers that matched the color of whatever the background was supposed to be behind Kong to hide whatever needed to be hidden. As shooting progressed, Kline discovered that Kong had a good and a bad side. When Kong was supposed to look ferocious, Kline would shoot him from the left. When he was supposed to be gentle, Kline would shoot him from the right.

One point of contention in photographing Kong was the frame rate at which he was filmed. Miniature scenes are usually filmed at high speed (often seventy-two frames per second or more) so that when they are projected at normal speed, the on-screen action will be slowed down considerably. The special effects team recommended that the miniature Kong be shot at a high frame rate in order to give his movements a ponderousness appropriate for a creature of his supposed size and weight, but Guillermin refused. He wanted Kong shot at close to normal speed so as not to interfere with the expressiveness of Baker's eyes, which he felt would look strange if their movement were slowed down.

SUITING UP   To prepare to play Kong, Baker would begin by putting in the contact lenses and then use makeup to blacken his eyelids and the area around his eyes. Next he would put on the padded undersuit, the rubber chest, and whatever mask he was using that day. If necessary, the cables would be threaded down through the padded undersuit, after which Baker would then put on the outer fur, which had a big hole in front to accommodate the chest. The suit was then zipped up (the zipper was in the back) and attached to the chest with Velcro. Finally, Baker would don the gloves and the feet. The arduous process took about forty-five minutes and required the help of a team of four assistants. Once ready, Baker would be led to the set and put into position, at which point the cables would be attached to the control panel. Will Shephard followed the same basic procedure, although as he usually only used the stunt head, he didn't have to accommodate the cables.

DIRECTION   The miniature scenes began filming on April 26, 1976. The first scene shot was the sacrifice scene, in which Kong crashes through the trees, approaches the wall, picks Dwan up from the altar, and carries her off into the jungle. The original plan had been for the second unit to film all of the miniature components of a scene at the same time the main unit was shooting the full-scale portions. This was the reason that a miniature expert like Harold Wellman was hired as the second unit's director of photography. In practice, however, the plan didn't work out. William Kronick began directing the miniature sequences, but Guillermin—perhaps realizing that, with the Big Kong not working out, the man in the suit was going to be more central to the film than originally envisioned—soon decided to direct most of them himself.

Second Unit director William Kronick guiding Will Shephard through the breakout scene.

Directing the miniature Kong was a complicated process. First Guillermin would tell Baker how he wanted him to move his body, head, and eyes. Then Guillermin would tell Carlo Rambaldi's team of operators what facial expressions he wanted Kong to make. This was not an easy thing to do because Guillermin didn't speak Italian and the operators didn't speak English. As a result, instructions usually had to be given through an interpreter (often Federico). The operators would then move the appropriate levers to push and pull Kong's features into the correct position. Richard Kline reports that the operators would "live" each scene by closing their eyes and enacting the expressions they were trying to create as they moved the levers. "It was an amazing thing to watch," he recalls appreciatively. Baker then had to coordinate his movements with what the Italians were doing, a process made more complicated by the fact that he couldn't see or hear well and also couldn't speak Italian.

PERFORMANCE   The tag team approach to acting Kong that Baker envisioned didn't work out either. During the shooting of the initial Kong scenes, Baker and Shephard traded off, but Guillermin was dissatisfied because he could see the differences in the two men's performances. He preferred Baker's approach and insisted on using him in most of the shots. From this point on, Baker worked primarily with Guillermin, Kline, and the main unit, while Shephard, now more of a stunt double than a relief performer, would work on specific action scenes with Kronick, Wellman, and the second unit.

One of the first things Guillermin and Baker had to do was decide on a walk for Kong. Baker wanted him to walk on all fours like a real gorilla, but Guillermin thought Kong should walk in an upright manner as he did in the original film. They experimented with various approaches and finally settled on a gait in which Baker would bend his knees, splay his feet, and roll his shoulders while he walked. Guillermin was happier with this solution than Baker was. They also disagreed on the way Kong should thump his chest. Rick wanted to do it in an open-handed manner the way real gorillas do, but Guillermin wanted him to do it close-fisted the way movie gorillas do. Despite these disagreements, Guillermin and Baker got along very well. Baker liked Guillermin a lot and Guillermin was in awe of Baker's uncanny ability to portray a gorilla, especially the way he could communicate a wide range of emotions using only his contact lens–covered eyes. (Early on, consideration had been given to using a real gorilla to shoot the close-ups of Kong's eyes, but when Guillermin saw what Baker could do, that plan was abandoned.)

The wear and tear on Baker was considerable. To begin with, he had big problems with the scleral contact lenses. They rubbed against his corneas and against his upper and lower eyelids (which remain calloused to this day), so he wasn't supposed to wear them for more than thirty minutes at a time. Initially he tried taking them out between shots, but to do so he first had to remove the mask and all of the makeup around his eyes. Removing the mask was time-consuming and wiping away the makeup made his face raw, so eventually he just started leaving the lenses in. Adding to his troubles, during the first week of shooting, Baker found that his eyes were burning all of the time. He went to an optometrist, who told him that the scleral lenses were preventing oxygen from getting to his eyes. The optometrist drilled a hole in the center of the pupil to let air through and the problem cleared right up. Unfortunately, this created another problem. The lenses were filled with liquid, which leaked out of the holes and into Baker's eyes, causing a halo to appear in his vision field that gave him a headache and made him feel nauseous. When the halo effect was combined with the mask's overhanging brow and extended cheekbones, Baker could barely see anything when he was in the suit.

He also had trouble breathing. The masks were closed and cramped and it was quite difficult to get any air in or out. A tube was inserted in the mask's muzzle to help Baker get some fresh air between takes, but most of the time he was left to breathe his own carbon dioxide. The problem was exacerbated when a fresh batch of Spray 'N Tips was sprayed onto the suit before each take—often directly into Baker's face. The cables were also a problem. The big bundle protruding from Kong's head was very heavy and upset Baker's balance. It also had a tendency to snag on pieces of the set and yank Baker over backward at the most inopportune moments. The mechanics in the masks tugged on Baker's face and rubbed against his skin, giving him scabs. To cope with all of this, Baker would go to the small wooden dressing room that had been set up for him (after much protest) on the corner of the stage, close his eyes and attempt to meditate to keep from freaking out. But even this modest escape had its disadvantages. One time when Baker was in his dressing room, everyone forgot about him and went to lunch. He couldn't get out of the suit on his own, so once he discovered he was alone he was stranded.

As Baker had predicted, the bearskin suit was incredibly hot and the intense studio lights only made matters worse. Baker would sweat intensely, often losing up to five pounds of water weight a day. The situation was especially bad when he was filming in front of the blue screen, which required much more light than regular shooting. It was often so hot that Kong's rubber feet would fill up with water and cause Baker to start slipping around. Exacerbating this situation was the fact that he was required to wear the suit for hours on end and often all day long even when he wasn't being used. In an attempt to keep cool, Baker would sit in front a fan and attempt to force some cool air through the seams and joins of the suit, usually without success. He says now that he's surprised that he didn't do permanent damage to himself.

Finally, while filming Kong's battle with the helicopters atop the World Trade Center, Baker got hit on the arm by a two-by-four that fell from the soundstage rafters high above him. Although he sustained a massive bruise, the padded undersuit insulated him enough to prevent a break—or so he thought. Many years later, Baker had some trouble with his shoulder. His doctor ordered an X ray, which revealed that Baker's collarbone had actually been broken during the incident.

Because he didn't work as much as Baker, Will Shephard had an easier time but he still had his problems. The heat caused him to sweat as much as it did Baker. He also had difficulty breathing, especially when he fell into the chloroform-filled pit (which was actually filled with dry ice and fog from the fog machines). Shephard also had trouble keeping his mask on—because it was made to fit

Baker, it tended to slip around on him. One thing Shephard didn't mind was wearing the contact lenses—he described the halo effect as "a real trip."

Filming on the miniature Kong scenes continued long after the end of principal photography and didn't wrap until October 20, 1976. In the end, Rick Baker found the *King Kong* experience a frustrating one. It was physically exhausting, the collaboration with Rambaldi was difficult, and he was disappointed that he was unable to realize the ultimate gorilla suit he had originally envisioned (a dream he would continue to pursue in films such as *Kentucky Fried Movie* (1977)—in which he played a gorilla named Dino—*The Incredible Shrinking Woman* (1978) and *Greystoke: The Legend of Tarzan, Lord of the Apes* (1984) and finally fulfill on *Gorillas in the Mist* and the 1995 remake of *Mighty Joe Young*). Despite all of this, and despite having misgivings about the finished film, he does admit that he also had a lot of fun. "At least I got to stomp around in miniature sets, throw cars, and break stuff," he says now with a smile. Will Shephard has a more positive view of the experience. He says he learned a lot about filmmaking and loved talking to the MGM old-timers, who told him great stories about Hollywood history. Like Baker, he also got a real kick out of playing Kong. "Putting on the Kong suit and walking out among trees that only came up to my waist was…well, it was something!"

OPTICAL EFFECTS   As soon as the miniature footage for each scene was completed, it was turned over to Frank Van Der Veer. The optical effects were produced on the same grueling schedule as the rest of the film. The team at Van Der Veer Photo Effects worked around the clock, seven days a week to make the Christmas deadline. The time pressure often made extreme measures necessary. Richard Kline recalls an afternoon late in the schedule when Van Der Veer called, saying he needed a shot of the Manhattan skyline to use as a background plate for a composite he was working on. No such shot could be found, so Kline immediately went to the Los Angeles airport, flew to New York, and went to a location across the river from Manhattan where a camera crew was waiting for him. Kline took the shot, returned to the airport, boarded the first flight back to Los Angeles and went straight to the lab when he landed. Van Der Veer had the shot in his hand the first thing the next morning.

Van Der Veer's workload was not helped by the difficulty he sometimes had in convincing other members of the production to accommodate to the special needs of the optical department. For example, in one blue screen scene, Jessica Lange was dressed in jeans and a yellow sweater, even though Van Der Veer had warned that blue and yellow were the two worst possible colors to use with blue screen. Van Der Veer made the shot work, but it took a lot more time and effort than it would have if his advice had been heeded.

The optical effects team worked right up to the last minute, finishing the final shot just hours before the film had to be locked for printing. Barry Nolan characterized the experience as "exhausting" and the pressure caused some of the shots to be rushed through at the end, resulting in some unavoidable compromises in quality. Still, in the end, they made the deadline with quality work that ultimately won an Academy Award.

SC. — 57X DWAN PUNCHES

MAN IN SUIT — DWAN ON FULL SCALE HAND IN MIN. SET ON BLUE SCREEN PLATE

SC. — 57XA

DWAN ON FULL SCALE HAND IN MIN. SET

A SPECIAL EFFECTS OVERVIEW

The first optical effect shot in *King Kong* '76 is the first view of the Great Wall, which is a matte-painting shot. The closer shots of the wall in the same sequence also feature a matte painting.

THE SACRIFICE SCENE This scene was full of firsts. To begin with, it is the first miniature Kong scene shot for the film, as well as Kong's first appearance in the story. In several interviews given at the time of the film's release, Guillermin was quoted as saying that his hardest creative task on the film was to determine the proper way to introduce Kong. He finally decided to use an enormous close-up showing only the giant ape's eyes and a portion of his snout. Guillermin said he hoped that this would give the impression that Kong was "the biggest thing on earth"—so big that he couldn't be contained in a single shot. The sacrifice scene also contains the film's first blue screen shot—the full reveal of Kong as he beats his chest and roars in front of Dwan on the altar. To create this image, Jessica Lange was filmed on an altar placed in front of the blue screen and composited with Rick Baker, as Kong, on the background plate.

The film's first split screen shot is the long view of Kong beating his chest as the natives look on from the top of the Great Wall. To create the shot, the natives were filmed standing on the full-scale Wall and then joined with a shot of Baker-as-Kong in the top part of the frame standing in front of the miniature altar. The shot of Kong sniffing Dwan was filmed—as were all of the shots of the miniature Kong holding the full-scale Dwan—with Lange in the Big Hand in front of the blue screen. Baker then posed for the background plate on the miniature set with his own arm held behind his back, looking down at both a girl and a hand that weren't there. When the two were composited, it appeared that the Big Hand was part of the miniature Kong's body.

The Dwan that Baker carries off in the long shot at the end of the sequence was a six-inch-tall cable-operated doll created by Rambaldi and Raponi that was capable of making a variety of movements. Another Dwan doll was made that attached to one of the Kong gloves and could be operated by controls built inside the glove, but neither doll was much seen in the finished film.

THE GLADE SEQUENCE The opening shot of the scene, in which Kong wakes up and rises up out of frame, revealing Dwan sleeping in a cave behind him, was filmed using miniature projection. Jessica Lange had been filmed previously and then projected onto a tiny rear screen built into the cave behind Baker on the miniature glade set.

For the shots looking over Kong's shoulder as he toys with Dwan, Baker performed in front of a blue screen and was composited with a background plate of Lange on the full-scale glade set. A video monitor was set up in front of Baker so that he could view the composite image and know where to place his hand, but Baker had such a hard time seeing out of the mask that he couldn't use it. The shot of Dwan trying to run away from Kong was filmed against a blue screen and composited with a plate of Baker-as-Kong catching up to her in two quick

FACING PAGE, CLOCKWISE FROM TOP: Federico De Laurentiis points to Rick Baker during a rehearsal for the miniature sacrifice scene as Dino De Laurentiis looks on.

Jessica Lange and the Big Hand in front of the blue screen.

Storyboard for the glade scene indicating the live action element to be filmed (bottom) and the final composite (top).

strides. For the solo shots of Dwan in Kong's hand, Lange was filmed in the Big Hand in front of the blue screen and composited with background plates of the miniature trees used in the sequence in which Kong is first seen approaching the sacrificial altar. When filming the plate for the shot in which Dwan punches Kong on the snout, Baker had to jerk his head back subtlety as if he had been hit, which was very hard to do encased in all that foam rubber. A full-scale insert was also filmed of Lange punching the nose of the Big Kong.

The shot in which an angry Kong slams his fist down on the bank of the mud puddle after Dwan has run away from him was a split screen shot. The split, made along a rounded line that went around the outside of the puddle, is almost undetectable. Rick Baker slammed his fist down on the miniature set and Jessica Lange reacted on the full-scale set. To sell the effect, a special effects crew positioned an air cannon on the portion of the full-scale set that would be hidden by the split and fired a blast of dust at Jessica. In the final composite, it looks as if it is the force of Kong's pounding that blows the dirt onto Dwan.

THE WATERFALL SCENE

All of Kong's shots for this scene were done on a miniature set constructed in front of the blue screen. To film the background plates, a cameraman was sent to Brazil to film a real waterfall. He wasn't heard from for over the month and the crew feared the worst, but he turned up eventually, having shot some spectacular footage. The waterfall scene contains one of the most complex blue screen shots in the entire film — the view of Kong holding Dwan under the falls. Baker-as-Kong was on the background plate, composited with a shot of the Brazilian falls. Jessica Lange was filmed in the Big Hand in front of the blue screen with real water cascading down on her. Barry Nolan reports that trying to pull mattes from white, moving water photographed against a blue backing was one of the film's biggest challenges.

THE LOG SCENE

For the overhead shots of the search party crossing the log, the floor of the full-scale set was covered with blue screen material. The men were photographed crossing over the screen on the log and then composited with a matte painting of a deep ravine. A blue screen was then repositioned along one side of the full-scale set to film the shot of Jeff Bridges as he sees Kong for the first time and then for the shots of Kong twisting the log as the men begin to fall, all of which were later composited with shots of Baker-as-Kong filmed on the miniature ravine set. For the overhead shots of the crew falling into the ravine as Kong shakes them off the log, the actors and the stuntmen were hung on wires and dropped into the blue-lined pit. Seven different matte paintings were used to establish the depth of the ravine. The shots of Jack trying to avoid the miniature Kong's hand were originally supposed to be done as miniature projection shots, but the image failed to register, so a miniature blue screen was placed in the cave and later composited with footage of Bridges filmed on the full-scale set.

THE CRATER SCENE

For Kong's lair, an impressive set based on an actual Hawaiian volcano was built on Stage 15. Close shots of Baker were shot to serve as background plates for the scene in which the Big Hands peel away

ABOVE: John Guillermin directs Jeff Bridges as the actor balances precariously in the ravine set.

BELOW: Jeff Bridges confronts the Big Hand.

Dwan's clothes. The over-Kong's-shoulder shots of Dwan in the same scene were filmed using forced perspective. Both Baker and Shephard were used in different takes of shots looking down past Kong's head and right shoulder at Jessica Lange cradled in the Big Hands below. Both men were placed on a platform raised twenty-five feet off of the floor of the full-scale crater set. The camera was positioned behind them, shooting down at Lange. Baker/Shephard blocked the cranes holding the hands, making it appear, from the camera's point of view anyway, that the miniature Kong and the Big Hands were one. While filming this scene, one of the Big Hand's heavy metal fingers came down too hard and hit Lange on the head, giving her a pinched nerve that lasted for weeks.

THE SNAKE FIGHT Glen Robinson's team built four snakes for this scene, all of them sculpted by Don Chandler. The first was thirty-two feet long and contained an air hose that caused it to shake menacingly as it rolled along a track. A second snake was loose and moved by wires like a puppet. A third snake was rigged with a device that would make its mouth open in a menacing manner when its throat was squeezed and was used for specific close-ups. A

Kong caresses Dwan during the crater scene.

Will Shephard wrestles with the big fake snake.

fourth was designed for Kong to rip apart at the jaw in the final shot of the fight.

For the shot in which Dwan first sees the giant snake, a blue screen shot of Lange was composited with a plate of the track snake rolling into the miniature crater. Miniature projection was used for the second and last time in the film for the shot in which Dwan runs behind Kong as he grabs hold of the advancing snake. As in the glade scene, the shot of Lange running was filmed ahead of time and then projected on to a screen behind Rick Baker as he seized the snake. The actual fight was filmed using the wire snake. While the track snake had worked superbly, the wire snake was a major disappointment. The wires didn't work very well, forcing Baker to make the snake look alive by shaking it, which was next to impossible using his glove-covered hands. On top of this, the wire snake's skin wrinkled visibly when it wrapped around Kong. It didn't look at all convincing and filming of the scene was postponed after the first few shots in order to give the production team time to figure out a new approach. Different suggestions were made as to how to approach the scene (including one to put a little person into a Kong suit and match him with a real boa constrictor), but ultimately a decision was made to cut the wire snake into pieces, wrap it around Kong, and then film the remainder of the fight in a series of close-ups. William Kronick and Will Shephard completed the sequence, which took an entire day and which Kronick describes as a "bitch to shoot."

KONG BREAKS THROUGH THE WALL This was the second miniature Kong scene filmed and was done right after the sacrifice scene. For the over-the-shoulder shots of Kong charging the wall as Wilson scrambles to safety,

Baker was filmed walking on a treadmill in front of a blue screen and composited with a shot of Grodin on the full-scale Wall. Kronick directed both Baker and Will Shephard in various full body shots of Kong pounding the miniature Wall, while Guillermin directed Baker in some additional close-ups. Shephard did Kong's actual break through the gate. Because of the need to convey the size and weight of the chunks that flew off the wall as Kong hit it, this was one of the few miniature sequences shot at high speed (approximately seventy-two frames per second). The result was extremely effective. The full-scale Dwan, Jack, and *Petrox Explorer* crew was placed in front of the miniature wall via a split screen.

Because the producers didn't want Baker getting hurt, Shephard did Kong's fall into the pit, which was about three and a half feet deep and five feet wide and had gym mats lining the bottom. Dry ice and fog machines generated the "chloroform." On the first take Shephard, a former swimmer, did a turn as he fell to allow him to land on his back. Kronick told him to do it again, this time with "less ballet." On the second take, Shephard went into the pit face forward. Unable to hear, he waited what he thought was a reasonable amount of time and then started to get up, only to realize that Kronick had not yet called "Cut." Angry that he had messed up the shot and would have to do it over again, Shephard slammed his fist down into the gym mats. Much to his surprise, this is the shot that was used in the final film, where it looks like Kong is slamming his fist in hopeless frustration as he is overcome by the chloroform fumes. These shots were composited with blue screen shots of the actors as they look on.

THE SUPERTANKER SCENE   The miniature supertanker set was built on Stage 14. For the opening shot of Kong's food being dropped into the hold, miniature fruit was filmed at a rate of ninety-eight frames per second to give the impression it was falling from a great height. For the whimsical scene in which Dwan's scarf drifts down to Kong in the hold, a "miniature kerchief" was used that was unfortunately so grossly out of proportion that it looked more like an area rug than a bandana.

Jessica Lange filmed the over-the-shoulder shot of Dwan looking down from the deck at Kong in the hold in front of a blue screen covered with a mock-up of the grate, footage that was later composited with a high angle plate of Kong in the miniature tanker set. Baker played Kong throughout the supertanker scene, although Will Shephard did do a few takes of the jump-up-and-fall-back Kong does that dislodges Dwan from the grate and causes her to fall into the tank. The reverse angles of this shot were done in front of the blue screen and composited with shots of Lange on the full-scale grate. For the shot in which Kong catches Dwan as she plummets, Jessica Lange was hung by wires in front of the blue screen and the Big Hand brought up into the shot beneath her as she mimed falling. The shot was later composited with a rapid pan up the side of the miniature tanker that made it look like the wall was rushing by.

A shot of Lange walking away from the blue screen was composited with a shot of Kong in the miniature set forlornly watching her go. The final shot in the sequence featured Lange climbing up a ladder placed in front of the blue

Rick Baker as Kong on the miniature supertanker set.

ABOVE: Side by side comparison shows the vast difference in appearance between the miniature and full-scale Kongs.

FACING PAGE: Kong trashes the elevated train.

screen composited with a longer shot of the miniature Kong. Three matte painting were used to augment the full-scale supertanker set, which in reality consisted only of two eight-foot walls and a ladder that ran up to a grate at the top of the soundstage.

THE PRESENTATION SCENE The presentation scene contained the greatest number of split screen shots in the entire film. The first was of a marching band parading in front of the Manhattan skyline. The band in the bottom part of the screen was filmed on the back lot in Culver City and combined with a still photo of New York City in the top portion of the frame. The second features Baker-as-Kong breaking out of his cage married to a shot of the audience reacting on the back lot. The third split screen shot shows Kong stepping off his pedestal after he breaks free from his chains. Baker-as-Kong was filmed on the miniature set and joined with a shot of Jessica Lange and Charles Grodin standing at the full-scale altar. The final split screen shot in the sequence features Kong roaring at the full-scale crowd just before they panic. One of the cameras used to film the splits in this sequence had bad registration, which caused the image on one side of the split to shake against the image on the other.

For the shots of Kong stomping on audience members, Baker-as-Kong was filmed walking on a blue screen and then composited with a background plate of several extras dropping to the ground and writhing in pain. A wide shot of the crowd fleeing was also filmed against a blue screen and composited with a plate of Baker-as-Kong advancing toward the camera. The presentation scene was especially challenging for Baker because he had to match the movements of the Big Kong as he was smashing his way out of the cage and make it look realistic. Given how slow and stiff the big robot's movements were, this was not an easy task.

THE ELEVATED-SUBWAY SCENE For the scene in which Kong destroys an elevated-subway train, Glen Robinson and his team constructed a large section of track, as well as several miniature subway cars complete with

70s-era graffiti. One of the cars was rigged with a wire that did most of the actual lifting in the shot where Kong picks it up and throws it into a building. Robinson's crew also rigged a series of big explosions designed to go off when the car hit the building. Baker recalls the explosions as being so intense that on several occasions he became convinced that his suit had caught on fire, although, thankfully, that wasn't the case. To enhance the scene's realism, miniature people were placed on rods and moved in and out of the windows of the miniature apartment buildings as Kong rampaged.

CROSSING THE EAST RIVER Baker performed the shot of Kong walking down to the river from the Queens waterfront in front of the blue screen and was then composited with a shot of the East River and the 59th Street Bridge filmed by the second unit in New York.

The scene in which Kong wades across the river was shot in a tank on one of the MGM soundstages. When Baker first tried to wade into the water, his foam rubber undersuit made him buoyant, which caused him to bob up and down on the surface. To stabilize him, the crew squeezed the undersuit like a sponge to get it to absorb the water. Although this finally allowed Baker to enter the water, it also caused the suit to weigh about 500 pounds. While Baker could manage well enough while submerged, the extreme weight caused his knees to buckle as soon as he cleared the water. During the scene, Baker had to walk across an

underwater platform from one side of the tank to the other. After Baker expressed concern that he might slip off the platform, fall to the bottom of the tank, and drown, the crew placed a diver in the pool with an emergency tank of air to feed Baker if he fell. While Baker certainly appreciated the gesture, he was never quite certain how the diver planned to get the hose from the air tank past the Kong mask and into his mouth in time. Luckily, he never had to find out.

A miniature model of a power station was placed on one side of the tank and rigged to spark as Kong touched it. Since Baker was soaking wet when he did the shot, he was naturally very concerned about being electrocuted. When the shot was done, Guillermin told Baker he never saw Kong move so fast.

RECAPTURING DWAN Background plates of Baker-as-Kong peering into a Sutton Place bar were composited with a foreground shot of a blue screen covered by a mock-up of the bar's window. The shot of Kong marching away from the bar toward the World Trade Center holding Dwan was filmed in front of the blue screen and then composited with a second unit plate of the actual twin towers. Kong's walk down Fifth Avenue was filmed on a blue screen set featuring a miniature building in the foreground and composted with a still of the actual Fifth Avenue retouched to make it look like all of the lights had gone out. A faux-tracking shot of Kong carrying Dwan through the streets on his way to the World Trade Center was created by filming Baker-as-Kong as he walked in place on a treadmill in front of the blue screen and joining the resulting shot with one of Lange in the Big Hand that was moved up and down optically to make it look as if Kong's hand was bouncing as he walked. Both images were then composited with a rapidly moving tracking shot of several Manhattan buildings. Unfortunately, the elements didn't line up properly, so the shot was dropped.

THE WORLD TRADE CENTER To construct the World Trade Center miniatures, Dale Hennesy obtained the blueprints and architectural drawings of the real buildings, which allowed him to reproduce all aspects of the building in exact detail. In actuality, several sets were created. The first was a recreation of the main plaza that was built on the back lot and included a three-sided reproduction of the South Tower and a one-sided reproduction of the North Tower.

For the shot of Kong standing in the plaza holding Dwan in his hand as he looks up at the towers, both Jessica Lange and Rick Baker performed in front of the blue screen. A shot of Baker-as-Kong was placed over a shot of Lange in the Big Hand and then composited with a background plate of the actual buildings. Although most of the background plates seen in the film were moving images, the World Trade Center plate in this shot was a still photograph that was blown up into a large-format transparency, lit from behind, and then rephotographed onto motion picture film. This shot contained one of the film's most poignant interludes—the brief moment when Kong, sensing danger, looks around, spots the army waiting in the shadows to ambush him, and lets out a terrific roar that combines noble defiance with bewildered fear. The final effect is oddly touching.

Baker did the initial shot of Kong crossing the plaza to begin his ascent and Shephard did the actual climb. To facilitate this, a cable was hooked to a belt

Shephard wore inside his suit. A winch then pulled Shephard up the side of the miniature South Tower as he moved his arms and legs to make it look like he was climbing. An unusual shot at the beginning of Kong's climb featured a blue screen shot of Jessica Lange clinging to the shoulder of the Big Kong layered over another blue screen shot of the miniature Kong moving his arm up and down in a climbing motion. Both shots were then composited with a plate featuring a tilt-up on the side of the real building. The idea was to make it look like the Big Kong was actually climbing. Although the action and speed of the two elements never quite match up, it was an ambitious attempt nonetheless.

A section of the middle of the South Tower was constructed for the shots of Kong making his way up the side of the building. These shots were filmed in front of a blue screen and composited with plates of the city in the background or the plaza below. The shot of Jack watching as Kong climbs past the observatory windows was shot on a blue-backed window set and then layered over another blue screen shot of Rick Baker climbing a scaffold. Both shots were then composited over a transparency of the New York City skyline.

Miniature rooftops of both towers were also constructed. Baker filmed the shots of Kong reaching the top of the South Tower and his subsequent interplay with Dwan. Will Shephard did the scene in which Kong is attacked by the U.S. Marines. The shots of the marines firing a flamethrower at Kong were filmed in front of a blue screen and composited against reaction shots of Shephard as Kong. For the shot in which Kong is actually hit by the flames, an explosive charge was rigged to the back of Shephard's suit and timed to ignite in synch with the flames. Worried that the suit would catch fire, Shephard insisted that crewmembers stand by with buckets of water at the ready before he would agree to perform the shot. For the shot of Dwan bouncing in Kong's hand as he runs across the roof, Lange was filmed in the Big Hand in front of the blue screen alongside the chest of the Big Kong. Both the chest and the hand were jiggled up and down during the shot and then composited over a plate of the city skyline, which was optically jiggled as well.

To film the beginning and end of Kong's leap from one tower to another, Will Shephard was rigged with wires that carried him away from the roof of the miniature South Tower and swung him toward the side of the North Tower. The actual leap was filmed atop two MGM soundstages. Shephard was originally asked to make the leap, but refused because he wasn't a stuntman. Instead, the film's stunt co-coordinator Bill Couch donned Baker's Kong suit and leapt between the two buildings on a wire. Baker recalls that Couch did not enjoy being encased in the suit even for the short amount of time it took to do the leap and spent much of the evening on the verge of freaking out. The final shot was optically reduced and matted into a shot of the actual towers. For the close-up of Dwan's scream as Kong makes his leap from one tower to another, Lange was again filmed on the shoulder of the Big Kong and then composited against an aerial shot of the actual building. Baker filmed the shots of Kong lobbing hunks of air-conditioning equipment at the marines and forced perspective was employed for the shot looking over Baker-as-Kong's shoulder as the debris lands on the marines, causing their flamethrower to explode.

Kong (Rick Baker) sends a model helicopter crashing into the side of Dale Hennesy's miniature recreation of the World Trade Center's North Tower.

The shots of the army helicopters approaching the Trade Center to kill Kong were filmed at Los Alamitos Air Force Base. A forty-foot-tall platform was erected on a runway and Baker was placed atop the platform dressed in his Kong suit. Three real helicopters then flew toward the platform from a starting point a mile away. To light their approach, Richard Kline positioned ten arc lights in a straight line from the takeoff point to the platform. Operators would train the lights on the choppers and track them as far as they could, at which point the next light in the chain would pick them up. The goal was to make it look as if the helicopters were being lit by the ambient light of the city that was allegedly below them. Kline used a split-diopter (a special filter that allows a single lens to focus on two different planes at the same time) to keep both Baker and the helicopters in focus in the same frame. As the helicopters approached, they fired hundreds of blanks at Baker, who wore a plastic shield in front of him to keep from being hit by the hot shell casings.

For the shots of the helicopters circling Kong as he swats at them, the original plan had been to use radio-controlled helicopters. For this reason, the Trade Center rooftop sets were originally constructed outdoors. Three six-foot-long helicopters were constructed, but once they were completed, the operator couldn't guarantee that he would have enough control over the helicopters to keep them from slicing up the actors, so the plan was scrapped. The sets were rebuilt inside a soundstage with a raised roof. Model helicopters run by electric motors were hung from a track attached to the stage ceiling and flown around Baker on wires. Lange was inserted into some of these shots via split screen.

For the scene in which Kong sends one of the helicopters crashing into the side of the North Tower, Baker was positioned on the edge of the roof so that Kong would appear in the shot as the chopper spiraled into the building. Since Baker couldn't see where he was stepping, the crew tied a rope around his waist to keep him from falling. To film Kong being hit by bullets from the choppers, the crew fired wax pellets filled with fake blood at Baker. When the pellets hit, they burst and sprayed blood across Kong's chest in a very realistic approximation of bullet hits. Baker felt the technique was very effective, but spent the entire shoot hoping that one of the pellets wouldn't hit him in the eye. The close-ups of Kong with the helicopters behind him were filmed against the blue screen and then composited with moving plates of the real helicopters. The very first shot, in which a chopper flies past Kong as he swats at it, has a three-dimensional quality and is quite impressive, but the rest of plates don't match up well with the static foreground shots of Kong. The contrast between the foreground and background is off as well. For those reasons, these are the least successful blue screen shots in the entire picture.

To film Kong's fall from the roof of the North Tower, Will Shephard was hung from wires in front of the screen and flailed his arms and legs as the camera zoomed in on him. This footage was then composited with a transparency of the actual building. Kong's death scene was filmed by having Baker lie on a platform covered with Styrofoam chips that were intended to represent pieces of the smashed Trade Center Plaza and moving the camera in close to record Kong's final death throes.

POSTPRODUCTION

Academy Award–winning film editor Ralph E. Winters (*King Solomon's Mines*, *Ben-Hur*) assembled the film, aided by assistant editor Robert Pergament. Because of the tight December deadline, the film was edited as it was being shot. In fact, about half of the film was actually fine cut and locked before the end of principal photography, a process made easier by production manager Terry Carr's efforts to ensure that the film was shot largely in continuity.

For Winters, the hardest part of the job was coordinating all of the different elements that went into the optical effect shots. He had to determine the start and end points for every piece of film used in each effect shot, synch them together, and then mark them so that the optical effects team would know where to start and shot each one when they made the composites. It was incredibly tedious work that required intense focus and precision. Assistant editor Margo Anderson acted as the liaison between the editing room and Van Der Veer Photo Effects.

Winters also had to judiciously edit the various appearances of the various Kongs. Many full body shots of the miniature Kong had been filmed, but because the length of the performer's legs made it obvious that Kong was really a man in an ape suit only a few were used. For most of the scenes in which Kong had to move about, medium shots featuring only his upper torso were employed. Most of the emphasis, however, was given to the close-ups of Kong's magnificently expressive face. The footage of the Big Kong was also a challenge for Winters. Because it performed so poorly, there weren't many usable shots and, since neither its appearance nor its movements came any-where close to resembling Baker in the ape suit, Winters had to work hard to match what few shots he could, but it was an uphill battle all the way.

A few minor scenes were cut to speed the film's pace, including a scene from the beginning of the movie in which Jack drugs a sailor in a Surabaya bar in order to get his *Petrox Explorer* crew shirt; a scene of the Petrox drillers play-ing cards on the deck of the ship on the morning after the storm; a sequence in which Jack discovers Garcia and Timmons spying on Dwan in the shower, prompting him to drop Garcia overboard; a brief scene of Bagley analyzing oil in his shipboard lab; another of Jack and Dwan trying to steal a car from a Queens street as they escape from Kong; a scene in which Kong tosses a car into a building; a scene showing some jet pilots readying their planes to take off to fight Kong, only to have their commander cancel the mission and send up some helicopters instead; and a brief scene in which Jack commandeers the bike that he rides to the World Trade Center. Finally, to give Kong more of a victory dur-ing the end sequence, Kong's attack on one of the helicopters was recycled. The scene was presented once in a close-up and again in a long shot to make it look as if Kong destroyed two helicopters instead of one.

SOUND EFFECTS James J. Klinger created and edited the film's sound effects. Kong's distinctive roar was created by playing the sound of a trumpet backwards and mixing it in with a variety of other animal sounds.

MUSIC At the start of preproduction, Academy Award–winning composer John Barry (*Born Free*, the James Bond films) was engaged to compose and conduct the score (Guillermin and Barry had worked together sixteen years earlier on *Never Let Go*). Barry's first task was to compose the music for the sacrifice scene, which was actually played on the set as the scene was filmed. Following this, Barry turned his attention to the rest of the music. As with all other aspects of the production, no attempt was made to imitate the original film's groundbreaking score. In keeping with the film's "Beauty and the Beast" emphasis, De Laurentiis and Guillermin asked Barry to compose a romantic theme for the picture. Barry agreed, although he felt that the theme should also have a sense of power and strength to balance out the sweetness. Once the theme was written, Barry used it to build a lush score that perfectly captured the spirit of romance and adventure the filmmakers were trying to achieve.

The score was created in a very unusual way. Normally, a film composer will wait until editing on a film had been completed before starting work. This allows him to create music that will perfectly match the mood and rhythms of the finished film. However, because of *Kong*'s sped-up postproduction process, a special arrangement was made for Barry to compose the score two reels at a time. As a result, the recording sessions, which normally take place in a few weeks at the end of the schedule, were spread out over an eight-month period. The first four were held between March 29 and April 12, 1976, on the MGM scoring stage and the last nine were held between July 22 and November 5, 1976, at the Burbank Studios.

PREVIEW A sneak preview was held in Denver a few weeks before the film's release. Some of the special effects sequences weren't yet complete and the sound mix hadn't been finished. Despite these problems, the film was reasonably well received. Still, based on the audience reaction, a few additional changes were made. The first involved the ultimate fate of Fred Wilson. In the original cut, after Kong breaks loose in the presentation scene, Wilson is confronted by the Petrox Chairman of the Board. Furious at the havoc Kong has caused and the billions it's going to cost the company, the Chairman fires Fred and threatens to ruin him. Intimidated, Fred hurries away from the Chairman and runs smack into Kong. Recognizing his tormentor, Kong lifts up his foot and then stomps it down, seemingly on top of Fred. However, when Kong lifts up his foot, we see that he actually missed Fred and only squashed his hat. Kong moves off, leaving Wilson to face a bleak and miserable future. The preview audience was very disappointed by this ending. Grodin had done such a good job of making Fred despicable that the audience wanted him to die. Accordingly, all of the material involving the Chairman was removed (although he remains listed in the film's closing credits) and the shot of Kong lifting his foot was cut before it can be seen that he hadn't actually stepped on Fred, making it appear that Wilson has been killed. The resolution of the relationship between Jack and Dwan was also altered. Originally, in the Sutton Place bar scene, Dwan asks Jack if their relationship has a chance. Jack replies that it does only if Kong survives. If not, Jack feels that they will be so haunted by him that they will not be able to stay together. After Kong dies, Jack pushes through the crowd toward Dwan, but when he sees that Kong is dead and

Kong News

NUMBER 2, OCTOBER 1976 • NEW YORK, N.Y. & HOLLYWOOD, CALIF. • PARAMOUNT PICTURES

Creation of "King Kong" monster is a tribute to the genius of the men who make movie magic

He may not be the handsomest movie star in Hollywood history, but he certainly is the biggest and hairiest, standing 40 feet tall and covered with acres of fur. He is a star in his own right, according to producer Dino De Laurentiis.

He is King Kong, the greatest movie monster of them all.

He wasn't even born a year ago. But he was alive in the minds of Carlo Rambaldi and Glen Robinson, who had been hired by the producer to come up with a mechanical monster big enough to fill the screen in a multi-million dollar contemporary version of the classic "King Kong" story of beauty and the beast.

If Kong has any nationality, he is an Italian-American. Rambaldi is one of the most famous special effects designers in the Italian film industry, and Robinson, a Hollywood native, is a two-time Academy Award winner for "Earthquake" and "The Hindenburg."

Discussions among Rambaldi, Robinson and De Laurentiis led to an agreement that Kong had to be monster-size and mechanical, having moving arms and legs. The original intention was to have an aircraft company build King Kong from the designs evolved by Rambaldi and Robinson, but when it became necessary to rush the film into production, the decision was to have Kong coming alive on a Hollywood backlot.

Work on the Kong monster began in January, 1976, months earlier than had been originally anticipated, and at his birth on that day, he was just a pile of aluminum and wires waiting to be shaped by the skilled hands of a hundred craftsmen assembled in the workshop by Robinson.

The dimensions of Kong, a tribute to the genius of the men who make

movie magic, are staggering. He weighs 6½ tons. His skeleton is metal, mostly aluminum. His inside contains 3,100 feet of hydraulic hose and 4,500 feet of electrical wiring. His chest is 20 feet wide and his arm span is 20 feet.

He is fully functional, the first such creature conceived by Hollywood. His arms can move in 16 different positions. He can walk and turn at the waist. His eyes and mouth move. He is a very human monster, terrifying when aroused, but with the soul of a romantic lover.

The secret to his ability to move is in the proportional balance in the hydraulic valves, according to Robinson, who believes Kong should retain some of his mystery and not everything about him should be made public. But the master builder said these valves are operated by wires running through a crane to a control panel operated by six men.

While marveling at the mechanical wizardry of her ardent pursuer, Jessica Lange, who spends much of the film literally in his hand, had

(Continued on page 4)

Having fallen 107 floors from the top of the World Trade Center, King Kong finds peace at last, in death.

An issue of the King Kong newsletter.

that she is surrounded by photographers, he stops, looks at her regretfully and then turns and walks off into the crowd. Coming so soon after the death of Kong, this ending was just too much of a downer for the audience, so the conversation in the bar was eliminated, as was the shot of Jack walking off into the crowd. In the final film, it appears that Jack is pushing through the crowd in an attempt to get to Dwan, but the sheer mass of people prevents him from doing so.

The film was finally locked just a few short weeks before release at a running time of 135 minutes. At a final cost of $23 million, it was the most expensive film ever produced at that time.

RELEASE

Spearheaded by Gordon Armstrong, Dino De Laurentiis's publicity head, the promotional campaign for *King Kong* began over a year before the film's release with the publication of the joint De Laurentiis/Paramount "There still is only one King Kong" ad. At the suggestion of Gordon Weaver, Paramount's vice president in charge of world wide marketing, a coupon was placed at the bottom of the ad that readers could send in to receive a free color copy of the poster. Sixty thousand coupons were received in a matter of days. On New Year's Eve 1975, the producer and his United States distributor leased the electronic ticker in Times Square and programmed it with the following message: "Paramount Pictures and Dino De Laurentiis wish all America a Happy King Kong New Year." A King Kong newsletter was later sent to all of the people that ordered the poster. The newsletter contained pictures of the cast and crew, as well as articles written by the film's publicist Bruce Bahrenburg that kept readers up to date on the progress of the production.

In the wake of the original ad, Berkey revised his illustration, refining it and adding more detail to his drawing of Kong, the World Trade Center and the city behind them. This revamp was also revamped—Kong was originally shown with a foot on each of the Twin Towers and holding an airplane in his hand as more planes buzzed around him. This version of the poster was used in some overseas markets, but for the United States, Canada, and Great Britain, Berkey removed some of the planes and replaced them with helicopters. The plane in Kong's hand was replaced by a burning fuselage and finally a shadow was removed from under Kong's rear foot so it would look like he was leaping from one building to the other rather than straddling them. It was felt these changes more accurately reflected the storyline of the finished film. This illustration became the key piece of art for the film and appeared on so many products, magazine, and book covers in the next year that it became practically ubiquitous. Once the poster—which featured the tagline "The most exciting, original motion picture event of all time"—was complete, Paramount commissioned Berkey to do a series of additional paintings depicting various scenes from the movie: Kong battling the snake, Kong smashing through the Great Wall, Kong breaking out of his cage in Shea Stadium, Kong destroying a subway train, Kong wrecking boats as he crosses the East River, and a dramatic overhead view of Kong climbing the World Trade Center. With the exception of the Shea Stadium and the World-Trade-Center pictures, Kong had the exact same face in all of these illustrations. Berkey had painted different faces on the pictures, but the Paramount marketing department replaced them all with the face from the original poster in order to achieve consistency. All of these illustrations appeared on a wide variety of Kong-related merchandise.

The Big Kong also generated tremendous publicity. From the very beginning of production, De Laurentiis's publicists began circulating stories that contained exact details of how the Big Kong was built and some rather exaggerated claims about what it could do (many early stories claimed it could actually walk). However, since construction on the robot was not actually finished until the end of the production, most of these stories were rather vague about the precise status of the robot and its exact role in the making of the film. Initially, to maintain suspense, the studio wasn't going to release any photos of the Big Kong until the film was about to open. At first this wasn't a problem because

ABOVE AND ON FACING PAGE:
Some of John Berkey's conceptual paintings.

there was no Big Kong to take pictures of, but when the production arrived in New York, De Laurentiis was so pleased by the look of the Styrofoam Kong that he wanted to invite the press to take pictures of it. Worried that the Styrofoam Kong would look fake, Paramount said no, but Armstrong notified the press anyway and before long photos of Kong were appearing everywhere. They were very well received. Once the Big Kong was finished, pictures of it were widely circulated as well, to equally positive reaction. So, while the Big Kong may have been a failure as a working prop, as a publicity tool, it was a terrific success.

Reveling in all of the attention the Big Kong was generating, the producers understandably wanted to keep the fact that most of the Kong shots in the movie were being done with a man in an ape suit a secret. Although a few rumors did circulate, they were able to do so until a reporter from *Time* magazine came to the set in the middle of production to do a story on the movie. Initially, no mention was made of Rick Baker and his suit. Instead, the reporter's attention was directed to the Big Kong, which was, at that point, unfinished. Later, the reporter was shown some scenes from the film featuring Kong. The reporter was curious as to how these scenes were filmed, since the Big Kong was clearly not ready. At this point, the producers had no choice but to introduce the reporter to Baker and show him the ape suit. Baker feels that this why he received a credit on the final film, since he wasn't originally supposed to. Even so, the credit was a deliberately vague one that did not specify Baker's role in the production. (It read: "The producer wishes to acknowledge that Kong has been designed and engineered by Carlo Rambaldi and constructed by Carlo Rambaldi and Glen Robinson with special contributions by Rick Baker.") When the *Time* article appeared that October, the secret was out, but surprisingly didn't make much of a difference. Most of the publicity continued to focus on the Big Kong and the public continued to eat it up.

De Laurentiis himself was also the focus of much of the prerelease publicity. The story of his fabled European career and the tremendous success he had achieved since arriving in America just a few short years before was repeated many times in the months before the film's release, as was his desire to make his *Kong* the highest grossing film of all time. By the time of the film's release, De Laurentiis had become a "star" in his own right, and was arguably the most well-known movie producer on the planet. The film's other star, Jessica Lange, was sent on a six-week promotional tour that took her to thirty-one cities on three different continents. As the film's release drew closer, coming attractions posters and standees began appearing in theaters worldwide, along with a trailer featuring scenes from the beginning of the film (as the end had not yet been completed). Kong appeared on the cover of many magazines that went on sale in December. Commercials began running on television and radio two weeks before the film's debut and reached saturation point by the weekend of the release.

THE OPENING   A few days before the film was released, a gala premiere was held in New York. The after party was televised live as a segment of NBC's *The Big Event.* Finally, on Friday, December 17, 1976, *King Kong* opened worldwide in 1,200 theaters in the United States and in another 1,000 theaters overseas. At that time, it was the biggest simultaneous release in film history.

REVIEWS AND ANALYSIS The critical reception was mostly positive. Reviews ranged from respectful to raves:

"The Dino De Laurentiis–John Guillermin version of *King Kong* is one of the most fabulously successful remakes in the brief history of motion pictures! Faithful in substantial degree not only to the letter but the spirit of the 1933 Merian C. Cooper-Ernest B. Schoedsack-Willis O'Brien original, this new version neatly balances superb special effects with solid dramatic credibility." — Art Murphy, *Daily Variety*

"It's a romantic adventure fantasy—colossal, silly, touching, a marvelous Classics-Comics movie…a pop classic that can stand in our affections right next to the original version." —Pauline Kael, *The New Yorker*

"One of the year's ten best! A truly spectacular film! The new *King Kong*, for all its monumental scale retains the essential, sincere, and simple charm of the beauty and the beast story. The attitude toward the original that permeates the remake is respectful, not mocking. *Kong II* is grand and tender. The ending has an emotional complexity to equal the dazzling complexity of the special effects. Despite the hype and hooraw, you are likely to be moved." —Charles Champlin, *Los Angeles Times*

"The result is enjoyable enough on its own terms as well as highly respectful of the adventurous spirit and wonder of the original. Even buffs will have to admit that there's room for both." —Bartholomew, *Film Bulletin*

"A dazzling display of what the special effects people can do. John Guillermin, the director, and Lorenzo Semple, Jr., the writer, display real affection for old-time movie magic and nonsense." —Vincent Canby, *New York Times*

There were some negative notices, but even those had some nice things to say. *Time*'s Richard Schickel, who felt the new Kong was too sympathetic and not terrifying enough, wrote:

"The special effects are marvelous, the good-humored script is comic bookish without being campy, and there are two excellent performances (Grodin and Kong)."

Even *Newsweek*'s Jack Kroll, who gave the film one of its few outright pans, admitted that it "…does have a certain thunderous fun." Most of the bad reviews—Kroll's included—did not take issue with the specifics of the film itself, but instead simply dismissed it for not being the original film. It's not, of course, but, as has been stated many times in these pages, it was never trying to be. As Dino De Laurentiis, John Guillermin, and Lorenzo Semple, Jr., intended from the beginning, their *King Kong* is a very different film from Merian C. Cooper and Ernest Schoedsack's *King Kong*—one that deserves to be judged on its own terms.

To begin with, *King Kong* '76 is not so much a remake as a variation on a theme. The original *Kong* is primarily a monster movie. *Kong* '76 is first and foremost a love story; this is simultaneously the film's greatest strength and its greatest weakness. Making Kong's love for Dwan the primary focus of the movie puts the central absurdity of the premise on display in a very blatant way that is occasionally a bit silly. At the same time, it brings the emotional content of the story to the fore in a way the original film never did. As a result, the film is surprisingly moving and the ending even more tragic.

It helps that the film is extremely well made. Semple's screenplay honors the Kong legend and then enhances it by fleshing out a relationship between Kong and Dwan that had only been suggested in the original. It also adds a cryptic piece of faux folklore ("From thy wedding with the creature who touches heaven, lady God preserve thee.") that is a worthy companion to Cooper's venerable ancient Arabian proverb. The characters and storyline have been updated in a thoughtful, intelligent manner, and the dialogue is both witty and clever. The script is highly romantic and takes a very poignant view of Kong (which is most in evidence in the supertanker sequence). Not everything works—the dinosaurs are missed, a few of the jokes fall flat, and some of the attitudes and characterizations have not aged well—but the story's structure is solid and its power to move remains intact. Guillermin's direction is impressively sharp and precise. The widescreen shots are expertly composed to make the most of the adventure and spectacle and give the film a truly epic feel. Guillermin keeps a firm grip on the film's pace and tone, nicely balances the action and the drama, and does a splendid job of realizing the story's lyricism. There are a few lapses—the scenes shot on location do not always intercut smoothly with those filmed on the stages, Kong's fight with the snake is weak, and both the log and the presentation scenes are awkward and rushed. On the other hand, the sacrifice scene is tremendous—the ceremony itself is both spectacular and terrifying and Kong's approach generates great suspense and anticipation, of which the payoff is the giant ape's thrilling and totally convincing first appearance. The waterfall scene is sweet and endearing and the wall breakthrough, the elevated-subway sequence, and Kong's battle with the marines atop the World Trade Center are all terrifically well done and exciting. Kong's death is touching, and the final pullback from Dwan and Kong as the crowd swarms around them is magnificent and everything a Kong movie should be.

The film's other creative elements are equally strong. Richard Kline's cinematography is spectacular—the Hawaiian footage is terrific, as is the sacrifice scene, and Kline's use of soft light and modest diffusion greatly enhances the film's fairy-tale quality. Dale Hennesy's miniature and full-scale sets—especially the wall and his re-creation of the World Trade Center—are terrific. Ralph Winters's editing is crisp and John Barry's music is romantic, thrilling, and at times even terrifying. The acting is also good. Bridges projects an earnest sincerity that solidly anchors the film. Grodin is deliciously funny, but never loses his sense of menace. After a tentative beginning, Jessica Lange finds her feet and gives a memorable performance as an overwhelmed young woman who finds herself unexpectedly touched by this strange creature who has taken a liking to her. Ed Lauter, Julius Harris, Jack O'Halloran, John Randolph, and especially Rene Auberjonois all bring great presence and character to their sup-

The cover of *Time* magazine's October 25, 1976, *King Kong* issue.

porting roles. Finally, Rick Baker overcomes layers of foam rubber and bearskin to imbue Kong with heart, soul, and a certain tragic majesty.

Ultimately, of course, a Kong film has to be judged by the quality of its special effects. While some of the material in the last third of the film was clearly rushed, the overall quality of the optical work is superb—the blue screen shots are some of the best ever done and the split-screen, matte painting, and miniature projection work are all excellent. As for Kong himself: The Big Kong was, of course, a misfire and, in spite of its publicity value, should have been cut from the film. On the other hand, the Styrofoam Kong is terrific. Although made from the same molds, it is much better looking than the Big Kong and is completely convincing in the film's closing shots. The Big Hands are also terrific. Limber, agile, and surprisingly graceful, they were as successful a mechanical construct as the Big Kong was not. The Kong suit is more problematic—it looks wonderful in some scenes, but misses the mark in others. Certainly, more could have been done to disguise the human performer inside, and the miniature scenes suffer from not having been filmed in slower motion, because Kong only occasionally appears to move with the weight and ponderousness that a creature of his alleged size should. The masks, on the other hand, are magnificent—Baker's design and execution are terrific, Rambaldi's cable work is tremendously effective, and the combination of the two gives Kong's face an astonishing range of expression that is directly responsible for much of the film's emotional impact. Because of the huge special effects revolution sparked by the release of *Star Wars* just six months after *Kong* opened, *Kong*'s significant effects achievements tend to be overlooked, but in many ways it is a landmark film—the last to employ the noncomputerized, nonmotion controlled optical work that had been practiced in Hollywood for generations, and the first to employ the sophisticated approach to creature design, makeup, and mechanical effects that endure to this day. Viewed from this perspective, Baker's and Rambaldi's work can be considered as groundbreaking and innovative in their field as O'Brien's was in his.

BOX OFFICE The film earned $6.9 million in its first three days of release. By its twelfth day of release, it had grossed $31.8 million ($19.8 million in the U.S. and Canada and $12 million in the rest of the world) and by March 1977, the film had earned $88 million. It ultimately grossed a bit more than $90 million and returned $36,915 in rentals to its producers. While its take did not beat *Jaws*, it was the third highest grossing movie of 1976 (behind *Rocky* and *A Star Is Born*) and was, by all measures, a terrific success.

AWARDS Although the Academy did not act on De Laurentiis's suggestion that Kong himself be nominated as Best Actor, the film did receive two Oscar nominations: Richard Kline for Best Cinematography and Jack Solomon, Harry W. Tetrick, William L. McCaughey, and Aaron Rochin for Best Sound Recording. Dale Hennesy and Mario Chiari were nominated for a British Academy of Film and Television Arts (BAFTA) award for Best Production Design/Art Direction and Jessica Lange won a Golden Globe for Best Acting Debut in a Motion Picture—Female.

The film also won an Academy Award for Special Achievement in Visual Effects, an award that generated a considerable degree of controversy. At the time, Visual Effects was not a regular Academy category. Instead, the Academy's Visual Effects Committee would review the year's releases and, if it found a film to be deserving, would recommend that the Academy's board of govenors give it an award. Although the board was not obligated to follow the committee's recommendation, it usually did. Dino De Laurentiis nominated Carlo Rambaldi, Glen Robinson, and Frank Van Der Veer for their work on the film. Because the producers were still emphasizing the Big Kong and downplaying the ape suit, Rick Baker was not included in the nomination, which upset Baker a great deal. However, when the Visual Effects Committee was evaluating *Kong*, it became curious about Baker's credit at the end of the film and called him in to find out exactly what he had done on the project. Following Baker's explanation, the committee decided not to recommend the film for an award, since the Big Kong that was the focus of the nomination had only been used in a few shots. A short time later, the Academy's board of governors decided to give the film an award anyway, which prompted famed animator and special effects artist Jim Danforth (*When Dinosaurs Ruled the Earth*) and several other members of the special effects branch to resign from the Academy in protest. Danforth wrote a letter to the Academy's Board of Governors in which he stated "Rick Baker was not in any way in my opinion to be considered a 'special visual effect.'" Danforth accused the board of caving in to pressure from De Laurentiis and Paramount, an accusation that board member Linwood Dunn (who had, of course, worked on the original *Kong*) denied: "All the committees…are affected by pressure, but we listen, discuss, and make our decisions based on the facts." Another board member conceded that De Laurentiis had sent a letter, but only to ask that the film be given "a fair shake." The board member went on to say: "I've seen *King Kong* and I thought the stuff was marvelous." Danforth proposed that Baker be given a special award for makeup instead, but the board declined. While Baker certainly did deserve an award for his work, there is no doubt that—whatever one's opinion of the Big Kong—the Big Hands, the masks, and Frank Van Der Veer's stellar optical work were worthy achievements that indeed merited an Oscar.

For those that worked on it, *King Kong* '76 was a memorable experience. The cast and crew were extremely proud of the high quality of the work they created in the face of such overwhelming pressure, as well as the fact that they had met what had seemed at the outset like an absolutely impossible deadline. Rene Auberjonois recalls it as being "A great experience." Richard Kline says: "I was proud to be a part of it." And Brian Frankish sums up the feelings of many when he said: [*King Kong*]…was a really good film to be on. It was thrilling. It was really something…"

LEGACY

For Dino De Laurentiis, John Guillermin, Carlo Rambaldi, and Barry Nolan, there would be another Kong adventure to come. As for the other members of the production: Lorenzo Semple, Jr., wrote the screenplays for the Dino De Laurentiis productions of *Hurricane* (1978) and *Flash Gordon* (1980), as well as the script for Sean Connery's James Bond comeback *Never Say Never Again* (1983) and John Guillermin's *Sheena* (1984). Rick Baker went on to become one of the most respected and in-demand creator of makeup and creature effects in the entertainment business, winning the first ever Academy Award for Makeup for his work in *An American Werewolf in London* (1981) and additional Oscars for *Harry and the Hendersons* (1988), *Ed Wood* (1994), *The Nutty Professor* (1996), *Men in Black* (1997), and *How the Grinch Stole Christmas* (2000). Richard Kline continued his career as a cinematographer, working on films such as *Who'll Stop the Rain* (1977), *Star Trek: The Motion Picture* (1979), and *Body Heat* (1981). He is also a highly respected director of television commercials. John Barry continues to compose scores for motion pictures and won additional Oscars for his work on *Out of Africa* (1985) and *Dances with Wolves* (1990). William Kronick went on to direct many more documentaries, including the award-winning *To the Ends of the Earth* (1983), as well as the second unit on Dino De Laurentiis's *Flash Gordon* (1980). He has recently published his first novel, *A Cry of Sirens*. Christian Ferry continues to produce films, mostly in France, and worked with John Guillermin again on *Sheena*. Fred Sidewater remained with Dino De Laurentiis until 1988, and is now an executive vice president of UFA International.

The members of Jack Grossberg's production team all continue to work as producers, production managers, and assistant directors. The expertise Terry Carr developed on *King Kong* made him a sought-after producer and consultant on special effects pictures such as *Predator 2* (1990). Brian Frankish executive produced *Field of Dreams* (1989). Scott Thaler's most recent project is *Sahara* (2005). David McGiffert went on to become one of the premier first assistant directors in the business, working on films such as *Tootsie* (1982), the *Back to the Future* trilogy, and *Batman Returns* (1992). Gary Martin is in charge of physical production at Columbia Studios, and Jeffrey Chernov is now a production executive with Spyglass Entertainment. As Chernov says, "A lot of great careers came out of that movie."

As for the cast, Jeff Bridges continued his impressive career as a leading man and character actor, appearing in more than sixty films, including *The Fabulous Baker Boys, Fearless, The Big Lebowski, The Fisher King,* and *Seabiscuit.* He was nominated for an Academy Award as Best Actor for his work in *Starman* (1984) and as Best Supporting Actor in *The Contender* (2000). Playing the camera-wielding Jack Prescott rekindled in Bridges a boyhood interest in photography. He began taking pictures of various aspects of the production, a practice he continued on his other films, and in 2005 published a collection of these on-set photos called *Pictures.* Charles Grodin continued to work as an actor, writer, and director until 1995, when he retired from acting and began hosting a current affairs show on the CNBC cable news network. He went on to do commentary for CBS, wrote several best-selling books, and currently tours the country as a public speaker. After a few dry years following *Kong,* Jessica Lange jump-started her acting career with a role as the Angel of

Death in *All That Jazz* (1979) and a powerful performance as a murderous adulteress in the explicit 1981 remake of *The Postman Always Rings Twice* opposite Jack Nicholson. She went on to become a well-respected film and stage actress and was nominated for an Academy Award for her work in *Frances* (1982), *Country* (1984), *Sweet Dreams* (1985), and *Music Box* (1989). She won a Best Supporting Actress Oscar for her role in *Tootsie* (1982) and a Best Actress Oscar for *Blue Sky* (1994). Rene Auberjonois starred in the long-running television series *Benson* and *Star Trek: Deep Space Nine* and is currently a series regular on *Boston Legal*. Ed Lauter appeared in films such as *Born on The Fourth of July* (1989), *The Rocketeer* (1991), and *Leaving Las Vegas* (1995) and continues to work as a character actor. Jack O'Halloran appeared in the films *March or Die* (1977), *Superman* (1978), and *Superman II* (1981) and is now a novelist living on the Isle of Man. John Lone starred in the Dino De Laurentiis production of *Year of the Dragon* (1985) and Bernardo

King Kong '76's Beauty and her hydraulically-operated Beast.

Bertolucci's *The Last Emperor* (1987). Will Shephard currently teaches acting at the California State University at Monterey Bay.

Sadly, many members of the production have passed away. Federico De Laurentiis died in a plane crash in Alaska in 1981, an event that reportedly devastated his father. Dale Hennesy passed away in 1981, Frank Van Der Veer and Charles Bludhorn in 1982, Mario Gallo in 1984, Mario Chiari in 1989, Harold Wellman and Jorge Moreno in 1992, Jack Grossberg in 2001, Glen Robinson, Jack Solomon, John Agar, and Dennis Fimple in 2002, John Randolph, Julius Harris, and Ralph E. Winters in 2004, and Terry Carr in 2005.

Shortly after the release of the film, Fred Sidewater leased the Big Kong to an amusement park in Buenos Aires for $100,000. After its year-long engagement was over, the Big Kong was returned to the United States and placed in storage. Stripped of its exterior detail, the robot ended its days on a junk pile on the back lot of the studio De Laurentiis built in Wilmington, North Carolina, along with the Big Hands and the man-sized costumes. The Styrofoam Kong met a similar fate. After a promotional visit to Paris, the picked-over model was returned to California and stored in a warehouse near the Los Angeles airport until summer 1977, when De Laurentiis made a deal with Rizzoli Books to feature it in a Kong exhibit at an amusement park in Rimini, Italy. At the end of the engagement, the Styrofoam Kong was apparently sold to filmmaker Marco Ferreri, who brought it back to New York to use in a scene in his film *Bye, Bye Monkey*. After that, it was apparently junked. In the late 1970s, MGM's Lot 2 was sold to a real estate developer, who leveled all of the sets and built a housing development on the site. Gary Martin reports that when one of the developer's bulldozers first broke ground, it ran smack into the concrete base of the Great Wall (which was left in place when the structure was demolished) and broke a blade. The MGM lot itself was sold to Columbia Pictures in the late 1980s. *King Kong*'s most significant location was destroyed on September 11, 2001, when

"When Kong dies...."

terrorist hijackers destroyed the twin towers of the World Trade Center, an event that has given the film's ending an unintended poignancy.

As for the film itself, *King Kong* '76 made its television debut in 1978 as a two–part presentation on NBC (which paid De Laurentiis $19.5 million for the rights to two showings over five years—at the time the highest amount any network had ever paid for a film). To pad the movie out to fill a four-hour time slot, many of the scenes cut from the original release were reinstated. NBC repeated the film in 1983 to take advantage of the publicity surrounding Jessica Lange's double Oscar nominations that year for *Tootsie* and *Frances*. Unfortunately, that was the end of its run. Unlike the original film, *Kong* '76 was never re-released to theaters or widely syndicated on television.

Despite the film's generally positive reception and worldwide success, its reputation has suffered tremendously in the years since it was released. This bad rap began with a comment Charles Bludhorn made to a group of Gulf & Western stockholders in the spring of 1977 stating that he was very disappointed the film had not grossed more than *Jaws*. The comment was widely reported, usually without the *Jaws* qualifier, which created the impression that Bludhorn had said that the film was a financial flop. For some reason, this idea took hold and, all evidence to the contrary, is now routinely reported as fact. The slide continued after the film had ended its theatrical run. At that point, the only people that still talked about it on a regular basis were disgruntled sci-fi fans, who continued to compare it negatively to the original film and who falsely asserted that the film was massacred by the critics when it first came out. As with the false impression of the film's financial performance, this idea, wrong as it is, has been repeated so often that it has become the accepted wisdom.

Happily, the film has begun to enjoy a bit of a renaissance in recent years. It is out on DVD, has been appearing more regularly on television, and has many Websites devoted to it. This newly heightened profile is well deserved because, while *King Kong* '76 can't match the thrills, surprise, and iconic impact of the original film, it does provide viewers with spectacle, excitement, humor, and enormous affection for a beloved character. It may not be a classic, but it is, as Richard Schickel described it in *Time*, "a confidently conceived, exuberantly executed work of popular movie art."

■ ■ ■

"YOU ARE DEALING WITH A LADY"

The Making of *King Kong Lives*

1976. King Kong makes his last stand atop the World Trade Center. As Jack Prescott and Dwan look on in horror, helicopters fire round after round into Kong's chest. Severely wounded, Kong topples from the top of the North Tower and crashes to the plaza below. As a crying Dwan approaches Kong, he turns to face her as his wounded heart begins to slow…FADE OUT

FADE IN: 1986. A comatose Kong is on life support in a research lab at the Atlantic Institute, an Ivy League university somewhere in Georgia. Dr. Amy Franklin is the head of a project to replace Kong's real heart—which was damaged beyond repair by the army's bullets ten years before—with a giant artificial heart. After years of work, the $7 million device is finally ready,

Release poster for *King Kong Lives*.

but Amy can't operate because Kong's blood volume has deteriorated during his long coma. He requires a blood transfusion, but there is no known species whose blood will transfuse with Kong's. "Only one thing can save Kong now," Amy tells Dr. Ingersoll, the president of the Institute, and Dr. Benson Hughes, the head of primate research. "What's that?" Hughes asks. "A miracle," Amy replies.

CUT TO: Borneo. Hank "Mitch" Mitchell, an unsuccessful diamond prospector, makes his way through the jungle. Deciding to stop for a nap, he lays down among some trees, only to find that his bed is actually the palm of a giant female gorilla. The massive ape chases Mitch through the foliage and is about to catch him when some local natives appear and fell the creature with a volley of anesthetic-tipped blow darts.

Learning of the female's existence, Hughes and Ingersoll contact Mitchell and ask that he allow them to transfuse the female's blood into Kong, but the prospector is only interested in selling his captive to the highest bidder. Worried that any sort of excitement or arousal will endanger Kong's recovery, Amy cautions Ingersoll and Hughes not to bring the female ape to the institute, but when Mitch threatens to sell the female to Harvard, Amy is overruled. Now dubbed Lady Kong, the female is brought to Georgia by cargo plane. Mitch, whose affection for his charge is growing, calms a distressed Lady Kong as the plane taxis to a stop on the airport runway. As Lady Kong is unloaded, Amy and Mitch meet for the first time. Amy makes it clear that she has little use for Mitch, whom she regards as nothing more than an opportunist out to make a buck.

Lady Kong is brought to the lab, where her blood is transfused with Kong's. After the procedure, Lady Kong is moved to a warehouse on the other side of the Atlantic Institute campus, where she will be housed until a permanent enclosure can be constructed. With Kong now strong enough to survive an operation, Amy begins the transplant. Using giant surgical instruments, Amy cuts open Kong's chest, removes his wounded heart and replaces it with the artificial one. The operation is a success and the campus erupts in celebration. Several nights later, Kong finally regains consciousness. Sensing Lady Kong, he becomes restless and tries to get up. This action places a strain on his new heart, so Amy knocks him out with a large dose of Thorazine. She reports to Ingersoll and Hughes and tells them that Lady Kong must be relocated or else Kong's recovery will be endangered. Ingersoll brings in a team to move Lady Kong. Despite Mitch and Amy's pleas, Ingersoll and the team treat Lady Kong roughly as they enclose her in a net. Lady Kong begins to cry out. Back in the lab, Kong reawakens to the sound of her cries. Breaking his bonds, he smashes out of the lab, heads for the warehouse, and crashes through the wall. As he does, he and Lady Kong lock eyes and fall instantly in love. Knocking aside all manner of men and machine, Kong frees Lady Kong from the net. When a SWAT team takes aim at Kong and attempts to shoot him, Mitch—who is now squarely on the side of the apes—foils them by ramming a truck into their vehicle. Kong picks Lady Kong up, carries her out of the warehouse, and off into the wilderness.

Assigned to capture the two giant apes, gung ho army Colonel R. G. Nevitt leads a battalion into the countryside. Meanwhile, Hank and Amy run a military roadblock and hike into the woods, hoping to find the apes before Nevitt does. Deep in the woods, Kong and Lady Kong take refuge in a spot called Honeymoon Ridge, where Kong courts Lady Kong and she tends to his wounds. Hank and Amy find the gorillas with the help of a device Amy has constructed that can monitor Kong's heartbeats and adjust the mechanical heart's rhythm by remote control. Watching from a distance as Kong and Lady Kong frolic, Mitch realizes that the two apes could survive quite nicely if a preserve could be set aside for them somewhere. Touched by Mitch's concern for the apes, Amy begins to warm to him and the two have a love scene of their own. The next morning, Kong goes off to forage for food. Meanwhile, Nevitt's team locates Lady Kong and sprays her with knockout gas. As soldiers start wrapping Lady Kong in a net, Kong returns. Nevitt's men hold Kong off with grenades and flamethrowers as a helicopter airlifts Lady Kong away into captivity. Nevitt then orders his men to capture Kong, but the furious gorilla escapes by climbing a nearby mountain. Reaching the top of the mountain as a storm approaches, Kong begins hurling boulders down on Nevitt and his men. Amy and Mitch are captured as Nevitt orders his men to kill Kong. Before that order can be carried out, Kong surprises everyone by jumping off the mountain and plunging down into a raging river below. Swept along in the current, Kong hits his head on a rock, goes under, and disappears. He is presumed dead.

Nine months later: Amy and Hughes visit Lady Kong, who is being held in a missile silo on an army base under Nevitt's command. They are shocked to

CAST AND CREW: *King Kong Lives*

King Kong: Peter Elliott; Lady Kong: George Yiasoumi; Hank Mitchell: Brian Kerwin; Amy Franklin: Linda Hamilton; Colonel Nevitt: John Ashton; Dr. Ingersoll: Peter Michael Goetz; Dr. Benson Hughes: Frank Maraden; Major Peete: Jimmie Ray Weeks; Mazlansky: Robin Cahall; Baby Kong: Benjamin Kechley; Surgeons: Nathaniel Christian, Mac Pirkle; Crew Chief: Marc Clement; TV Reporter: Rod Davis; Cell Guards: Duke Ernsberger, Mike Starr; Native Woman: Margaret Freeman; Hunters: Wallace Merck, Leon Rippy, Herschel Sparber, Dean Whitworth; Girlfriend: Mary Swafford; Boyfriend: Jimmy Wiggins; Stunt Coordinator: Bud Davis; Stunts: Kenny Bates, Monty Cox, Greg Gault, Joe Gilbride, Randy Hall, Chuck Hart, Bruce Moriarty, Beth Nufer, Don Pulford, Dar Robinson, Dennis Scott

Directed by: John Guillermin; Produced by: Martha Schumacher; Screen Story and Screenplay: Ronald Shusett and Steven Pressfield; Executive Producer: Ronald Shusett; Creatures created and constructed by: Carlo Rambaldi; Music Score Composed by: John Scott; Production Designer: Peter Murton; Director of photography: Alec Mills, B.S.C.; Miniature Unit Director/Cameraman: Robin Browne, B.S.C.; Visual Effects Supervisor: Barry Nolan; Film Editor: Malcolm Cooke; Sound Editor: Colin Miller; Unit Production Manager: Lucio Trentini; First Assistant Director: Brian Cook; Casting: Donna Isaacson and John Lyons; Casting Associate: Michelle Guillermin

Location Manager (Wilmington): Alexander Johnston; second unit Director: Bud Davis; Assistant Director (second unit): Bruce Moriarty; Camera Operator: Mike Brewster; Key Grip: "Chunky" Huse; Best Boy Rigger: Steve Graves; Grip: Jim Cody Harrington; Still Photographer: Richard Foreman Jr.; Editing Assistants: Kerry Kohler, Daniel Candib, Jonathan Chibnall; Set Decorator: Hugh Scaife; Set Dresser: Robert Beck; Set Designer: Jeff Ginn; Miniature Unit Supervisors: David Jones; David Kelsey; Model-makers: Rod Schumacher, David B. Sharp, Kevin Scott Mack, Gus Ramsden; Lead Man: John D. Kretschmer; Plaster Foreman: Brian Kontz; Make Up Artist: Jeff Goodwin; Special Effects Makeup: Dean Gates; Special Effects: Steve Lombardi, Robert Bass, Doug Beswick, Casey Cavanaugh, Frank Ceglia, Joe Digaetano, William D. Harrison, Larry Reid, Joe Lombardi; Released by: De Laurentiis Entertainment Group; Running time: 105 minutes.

find her depressed and crying. Amy begs Nevitt to let her attend to Lady Kong, but Nevitt refuses. Meanwhile, we learn that Kong has survived and is living in the middle of a vast swamp. He survives by snacking on alligators. Mitch returns from Borneo, where he has arranged for the Institute to buy ten thousand acres of land in order to construct a preserve for Lady Kong. When Amy tells him that Nevitt is again refusing to let them see Lady Kong, a furious Mitch tries to force his way onto the base, but is rebuffed by Nevitt's men. Mitch is devastated as he hears Lady Kong begin to moan from inside her silo. Deep in his swamp, Kong also hears Lady Kong's cries and decides to go after her. His emergence from the swamp startles the residents of a local fishing resort and news of Kong's return brings out hoards of redneck hunters determined to capture the giant gorilla. As Amy and Mitch search for Kong, an especially vile group of hunters trap him by dynamiting both walls of a local gorge. The resulting avalanche buries Kong in rubble up to his neck. The hunters torture Kong, who responds by erupting from the rock and striking back at his tormentors; tearing one in half and biting the head off another. The stress of this encounter causes Kong's artificial heart to malfunction. Mitch and Amy locate Kong as he flees the scene. Amy tries to fix Kong's heart, but before she can, the giant ape stomps on the monitor and destroys it. Horrified, Amy declares that Kong's heart won't last another day.

Kong makes his way across the countryside toward the missile base, causing the local residents to panic. Determined to stop him, Colonel Nevitt assembles his men along a gorge at the edge of the base. Kong distracts them by throwing dirt into the air and creating an enormous dust cloud. Unable to see, Nevitt and his men begin firing blindly. Kong eludes them and heads for the silo. Meanwhile, Amy and Mitch sneak into the silo, where they learn that Lady Kong is in the advanced stages of pregnancy. Determined to help her escape, they activate the silo elevator and begin rising toward the concrete doors at the top of the shaft as the overhead doors open. Trying to head off the escape, one of Nevitt's men starts to close the doors. Panicking, Lady Kong picks up Mitch and holds him close. Just when it looks like they're not going to make it, Kong appears at the top of the shaft and pulverizes the doors. Reaching down, he grabs Lady Kong—who is still holding Mitch—and pulls her up. The two giant apes escape as Nevitt and his men approach in the distance.

With Amy in hot pursuit, Kong and Lady Kong make their way to a nearby farm. As her labor begins, a stricken Lady Kong drops Mitch and crashes down into a barn. As she lies moaning in pain, Kong sees Nevitt and his men approaching. Amy and Mitch try to call Nevitt off, but the now-mad colonel is determined to kill the apes. When Nevitt's men begin firing, Kong attacks. As bullets tear into him, Kong destroys a variety of tanks, jeeps, and heavy weaponry and finally stops the attack. Kong then chases Nevitt into a nearby cemetery and pounds him into the ground with his fist. As his heart begins to give out, Kong staggers back to the barn in time to see Lady Kong give birth to a male baby. At Mitch's urging, Lady Kong shows Kong his son. At Amy's urging, Kong reaches for the infant. Kong wraps his hand protectively around the baby, smiles, and dies.

CUT TO: Borneo, several months later. Lady Kong and her son are living peacefully on the preserve Mitch obtained for them, with Lady Kong somberly mourning her lost mate. Young Kong tries to cheer her up. He is unsuccessful until he imitates his late father by pounding on his chest and roaring, which finally brings a smile to Lady Kong's face. The film ends with the young ape swinging happily off into the trees.

THE RETURN OF KONG

Dino De Laurentiis first began talking about doing a sequel to his *King Kong* in the run-up to that film's release in late 1976. Articles in several newspapers and magazines at the time reported that De Laurentiis, interested in utilizing the various incarnations of Kong still at his disposal, had allegedly hired Lorenzo Semple, Jr., and another writer, Joanna Crawford, to pen a script alternately identified as *King Kong II* or *King Kong in Africa*. In his January 4, 1977, column, Earl Wilson reported that De Laurentiis planned to begin production on the film later that year for a 1978 release. Semple confirms that a sequel was discussed, but says that there was never a script. Instead, he says that he and Crawford wrote just a few pages of notes outlining a Frankenstein-like story in which Kong was brought back to life by scientists and then came under the sway of some evil villains. De Laurentiis approached both Jeff Bridges and Charles Grodin about starring in the film, but Jessica Lange made it clear during the press junket for *King Kong* that she had no interest in appearing in a sequel. De Laurentiis joked that he would have Semple write in a scene in which Dwan, now a big star, would come to see the newly revived Kong, who would pick her up just like the old days and then promptly eat her. Despite all of these discussions and announcements, the proposed sequel never materialized. The reasons were never made public, but, De Laurentiis's disappointment over *King Kong*'s failure to beat *Jaws* at the box office was undoubtedly a factor. The fact that De Laurentiis needed Universal's permission to produce a sequel probably also played a part in the decision, since at the time De Laurentiis and Universal were involved in another tussle, this one over De Laurentiis's plans to produce a film about a killer whale called *Orca* (1977). Since Universal was complaining that De Laurentiis's film was a blatant rip-off of *Jaws*, it is safe to assume that the studio wasn't eager to cooperate with him on other projects at that time. Whatever the reason, the idea of doing a sequel fell by the wayside.

In the years that followed *Kong*, De Laurentiis continued producing movies at a prodigious rate, including two more giant monster movies (the aforementioned *Orca* and the 1977 Charles Bronson starrer *White Buffalo*), as well as *King of the Gypsies* (1977), *Hurricane* (1978), *Flash Gordon* (1980), *Ragtime* (1981), *Conan the Barbarian* (1982), *The Dead Zone* (1983), and *Dune* (1984). Some of these films were successful and some were not. Many were produced with his daughter Rafaella, who began working with De Laurentiis after Federico's death. Ever the entrepreneur, De Laurentiis also opened several branches of a combination gourmet restaurant/high-end grocery store called the DDL Foodshow in New York and Los Angeles. He also found a new love. Following Federico's death, De Laurentiis's marriage to Silvana Mangano ended and he began a relationship with Martha Schumacher. A former model from Ohio, Schumacher entered the administrative end of the film industry in the late 1970s as a production accountant. She worked on a series of films before getting a job in De Laurentiis's New York office during the production of *Ragtime*. After Schumacher and De Laurentiis became involved, she began working with him as the associate producer of *Firestarter* (1983) and the producer of *Cat's Eye* (1985), *Silver Bullet* (1985), *Raw Deal* (1986), and *Maximum Overdrive* (1986).

Firestarter was produced in Wilmington, North Carolina. Located on the Carolina coast, Wilmington turned out to be an ideal place for motion picture production. It was close to an airport and to a variety of scenic locations, including mountains, forests, and beaches. Making the area even more attractive was the fact that North Carolina is a right-to-work state, which meant that producers working there can hire non-union workers, allowing them to produce movies for much less than they would be able to in heavily unionized Hollywood or New York. When *Firestarter* wrapped, De Laurentiis bought a warehouse complex and, with Schumacher overseeing the project, transformed it into a full-scale production facility complete with soundstages, workshops, offices, and postproduction facilities.

Not long after the facility opened, De Laurentiis was offered the opportunity to acquire the distribution arm of Embassy Pictures, a mini studio that had recently been acquired by the Coca-Cola Company. Coca-Cola had bought Embassy in order to acquire its valuable film library, but, as it also owned Columbia Pictures, it had no need for another distribution unit. Getting films into theaters is one of the keys to success in the motion picture industry. Doing so requires significant financial and organizational resources beyond the means of most independent producers, who usually distribute their films through the major studios, to whom they pay a significant percentage of their returns as a fee. The idea of distributing his own films and turning his company into a full-fledged movie studio appealed to De Laurentiis, so he decided to go ahead with the deal. In October 1985, De Laurentiis officially purchased Embassy Pictures and renamed it the De Laurentiis Entertainment Group (DEG). He then sold his new company all of the assets of his old one, including the Wilmington facility and many of the projects he currently had in development, and immediately began making plans to produce an ambitious slate of twenty-two films. In order to raise the $500 million he needed to produce these pictures, De Laurentiis planned to take the company public and sell $300 million in stock. The rest of the money would be raised through a series of tax shelters. At a press conference announcing the formation of his new company, De Laurentiis announced that one of DEG's first productions would be a sequel to his *King Kong*.

DÉJÀ VU ALL OVER AGAIN   Since 1982, De Laurentiis had been working with screenwriter Ronald Shusett on a screen adaptation of Phillip K. Dick's short story "I Can Remember It for You Wholesale" called *Total Recall*. Shusett, who had worked both in the theater and in real estate, had been making a career for himself as a writer and producer since the early 1970s. He was best known for his work as cowriter (with Dan O'Bannon) and executive producer of *Alien* (1979). *Total Recall* was an expensive project, so Shusett and De Laurentiis spent several years trying to find a cofinancier. With the advent of DEG, De Laurentiis was able to fund the project on his own, so they then began searching for a top-level star or a director that De Laurentiis could present to his board as justification for the large budget. Shusett recalls that they were in the middle of this process when, one morning in 1985, De Laurentiis, quite out of the blue, said "I want to do a sequel to *King Kong* and I would like you to write it."

It's not clear why De Laurentiis suddenly became interested in reviving a project that had been dormant for so many years. Shusett recalls De Laurentiis mentioning in their initial conversation that he wanted to make use of the Kong constructs left over from the first film. When De Laurentiis sold the assets of his old company to DEG, the Big Kong and the various other incarnations of the great ape were included in the deal, so they were shipped from storage facilities in Los Angeles to the Wilmington lot. It's possible that the sight of all of this Kong paraphernalia inspired De Laurentiis to revive his "Big Monkey." Another possible factor was that Universal was planning to open a King Kong attraction at its Hollywood and Florida amusement parks in summer 1986. A new movie would be great promotion for the ride and, while Universal wasn't interested in spending the money to produce a movie itself, the company might have been more willing that it had in the past to allow De Laurentiis to do so. In addition, De Laurentiis's new company needed a reasonable flow of cash to keep his new stockholders happy and to pay for future production. The best way to do this was to make successful movies. Despite its reputation as a flop, *King Kong* '76 had been very successful, so a sequel may have seemed like a safe bet—if it did even half the business of what the first film had done, it would give the new company a sizeable financial boost. Finally, it may have been that De Laurentiis just liked the idea of doing another Kong movie. At the time of the film's release, Martha Schumacher was quoted as saying: "Dino really loves Kong and has been looking to resurrect him for ten years." Whatever the reason, De Laurentiis decided it was time to bring back the great ape.

But first, he had to figure out how to do it. De Laurentiis told Shusett that he had batted around sequel ideas with several writers over the years, but that they had always run into the same problem: How could they convince an audience that Kong survived or could be brought back to life after falling off the World Trade Center? No one had ever been able to figure out a believable solution. De Laurentiis wasn't interested in doing a *Son of Kong*–like sequel about another giant ape—he wanted to do another movie about Kong himself. De Laurentiis told Shusett that if he could figure out a way to revive Kong, then he (De Laurentiis) would pay him to write the script. Shusett knew there was no realistic way of reviving Kong, but felt he could come up with something that was reasonably believable within a fantasy context. In 1982, Dr. Robert Jarvik had made history with his creation of the first artificial heart. Shusett came up with the idea to give Kong his own artificial heart—albeit one as big as a Volkswagen. Shusett felt that this would bring Kong back in a way that most audiences would accept. He pitched the idea to De Laurentiis, who loved it and immediately commissioned a script. De Laurentiis's only proviso was that he wanted a good deal of the story to be set in the wilderness so that they could save money by shooting in the countryside around the Wilmington studio and by not having to build a lot of miniature city sets.

THE SCRIPT   At the time, Shusett had been working with another writer named Steven Pressfield (who would later write the novel *The Legend of Bagger Vance*) on several projects, including a rewrite of *Total Recall*, so the two of them got to work figuring out the rest of the story. As Lorenzo Semple, Jr., did before them, the duo had to first determine the tone of the piece. Shusett knew that the notion of giving Kong a giant artificial heart could not be played absolutely straight—it was, as Shusett describes it, "too bizarre and funny." So they decided to take a "semi-satirical" approach to the material. As inspiration, Shusett looked to, of all things, *Raiders of the Lost Ark*. As Shusett explains: "I read once that *Raiders*…was a spoof of an action movie, but at the same time, it was also an action movie. That was exactly what I was going for, but that's a hard pin to hit." Once Kong was revived, Shusett knew they would need a hook to hang the rest of the story on. Not wanting to be derivative of other Kong movies, they came up with the idea of giving the king a queen. As the story evolved, they decided to have a male hunter discover a female ape who is almost as tall as Kong. The hunter would bring the female, nicknamed Lady Kong, back to captivity to raise Kong's spirits, because, although Kong is alive, he has become depressed because he has been locked away in a research facility. In keeping with the spoofy tone, Shusett thought it would be funny to include a running gag in which Lady Kong would fall in love with the hunter in the same way that Kong fell in love with Ann/Dwan and that every chance she got Lady Kong would pick up the hunter and attempt to carry him off as Kong did with Fay Wray/Jessica Lange. "Essentially, the joke would be that, in this picture, Fay Wray is a man." Lady Kong's affection for the hunter would, of course, make Kong jealous. To provide an emotional kick at the end, they decided that Kong and Lady Kong would eventually mate and produce a male child and that Kong would die cradling his son, passing the torch and paving a way for yet another sequel.

It took Shusett and Pressfield a few weeks to write an outline, which they then fleshed out into a full-fledged screenplay. In the process, some of the initial ideas were reworked. Lady Kong's existence was explained with a line theorizing that Borneo and Kong's island had once been part of the same landmass. (This still doesn't explain the existence of giant apes in the first place. In the 1933 original and its sequel, Kong and the dinosaurs are holdovers from prehistory. Semple's script never explained where Kong came from. None of the films have ever addressed what happened to the rest of his kind.). Rather than have Lady Kong brought to civilization to cheer Kong up, she would instead be brought in to provide Kong with a blood transfusion to give him the strength to survive his surgery. The hunter—now named Hank Mitchell—was given a love interest of his own, a female vet named Amy Franklin who performs Kong's transplant. All four protagonists were given an antagonist—U.S. Army Colonel Nevitt, who is hell-bent on destroying both Kongs. The subplot in which Lady Kong falls in love with Hank was eliminated (although she was still allowed to pick him up once near the end) in order to clear the way for an unambiguous relationship with Kong, a relationship which allowed the writers to include a visual joke in which Kong picks Lady Kong up and carries her off in the same way that Rhett Butler carried off Scarlett O'Hara in *Gone With the Wind*. De Laurentiis liked the finished script—now called *King Kong Lives*—and approved it. Now he had to find a director. He surprised many people by turning to a man he had once swore he would never work with again.

John Guillermin—1986.

THE RETURN OF JOHN GUILLERMIN Following *King Kong*, John Guillermin went on to direct a well-received version of Agatha Christie's *Death on the Nile (1978)*—producers John Brabourne and Richard Goodwin's sequel to their 1974 production of *Murder on the Orient Express*—with Peter Ustinov (replacing Albert Finney) as the brilliant Belgian sleuth Hercule Poirot. Following this, Guillermin made *Mr. Patman* (1980), a dark drama filmed in Canada starring James Coburn. In 1984, he directed the ill-fated Tanya Roberts starrer *Sheena*, which was co-written by Semple. During the production of *Sheena*, Guillermin's son Michael was killed in a car accident. When he returned to work, Guillermin began developing a version of James Clavell's novel *Tai Pan* with Sean Connery as the proposed star, but the producer went bankrupt and sold the project to DEG. De Laurentiis soon decided that he didn't want to proceed with *Tai Pan* (although he did reactivate it a few years later with Daryl Duke as director and Bryan Brown as the star) and offered Guillermin *King Kong Lives* instead. Knowing how difficult their relationship was on the first film, one of De Laurentiis's associates asked him why he was willing to work with Guillermin again. Referring to a mellowed affect he detected in the director since the death of his son, De Laurentiis, who had, of course, lost his own son, replied that he felt Guillermin was a changed man and that he wanted to give him a chance.

PREPRODUCTION

Preproduction officially got underway in November 1985. With an entire studio to run, De Laurentiis didn't have the time to personally produce the film as he did in 1976, so the first order of business was to find a producer. Initial trade announcements named veteran production manager and line producer Fred Caruso, but ultimately Martha Schumacher was given the assignment. Ronald Shusett was given an executive producer credit (Shusett always negotiates for a producer credit on the films that he writes so that he can have input into the production). Lucio Trentini was named production manager, and Brian Cook signed on as the first assistant director.

In addition to Guillermin, De Laurentiis brought back two other key mem-

Carlo Rambaldi—1986.

bers of the *Kong '76* team: Carlo Rambaldi and Barry Nolan. In the years since *Kong*, Rambaldi had relocated from Italy to Northridge, California, and used his unique talents to create "Puck," the alien who waves to François Truffaut at the end of Steven Spielberg's *Close Encounters of the Third Kind* (1977) and to animate the head of H.R. Giger's vicious xenomorph in *Alien* (1979), for which he won a second Oscar. Rambaldi then spent several years designing and building ape masks and costumes for an aborted version of Robert Towne's Tarzan epic *Greystoke* (which was eventually produced in 1984 as *Greystoke: The Legend of Tarzan, Lord of the Apes* and featured apes created by Rick Baker). In 1982, Rambaldi created his most famous character for *E.T.: The Extraterrestrial* and won a third Oscar for his extraordinary work on that film. For *King Kong Lives*, Rambaldi would be responsible for realizing three different giant apes: King Kong, Lady Kong, and their son. To assist him, Rambaldi brought along his sons, Allesandro and Vittorio. After Frank Van Der Veer's passing, Barry Nolan had become the chief visual effects supervisor at Van Der Veer Photo Effects and had supervised the optical effects on De Laurentiis's productions of *Dune* (1984), *Cat's Eye* (1985), *Red Sonya* (1985), and *Maximum Overdrive* (1986).

Because DEG was a nonunion facility, creative personnel could not be brought in from Hollywood or New York, so the production instead imported many key people from England. To design the production, Guillermin brought in his friend Peter Murton, who was the production designer of films such as *The Man with the Golden Gun*, *Superman II*, and *Superman III* and who had designed *Death on the Nile* and *Sheena* for Guillermin. To photograph the film, Guillermin hired Peter MacDonald—a legendary British camera operator who had worked for years with the equally legendary cinematographer Geoffrey Unsworth on films such as *Cabaret* (1972), *A Bridge Too Far* (1977), and *Superman* (1978). After Unsworth died in 1978, MacDonald forged a new career for himself as a second unit director and cinematographer and had recently directed and photographed the spectacular helicopter chase battle for 1985's *Rambo: First Blood, Part II*. MacDonald recommended that noted second unit director/cinematographer Robin Browne be brought in to supervise the filming of the miniature Kong sequences. Browne had directed and photographed the extraordinary parachute sequence on *A Bridge Too Far* and the miniature dam sequences on *Force 10 from Navarone* (1978). The rest of the crew was hired locally. To prepare everyone for the task ahead, Guillermin screened the 1976 *King Kong* to show what had been done then and what he wanted done better this time.

BUDGET The film's initial budget was set at $22 million—a reasonable amount for a large scale, special effects filled picture at that time. Plans were made to film on location in Jamaica and Brazil (for the jungle and game preserve sequences), Tennessee (for the U.S. mountain scenes), and at the DEG Studios in Wilmington (for all of the interiors and miniatures).

CASTING Casting Directors Donna Isaacson and John Lyons, along with associate Michelle Guillermin (John's daughter), helped assemble the cast.

Linda Hamilton as Dr. Amy Franklin and
Brian Kerwin as Hank "Mitch" Mitchell.

Stage and television actor Brian Kerwin, who had just given an impressive performance as Sally Field's ne'er-do-well ex-husband in Martin Ritt's *Murphy's
Romance*, was cast as Hank Mitchell. Kerwin recalls how he got the role: "I was
just coming off *Murphy's Romance*, which was a pretty darned nice prestigious
film and this was the next one. The script came and I read it and I thought,
'This is pretty awful.' I didn't want to do it, but my agent told me I should consider it because they offered me a lot of money and it would be my first lead in
a movie. I said, 'Gosh, you're right. A feature film and I'm the lead.' It never
occurred to me that I wasn't the lead. The monkey was the lead. I was just set-
dressing." Money and billing aside, there was another reason Kerwin accepted
the part. "One of my whole motivations for doing the film was that I got to be
picked up. There are very few people in the world who get to be picked up by
King Kong." Linda Hamilton, fresh from her role as Arnold Schwarzenegger's
target, Sarah Connor, in James Cameron's *The Terminator* (1984) was cast as Dr.

Amy Franklin, and John Ashton, who had just appeared alongside Eddie Murphy in *Beverly Hills Cop*, was cast as Kong's nemesis, Colonel R. G. Nevitt. Veteran screen and television character actor Peter Michael Goetz, a member of the prestigious Guthrie Theater Company of Minneapolis, was cast as Atlantic Institute head Dr. Ingersoll and stage actor Frank Maraden was cast as Amy's superior and ally, Dr. Benson Hughes.

CREATING THE KONGS   To bring Kong and his family to life, the creative team decided to take the same basic approach they took in 1976: The apes would be portrayed primarily by actors wearing costumes and expressive masks, and optical effects would be used to marry footage of the miniature apes with full-scale humans when required. There would also be a full-scale mechanical hand (only one this time), as well as some sort of full-scale representation of Kong and Lady Kong (but not a giant robot). Although all of the

TOP: John Ashton as Colonel R. G. Nevitt.

RIGHT: Peter Elliott as King Kong.

George Yiasoumi as Lady Kong.

various mechanical incarnations of Kong from the 1976 film had survived, none of them were in particularly good shape. Some consideration was given to refurbishing them, but ultimately the decision was made to start over again from scratch. Rambaldi had three months to design and build various incarnations of three different Kongs. With Rick Baker and Glen Robinson out of the picture, this time Rambaldi was completely on his own.

THE KONG SUITS By the time *King Kong Lives* went into production, the suits and masks from *Kong* '76 has disintegrated (foam rubber does not have a long shelf life), so Rambaldi had to start from scratch on them as well. The suits were fabricated in the same manner as they had been in 1976: body molds were made of the performers, which were used to produce plaster statues. The ape's bodies were then modeled on the statues in clay. Casts were taken of the final shapes and used to produce foam rubber pieces, which were attached to a spandex body suit to create a padded muscle suit. A foam rubber chest was also cast and attached to the muscle suit. A fur suit was worn over the muscle suit and attached to the chest. Gloves and shoes simulating hands and feet completed the costume. This time around, Rambaldi incorporated many of the design suggestions he had rejected in 1976. To begin with, the muscle suit was made up of individually cast pieces to allow for more definition and flexibility. The chest was more rigid and better defined. Bearskins were abandoned and Kong's fur was instead made out of individual strands of Icelandic Yak hair attached to a piece of spandex. The strands were not individually hand-knotted onto the spandex in the Rick Baker style, but instead were loop-knotted together to form swatches; the swatches were then sewn onto the spandex in layers. Two kinds of arm extensions were built into the gloves: Mechanical extensions that utilized cables operated by ring pullees to move the hands were worn for long shots and finger extensions attached to thimbles were used for close-ups. For the scenes in which Kong walks on his knuckles, another set of gloves were used that contained fixed position supports for the actors to lean on. The actors used hand-grips to hold onto the supports, which were attached to flat rubber hands that were capable of making some minimal wrist movement. All of the different gloves joined the costume at the elbow rather than at the wrist.

THE KONG MASKS Rambaldi followed the same basic procedure to produce the masks that he and Baker used on the first De Laurentiis Kong: Cable-operated mechanics used to create expressions were attached to a "skull" (this

Benjamin Kechley as Baby Kong.

time made of hard plastic rather than fiberglass) that was then covered by foam latex "skin" and hair. Cables protruding from the back of the mask were connected to an electronic box on the actor's back. A set of detachable cables were plugged into the box, dressed out through the back of the costume, and connected to a master operating switch located approximately thirty feet away. The biggest difference between the Kong of 1976 and the Kong of 1986 was that the first Kong required three different heads to create his full range of expressions, whereas Rambaldi had created new mechanisms that allowed a single head to generate all of the new Kong's looks. One fully-articulated head each was created for King Kong and Lady Kong. In addition, another semi-articulated Kong mask, called the Roar Head, was created for use in medium shots. Mechanisms built into the Roar Head's jaw allowed the actor to open and close Kong's mouth. While the Roar Head did not have the full range of expression that the fully-articulated head did, it did permit the actor to give Kong some life without having to drag a bundle of cables around behind him. Finally, a nonarticulated stunt head was created for long shots and action scenes. Scleral contact lenses were again worn by the actors to create the apes' eyes. Several sets of lenses were originally created by a firm in North Carolina, but they were poorly made and uncomfortable to wear, so new sets were created in England and shipped over.

THE APES' APPEARANCE The creative team wanted the 1986 Kong to look as much like the 1976 Kong as possible, something that proved rather difficult to accomplish. Rambaldi sculpted Kong's face repeatedly, but couldn't get it to match. The situation was looking dire until Barry Nolan came across the molds used to create the '76 Kong on the backlot dump. Rambaldi was able to use these molds to produce skins that more closely matched the original Kong's face. The thicker foam rubber required to accommodate Kong '86's greater range of expression did alter his appearance to some degree, however, as did a different hairstyle and finish paint. Kong's head was also made smaller in relation to the rest of his body, while his shoulders were broadened. Kong '86's fur also remains a deep black throughout the film, as opposed to the brownish coloration that Kong '76 sported. Lady Kong was smaller than Kong, and the fur on her head and shoulders was auburn rather than black. She also sported a rather unseemly pair of breasts. A second chest was created for later scenes in which Lady Kong is pregnant. This chest had a rounded belly and fuller breasts.

Baby Kong was redesigned three times. The first version had the round, soft look of a typical infant gorilla, but this version was rejected as being too cute. A second version was also rejected, but not until after the birth scene had been shot (a small, mechanized version of this design can be seen briefly in the shot when Lady Kong first lifts the baby into view). The third and final version was shot on rebuilt sets after principal photography had officially wrapped. Based on the logic that Baby Kong would grow up to become the new King, he was designed to look more like his father than his mother. Baby Kong was also much smaller than the offspring of two creatures the size of Kong would realistically be. This was done because Guillermin wanted to create an emotional connection between father and son by having Kong wrap his hand protectively around his young son as he dies, something that wuld not have been possible if Baby Kong had been the proper size. A slightly more developed Baby Kong was created for the film's closing scene in which the young ape roars like his father and swings off through the trees.

THE BIG HAND #2 The Big Hand created for *King Kong Lives* used the same basic design as the Big Hands of *King Kong* '76, but this one was made of much lighter materials and so required less hydraulic pressure in the cylinders in order to move. As a result, the fingers were much more limber and moved much more quickly. The Big Hand was attached to a Chapman Super Titan Crane that lifted it up and down and could rotate it 120 degrees.

THE BIG KONG #2 Having learned their lesson back in 1976, the producers wisely decided that there would be no giant robot this time around. Instead, a mannequin—or rather a balloon—would be used to represent the prone Kong in several scenes. To create the new Big Kong, Rambaldi and production designer Peter Murton poured a latex mixture into the molds of the 1976 Big Kong (which, like the mask molds, were found on the backlot dump) to create rubber Kong pieces a quarter of an inch thick. These pieces were attached to one another and then pressurized. Wooden firmers were placed inside the body to allow actors to walk on it when necessary. The resulting 6,000-pound inflatable giant was then covered with strands of synthetic fur twelve inches long. For shots in which Kong would have to breathe, crew members were placed inside the chest to push it in and out on cue. Because some

RIGHT: The crew prepares the new Big Kong for its flight across Tennessee.

FACING PAGE: Brian Kerwin and Linda Hamilton have differing reactions to being trapped in Carlo Rambaldi's newer, lighter, Big Hand.

shots of a full-scale Lady Kong were also required, two different heads were created for the Big Kong—one for Kong and one for Lady Kong. Kong's head was equipped with cables that allowed his eyelids to flutter slightly during the scenes in which Kong is supposed to be comatose. A crew member was placed inside the head to open and close Kong's mouth when required. The two heads could also be mounted on wooden scaffolds to allow for the creation of some impressive over-the-shoulder shots. The two-heads-on-one-body approach required Lady Kong to sport some rather unusual coloration. Because the fur on the Big Kong's body was black, the fur on Lady Kong also had to be black, while the fur on her head was auburn—a two-toned look that is decidedly ungorilla-like. It also caused Lady Kong to lose her breasts in the full-scale long shots, an unusual occurrence indeed.

EXTRA LIMBS A separate pair of free-standing arms and legs were created for use on the full-scale sets.

KONG'S HEART The giant heart that is removed from Kong's chest is a large-scale version of a real ape's heart. It was made of foam rubber, with a latex skin.

KONG'S ARTIFICIAL HEART The giant artificial heart was a fantasy creation—it was not based on any real conception or design for an artificial heart, but was instead designed simply to look impressive. It was made from steel and fiberglass.

OPTICAL EFFECTS

King Kong Lives used the same optical effects techniques used on *King Kong* '76—blue screen, split screen, and matte painting. The only technique not reused was miniature rear-screen projection.

To incorporate the full-scale performers and the miniature performers into the same shot, the filmmakers originally wanted to use the Introvision process. First used on *Outland* (1981), Introvision was a sophisticated front-projection technique that not only projected an image behind the foreground characters, but also allowed projected portions of the plate in *front* of the foreground characters as well. In the final image, it appeared that the actors had actually been inserted *into* the background plate. This not only created a more realistic effect, but also allowed producers to save money on sets and locations because they could place actors into less expensive models or paintings instead. As with regular front projection, Introvision allowed for instant results without having to do optical composites. It was an ideal technique for a King Kong film and DEG was very interested in using it, but the licensing fee was too high, so the production decided to stick with blue screen instead.

Because there wasn't as much interplay between the giant apes and the humans as there was in *King Kong* '76, *King Kong Lives* had much less blue screen work than the previous picture. Whereas *Kong* '76 had approximately

300 blue screen shots, *King Kong Lives* had between 70 and 100. A new and improved blue screen was constructed for the film. At 90 x 40 ft., it was the biggest blue screen in the world at that time. The screen for *Kong* '76 was front-lit with twenty large arc lights, a time-consuming process that generated tremendous heat. The *Kong Lives* screen was translucent and lit from behind by a bank of twelve hundred florescent tubes. This provided more even illumination and was much cooler. The lights were automated and could be run from a single control box, which made it much easier and quicker to set up. In addition, the screen was so big that the actors and foreground sets could be moved far enough away to avoid blue spill and still have the blue screen completely fill the background. As on *Kong* '76, a video system was used to align the background and foreground elements of the blue screen shots. Rough versions of

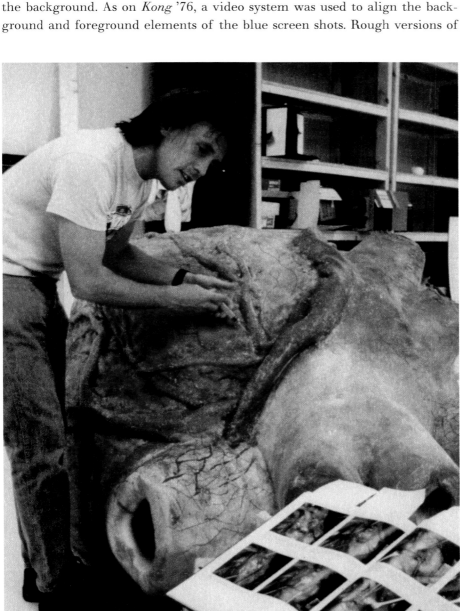

Kong's big heart, which Brian Kerwin considered making into a coffee table.

many of the effects shots were videotaped beforehand and used as a guide for the shooting of the background plates, which helped ensure an even better match when the foreground scenes were finally put on film. The same matting and color-separation techniques that were used to create the blue screen shots in *Kong '76* were employed again for *Kong Lives* and achieved the same generally seamless results. Once again, the alignments were generally excellent; there were no fringing, visible matte lines, chopping off, or halos.

The split-screen shots in *Kong Lives* employed a novel new technique devised by Barry Nolan that in its way was as groundbreaking as Frank Van Der Veer's soft-edge matte technique. Traditionally, the elements of a split screen shot were lined up along a hard edge to allow for a very precise, although sometimes noticeable join. For *Kong Lives*, Nolan figured out a way to create a soft-edge join between the elements along an irregular line. Part of this technique involved using Vaseline to slightly blur the edges of the joins. This made it much harder to spot the split and created a much more convincing final shot.

PRINCIPAL PHOTOGRAPHY

DEG released an official statement announcing the production on January 13, 1986. That statement indicated that shooting would begin at the end of March and continue for four months.

BUDGET PROBLEMS Unfortunately, the production ran into budget problems before filming even began. In spring 1986, DEG stock went on sale and quickly brought in the hoped for $300 million. However, the laws governing tax shelters were changed shortly thereafter, which prevented the company from raising the additional $200 million it needed to produce its current slate of pictures. To save money, some expensive films were postponed or sold off (including *Total Recall*, which was sold to Carolco, which eventually made the film in 1990), and the budgets on all current DEG productions were cut back. This development had a strong negative impact on *King Kong Lives*. The budgets for

The Big Kong on location in Tennessee.

all of the departments, including special effects, were trimmed considerably. To compensate, plans for shooting in Brazil and Jamaica were eliminated—the film would now be made completely in Tennessee and Wilmington. In addition, several elaborate sets were streamlined or dropped; a major stunt was cut from the sequence in which Mitch discovers Lady Kong (Mitch was originally supposed to fall of a cliff and be saved by Lady Kong), and some aerial work was trimmed from the sequence in which Mitch calms the panicky Lady Kong during their flight to America. Two costly sequences—one in which the dying Kong's body is loaded on to a truck and driven away from the World Trade Center at the beginning of the film and another in which Mitch and Amy engage in an aerial chase with army helicopters—were eliminated entirely.

TENNESSEE Production began in Tennessee on March 31, 1986. Locations in Pigeon Forge and Fall Creek Falls State Park were used to film scenes depicting the massing of Colonel Nevitt's forces and the attempts of Hank and Amy to find Kong and Lady Kong before Nevitt does. The soldiers in these scenes were played by members of the North Carolina National Guard. Eager to attract more motion picture production to his state by demonstrating a willingness to cooperate with filmmakers, North Carolina's governor loaned the production both men and equipment, including many of the helicopters used in these and subsequent sequences. The national guardsmen were dressed in rented U.S. Army uniforms.

Shooting continued with the sequence in which Nevitt's men capture Lady Kong and carry her off by helicopter. This sequence marked the first use of the Big Kong in the film, which had been fabricated in Wilmington and then shipped to Tennessee. The Big Kong was assembled (with the Lady Kong head) in an abandoned amusement park about ten miles away and then airlifted to the location by a very large helicopter. The sight of a giant gorilla soaring across the countryside stopped traffic on the highways for miles around. Getting Lady Kong airborne proved to be a difficult task. To begin with, the downdraft from helicopter blades pressed down on the giant carcass, creating an even stronger resistance for the chopper to overcome than just the drag from the ape's 6,000 pounds. Plus, in order for the helicopter to fit into the same frame as Lady Kong, the cable connecting the chopper to the net could only be about forty feet long, but the helicopter had trouble maintaining its altitude if it dipped below eighty feet, so it took some deft maneuvering to hoist Kong's queen aloft.

The Tennessee shoot concluded with the full-scale components of the sequence in which the army battles Kong before his seemingly fatal leap into the gorge. Since these scenes were supposed to occur in the middle of a storm, wind machines were brought to location and employed along with artificial boulders and flamethrowers. Rain and lightning were then superimposed over the entire sequence in postproduction. While the first unit was busy filming these scenes, Robin Browne and Barry Nolan shot background plates for the blue screen and split-screen portions of the sequences. Peter Murton also directed a few brief second unit scenes during this phase of production.

Just before the unit returned to Wilmington, Director of photography Peter

MacDonald took ill and was rushed to the hospital. MacDonald underwent an emergency appendectomy and then went home to England to convalesce. British cinematographer Alec Mills was hired to replace MacDonald. Mills was a veteran camera operator and cinematographer who had worked on many of the James Bond films, as well as the third Star Wars film *Return of the Jedi*. He had a positive experience working with John Guillermin as camera operator on *Death on the Nile*, which is why he suspects he was asked to take over on *King Kong Lives*. Although it can often be quite difficult to join a production already in progress, Mills recalls that the crewmembers were all very welcoming and capable, which helped make the transition a smooth one. Mills decided to shoot the film in a crisp, realistic fashion, with little or no diffusion or filtration.

DEG STUDIOS The biggest soundstage on the DEG lot was used to build the production's biggest set—the operating theater where the heart transplant scene takes place. The set itself was so big that it completely filled the 20,000-square-foot stage—in fact, the set's and the stage's walls were one in the same. Production designer Peter Murton created an impressive, multilevel set, complete with an overhead walkway and modular playing areas. The Big Kong—this time with his male head attached—was placed in the center of the set and surrounded by millions of dollars of expensive medical and computer equipment loaned to the production by local hospitals and manufacturers. The first new shot of the film (after the flashback opening)—an elaborate shot that begins on a close-up of Kong's heart pumps and then lifts and widens to reveal both Kong and the operating theater—was filmed on this set. This sort of intricate, ever-changing shot was a Guillermin specialty and is arguably the most impressive in the entire film.

The operating theater was also the setting for the heart transplant itself. For the scene, a giant surgical saw was constructed and used to cut open Kong's chest. A set of equally giant claws was used to reach into Kong's chest cavity and lift out the giant foam rubber heart. Thousands of gallons of fake Kong-blood were used during this sequence, the sight of which caused one of the extras on the set to pass out. The oversized artificial heart was then rolled in on a track and lowered into Kong. For the shot in which the heart is actually installed, the camera was placed within a mock-up of Kong's chest to capture a truly "inside" look. For most of the people involved, the transplant sequence was the most memorable in the entire film—both for the sheer size of Kong, the set, and the surgical implements, as well as for the audacity of the entire concept. Alec Mills reports that this was the most challenging scene to light, as well as the most enjoyable to work on. When the scene was over, Brian Kerwin asked the prop men if he could have Kong's heart. "I thought I could take it home and make a coffee table out of it or something. They said sure, but I couldn't justify the expense of shipping it back to LA." The operating theater set was later used to film the full-scale sections of the scene in which Kong escapes. For the shot in which the sedated Kong begins to wake up, the Big Hand was positioned behind the Big Kong and, on cue, raised up into the air behind an unsuspecting guard to create a totally convincing illusion.

The soundstage adjacent to the one that housed the operating theater was dressed to create the warehouse in which Lady Kong is kept during Kong's operation (once again, the walls of the stage were the walls of the set). For the later scenes in which Ingersoll's men attempt to move Lady Kong, the free-standing arms and legs were placed in the set to give the actors a full-scale portion of the great ape to interact with. For the scenes in which Kong bursts in and frees Lady Kong, stuntmen spent several days overturning vehicles and falling about in reaction to Kong's supposed attacks.

A full-scale section of the gorge was also constructed on one of the sound-stages to film portions of the scene in which the redneck hunters trap and torture Kong. For the over-Kong's-shoulder shot of the hunters firing their guns, the Big Kong Head was placed on wooden risers and covered with artificial boulders. The Big Hand was brought in for the scene in which Kong pulls the rocks out from under one of the fleeing hunters.

A section of the bluff overlooking Honeymoon Ridge was constructed on a soundstage to film the scene in which Mitch and Amy observe the courtship of Kong and Lady Kong, as well as the scene in which Mitch joins Amy in her sleeping bag. The interiors of the missile base were constructed on a sound-stage, including full-scale portions of the silo in which Lady Kong is kept. This set was used for the scene in which Mitch and Amy try to escape with Lady Kong. The Big Hand was brought in for the shot in which Brian Kerwin got to fulfill his Fay Wray fantasy by getting picked up by Lady Kong. One of the Big Feet was placed on a crane to film the scene in which Kong steps on Amy's heart monitor. Finally, a fake cemetery was constructed on the backlot to film the full-scale portions of the scene in which Kong pounds Colonel Nevitt into oblivion.

WILMINGTON, N.C. The Wilmington airport was used to film Lady Kong's arrival by cargo plane and for later scenes in which Mitch returns from Borneo after having secured the preserve. In the cargo plane scene, the Big Legs were placed inside the plane to make it look as if Lady Kong was inside.

A local military facility stood in for Colonel Nevitt's headquarters for the exterior portions of the missile base scenes and a nearby gorge served as the location for certain portions of the redneck hunter scenes. Scenes of the locals panicking when Kong emerges from the swamp were filmed at an area lake (the Big Legs were set up at the location for a shot in which a hotshot thrills his girlfriend by riding through Kong's legs).

The campus of the University of North Carolina at Wilmington was used to film exterior shots of the fictional Atlantic Institute campus, and local Wilmington locations were used for the full-scale portions of the brief vignettes depicting Kong stepping on a Lamborghini and interrupting a golf game as he makes his way across the countryside toward the missile base. Robin Browne's second unit spent several days filming the exteriors of the aerial sequence in which Amy and Mitch use an airplane to search for Kong.

THE ACTORS For the actors, *King Kong Lives* was not the most challenging of experiences. Quoted in a 1986 *Los Angeles Times* article on the production of the film, John Ashton summed up the feelings of most of the cast when he said, "This movie is about Kong, about special effects, and about jeeps being blown up. Acting is simply secondary in a picture like this." Far and away the biggest acting challenge was to find the correct tone. This was difficult because, while it was clear to Ronald Shusett and Steven Pressfield that they had written a spoof, apparently not everyone shared their vision. In an interview with *Cinefantastique* magazine at the time of the film's release, Martha Schumacher was quoted as saying: "[*King Kong Lives* is]...a serious picture. It's not a joke. It was taken very seriously and has the stamp of reality." Brian Kerwin confirms that this was the approach: "Nobody was trying to make a joke *at all ever* about it." This confusion over what note to hit made things very difficult for the actors and resulted in a film in which some of the performers underplay their parts, some are much too broad, and others are stuck uncomfortably in the middle.

As usual in a special effects picture, there was a lot of downtime for the actors. Kerwin found several enjoyable ways to fill the gaps. "I read every Travis McGee novel—there were twenty-two of them. I also watched every match of the U.S. open that year. And I did a play!" One of the actors in the cast...directed plays in the local theater. He said 'We're just finishing up *The Odd Couple* and we're gonna do *Cat On A Hot Tin Roof* next.' I said I'd always wanted to do *Cat*...and he said 'Why don't you do it?' I said I couldn't while I'm working on...(the movie)...and he said 'We'll work around it. It's community theater, where everybody has a day job.' So I did it. It ran for 12 performances. My Maggie was the worst actress I ever worked with in my life and my Big Daddy...was one of the best actors I ever worked with in my life. Later, I got a nasty letter from Equity saying I wasn't allowed to do it because it wasn't a union job."

PROS AND CONS *Kong Lives* was a much simpler, much less ambitious project than *Kong '76*. It was produced on a considerably more modest scale and the production team did not have to rush to meet a seemingly impossible deadline. As a result, *King Kong Lives* was a much easier film to work on.

As on the first film, most of the production team liked Dino De Laurentiis and enjoyed working for him. "[Dino's] very braggadocious and [can be] very stingy," Brian Kerwin says. "But the bottom line is, he's Dino De Laurentiis! He's a showman—like Barnum or something. I liked the guy." As before, people were impressed with De Laurentiis's dedication and commitment to the project. "Dino was very hands-on," said Peter Elliot, and Alec Mills recalls that "Dino wanted everything to be so correct!" The producer also received high marks. "I liked Martha Schumacher," Brian Kerwin recalls. "She was a neat lady." Other members of the production described Schumacher as being "charming," and "a joy to work with." Robin Brown recalls a time when the temperature on the uninsulated model stage reached 110 degrees. This was hard on the crew and even harder on the performers encased in the ape suits. Schumacher saw to it that an air-conditioning system was installed immediately, a gesture that was greatly appreciated by the sweltering workers and even more so by the hyper-perspiring Kongs.

The accommodations were also good. Most of the cast and crew stayed in and around Wilmington Beach, a seaside resort area. As Peter Elliot recalls: "I liked Wilmington…I had a really Norman Rockwell house right on the beach right down the road from Dino… and I loved the sun and the beach. I bought this old 1960 Pontiac convertible. I had a number plate on it—KONG! It [Wilmington] was a bit hicksville and the redneck element got a bit wearing— I actually saw Klu Klux Klan on the street corner and they weren't going to a fancy dress party—but for the most part [the residents] were incredibly friendly. I remember one night there I met someone at a bar who worked for the local Wilmington Shakespeare Company and he told me he did Shakespeare in his native accent!" Still, life in Wilmington did have a few drawbacks. "I got robbed," Brian Kerwin recalls. "Somebody snuck into my beachside apartment and stole money out of my pants while I was right there sleeping." Robberies aside, most of the cast and crew enjoyed their southern sojourn. An avid sailor, John Guillermin had a catamaran and would often go sailing during lunch breaks. Alec Mills speaks for many when he remembers, "…it was very enjoyable. The environment was good, the people were kind and the studio had a great canteen. What more could a man ask for?"

As pleasant as all of these things were, the production was far from trouble free. To begin with, North Carolina is an extremely hot and humid place in the summertime and temperatures often rose well above 100 degrees. In addition, there was also some tension between the British and American crews, although it never approached the level of animosity that existed between the Italians and Americans on *King Kong* '76. The biggest problem of course, was the ongoing impact of DEG's financial problems on the production. The studio has hoped that the cash flow from its initial releases would close its ever-widening funding gap. Unfortunately, all of films DEG released in the spring and summer of 1986 were failures. As money got tighter, *Kong Lives*'s budget continued to get cut back, negatively impacting all areas of the production. Some scenes were dropped, others were left uncompleted, and resources across the board became scarce.

WORKING WITH GUILLERMIN
As he had on several previous films, production designer Peter Murton enjoyed working with John Guillermin immensely: "We had a very acceptable, realistic relationship. He [John] is an incredibly practical director, as one knows from all the things he has done, but… I found him very, very friendly. [He was] very demanding…[and] if it didn't go quite right he'd have a tendency to raise his voice a little bit, but we had a good relationship. We used to spend our evenings playing billiards or table games together and it was a very relaxing kind of atmosphere. I found him a good person to work with." For other members of the production, however, Guillermin proved to be as a controversial figure on the set of this Kong as he had been on the last one.

By all reports, the mellower temperament De Laurentiis noticed in

John Guillermin supervises a set-up.

Guillermin held through preproduction, but once the cameras rolled, Guillermin's moods once again became mercurial. As one production associate who worked on both De Laurentiis *Kong*s recalls: "We had some good times, but then things started to unravel. Guillermin...was just as cantankerous as ever. He can be a nice man, but he could also really get nasty." Ronald Shusett had a few run-ins with his director: "[Guillermin is] strong-willed. A decent guy, but he is temperamental. I would give my input to him privately from time to time—never in front of the crew. In preproduction he accepted it, but during shooting he would get annoyed, so I stopped. I knew I shouldn't be around there. It wasn't beneficial." Guillermin was less explosive with the actors. As Brian Kerwin recalls: "[Guillermin] didn't yell and scream, but he was not a particularly fun director to work with. He wasn't mean or belligerent

John Ashton confronts the Big Hand.

or anything, but he was a very sour person." Guillermin's relationship with De Laurentiis was reportedly as strained on *King Kong Lives* as it was on *Kong '76* and his relationship with the crew was so bad at one point that some members of the art department allegedly made up hundreds of little rubber models of Guillermin and gave them out to everyone on the crew. From then on, whenever Guillermin would yell at them, crew members would hold the dolls behind their backs and twist them for the length of the rant. On one occasion, some special effects technicians put one of the Guillermin dolls in a radio-controlled truck and drove it off a cliff. On another occasion, someone attached a sign reading "Die Guillermin Die" to a doll and then hung it on the stage with a miniature noose. Guillermin reportedly saw this one and found it to be quite amusing.

As the production went on, Guillermin's behavior became more erratic. On several occasions he went home for lunch and didn't come back, leaving the crew to carry on without him. A few times he left and went sailing. One time, after a dustup with the production staff, he didn't come in at all for a few days. Most people understood that Guillermin was going through a hard time and were willing to excuse some of his more difficult behavior. "His son had died and this was him getting back on the horse," said one production associate. Even those who were not overly enamored of Guillermin respected his ability and sense of craftsmanship. "Guillermin was very professional at his job," the associate continues. "He knew what he wanted and made it pretty clear. John was a good director and he could be an okay guy, apart from his manners sometimes."

As the production continued, the budget difficulties, tonal problems, and personality issues began to take their toll. Many members of the cast and crew began to realize that the film wasn't working out. Brian Kerwin says: "We all knew it was going badly about halfway through. It was no big mystery. We all just sort of hung in there and half-heartedly tried to do our best. They [the producers] kept talking about how they were leaving the ending open with Baby Kong so they could do another one, which made me laugh because none of us wanted to be there on that one." Some bore the difficulties better than others. Linda Hamilton, for one, had a pretty rough time. "She was a nice lady," recalls Brian Kerwin. "I thoroughly enjoyed working with her—we were partners in our misery. But, especially when things started going bad, she didn't want to be there and she made that very clear. She was in a real bad mood the whole time."

WRAPPING UP A local farm was used to film the full-scale portions of Kong's final showdown with Colonel Nevitt and the sequence in which Lady Kong gives birth. A split-open replica of the barn was set up nearby and the Big Kong placed inside to film the exterior portions of Kong's death scene. While this scene was being filmed, Alec Mills received an offer to photograph the new James Bond film *The Living Daylights*. Having worked on the Bonds for so many years as a camera operator, this promotion was a dream come true and an opportunity Mills could not turn down. Robin Browne was asked to take over for Mills and so became the production's third official director of photography.

Following the barn sequence, the first unit moved to the New Hanover County Arboretum to film Mitch's introduction and the full-scale portions of the scene in which he is chased by Lady Kong. The Big Hand was brought to the location for use in these scenes. It was placed on the crane for the shot in which the hand erupts out of the jungle and sweeps into the air. It was then placed on a trolley and pushed along a track by some grips for the shots in which the hand chases a very perplexed Mitch.

The first unit wrapped at the end of July 1986, although some of the principal cast and crew returned in September for several additional weeks of blue screen work.

THE MINIATURE SCENES

Peter Elliott tosses boulders during the filming of Kong's confrontation with Colonel Nevitt.

CASTING THE KONGS Rick Baker did not reprise his role as Kong in *King Kong Lives*. De Laurentiis had approached him about doing a sequel prior to the release of *Kong '76*, but the offer came with a series of conditions that Baker refused to accept, including one that prevented him from building a gorilla suit for anyone (including himself) except De Laurentiis. Irritated by these demands, as well as by the dustup over the credits and the Academy Award nomination, Baker refused the offer, which put an end to the matter both then and a decade later. Instead, the role was given to Peter Elliott, an acrobat and veteran costume performer who appeared in the film *Quest for Fire* (1981) and did the primate choreography for *Greystoke: The Legend of Tarzan, Lord of the Apes* (1984).

Elliott was recommended for the job by Carlo Rambaldi. Elliott and Rambaldi had met when Rambaldi was working on the earlier, aborted version of *Greystoke* in the late 1970s. Elliott wore the costumes that Rambaldi designed for the project in a series of tests conducted over several years. When it came time to recast Kong, Rambaldi remembered Elliott and told Martha Schumacher about him. Schumacher gave Elliott a call at his home in London, and he soon found himself on a plane bound for Los Angeles. He read the script during the trip and remembers thinking "it was a jolly romp."

Elliott spent a week at Rambaldi's Northridge facility posing for life masks and body casts. He was then given the assignment of finding someone to play Lady Kong. When Elliott returned to England, he contacted George Yiasomi, an actor he had worked with on *Greystoke*. "I asked George if he wanted to come to America and be in a King Kong movie. He said 'Yeah, yeah!' Both men returned to Northridge a month later and did more work with Rambaldi, after which they flew to North Carolina to begin rehearsals. A third actor would later enter the mix when De Laurentiis decided that Elliott's eyes weren't big enough and as Elliott recalls, "Some Greek guy who had eyes like Marty Feldman" was flown in from London to shoot close-ups of Kong's eyes.

STORYBOARDS As he did on *Kong '76*, Guillermin storyboarded all of

K-27: FULL SHOT KONG (ON MIN. SET AGAINST REAL SKY) as he
       appears over brow of hill and stands looking down on
       the scene below him and rears with anger. MAN IN SUIT
       ON MIN. SET.

K-53: C.S. KONG. He is trapped! He bellows into the howling gate.
       (MAN IN SUIT ON MIN. SET AGAINST REAL SKY) STUDIO LOT.

K-8:   KONG & LADY KONG in their refuge. They have a domestic
       scene. DAY. MEN IN SUITS ON MINIATURE SET.

BARN-21: SIDE ANGLE KONG as he comes forward, torn by the deadly fire reaching
          down and up-ending a tank which bursts into flame. Vehicles turn away,
          MEN flee. MAN IN SUIT & MIN. TANK AGAINST BLUE (PLATE OF ARMY ON
          LOCATION).

A selection of storyboards for
King Kong Lives.

the Kong scenes during preproduction (many of the storyboards were drawn by Peter Murton's son, Simon). Guillermin then reviewed the boards with Murton, Rambaldi, and Nolan to determine what sets, optical processes, and Kong pieces would be required to realize them.

MINIATURE SETS In addition to all of the full-scale sets, production designer Peter Murton was required to create forty miniature sets for *King Kong Lives*. For Murton, this was the most challenging part of his assignment, because while the veteran production designer had certainly designed miniature sets before, he never had to do so many at the same time. The lack of an experienced team of model-makers made the assignment even more challenging—although Murton had brought in key members of his team from England, the bulk of the crew was made up of Wilmington locals who had never done this sort of work before. As on *Kong '76*, all of the miniature sets were built on platforms raised about five feet off the floor to allow the cameras to shoot up at the Kongs.

One of the main differences between *Kong '76* and *Kong Lives* was that the majority of the miniature sets in the latter were designed to mimic wilderness settings (based on the terrain in which the full-scale wilderness scenes were filmed) as opposed to cityscapes. This was a major challenge for the set builders, because it is extremely difficult to convincingly recreate natural objects (such as rocks and trees) using artificial materials, especially in small scale. In order to make the faux environments look as believable as possible, the production design team tried to incorporate as many real plants and other natural materials as they could into the sets in order to enhance their overall reality. In another change from convention, some of the miniature sets in *Kong Lives* were constructed outdoors (most miniatures—even those representing exteriors—are usually filmed indoors in order to give the cinematographer more control over the lighting). Most of these outdoor sets were used for scenes involving special effects, such as fire or explosions, that would have been too dangerous or difficult to create on an enclosed stage.

To determine the scale of the miniature sets, it was first necessary to determine how big Kong was supposed to be. The 1976 Kong was forty-two-feet tall in the island scenes and fifty-five-feet tall in the New York scenes. For *Kong Lives*, De Laurentiis, Schumacher, Guillermin, Rambaldi, and Murton jointly decided that Kong would be depicted as being sixty-feet tall. Because Peter Elliott was 5-feet tall (in a bent-over position) when he played Kong, the sets were built on a 1-to-12 scale (although this was adjusted when necessary to make Kong look more impressive). Modelmaker David Jones supervised the construction of the miniature buildings and landscapes, and David Kelsey supervised the construction of the "action" miniatures—those requiring electricity or motors or that were radio-controlled.

PHOTOGRAPHY One of Robin Browne's biggest challenges on *King Kong Lives* was to match the lighting on the miniature sets to the work Alec Mills did on the full-scale sets, which required the same sort of scaling down of

The miniature unit assembles some of the thousands of trees used in *King Kong Lives*.

lights and lenses that Richard Kline and Harold Wellman had to do on the previous picture.

Many of the miniature scenes in *Kong Lives* took place during the day. This was a big challenge for Robin Browne because the extremely bright lighting required to reproduce daylight tended to emphasize the artificial look of the miniature "outdoor" sets. To meet the challenge, Browne attempted to create an overcast look in many of the scenes, which produced some mild diffusion that softened the lighting and took the edge off the sets.

Browne also found that it was hard to light the Kongs because their black fur absorbed the light, causing the apes to appear on film as nothing more than black blobs. To bring out the detail in the ape suits, Browne had to use an intensive amount of light. While this allowed him to photograph the Kongs properly; it also overexposed the rest of the shots. To compensate, all of the miniature sets were painted darker than they were supposed to appear, so that they would look normal when overexposed. Even with this compensation, the contrast between the apes and the sets was sometimes so extreme that it had to be further adjusted by the optical effects team in postproduction. Another big challenge in photographing the Kongs was to find angles that hid the cables that emerged from the back of the apes' heads. As this was an especially big issue in full body views, the stunt and roar heads were usually used to film the long shots, which eliminated the problem.

Just like he did on *Kong '76*, John Guillermin wanted the Kongs filmed at twenty-four frames per second. As before, he was reluctant to overcrank because he didn't want the Kongs to look too lumbering or for their eye movements to appear too slow. In order to create a proper sense of size and weight, Browne and Elliott tried to create the same ponderous effect provided by slow motion through movement alone. As Elliott recalls: "[To give] weight to the walk, we added a hesitation and a sustain. We [also] glued foam to my feet and I [stepped] in…Fuller's earth so that I would create a dust cloud with every step."

DIRECTION As on *Kong '76*, the initial plan was for the main and miniature units to shoot simultaneously, with each unit being helmed by a different director. This time, however, the plan was actually implemented. Guillermin directed the main unit and left Robin Browne in charge of the miniatures. To ensure that the work of both units meshed into a cohesive whole, the two men reviewed the script and storyboards before shooting began, with Guillermin explaining in great detail what he wanted from each shot (Browne reports that Guillermin was most concerned with the quality of Kong's movements and in creating a sense of realism). During the shoot, both men reviewed each day's rushes so that Guillermin could give his input. Guillermin also made himself available for consultation during the day and would often drop by the model stage to see how things were going. Guillermin did direct a few of the miniature scenes himself—usually those involving key story points or those in which he wanted to match something he did in the full-scale scenes—including the scene in which Kong rescues Lady Kong from the warehouse, as well as the birth of Baby Kong and the death of King Kong. Most of the miniature-unit blue screen shots were filmed at the end of the schedule. Guillermin directed most of these shots as well.

In addition to Guillermin, Browne also worked closely with the art department and the modelmakers, whom he describes as having been "very supportive." He also collaborated with Carlo Rambaldi and his team of operators to create Kong's facial expressions. As on *Kong '76*, it took a lot of time and a great deal of experimentation to get the Kong masks to make the correct expressions. Finally, Browne and Elliott worked together to devise the movements for all the Kongs.

PERFORMANCE Like Rick Baker, Elliott wanted to play Kong in a realistic manner and have him walk on all fours like an actual gorilla. "I know I wanted to go more gorilla-like, particularly with some of the physical moves. When he was running and charging, I wanted to do more quadruped." This concept was discussed and approved before shooting began, but once the cameras started rolling, De Laurentiis and Guillermin decided that they wanted Kong to walk upright as he had in *Kong '76*. At this point, Elliott began to understand the challenges Baker faced a decade before. "I had liked Rick's performance [as Kong], but thought it was maybe a bit melodramatic. But when I came to do it, [I realized] Rick was right in the way [he did it] because that is what Dino wanted. [De Laurentiis would say,] 'He is Kong up there! I want it just the same as the first one!'" There was a bit of a creative tug-of-war between the two approaches before it was finally decided that there would be two separate behavior concepts for the Kongs. When they were in the wilderness, the pair would act more like real apes, but when they were around people, they would act in a more human-like fashion.

In addition to working on Kong's behavior and movements, Elliott also worked on the great ape's character, which he modeled on an unexpected source. "I played King Kong as though he had a real personality, and I prepared myself as an actor by basing it on James Dean. As a method actor, I thought that [what happened to] King Kong was incredibly unfair—he didn't ask to be taken out of his natural habitat and stuck in New York! It's not his fault! Basically, he was a giant, misunderstood gorilla."

As did Rick Baker before them, Elliott and Yiasoumi had to synchronize their body movements with the facial expressions on the masks. In order to do this, a television monitor was placed in front of the two men so that they could see the expressions on the masks as they were acting. For both performers, the hardest part of the job was disguising their human proportions—most specifically the length of their legs. For Elliott, this meant he occasionally had to compromise his agreement to have Kong walk upright. "I just found that if you just keep walking and walking, it really starts to hit you [that it is] a man in a suit, so anytime he ran I tried to drop to quadruped. I just didn't want to walk long, long, distances because it all starts to look comical."

Elliott and Robin Browne got on very well. Says Elliott: "Robin is a sweetheart. He's so patient...[and]...meticulous. He was [also] calm. John was quite passionate and Robin was more methodical—chalk and cheese! He gave...[us]...a lot more room and he was a lot easier to work with!" Browne was equally complimentary about his star. "[Peter]...had a remarkable ability to do an ape. It was amazing how he could tolerate the...difficult conditions on stage—the heat especially. Peter's input was invaluable—more so than even John Guillermin's. Five stars. Five thumbs up. Excellent man." Elliott also had a good relationship with John Guillermin, although it did get off to a rocky start. "We nearly came to blows once. We were working on puppeteering Baby Kong's face and...John was screaming and shouting 'Make him cry!' Of course, when you do any puppeteering you need a way of syncing it all together; you can't just say 'Cry!' John was screaming and I was talking to George...and I said something to him under my breath and he [John] saw me and he went 'What did you say?' I said, 'This is not how you do it!' and he screamed 'Do you think you could do it better?' and I said 'Yes. I think I could!' He said, 'Go on then!' so I...[had each puppeteer] make three different faces that when connected would make the crying. We'd been there two hours and it was terrible and then about ten minutes later it looked fantastic! John (then) said to me, 'You—come outside!' When we got outside he said, 'Well, well done! Nobody has talked to me like that in twenty-five years in the business. All right, are we friends then?' After that we got on fantastically."

WEAR AND TEAR   The miniature shoot lasted for six months. The days were long—work began at 7 A.M. and often continued until 8 P.M. Six-day workweeks were common. Peter Elliott describes a typical day: "Usually it was arrive, line up the first shot, and (rehearse) the actions, which is probably the only time [I was] out of the [Kong] suit for the whole day. [After rehearsal] I'd get changed and then pretty much we were full on shot after shot. There wasn't much sitting around. Once we were in the suits we'd rehearse once more—we tried to limit the length of time wearing the suit to the time we shot and we never stuck to it! Lining up the shots with the costumes on was a bit frustrating—some of the shots took a hell of a long time to set up. Once we got the shot lined up, I would go and put in lenses while [Rambaldi's crew would] lay the cables out and get the heads ready—there'd always be an issue of where you'd hide the cable—and then you'd get the head on and try and get the shot."

Yiasoumi and Elliott experienced most of the same hardships that Rick Baker and Will Shephard did—the suits caused the actors to become very hot, making them to lose approximately seven pounds in water weight a day; and the contact lenses were uncomfortable to wear and hard to see through. Yiasoumi and Elliott were able to remove their suits more often than Baker and Shephard. This was because their contact lenses had to be removed every three hours, which required that the suit (or at least the mask) come off as well.

Elliott found that being the "star" of the miniature unit was not always an enviable thing. "If you have a unit dedicated to you all the way through the movie, it creates immense pressure because if you stop, the whole unit has to stop! They wanted to keep you filming all the time—all day every day. I had PA (production assistant), this young kid, a lovely guy. They had him stand at the gate in the morning waiting for me to come in [to alert them so we could get started]. [From there] it was [always] a dash from one shot to another—you would finish one shot and they would want to line up another. I remember one day shooting I'd been on set for eight hours. I was completely exhausted. I said, 'I *really* have to have a break,' so I went to my trailer—called Club Kong, as I seem to remember—and I'd been there about five minutes, had gotten the suit off, and they came and said, 'Can you come out for a quick rehearsal?' I was like 'What? What do you want me in?' and they said whatever I was most comfortable in, so I came out stark naked! It didn't go down very well, especially as there were some women on the set. They were like, 'Right, take a break!' But, in general, it was a pretty continuous moving unit, most days were full on shooting. The only time I had time off was when Robin was occasionally used on the main unit for night shoots. It was a highly pressured job—full on, all day, every day."

OPTICAL EFFECTS   Once the miniature footage was complete, it was sent to Van Der Veer Photo Effects in Burbank. Most of the optical effects crew had worked on the first De Laurentiis *Kong,* so they knew what the problems were with all of the various processes they were using, and knew how to successfully deal with them. The schedule was reasonable and there were no impossible deadlines. Compared to *Kong '76,* the optical effects work on *Kong Lives* was, in the words of Barry Nolan, "a piece of cake."

A SPECIAL EFFECTS OVERVIEW

With the exception of a brief cutaway of Elliott as Kong filmed on the miniature operating-theater set, the film's opening sequence features the Big Kong (wearing the Kong head) on the full-scale operating-theater set.

THE CAPTURE OF LADY KONG   The scene in which Lady Kong is captured in Borneo was a mixture of full-scale work involving the following: Brian Kerwin and the Big Hand filmed at the Wilmington Arboretum; some miniature shots filmed at the arboretum featuring Yiasoumi as Lady Kong; and shots filmed with Yiasoumi on a miniature set back at DEG.

For the shot in which Lady Kong falls over after being knocked out by the natives, Brian Kerwin and the natives on a full-scale set were split screened into a shot of Yiasoumi falling forward on a miniature set. The split moved along with the cloud of dust that shoots out from under Lady Kong as she hits the ground via a hand-drawn, frame-by-frame matte.

THE AIRPORT   Lady Kong's arrival in Georgia via cargo plane was a mixture of full-scale shots using the Big Legs filmed at the Wilmington airport and miniature shots of Yiasoumi on a miniature set.

THE TRANSFUSION AND TRANSPLANT SCENES   The first blue screen shot in the film is the one of Yiasoumi as Lady Kong in the operating theater during the transfusion scene. To create this shot, Lady Kong was photographed against the blue screen and then composited with a plate of the medical technicians filmed on the full-scale set. A similar shot was done of Kong and used in the transplant scene.

There are also several blue screen shots of Linda Hamilton and other principal cast members looking at Kong through the windows of the operating-theater control room. To create these shots, the actors were filmed in front of a window set backed with blue and composited with shots of Elliott-as-Kong filmed on the miniature operating-theater set. The miniature operating theater was actually quite large—approximately 30 ft. x 20 ft. x 10 ft.

The blue screen process was also used for a few shots in which Kong interacts with the nervous night watchman at the beginning of the sequence in which Kong escapes from the operating theater. Elliott did all of his own stunt work in this scene, including Kong's climb up to the rafters and his eruption through the skylight. In fact, with only one exception, he did all of his own stunts throughout the filming. "I was an acrobat from an early age and I have always done all my own stunts. Once or twice I have tried to use stuntmen and they've all ended up looking like stuntmen. I've spent so many years doing what I do that while I'm in a middle of a stunt, I don't lose the character. For insurance reasons, I have a stuntman overseeing everything I do, but I [do the actual stunt]."

KONG RESCUES LADY KONG For the opening shots of this sequence, Lady Kong was placed into the full-scale warehouse via a split screen. The rest of the Kong portions of the scene were filmed on a miniature warehouse set that was 27 ft. x 17 ft. x 8 ft. The full-scale portions of the scene were filmed on a full-scale set that, like the full-scale operating-theater set, incorporated the actual walls of the soundstage. The low-angle views of the bulldozers closing in on Lady Kong were blue screen shots, as was a shot of Hamilton, Goetz, and Maraden looking up at Lady Kong as she struggles in the net.

Kong enters the scene in a highly effective long shot in which he smashes through the warehouse wall (which was made of sheet lead and wax). This shot was then composited with a blue screen shot of actors fleeing on foot and in a truck.

The blue screen process was also used to merge a foreground shot of several frightened warehouse workers running toward the camera with a background plate of Kong's foot as it steps on a miniature truck. As soon as Kong is done stomping, the camera immediately tilts up to show him freeing Lady Kong. The design and compositing in the shot are seamless and create the impression that all of this action is happening in one continuous shot filmed in a single location. This not only enhances the scene's realism, but also gives it a much greater sense of urgency and movement than would have been possible with a more usual, static optical shot.

THE COURTSHIP SCENE Robin Browne says that the courtship between Kong and Lady Kong on Honeymoon Ridge was the most difficult miniature scene in the film to pull off, because both the concept and the action were so unbelievable. Elliott choreographed the interplay between Kong and Lady Kong. Because the scene was so over the top, Elliott based the apes' actions on the behavior of real apes, but performed it with George Yiasoumi in a decidedly tongue-in-cheek manner.

THE RECAPTURE OF LADY KONG For the shot of Lady Kong grooming herself which opens this sequence, a view of Yiasoumi as Lady Kong filmed on the miniature Honeymoon Ridge set was split-screened into a full-scale shot filmed on location in Tennessee.

The grotto in which Kong is seen foraging as one of Nevitt's helicopters appears overhead was the first outdoor miniature set in the film. The helicopter was a large radio-controlled model, the first of several used in the sequence. Apparently, the filmmakers had fewer qualms about using such devices than their 1976 counterparts did, although that didn't mean that the performers felt any more comfortable about it. As Elliott recalls: "I do remember one flying around my head and thinking, 'That was quite dangerous.'"

The long shot of Lady Kong watching as Nevitt's forces approach her was a continuation of the split-screen shot that opens the scene. Yiasoumi performed the initial shots of Lady Kong being overcome by the knockout gas on a miniature set, before being replaced by the female-headed Big Kong for shots filmed on location in Tennessee.

The shot of Kong looming up on a ridge behind Nevitt's men as they wrap Lady Kong in a net was a sophisticated split-screen shot (the split ran along the tree line). Meanwhile, the contrast between the bright blue sky and the dark rope that dangles down from above in the foreground of the shot was so great that the rope ended up becoming its own holdout matte. When the optical effects team was compositing both sides of the split, they used the faux matte to lay the rope across the split. As a result, the rope actually appears to be dangling down across the miniature portion of the shot, greatly enhancing the scene's realism and its effectiveness.

The ridge that Kong perches on as Nevitt's men use hand grenades and flamethrowers to hold the beast back was the second of the outdoor miniature sets used in the film. The explosions and flames in this scene were all real. The use of real daylight to photograph these shots give them a surprisingly realistic look, but unfortunately fails to create any true sense of scale; as good as the shots look, Kong never appears to be anything other than man-sized.

The sequence in which Kong scales the mountain to escape from Nevitt's men contains the highest concentration of blue screen shots in the film. The most complex of these is a multi-element shot of Colonel Nevitt watching Kong climb the mountain as the storm begins to whip up. To create the shot, Elliott was filmed climbing up a blue-covered riser (a foreground miniature of the mountain was placed in front of the camera to hide the riser) and then composited with a panoramic background shot of the countryside. The final composite was then used as a plate for a blue screen shot of John Ashton looking on through binoculars.

Kong atop the miniature mountaintop.

The first matte painting in *King Kong Lives* appeared in the shot of Kong facing off against Nevitt's men as rain begins to fall. Elliott-as-Kong was filmed in front of a blue screen posing atop a miniature mountain and composited with a matte painting of the gorge. A full-scale shot of the army filmed on location was then split-screened into the matte painting. To complete the shot, rainfall was superimposed over the entire image. As ambitious as this shot was, all of the various elements failed to gel into a convincing whole.

THE CLIFF JUMP   Kong's leap off the cliff into the river to escape Nevitt was done by a stuntman who plunged down the face of a 175-foot-tall artificial cliff constructed on the DEG backlot. Robin Browne's unit did not shoot this scene. Instead a special stunt unit was called in from Los Angeles. The stuntman was attached to a wire connected to a decelerator that gradually slowed the speed of his fall and brought him to a gentle stop as he reached the ground. Although a great deal of money and effort went into it, the finished shot ultimately wasn't convincing. Robin Browne felt that it just didn't look realistic enough. Dino De Laurentiis was reportedly very disappointed in the final result.

Elliott performed the final part of the sequence, in which Kong plunges into the raging river. The river set was constructed in a tank on the backlot that was equipped with a series of outboard motors used to churn the water at appropriate moments. To create the storm, water was piped in for rain and a rigger fan was set up to provide an 80 mph wind. Dressed as Kong, Elliott had to leap from a cherry picker suspended approximately thirty feet above the tank. An air hose was rigged to go off when he hit the water in order to provide a bigger splash. Seeing all of this equipment set up to create movie magic thrilled Elliott. "I thought 'My god, this is the movie business!'" Once he hit the water, Elliott was required to disappear beneath the surface, come back up, get swept down the river, and then go under again.

Getting that shot proved to be a perilous enterprise. Recalls Elliott: "I nearly got killed doing that shot. At first the costume wouldn't sink (because the foam undersuit was so buoyant) and then all of a sudden it soaked up all the water and under I went! I couldn't get back up again, couldn't breath under the water. On the second or third take they wanted me to stay under water as long as I possibly could so they could…show the empty river. I made it to the bottom of the tank…and then…I suddenly got caught in the current sucking to the back of the [outboard] motors." Luckily, the motors had a guard in front of them that prevented Elliott from being pulled in and chopped up by the blades. Unfortunately, the suction was so strong that Elliott was unable to pull himself free. "I couldn't get away from the motors…They had divers outside the tank waiting in case I got into trouble and apparently (because the shot called for Elliott to stay underwater for a long time) the divers were standing there thinking, 'Oh wow, he's doing really well!' and then eventually one said, 'No, he's been in there too long!' My personal dresser was the first person to jump in to pull me out, followed by the divers. I was blue when they pulled me out." The near-death experience aside, Elliott really enjoyed doing the scene. "It was a fantastic shot. I thought 'Wow, this is action!' This was also the last scene they [were supposed to do] with me, so that night we went out and partied all night long and [then]…about ten the next morning we got a bloody message saying they got it wrong at the lab and we [would] have to do the shot again!"

THE SWAMP Because it was full of water, the miniature swamp was a challenge to construct. The entire raised set had to be reinforced to support the enormous weight of the water. Live caimans (miniature crocodiles) were brought in to portray the alligators Kong snacks on in the scene. Elliott used the Roar Head for the shots in which Kong holds the alligators in his mouth. During the shoot, one of the caimans escaped into the set, causing jitters among the set-dressing crew (the members of which were used to going barefoot in the water-filled set). The pile of alligator bones seen in Kong's lair were actually chicken bones, and the full moon Kong gazes at (in this and in other scenes in the film) was actually a beach ball that was painted white and suspended above the set.

KONG'S TREK TO THE MISSILE BASE The miniature fishing resort consisted of a few actual buildings supplemented with cut-outs made from photos of the full-scale location. The Lamborghini Kong steps on later in the sequence was an off-the-shelf, prefab model kit that, luckily for the film-makers, had actually been manufactured in the required 1/12 scale (an unusual proportion for commercial model kits).

THE GORGE SCENE Blue screen was also used heavily for the scene in which redneck hunters set off an avalanche in order to trap Kong. Thousands of miniature foam boulders were used to create the avalanche.

The miniature hunter that Kong rips in half when he strikes back at his tormentors was a six-inch figure built on a wire armature. The shot of Kong biting the head off another hunter that ends the sequence was created by shooting the hunter in the Big Hand against the blue screen and then compositing it with a plate of Elliott-as-Kong. A matte was made to match Kong's mouth that wiped the hunter out of the shot as Elliott leaned forward to bite him. When filming the full-scale portion of the shot, the hunter ducked down into the Big Hand and stayed there as Elliott pulled back, which made it look like the hunter (or the top part of him, anyway) had disappeared.

THE DIRT FIGHT The scene in which Kong throws dirt in the air to foil Nevitt's forces was a straightforward mix of miniature and full-scale shots. Fuller's earth was used to increase the size of the dust cloud.

THE MISSILE SILO The miniature missile silo was a challenging set to construct because the floor—which is actually an elevator—was required to rise up through the shaft during the scene. Since it would have been both expensive and impractical to incorporate a real elevator, the set was instead constructed inside a large chute. During filming, the silo walls were lowered into the chute to create the proper rising effect. The combination of the enclosed space, the hot lights, and the North Carolina humidity made this the most difficult and uncomfortable set for George Yiasoumi to work on. The silo doors that appear at the top of the silo (which were allegedly made of concrete) were actually constructed of breakaway plaster to make it easy for Kong to pulverize them.

The complex shot looking down over Lady Kong's shoulder at Amy and Mitch on the floor of the silo as it moved up through the shaft was created by filming Yiasoumi against a blue screen and compositing it with a matte painting of the silo floor. Brian Kerwin and Linda Hamilton were then split screened into the matte painting. The moving walls of the silo were shot on the miniature set and then split-screened into the final shot.

All of the shots in which characters look through the silo viewing port at Lady Kong were done in front of a blue screen. Brian Kerwin was lifted by the Big Hand in the full-scale set, but the rest of the shots of him in the hand were filmed in front of a blue screen.

Brian Kerwin gets his chance to ride in Kong's hand.

THE BARN The miniature farm set was built on a very large platform to facilitate the many miniature vehicles and effects required for the sequence in which Kong battles Nevitt's men for the final time. The miniature barn itself was based on a real structure that existed on the property where the full-scale portions of the sequence were shot. Proportionally, the real barn would have been too small for a real sixty-foot gorilla to fit into, so the miniature model was made one-and-a-half times bigger than the scale dictated it should have been to accommodate George Yiasoumi. Three different miniature barns were constructed to accommodate multiple takes of Lady Kong's fall into the building. The first take was shot at seventy-six frames per second, but Guillermin felt that the results were too slow, so the other takes were shot at a speed closer to the normal twenty-four frames per second. The set was rigged with air jets that blew out the sides of the structure and stirred up clouds of dust as Lady Kong touched down.

The over-Kong's-shoulder shot of Nevitt and his men arriving on the farm in their armored vehicles was a blue screen shot. Elliott wore the Roar Head throughout the sequence in which Kong battles the army in order to allow him to give Kong expression without tying him down to the cables as he threw around jeeps and overturned tanks. For the scenes in which Kong is hit by gunfire, Elliott was rigged with twenty-six squibs that were set off in sequence. The squib shots were filmed at twenty-eight frames per second—one of the few times Elliott was filmed at anything other than normal speed.

For the shot in which Kong finally pounds Nevitt into oblivion, Elliott-as-Kong smashed his fist down on a blue screen and then composited with a plate of John Ashton on the full-scale cemetery set.

THE BIRTH OF THE BABY AND THE DEATH OF KONG Blue screen was used throughout this sequence to composite shots of Lady Kong and Baby Kong, King Kong and Baby Kong, and the human actors with all of the Kongs. One of these shots—Hamilton in the foreground against a plate of Elliott-as-Kong reaching out to touch his newborn son—achieves a very convincing three-dimensional effect, as Kong actually appears to be reaching *past* Hamilton.

Two multi-element blue screen shots were featured in the birth sequence. The first was an over-the-shoulder shot of Lady Kong holding up the newborn, with Amy, Mitch, and the fallen Kong looking on. To create this shot, Lady Kong, Kong and the mechanical newborn (the one time it can be seen in the film) were filmed against a blue screen in a mock-up of the collapsed barn and then composited with a plate of the full-scale farm. This composite was then used as a plate and merged with another blue screen shot of Hamilton and Kerwin. The second multi-element shot showed Baby Kong hopping down Lady Kong's leg toward Amy, Mitch, and Kong. To create this shot, Elliott was filmed in front of the blue screen in the miniature barn mock-up and composited with another plate of the full-scale farm. This composite was then used as a plate for a blue screen shot of Baby Kong hopping on one of the Big Legs as Kerwin and Hamilton look on.

To film the massive close-up of Kong as he dies, Elliott had to hold himself in an extremely awkward position for an extended period of time while the shot was being prepared. The position put such a severe strain on Elliott's muscles that he was in agony much of the time.

Seven-year-old Benjamin Kechley, a local boy from Wilmington, was hired to wear the Baby Kong suit in this sequence. The suit itself was covered with KY jelly to create an afterbirth effect. Elliott trained Kechley and choreographed Baby Kong's movements in the scene.

THE RETURN TO BORNEO The final scene of Lady Kong and Prince Kong on their preserve in Borneo was filmed outdoors at the Wilmington Arboretum. Peter Murton and his team dressed the location with tropical plants to give the impression that the apes were in a rain forest.

The scene required young Kong to swing from vine to vine three times and then land on a tree branch twenty-five feet off the ground. To facilitate the stunt, the crew strung a cable between two trees from which the swinging vines were hung. A platform was built into each tree in order to give Elliott—wearing the older Baby Kong suit—a solid place to launch from and a sturdy place to land. A stunt like this would have been difficult for Elliott to pull off even if he hadn't been wearing a costume, but making matters worse was the fact that he could barely see out of the Baby Kong mask. To help Elliott out, the wiremen set all of the swinging vines at predetermined positions so that the actor could memorize where the vines were during rehearsals and grab for them without having to look during the actual take. Normally, a string of airbags would have been placed below the cable to break the performer's fall should he lose his grip. However, the distance Elliott had to travel would have required at least twenty airbags and the production couldn't afford that many, so Elliott decided to do the scene without any airbags at all because "Sometimes…you are better off knowing there's [no safety equipment below you] rather than inadequate safety equipment below you. That way you know you can't afford to let go."

POSTPRODUCTION

Postproduction began in Wilmington and was completed in editing rooms adjacent to Van Der Veer Photo Effects in Burbank. Doing all of the postproduction in a single location made it easier for Barry Nolan to consult with Guillermin and the editors as the optical shots were completed.

EDITING Veteran British film editor Malcolm Cooke (*Far from the Madding Crowd, Supergirl*), who had cut *Death on the Nile* for Guillermin and *Flash Gordon* for De Laurentiis, was hired to edit the film. Stock footage from *Kong '76*—a pared-down version of Kong's last stand atop the World Trade Center—was attached to the beginning of the film and faded out before Kong actually dies in order to lead into the new story. The first new footage in the film is the establishing shot of the Atlantic Institute (which is misidentified as the Atlanta Institute in the subtitle).

SOUND EDITING Cooke brought in Colin Miller, with whom he and Guillermin had worked on *Death on the Nile*, to edit the sound effects for the picture. Kong's distinctive roar from *Kong* '76 was not reused. Instead, Miller gave Kong a growl—a new sound effect created by mixing Elliott's voice with various animal roars and breaths. Variations on this growl were used throughout the film and even replaced the original roar in the stock footage from *Kong* '76. The voices for the other Kongs were created in the same way.

MUSIC The music for *King Kong Lives* was composed by John Scott. A friend of *Kong* '76 second unit director William Kronick, Scott came to the attention of the producers because he had recently composed the majestic score for *Greystoke: The Legend of Tarzan, Lord of the Apes* and his agents were marketing him as a specialist in ape movies. Scott went down to North Carolina and reviewed the film with Guillermin, who told Scott that he wanted a serious score for the film. Guillermin said he saw Kong and Lady Kong as real creatures with real feelings and he wanted those emotions reflected in the music. In addition, Guillermin wanted Scott to compose a theme for Kong that would be instantly identifiable to the audience and that would recur throughout the film. Because Guillermin saw *Kong Lives* as an entirely new film, no thought was given to reprising any of John Barry's themes from *Kong* '76.

After meeting with Guillermin, Scott got to work. "My method of composing is that I have to hear it in the head. I do sit at the piano on occasion and pick out what I hear, but it starts in the head and I write notes on paper. I'm inspired by the story I'm writing the music for. The way it's shot, the way it's cut—these are the things that influence what comes into my head. It doesn't just come of course, one has to work at it—you know what the old saying is: it's ninety-nine-percent perspiration and one-percent inspiration. I think that's very true. I had to work very, very, very hard. I probably wrote thirty tunes, thirty melodies, before I arrived at something I thought was of the simplicity or complexity of what I was looking for." Over the course of six weeks working in London and Los Angeles, Scott composed an upbeat, romantic score for the film, which he saw as "A film on a big scale—everything had to be larger than life. I just saw it as a great adventure, the continuation of the Kong story." Scott began the prologue with fast-paced music reminiscent of the kind used for old-fashioned serial cliffhangers to indicate that "something had gone before," and then introduced his new Kong theme in a quieter, gentler manner under the titles.

Because of the film's nonunion status, Scott could not record the score in either London or Los Angeles, so he instead traveled to the Bavaria Studios in Munich, where he conducted the Graunke Symphony Orchestra over the course of a few days. Scott enjoyed the experience of recording in Munich, although he considered the orchestra to be second class and feels the final product would have been better had it been recorded in London or Los Angeles. Scott enjoyed working with Cooke and Miller, who were already friends, and with Guillermin, whom Scott considers "a true artist" and who also became a friend.

PREVIEW Several preview screenings were held, all of which went badly. Ronald Shusett spent a great deal of time analyzing the audience's reactions and says that he thinks the biggest problem was that preview audiences couldn't tell if the movie was supposed to be funny or thrilling. "It wasn't completely campy, but the thrills weren't very exciting," he said. Another problem was that the action was repetitious. "It wasn't repetitious in the original *Kong* or in Dino's, because you had the cityscape. He [Kong] could go to the subway, get out of a Broadway theater, climb the Empire State Building, etc. Once he was out in the woods, though, it was just the same thing every time. Every fight with the army and all the running around in the woods was the same. On the page it looked exciting, but when you saw it, it was repetitious. It saved a lot of money, but... the audience got bored with it." In addition to all of this, Shusett says that the final nail in the coffin was that the audiences thought that the birth of Baby Kong and the death of King Kong—scenes meant to provoke strong emotion— were corny. "There were snickers," Shusett reports. Shusett was surprised by the negative reaction, because the response to the script had been so positive, but now feels that the script's structure was a big part of the problem. "It's one of the few times in my life that I completely miscalculated on how the audience would respond. Everybody loved the script. Nobody loved the movie."

As accurate as Shusett's analysis of the problems was, there wasn't much that could be done to fix them. At that point, all DEG could do was release the film and hope for the best.

RELEASE

The first official publicity done for the film was a press release issued on May 20, 1986, heralding the birth of Baby Kong. The text took the form of a traditional birth announcement: "Name: Baby Kong. Born: May 19, 1986, in Wilmington, North Carolina. Height: 84 inches. Weight: 200 pounds. Eyes: Brown. Hair: All Over. Father: King. Mother: Lady."

On May 12, 1986, Universal opened a King Kong attraction on its backlot tour in Southern California. A similar attraction was planned to open the following year in the company's Orlando, Florida, park. As part of the promotion for the ride, a syndicated television special was prepared called *King Kong: The Living Legend*. Hosted by Jonathan Winters and Jenilee Harrison, the special integrated footage from the original *Kong*, *Kong* '76, and on-set footage and clips from *Kong Lives*, as well as an interview with Martha Schumacher. The special also included behind-the-scenes footage of the construction of the theme park ride, giving more credence to the notion that the film was initiated, in part, as a promotional piece for Universal. The special played on local television stations around the country throughout the summer of 1986, promoting the ride and paving the way for the film. Some of the behind the on-set footage was shot by a Japanese film crew that spent a week on the set. Elliott recalls: "I remember a Japanese director—he followed me around and had the camera in my face the whole time. He would ask me questions and then scream ACTION! at me when he wanted me to answer. It was hilarious."

A fairly lengthy piece on the making of the film appeared in the *Los Angeles Times* in June 1986 and was distributed to other newspapers around the country as well. Carlo Rambaldi was the prime focus of the piece. In the aftermath of *E.T.*, Rambaldi had become quite famous and there was great interest in what he was going to do next. In some of these pieces, Rambaldi claimed that Baby Kong was going to be totally mechanical. While this may have seemed like a return to some of *Kong '76*'s mechanical monkey hype, Rambaldi was actually referring to the second incarnation of Baby Kong, which *was* mechanized, rather than the final boy-in-a-suit version, which was not filmed until after the main shoot had wrapped. Later stories made no mention of any robots of any kind.

By the time of the film's release, DEG was in serious financial straits. Most of the company's films had bombed and money was extremely tight, so the company didn't have the resources to mount the sort of huge print and television advertising campaign a film like *Kong Lives* requires. A promotional tie-in campaign was arranged with Nissan—which provided one of its King Cab pickup trucks for use in the production and featured the film in its advertisements—and a poster was prepared featuring a cartoonish illustration of Kong stepping on tanks and swatting at helicopters as he grabs for another ape hand (presumably Lady Kong's) that is reaching in from outside of the poster. Featuring the uninspired tagline "America's greatest hero is back—and he is not happy!" the poster had none of the iconic power and majesty of the 1976 poster and did a poor job of inspiring audiences to want to see the film. When the picture didn't test well, a decision was made not to throw good money after bad. As a result, only minimal advertising was done to promote the film in the weeks before it opened.

Looking for an inexpensive way to promote the film, DEG asked Brian Kerwin to make a few television appearances. "They asked me to go on the talk shows to pitch it [the movie]," Kerwin recalls. "I said, 'Well, I haven't seen it yet,' and they said, 'Yeah, well, we don't have a print of it yet we can show you.' Of course, I was very suspicious—it was two weeks before release, so of course they had prints. I said, 'I really want to see it before I go on a talk show and ask people to please go see the movie.' They just flat out refused. Finally I said, "I *won't* go on any show until I see a copy of it," and they just stiffed me. They just wouldn't show it to me. And they never had a [traditional cast and crew] screening, either. I finally ended up seeing it on Hollywood Boulevard the opening week. I put on a baseball cap and Groucho glasses and went in to Grauman's or the Egyptian or something for a matinee. There were about eighteen people in the theater. It was pretty bad."

OPENING   The film opened in 1,105 theaters on December 19, 1986—ten years and two days after the premiere of *Kong '76*.

REVIEWS AND ANALYSIS   The reviews were not kind:

"King Kong's revival after a decade serves as little more than a sequel in service to a possible sequel. Story and acting are too weak to outdo the 1976 remake and it will take more than curiosity over updated mechanics and effects to deliver anything but modest business. The pyrotechnics, machine gun barrages, and stomping of cars begins in earnest as Kong frees the female from her entrapment before the pair escape together in the woods. This would prove to be the moment when director John Guillermin loses all control of the picture. There's no logic to its [story] progression at all."—*Variety*

"The biggest missing link in this ill-developed production is the pedestrian, muddled script by Ronald Shusett and Steven Pressfield...Further trampling the cumbersome storyline is John Guillermin's witless and lumbering direction, bogged down with nonessential reaction shots and tonal changes at every juncture..." —Duane Byrge, *The Hollywood Reporter*

"The classic tale of nature betrayed decomposes into Southern Fried corn pone." —Deborah J. Kurk, *Los Angeles Herald-Examiner*

"Miniature work is shoddy, with absolutely no attention paid to scale... There is no script to speak of and the actors constantly appear to be looking for a telephone off-camera, trying to get a hold of their agents to find out how they got stuck in this...the most ill-advised film of the year." —*Box Office*

In addition to the bad print reviews, television critics Gene Siskel and Roger Ebert named the film one of the ten worst of 1986. Surprisingly, some reviewers did have a few nice things to say about the film:

"*King Kong Lives*, which was directed by John Guillermin, has a dull cast and a plot that's even duller, but the ape himself is in good form." —Janet Maslin, *New York Times*

"This sequel, directed by John Guillermin, is in good hands as long as Kong is on screen." —Patrick Goldstein, *Los Angeles Times*

The people who worked on the film gave their own mixed reviews: Ronald Shusett: "The satire and the thrills never blended and no one liked the movie at all." Peter Elliott: "I thought overall there were some great bits in it, but I was badly let down by a heart operation. The Kong and Mrs. Kong scene makes me cringe!" Barry Nolan: "It was corny—especially the heart transplant." Peter Murton: "To be honest I was saddened that the storyline they used was too humanistic—they made the Kongs too human in their reactions. The actual scriptwriting didn't make them as apelike in their reactions as I would've liked. There was that little lack of being totally, totally real." Robin Browne: "It was fun [but] I thought the film could have been more exciting. It's important for an audience to have sympathy for King Kong and perhaps that didn't come over. I could watch the original *King Kong* time and time again. I don't think I could watch *King Kong Lives* time and time again." Brian Kerwin: "The only fun I ever have with it is watching it with my kids and after about a half an hour even they say 'Okay, we've got Gameboys to play with here.' The only other fun is that somebody sent me a copy dubbed into Japanese. For me, this gives it the sense of a Kurasowa film and I say, 'Gee, this isn't as bad as I thought.'"

Composer John Scott gave the film its best review: "It's a long time since I've seen it, but I don't see it as being as bad as people tell me it was. In fact, it's always been thrilling to me. I saw them make it. I saw the sets in North

Carolina. I saw these miniature villages with him striding over it. It's so impressive, seeing the end result and knowing what it really looked like—the way they worked out all those proportions just leaves me aghast. So when I see the film I'm entertained in another way. I kind of believe in the story and I enjoyed it. I can't say I was disappointed in the film."

Unfortunately, the film deserves most of the brickbats it received, because, despite all of the effort that went into making it, *King Kong Lives* is a pretty terrible movie. The film's problems begin with its title. While one has to admire Dino De Laurentiis's determination not to simply rehash *The Son of Kong*, the decision to bring Kong back to life was a mistake. The notion that he could have survived the brutal helicopter attack at the climax of *Kong '76*, not to mention the 110-story fall from the top of the World Trade Center, is simply unbelievable. Plus, it robs the myth of much of its power—Kong's sacrifice of his life to protect his lady love is what gives the tale its tragic grandeur. If the great ape survives, then both the story and the character are diminished. While Shusett and Pressfield's attempt to make the resurrection idea work with their clever if preposterous notion of an artificial heart is valiant enough, perhaps what *King Kong Lives* ultimately proves is that there really may be only one King Kong story to tell.

In addition to the shaky premise, the script itself is poorly executed: The tone of the piece is all over the map—ranging from deadly serious to lightly comical to farcically broad. The plot is often illogical and, as Ronald Shusett points out, repetitive—an endless cycle of chases, captures, and escapes that quickly becomes tedious. The characters are all one-note (and in the case of the rednecks—especially the hunters—horrendously clichéd) and Colonel Nevitt is downright inexplicable—he comes out of nowhere full of an incredible hatred for Kong that is never explained and impossible to understand. The dialogue lacks spark and the humor falls flat.

The rest of the film's creative elements are equally lackluster. The direction is inconsistent—there are wide variations in tone and performance, the pacing is choppy, and, with the exception of the opening shot, the film lacks Guillermin's trademark visual flair. The performers—excellent actors all—do the best they can given the uncertain tone of the script and the direction. Plus, the film looks cheap. Peter Murton's full-scale sets and Alec Mills's lighting are fine, but the Wilmington, N.C.–area locations are drab and tacky and the film lacks an appropriate sense of size and scope. The miniature sets are well designed, but ultimately unconvincing. This is due in part to the impossibility of fabricating realistic-looking natural environments from artificial materials and in part to the script's insistence that the sets be filmed in simulated daylight, which serves only to emphasize their artificiality. Second unit director/cinematographer Robin Browne does the best he can with the miniature scenes, but he is hampered by the quality of the material he was given to work with.

This brings us to the film's biggest failure—the Kongs themselves. To begin with, the costumes are terribly unconvincing. Kong's too-broad shoulders, tapered waistline, and spindly legs make him look more like a Muscle

Beach bodybuilder than a gorilla (he also doesn't have a scar on his chest, a curious fact given that the film begins with him undergoing a massive heart transplant). Lady Kong's shriveled breasts, two-tone hair, and bulbous belly do nothing but inspire laughter and Baby Kong looks more like a primal man than he does an ape. The masks, so wonderfully supple and expressive in *Kong '76*, are stiff and lifeless (due, it seems, to the thick layer of latex needed to allow a single mask to stretch to make all of the required expressions). The apes are not well presented, either. Because the costumes are so bulky, their movements often seem stiff and awkward. The decision to have all the Kongs walk on all fours also doesn't work—because of the poor design of the costume, the human proportions of the performers' legs are even more apparent in the quadruped position than they are in the bipedal position. The size of the Kongs varies wildly from shot to shot (on some occasions they appear to be sixty feet tall, on others they appear to be hundreds of feet tall) and, as it was in 1976, the decision to film the Kongs at regular speed rather than in slow motion was a mistake, because the animals never appear to be as massive or move as ponderously as creatures of their alleged size should be.

Ultimately, however, it is the film's conception of the apes that sinks them (and the movie). The cutesy, over-anthropomorphized characterizations of the three giant apes—and all of the relentless smiling, mugging, and making of goo-goo faces that goes with them—are completely ridiculous and rob the beasts of not only of their dignity, but also of any ability they might have possessed to inspire fear, wonder, or awe. Peter Elliott and George Yiasoumi struggle valiantly to give the characters of Kong and Lady Kong credibility, but the decks are just too stacked against them.

Certainly the film does have its good points: The optical work is solid; the Big Kong—while it doesn't look anything like the miniature suits—is tremendously impressive and convincing, and John Scott's score is excellent. For the most part, however, *King Kong Lives* is a regrettable misfire.

BOX OFFICE   The film was a resounding flop, playing to mostly empty theaters and taking in only $1,172,942 in its first weekend (a poor average of about $1,000 per screen) and a total of only $4,791,220 over the course of its entire U. S. run, which was less than *Kong '76* made in its first three days. It had disappeared from most American screens by mid-January 1987. Retitled *King Kong 2*, the film did moderately better in overseas markets, especially Japan, where it featured a much-improved poster that captured much of the style and flavor of John Berkey's 1976 illustration. Overall, though, the film was a dud and did nothing to help DEG's continuing slide downward.

AWARDS   DEG submitted the film to the Academy of Motion Picture Arts and Sciences in the hope that it would be nominated best visual effects, but no nomination was forthcoming. Carlo Rambaldi was nominated for a Razzie Award for worst visual effects, but didn't win.

LEGACY

While *Kong '76* remains a source of pride for many who worked on it, the people who worked on *King Kong Lives* have mixed feelings about their participation in the film. In the biography, *Dino: The Life and Films of Dino De Laurentiis* by Tullio Kezich and Alessandra Levantesi, De Laurentiis refers to the film and the decision to make it as a "mistake." Ronald Shusett feels much the same way. "It was my least successful film," says Shusett. "I thought it would be a big hit. I didn't realize it would fall as flat as it did. Of all the movies in my career, it's the one that no one felt was any good or had any merit. I'm sort of embarrassed. I never missed the mark so much." Brian Kerwin wonders about the effect the film had on his career. "I've often questioned whether it was just a faux pas or a big mistake to have done it, because they cast *Platoon* while I was doing *Kong*, so I missed out on that. Also, Jim Brooks wanted to see me for *Broadcast News*. They set it up once in LA, but...[Kong]... wouldn't release me. They set it up two weeks later in New York. I could have just flown up, but stupidly I asked permission...so I missed out on that. So, I've often wondered if I shot myself in the foot. (In the end) it was stupid, but it was fun and I got money." On the other hand, Peter Elliott greatly enjoyed his experience playing a cinematic legend. "Do you know what? A lot of it was great fun. There's nothing more fun than dressing as King Kong and going and smashing up buildings and models, breaking through doors, stamping all over the place. Smashing through the lead door was a lot of fun! I...knew it was a hokey script, but overall it was just great fun!"

Following the failure of *King Kong Lives*, DEG continued to decline. Frustrated by the company's financial problems and by having his independence hemmed in by a board of directors, De Laurentiis resigned from DEG in February 1988. The company went into receivership six months later. Eventually, its assets—including the Wilmington studios—were sold off and the company was dissolved. The years following DEG were difficult ones for De Laurentiis. Although he and Martha Schumacher produced several more films, none of them did well at the box office. Things went much better in their privates lives—De Laurentiis and Schumacher went on to have two daughters and were married in April 1990. Things began to turn around for them professionally in 2000 with the success of the World War II submarine thriller *U-571*, which was followed by the *Silence of the Lambs* sequels *Hannibal* (2001) and *Red Dragon* (2002)—both produced for De Laurentiis's old nemesis, Universal Pictures. At the 2001 Academy Award ceremony, De Laurentiis was awarded the Irving G. Thalberg Award for Distinguished Motion Picture Production. As of this writing, Dino De Laurentiis is eighty-six years old and, in partnership with Martha, is still an active motion picture producer.

King Kong Lives was John Guillermin's last theatrical film. In 1988 he directed a television movie starring Kris Kristofferson called *The Tracker* for HBO, after which he retired. He reportedly spends his days building boats and indulging his great passion for sailing. Carlo Rambaldi continued to create cinematic creatures until the mid-1990s, when he retired as well. Rambaldi currently lives in Italy and remains proud of the work that he did for both De Laurentiis King Kong films, especially the fact that Kong's amazing facial expressions were all "real," and were created without the use of computers. Barry Nolan retired from the film industry in 1990 and lives happily in Southern California.

Peter Murton has continued his career as a premier art director and production designer and teaches at the National Film and Television School in London. Alec Mills went on to photograph both Timothy Dalton James Bond films—*The Living Daylights* (1987) and *Licence to Kill* (1989). He also directed the films *Bloodmoon* (1989) and *Dead Sleep* (1990). Immediately after *King Kong Lives*, Robin Browne reunited with Peter Elliott on *Gorillas in the Mist* (1988). He continues to work as work as a director, second unit director, and cinematographer on films and television commercials. Colin Miller went on to work on *The Living Daylights* (1987), *Mary Shelley's Frankenstein*

Dino De Laurentiis's Kong comes to the end of the road.

(1994) and many other films. Malcom Cooke has retired. Peter MacDonald recovered from his appendectomy and went on to direct *Rambo III* (1988) and to do second unit work on films such as *Batman* (1989) and the *Harry Potter* series. John Scott has composed the scores for films such as *The Deceivers* (1988) and *Time of the Wolf* (2002). He also rewrote his score for *King Kong Lives* as an orchestral suite, which he performs in concert around the world.

As for the cast, Brian Kerwin continues to work frequently in film, television, and the theater and feels that someone really should get to the bottom of the primal fascination people seem to have with giant apes. Linda Hamilton went on to star in the television series *Beauty and the Beast* and then reprised her role as Sarah Connor in *Terminator 2: Judgment Day* (1991). She has also appeared in the films *Mr. Destiny* (1990) and *Dante's Peak* (1997). John Ashton appeared in *Some Kind of Wonderful* (1987) and *Beverly Hills Cop II* (1987) and then in 1988 played none-too-bright bounty hunter Marvin Dorfler opposite Robert De Niro and *King Kong '76* star Charles Grodin in *Midnight Run*. He continues to work frequently in film and television. Peter Michael Goetz continues to appear on film, television, and in the theater. Sadly, Frank Maraden passed away in 1989. Peter Elliott played more gorillas in films such as *Gorillas in the Mist* (1988), *Congo* (1995), and *Buddy* (1997). He continues to play apes and creatures in films as well as teach animal study at the Central School of Speech and Drama in London. George Yiasoumi continues to play creatures and humans on film.

King Kong Lives was released on home video in 1987. Although it still plays occasionally on late-night television and was issued on DVD in 2004, it has, for the most part, been forgotten. Because of its brief, low-profile release, most people today aren't even aware that Dino De Laurentiis ever made a second King Kong film. The failure of *King Kong Lives* put an end to any plans De Laurentiis might have had to continue the saga and was the last Kong film to appear in theaters for almost twenty years.

■ ■ ■

THE LEGEND OF KING KONG
by Bo Goldman

FADE IN

1   EXT. PET SHOP - WEST 57TH STREET - NIGHT   1

The store window is trimmed in tinsel and silver balls and
colored lights, the letters "Merry Christmas" draped across
a cardboard Santa Claus and across a diapered cardboard baby
the numbers of the incoming year "1933."

Divided into two parts, in the larger one, puppies, in the
smaller part, a capuchin monkey rolling and swinging and
tumbling through the excelsior with joyous abandon in response
to a pretty set of fingers who tap and rap and wiggle against
the glass. Suddenly a hand reaches in from the store side of
the shop, lifts the monkey out, tucks him into a portable
cage and hands it to a 12-year-old girl who beams up at her
mother, a Park Avenue matron busy fishing in her pocketbook
for cash.

2   REVERSE ANGLE - FINGERS   2

Frozen on the glass, they belong to Ann Darrow, in her mid-
twenties, a lean and delicate beauty to her, a cloche and a
permanent frazzled at the edge, a dickie and a shirtwaist and
a faille skirt whose hem sags slightly, the run-down edges
of a depths-of-the-depression lovely whose hollow cheeks and
black circles reveal not a model, but an actress who hasn't
eaten for a day.

She watches ruefully as the monkey heads east with its new
owners, now she rises from her stooping position at the
window, heads in the other direction, into the smoky scurry
of the 5 PM Saturday shopping crowd.

3   ANOTHER ANGLE - ANN   3

Striding purposefully west, but we can see, with no real
destination as she passes fur shops and dress shops, painfully
checking them out of the corner of her eye, and now Charles
& Co., the fruiterer, just in time to see half a dozen Golden
Delicious lifted from their red tissue beds, and then a bottle
of marrons whose cap is quickly unscrewed and one of the con-
tents popped into a mink-hatted mouth.

She pushes on, past more apples, but this time the fruit is
on the curb side, sitting in shallow boxes which are slung
over the shoulders of vacant-eyed fedoraed men, their over
coats pulled up against the Christmas cold which seeps in
from the street, and out from the decorated store windows

CHAPTER

7

THE KONGS THAT NEVER WERE

Aside from the films already mentioned, several other Kong films have been planned over the years that, for one reason or another, never made it to the screen.

The opening page of Bo Goldman's screenplay of the never-produced *The Legend of King Kong*.

THE LOST ISLAND (1934)

The Lost Island was a one-reel, Technicolor parody of the original *King Kong* complete with singing and dancing numbers. What makes this film especially unusual is that all of the human characters were portrayed by marionettes designed to look like the famous stars of the day (for example, the Ann Darrow role was played by a marionette replica of Mae West). Kong was portrayed by Charles Gemmora, whose work had been such an inspiration to Rick Baker during the making of *King Kong* '76 (Gemora's appearance in *The Lost Island* is probably what gave rise to the long-standing rumor that he played Kong in the original film—a rumor Gemora steadfastly denied, which didn't stop people from repeating it). The dinosaurs were also portrayed by costumed actors. The film, which was directed by choreographer LeRoy Prinz and produced by *King Kong*'s Orville Goldner for the Christie Studio, proved to be more expensive to make than originally anticipated and production was stopped when the money ran out.

THE NEW ADVENTURES OF KING KONG (1934)

Following *The Son of Kong*, Cooper wanted to do another sequel, this one telling the story of how Carl Denham brought Kong to New York City. Based in part on an event that occurred during the voyage of the Wisdom II and following somewhat the structure of Edgar Wallace's original Kong treatment, the story begins with the *Venture* getting damaged off an island in the Malay Archipelago. As the crew works to repair the ship, the sailors are attacked by a series of strange and possibly monstrous creatures. In order to protect themselves, they release Kong from his chains. Kong battles the creatures and saves the day, after which the crew has to recapture him. The idea was met by a decided lack of enthusiasm from Schoedsack, who felt that they had already milked the concept dry, and Cooper eventually dropped it.

THE EIGHTH WONDER (1952)

Following the 1952 reissue of the original *Kong*, Cooper—then working for the Cinerama Company—became interested in doing a remake using the revolutionary widescreen process. To this end, he hired Willis O'Brien and gave him the task of figuring out how to adapt the stop-motion animation process for Cinerama. This was an enormous challenge, because Cinerama required using three separate cameras filming side-by-side in perfect synchronization in order to create a widescreen picture. Working with a Cinerama technician, O'Brien devised a set of complex interlocked motors that would allow him to pull off the complicated feat, but the technician died before the motors could be perfected and the project was put on hold. Cooper left Cinerama a short time later and the project was canceled completely.

'HAMMER' KONG I (1966)

Hammer Films, the premiere English monster-film studio that had produced color remakes of classic Hollywood horror films such as *Frankenstein*, *Dracula*, and *The Phantom of the Opera*, wanted to do a remake of *Kong* as its 100th film, but RKO—still enforcing its "no remakes" policy—refused to grant them the rights, so the studio did a remake of Hal Roach's *One Million B.C.* instead. The remake, which was titled *One Million Years B.C.*, featured stop-motion effects created by Ray Harryhausen and starred Raquel Welch in a famous prehistoric bikini.

'HAMMER' KONG II (1970)

Hammer decided to try again in 1970 and approached Ray Harryhausen about doing the animation, but RKO still wouldn't grant the rights and so the project died again and forever.

THE 'JIM DANFORTH' KONG (1974)

In 1974, animator/effects artist Jim Danforth (who had worked with Willis O'Brien on 1963's *It's a Mad, Mad, Mad, Mad World*) and writer/director/special effects artist Steve Barkett became interested in doing their own *Kong* remake. Barkett contacted Daniel O'Shea and was immediately rebuffed. Undaunted, Barkett researched the Kong rights and discovered that RKO-General did not own the copyright on the *King Kong* novelization, which was instead owned by the estate of Merian C. Cooper. Looking into the matter further, Barkett discovered that Cooper had (apparently inadvertently) not renewed the copyright when it expired in 1960, which meant that the novel was now in the public domain. In Barkett's estimation, this meant that he and Danforth could produce a Kong film based on the novel without violating RKO-General's copyright. (Barkett also discovered evidence that suggested that RKO-General might have allowed its copyright on the film to lapse, although the facts in that case were much less clear.) When RKO-General found out that Danforth and Barkett were planning to proceed with their project, it allegedly threatened to sue them. Although Barkett and Danforth were confident that they were on solid ground, neither had the money required to mount a legal defense and so they decided not to proceed.

THE LEGEND OF KING KONG (1976)

This was, of course, the film that sparked the titanic battle between Universal and Dino De Laurentiis. When Universal had first announced its intention to do a remake, Jim Danforth approached the studio's executives and offered them his services as an animator. Danforth allegedly told the executives about his own attempt to mount a remake two years earlier; presumably this is how Universal found out about the lapsed copyright on the novelization that became the basis of its counterattack against De Laurentiis and RKO.

While it is, of course, impossible to know how the film would have turned out if it had actually been produced, Bo Goldman's script was quite good. Set in 1933, it was a faithful adaptation of the original Kong storyline as represented in the novel (although, like Lorenzo Semple, Jr., Goldman made Kong much more sympathetic than he was in the original film). Goldman expanded some elements (mostly involving Denham's show business career) and changed others (the *Venture* was renamed the *Panama Queen*, a Triceratops was substituted for the Tyrannosaurus rex in the glade fight and a Parasaurolophus was substituted for the Brontosaurus in the swamp scene). The characters were also fleshed out to a much greater degree that they were in the original: Ann is nowhere near as naïve (like Jack Prescott in *King Kong* '76, she refuses to participate in Kong's exploitation at the end) and, as Semple did with Wilson, Goldman turned Denham into an out-and-out villain and had Kong kill him in the end (Denham hitches a ride in one of the fighter planes so he can film the attack on Kong as the giant ape stands atop the Empire State Building. When Kong grabs hold of the plane, Denham falls out and continues filming as he falls to his death). Because Goldman could not use any of the elements that were unique to the film, he did not include the elevated-train sequence, which he replaced with an ingenious scene set in a construction site in which Kong battles a vintage 1930s steam shovel that looks like a mechanized version of a T-rex.

Although Universal hired Jim Danforth as a consultant, the studio ultimately decided that stop-motion was too expensive and opted, as De Laurentiis had, to use a man in an ape suit to film the Kong scenes. Gorilla-suit performer Bob Burns was called in to film some test scenes on a hastily constructed jungle set wearing the Bionic Bigfoot costume from the *Six Million Dollar Man* television series (since Andre the Giant, who played Bigfoot, was a much bigger man than Burns, the arms and legs of the suit had to be pinned up before it would fit him) and an ill-fitting face mask. Burns recalls being asked to jiggle as he performed in order to simulate the movement of stop motion animation. To save money on the cost of miniature sets, the studio also considered using a little person in an ape suit, since the sets would then only have to be half the size. Neither of these approaches worked out and an elaborate hand-tied fur suit was later built to fit Franco Columbo, a five-foot-tall wrestler and bodybuilder with incredible muscles who would be able to wear the suit without padding (Rick Baker reports that he once saw Columbo's suit and thought that it looked pretty good). No mask was made for Columbo—the plan was for Kong's face to be created using appliance makeup.

Although Peter Falk and Susan Blakely were mentioned as possible candidates to play Denham and Ann, and even though the studio listed the film as an active production in January 1976, the truth is that no actor was ever cast for the film, no sets were ever built, and no footage was ever shot. Universal would have to wait almost thirty years before it would get a chance to bring its Kong to the screen and when it did, it would be a vastly different production than the one the studio planned in the 1970s.

'ROGER CORMAN'S' KONG (1976)

During the De Laurentiis–Universal battle, low budget exploitation filmmaker Roger Corman—jumping on the "the book is in the public domain" bandwagon—announced that he was going to produce his own *Kong* remake based on the Lovelace novel. This project apparently never got much further than that announcement.

KINGUKONGU TAI GOJIRA/
KING KONG VERSUS GODZILLA (1991)

In 1991, Toho considered remaking *KinguKongu Tai Gojira* as part of its new series of Gojira films, but could not obtain the rights to the Kong character.

GOJIRA TAI MEKANIKONGU/
GODZILLA VERSUS MECHANI-KONG (1994)

Unable to obtain permission to use Kong, Toho considered pitting Gojira against Mechani-Kong instead, but the company's lawyers decided that the similarity between Kong and Mechani-Kong was too close and so the project was called off.

'THE JOHN LANDIS' KONG (1990s)

Before Universal decided to offer *King Kong* to Peter Jackson in the mid-1990s, word circulated that John Landis, the director of *Animal House* and *The Blues Brothers* and an avowed King Kong fan, was going to produce a remake for Universal. It is not clear how far the project got before it was canceled.

■ ■ ■

CHAPTER

8

THE SONS OF KONG

Apart from the official canon, there have been many other films and television shows directly—and sometimes indirectly—related to Kong. Here is an overview.

Release poster for *Mighty Joe Young* (1949).

OTHER KONGS

MIGHTY JOE YOUNG (1949)

While *Mighty Joe Young* is not technically a King Kong film, it is usually counted as one because it was created by many of the same people that made the original *Kong*. Filmed as *Mr. Joseph Young of Africa*, the film tells the story of Jill Young, the daughter of an American explorer living in Africa. As the film begins, Jill buys a baby gorilla from some passing natives. The baby, whom Jill names Joe, grows into a ten-foot-tall adult who looks ferocious on the outside, but is sweet and gentle at heart (Joe's favorite song is "Beautiful Dreamer"). When nightclub owner Max O'Hara comes to Africa with a team of cowboys led by Gregg Johnson to capture animals for his new Hollywood hot spot, he decides that Joe would be an ideal featured attraction. O'Hara convinces Jill to bring Joe to America. Joe becomes part of nightclub act that pits him against a team of strongmen in a comical show of strength. After some meddlesome drunks ply Joe with liquor, he goes on a tear and wrecks the club. Following this incident, in which many people are hurt, the authorities decide to put Joe down. To save the giant ape, Jill, Gregg, and Max break Joe out of his holding cell and load him in a truck, intending to drive him to the port, where a ship is waiting to take him back to Africa. Before they can get very far, however, their plan is discovered and the police come after them. A wild chase ensues, during which the fugitives come upon a burning orphanage. Joe braves the fire to rescue two children trapped on the top floor of the orphanage and risks his life to shield them from harm when the building collapses. Joe's heroic deeds earn him a pardon, after which he, Jill, and Gregg return to Africa to live happily ever after.

The story for *Joe Young* was conceived by Merian Cooper and the screenplay was written by Ruth Rose. Cooper produced the film with director John Ford, while Ernest B. Schoedsack directed. Other Kong alumni that worked on the film included Linwood Dunn, Ted Cheesman and Walter Elliott. Robert Armstrong starred as Max O'Hara, along with Terry Moore (Jill) and Ben Johnson (Gregg). The live-action shoot took six months to complete and was marked by considerable friction between John Ford and Ernest Schoedsack (Schoedsack felt Ford was trying to tell him how to direct). Things got so bad at one point that Schoedsack actually quit the film, although Cooper talked him into coming back. Following this incident, Ford reportedly backed off. Because he was nearly blind, Schoedsack required some assistance from Cooper and O'Brien on the set, but still did a masterful job directing the film.

The film's stop-motion special effects were produced by Willis O'Brien, who was assisted by a young animator named Ray Harryhausen. When Harryhausen was thirteen years old, he saw *King Kong* during its original run and became fascinated with stop-motion animation. He began making his own films and eventually worked up the courage to contact O'Brien, who gave the young man advice and encouragement. Harryhausen got his first professional job working on George Pal's Puppetoon series and then, after the war, made a series of short animated fairy tales that were acquired by a nontheatrical distributor. Harryhausen remained in contact with O'Brien and when *Joe* came along, O'Brien invited Harryhausen to work on the film as his assistant. O'Brien was so busy planning and supervising the effects that he didn't have time to do the actual animation, so Harryhausen ended up doing about eighty percent of the animation, while another assistant named Pete Peterson did the remaining twenty percent.

Marcel Delgado created seven Joe models for the film. Four of the models were fifteen-inches tall, one model (used for long shots) was ten-inches tall, and another (used for even longer shots) was five-inches tall. The final model was a large scale torso-only model made for making close-ups that was never used. Delgado designed all of the armatures, which were very intricate and cost $1,200 each to make. The finished models were covered with fur of unborn lambs that had been rubberized by a special process created by taxidermist George Lofgren. Lofgren's treatment prevented the animator's fingerprints from imprinting on the fur and thus prevented the rippling effect that afflicted Kong and Kiko. Delgado also constructed a series of miniature lions, horses, and cowboys that were used in the film.

The animation was produced in a workshop on the old RKO-Pathe lot and took fourteen months to complete. Because of time constraints, O'Brien was unable to make much use of the miniature projection process, so most of the film's composite work was done on the optical printer. Released in 1949, *Mighty Joe Young* did well at the box office, but not well enough to earn back the $2.5 million it cost to produce the film. Because of this, a planned sequel called *Tarzan Meets Joe Young* was canceled. On March 23, 1950, O'Brien won an Oscar for his work on the film—the only one he ever received.

THE KING KONG VOLKSWAGEN COMMERCIAL (1971)

In 1970, when Hammer was considering doing a remake of *Kong* for the second time, American animator David Allen, who had just finished working on Hammer's production of *When Dinosaurs Ruled the Earth*, wanted to do the animation for the film and decided to produce a color recreation of Kong's battle with the biplanes atop the Empire State Building as an audition piece. Allen produced a superb replica of Marcel Delgado's Kong figure (with brown fur) to use in the test, which he completed by splicing in sound effects from the original film.

Allen produced the test at Cascade Pictures, where he was then working (animating, among other things, the Pillsbury Doughboy). In return for allowing him to use the studio, Allen gave Cascade permission to include his Kong footage in the company's demonstration reel. Hammer's Kong project never went forward, but Doyle Dane Bernbach, the ad agency representing Volkswagen, saw Allen's Kong in Cascade's demo reel and (after licensing the character from RKO) commissioned the company to produce a sixty-second King Kong television commercial to advertise its new 411 hatchback. The commercial—which was designed to show how big and roomy the 411 was— opened with Kong atop the Empire State Building fighting off airplanes. As in the original film, he reaches out and grabs one of the planes, but instead of destroying it, he instead tucks it under his arm, grabs Ann Darrow, and climbs back down the Empire State Building. Reaching the street, Kong crosses over

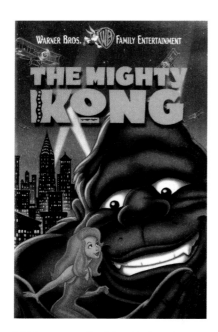

VHS cover art for *The Mighty Kong* (1998).

to a Volkswagen 411 parked at the curb, tosses the airplane into the trunk, puts Ann in the passenger seat, and then hops in the driver's seat. Kong then puts the car in gear and drives away.

Working at Cascade, Allen produced the animation for the commercial over a one-month period while another unit shot the live-action portion of the spot (which featured Victoria Riskin—the daughter of Fay Wray and Robert Riskin—as Ann Darrow). To complete the commercial, two nonanimated close-ups of Kong's hands—one showing him opening the trunk and stowing the biplane and the other showing him shifting the car into gear—were required. Allen approached well-known gorilla suit performers George Barrows and Janos Prohaska about playing Kong. Both declined, so Allen turned instead to one of Cascade's newest employees—a very young Rick Baker. Baker designed and built a Kong arm and hand, which he wore himself during the shoot. This was Baker's first opportunity to play Kong, although it obviously wasn't his last.

Creatively, Allen's commercial was a tremendous success, but the spot was pulled after only three airings. Explanations for the cancellation were vague—one implied that the commercial misled the public as to the actual size of the car, another that the Kong footage was so strong that people forgot what product the commercial was advertising. Allen animated Kong's last stand atop the Empire State Building once again in the 1996 IMAX film *Special Effects: Anything Can Happen.*

IT WAS BEAUTY KILLED THE BEAST (1992)

This was a short (twenty-five-minute) documentary on the making of the original *Kong* produced by Turner Home Entertainment for the film's sixtieth anniversary video release. Featuring interviews with Murray Spivak and Linwood Dunn, the film is pleasant but—due to the lack of behind-the-scenes footage or a wider range of interviews (sadly, most everyone that worked on the film had passed on by the time the film was made) —rather superficial presentation.

THE SECOND MRS. KONG (1994)

This was an opera with music composed by Sir Harrison Birtwistle and a libretto written by Russell Hoban. Set on the Egyptian Island of the Dead, the story focuses on a character called The Idea of Kong (waiting to be brought into the real world by Merian Cooper), who falls in love with the *Girl with a Pearl Earring* from the Vermeer painting. After contacting Pearl (who lives in the real world) via computer, The Idea of Kong decides to cross over into the real world to find her. He ends up battling with another character called The Death of Kong before finally meeting up with Pearl. The piece debuted at the Glyndebourne Opera in England in 1994.

THE MIGHTY KONG (1998)

This was a direct-to-video, animated musical retelling of the *Kong* story for children, with songs by Disney veterans Richard M. and Robert B. Sherman

(*Mary Poppins, The Jungle Book, Chitty Chitty Bang Bang*, and other works). Written by *King Kong Escapes* screenwriter William J. Keenan and featuring the voices of Dudley Moore as "C.B." Denham and Jodi Benson (the voice of Ariel in Disney's *The Little Mermaid*) as Ann Darrow, the film streamlined the plot, removed all of the original's harsher elements (Kong's battles with the dinosaurs are now mere scuffles and no dinosaurs or natives are killed), added a lot of "kid-friendly" elements (including an insufferably wide-eyed cabin boy and an anthropomorphized cabin monkey), and increased the "cute" quotient to near-red line proportions. It appropriated the waterfall sequence from *King Kong* '76 and, most significantly, replaced the tragic ending with a happy one in which Kong survives to the great delight of one and all. Produced by a company called Lana Film and featuring Japanese animation, the film was released in summer 1998 in order to capitalize on the release of Tri-Star's Americanized *Godzilla* remake, the anticipated success of which was expected to increase audience demand for big monster movies. Unfortunately, *Godzilla* proved to be a dud, as did *The Mighty Kong*.

MIGHTY JOE YOUNG (1998)

This respectful remake of the original *Joe Young* featured some impressive ape effects created by Rick Baker—including a man-sized Joe costume and two full-scale animatronic Joe puppets—that were augmented by a computer-generated ape produced by Dreamquest Images and Industrial Light & Magic. Directed by Ron Underwood (*Tremors*), the updated story made Jill (played by Charlize Theron) the daughter of a Dian Fossey–like naturalist who is killed by an evil poacher. Years later, when the poacher comes after Joe, Jill and adventurer Gregg O'Hara (Bill Paxton) bring him to a nature park in the United

Charlize Theron, Bill Paxton, and Rick Baker's Big Joe in *Mighty Joe Young* (1998).

TOP: *Kong: The Animated Series*

BOTTOM: Totally misleading DVD cover art for the camp extravaganza *Queen Kong* (1976).

States to protect him. The poacher tracks Joe down and torments him, causing Joe to go on a rampage that destroys a fundraising gala. Deciding to take Joe back to Africa, Jill—with Greg's help—sneaks Joe out of the park. The escape goes awry, but Joe is redeemed when he saves a young boy trapped on a Ferris wheel located on a burning amusement pier. The film featured cameos by Terry Moore and Ray Harryhausen.

KONG: THE ANIMATED SERIES (2000–2001)

This series from European-based Bohbot Animation focused on a clone of the original Kong created after Kong's fall from the Empire State Building by Dr. Lorna Jenkins. Dr. Jenkins takes the new Kong to Kong Island, where she keeps him hidden from the world. The island contains another secret—an evil god named Chiros, who is kept imprisoned by the magical Primal Stones. Years later, Dr. Jenkins's grandson Jason visits the island with his college professor, the evil Dr. Ramon De La Porta. De La Porta steals the Primal Stones, freeing Chiros and upsetting the island's balance of power. Jason and Kong, along with several of Jason's friends, set out on an around-the-world journey in an attempt to capture De La Porta and reclaim the stones. Jason carries a Cyber-Link that allows him to genetically merge with Kong at crucial moments. Forty episodes of the series were produced and aired in over eighty countries around the world, including France and the United States, but production was ended after one year due to poor ratings. The show later spawned a popular video game.

SPOOFS

KING KLUNK (1933)

This film was made as part of Universal's Pooch the Pup series (Pooch the Pup played Denham). The film, released in summer 1933, was co-directed by Walter Lantz, the future creator of Woody Woodpecker.

QUEEN KONG (1976)

Directed by low-budget schlockmeister Frank (Farouk) Agrama, this campy musical spoof was a low-budget quickie made to cash in on the publicity surrounding the release of *King Kong* '76. As is obvious from the title, the film switched the genders of all of the major characters: Carl Denham became Luce Habit (played by British B-movie actress Rula Lenska, best known for her role in the 1970s British television series *Rock Follies*) and Ann Darrow became Ray Fay (played by Robin Askwith star of several of England's ribald *Confessions of...* series). Featuring a dreadful ape costume (complete with breasts), even worse miniature sets and special effects, horrible acting, lousy set pieces, terrible songs, a dreadfully slow pace, and a series of totally inane jokes, puns, and double entendres, *Queen Kong* is a truly awful film. What saves it is the fact that everybody involved seemed to know they were making a bad movie and didn't let it bother them. Unhappy with the producer's blatant attempt to capitalize on his film, Dino De Laurentiis sought and was granted an injunction against the film, which went unreleased until its appearance on DVD in 2003.

RIP-OFFS

Spoofs pay tribute to the film they are making fun of. Rip-offs, on the other hand, just steal the idea outright. Kong has inspired more than its fair share of these unauthorized appropriations.

KONGA (1961)

C-movie producer Herman Cohen (*I Was a Teenage Werewolf*, *I Was a Teenage Frankenstein*) co-wrote and produced this film under the title *I Was a Teenage Gorilla*, even though there are no teenagers of any consequence in it. Starring British actor Michael Gough (who would later portray Bruce Wayne's butler Alfred in the Tim Burton/Joel Schumacher *Batman* movies of the 1980s and 90s), the film tells the story of research scientist Dr. Charles Decker, whose plane crashes in Africa. A year later, Decker is rescued, along with a chimp he has adopted as a pet and named Konga. During his exile, Decker discovered a serum that increases the size of any living thing injected with it. Upon returning to England, Decker injects Konga with the serum, which somehow turns the little chimp into a full-sized gorilla (played by an actor in a standard-issue gorilla suit). Decker then uses the gorilla to kill off his enemies. When Dr. Decker's female lab assistant—who is in love with the good doctor—finds him romancing another woman, she jealously injects Konga with the rest of the serum, causing the ape to grow to Kong-like proportions. Picking up Dr. Decker, Konga goes on a tear around London before finally being shot down in front of Big Ben, whereupon he shrinks back down into a (now stuffed) chimpanzee. Unfortunately, the synopsis is much more entertaining than the film itself.

KING KONG (1962)

India's gargantuan "Bollywood" film industry has a long history of "unofficially" remaking foreign films for the local market. In 1962, *Kong* was remade in a version starring World Wrestling Champion Dara Singh.

TARZAN AND KING KONG (1966)

Dara Singh returned four years later in an illegal Indian sequel to the illegal Indian remake. This time, Singh played Tarzan.

THE MIGHTY GORGA (1969)

A turgid, low-budget thriller about a circus owner that travels to Africa to capture a giant gorilla so he can bring it back and put it in his show. The gorilla is played by an actor (who was also the film's director—David L. Hewitt) in a truly awful suit.

A•P•E• (1976)

This made-in-Korea quickie produced by Denver-based Key International Pictures was originally announced as *The New King Kong*, and, like *Queen Kong*, was designed to cash in on all of the publicity surrounding *Kong* '76. The

Some of the cutting-edge special effects from *A˙P˙E˙* (1976).

Poster for *Mighty Peking Man* (1977).

threat of legal action by Dino De Laurentiis (who was in no mood to mess around after his battles with Universal and the producer of *Queen Kong*) prompted Key to change the title to *A*P*E** (after briefly considering what surely has to be the best alternate title in movie history—*Attack of the Giant Horny Gorilla*).

The film begins on a ship that has already visited a mysterious uncharted island and is now bringing back a giant ape that was discovered there. The giant ape escapes by somehow blowing up the ship, after which it battles a great white shark (*Jaws* was still in theaters when the film was made), before wading ashore and beginning a rampage through the Korean hinterlands. Eventually, the giant ape meets and falls in love with a blonde American actress filming a movie (played by Joanna De Varona, who would later change her name to Joanna Kerns and star in the long-running *Growing Pains* television series). The giant ape kidnaps the actress, which leads to a showdown with some miniature models and stock footage meant to represent the American army.

The production—which was originally meant to be presented in 3-D—is extremely cheesy, and the effects and the ape suit are terrible (Rick Baker was allegedly approached about making the costume, but was already busy working on *Kong '76*). The film begins with a reasonably serious tone, but then quickly degenerates into a dreadfully campy spoof. It appears that the producers intended to make a serious movie, but once they saw how bad the initial rushes looked, decided to switch gears and start goofing on themselves before the audience could. At one point during the film's climactic battle, the giant ape turns to the camera and gives the audience the finger, which pretty well sums things up.

MIGHTY PEKING MAN (1977)

Another attempt to cash in on the De Laurentiis Kong, this Hong Kong–made film actually rips off both *Kong* and *Mighty Joe Young*. After hearing reports that a Himalayan village has been attacked by a giant anthropoid, a shady producer hires an explorer to lead an expedition into the mountains to capture the creature. The explorer eventually encounters the giant anthropoid (which is supposed to be an oversized missing link) and his primitive, Sheena-like, blonde human companion—a female whom the giant anthropoid rescued from a plane crash when she was a baby. The explorer brings the giant anthropoid and the primitive, Sheena-like, blonde girl back to civilization, where the giant anthropoid is put on display before finally…well, you know. *Mighty Peking Man* is a better made movie than *A*P*E**, with a much higher level of production value and cinematography, but this strangely glum and at times unpleasant film is no where near as much so-bad-it's good fun as that previously-mentioned epic.

While some films have stolen *Kong*'s premise, others have appropriated its title in the hope that the name-recognition would drum up some business for productions that otherwise have nothing to do giant apes. Some examples: *King of Kong Island* (1968—about a mad scientist that performs mind-control experiments on gorillas); *King Kong's Faust/King Kong's Fist* (1985—about a group of filmmakers attending a German film festival); and *Las Munecas del King Kong/The Dolls of King Kong* (1981—a Mexican film about murderous toys).

KING KONG REFERENCES

There have been many Kong references in various works of popular culture. Here are some of the most notable:

THE WINDMILLS ARE WEAKENING (1965)

This Bob Newhart album contains the comedian's classic "King Kong" routine in which a befuddled night watchman at the Empire State Building calls his supervisor and asks for help in dealing with a fifty-foot-ape he discovers climbing up the outside of the famous landmark.

THE GODFATHER, PART II (1974)

The "Superman" stage show that Michael Corleone watches in a sleazy Havana nightclub is based on Kong's sacrifice scene. At one point the music played by the club's house band reprises Max Steiner's score.

SATURDAY NIGHT LIVE (1976–1977)

This classic NBC television comedy show presented two Kong-related routines during its second season. The first appeared on the November 27, 1976 broadcast and featured cast member Garrett Morris singing a song called "The King Kong Dirge" to a drumbeat accompaniment. The second, which appeared on the January 22, 1977 broadcast, was a spoof of NBC's popular late night interview program *Tomorrow*, in which Dan Aykroyd played Tom Snyder, the chain-smoking host of the program, and John Belushi played his guest, an inexplicably wheelchair-bound Dino De Laurentiis, who manically touts the virtues of his new Kong by frenziedly repeating DeLaurentiis's by then familiar "When Kong dies, everybody cry…" quote.

SEINFELD (1989–1998)

For several seasons of this long-running sitcom, a small poster from *King Kong* '76 hung on the wall of the show's main living room set.

JURASSIC PARK (1993)

The entrance to the dinosaur amusement park is designed to look like the gate in the Great Wall from the original *Kong*. Jeff Goldblum's character makes mention of this as he passes through it.

THE LOST WORLD: JURASSIC PARK (1997)

The ship that brings the captured *T-rex* to San Diego is called the SS *Venture*. The entire dinosaur loose in the city climax of the film is also an obvious nod to the greatest prehistoric monster-run-amok film of all time.

DINOSAUR SUMMER (1998)

A sequel to Sir Arthur Conan Doyle's *The Lost World*, this young adult novel by author Greg Bear and illustrator Tony Diterlizzi about an expedition back to Professor Challenger's dinosaur-filled plateau features Merian C. Cooper, Ernest B. Schoedsack, Willis O'Brien, and Ray Harryhausen as supporting characters.

THE CIDER HOUSE RULES (1999)

Michael Caine's Dr. Wilbur Larch entertains the orphans in his care by screening the 1933 *King Kong* for them in this 1999 drama.

SKY CAPTAIN AND THE WORLD OF TOMORROW (2004)

There are three delightful *King Kong* references in this computer-generated sci-fi adventure. In the sequence when the giant robots attack New York, an ape-like figure can be seen scaling the Empire State Building in the background of one of the shots. During a later underwater sequence, the camera passes over a sunken ship named the SS *Venture*. The ship has a giant cage chained to one of its decks. The bars of the cage are bent, indicating that something very big and very strong broke out of it. Finally, the jungle on the mysterious island where Jude Law and Gwyneth Paltrow find themselves at the end of the film is designed to resemble the Byron Crabbe/Mario Larrinaga Gustave Doré-inspired jungles from the original *Kong*.

■ ■ ■

CHAPTER

9

THE COLLECTIBLE KONG

The King Kong films have generated an enormous amount of collectible merchandise over the years. In this chapter, we'll take a look at some of the items the movies have spawned.

A King Kong pepper shaker and an Empire State Building salt shaker from the 1980s.

KING KONG

At the time of *Kong*'s release in 1933, film merchandising was not the potent force that it would later become. In those days, most cinema-related products were tied to stars rather than to any one particular movie. For example, an extensive line of Charlie Chaplin merchandise was produced in the 1910s and 20s, followed by a steady stream of Shirley Temple and Mickey Mouse–related products in the 1930s. When it came to individual films, however, far fewer items were available.

Modern manufacturers like movie merchandising because the film their products are based on serve as an effective advertisement for those products. Being connected to a popular movie that plays in theaters over a long period of time can be highly profitable. In the early days of Hollywood movies, however, theater programs changed twice a week—and most films were in and out of a neighborhood theater in just a few days—so a film's value as a promotional tool was negligible. For this reason, most manufacturers of the period weren't interested in producing movie tie-ins. (There were a few exceptions: for example, if a new movie were based on a novel, occasionally a commemorative edition of the book—sometimes containing stills from the film—would be published to coincide with the picture's release; or if a movie contained a popular song, then a recording might be issued or the sheet music widely published.) These are the reasons why so few pieces of official Kong merchandise were manufactured when the film was first released. In fact, there were only two items.

The first, of course, was the novelization by Delos W. Lovelace. A unique and rather strange literary genre, the novelization—a book based on the screenplay of a film or television show—originated as a way of giving films based on original scripts the same prestige as those based on novels. A book of a film was usually published well ahead of the film's release to give the impression that it was based on an already-published work. Although novelizations would later become quite popular (especially in the 1970s and 80s), they were quite rare in the 1930s. Still, Merian Cooper was confident that a book with Edgar Wallace's name on it would be a best-seller (since all of Wallace's books were) and, because of that, would also be a terrific promotional tool. As previously mentioned, this is one of the reasons Cooper chose Wallace to work on *Kong* in the first place. After Wallace died, Cooper didn't give up on the idea, so he hired Lovelace to write the book instead. A close friend of Cooper's since his newspapers days, Lovelace, a former reporter turned short story writer and novelist, was married to Maud Hart Lovelace (also a novelist and the author of the Betsy-Tacy novels—a popular series of books about two young girls growing up in turn-of-the-century Minnesota), with whom he had a daughter named Merian. Cooper paid his friend $600 to write the novel, which Lovelace finished in a matter of months. Lovelace based the novel on Ruth Rose's first complete draft of the script, so it differs from the finished film in several respects. It includes most of the bits Cooper cut from the film, including the *Arsinoitherium/Styracosaurus* scene (although Lovelace replaced both of

A 1976 reprint of Delos W. Lovelace's novelization.

THE APE THAT HAS THRILLED MILLIONS — THE GREAT ORIGINAL HIMSELF — THE ONE AND ONLY —

KING KONG

Conceived by EDGAR WALLACE and MERIAN C. COOPER
Novelization by DELOS W. LOVELACE
With 16 pages of splendid new art!

them with a *Triceratops*), the spider scene, the giant snake, and Jack and Ann's escape down the falls. The novel also includes some scenes that never made it into the movie, such as the asphalt pit scene and Kong's escape from the police across the rooftops of Manhattan. In addition, the novel did not include the elevated-train sequence, the name of Captain Englehorn's ship is the *Wanderer*, and Denham delivers his closing line from atop the Empire State Building. Because Cooper still wanted to take advantage of Wallace's name, the final credit on the book reads: "Conceived by Edgar Wallace and Merian Cooper. Novelized from the Radio Picture by Delos W. Lovelace." The novel was published in December 1932 by Grosset & Dunlap.

The second piece of Kong-related merchandise that appeared in 1933 was a collection of sheet music based on Max Steiner's score. The pieces included *The King Kong March*, *The Aboriginal Sacrifice Dance*, *The Forgotten Island*, and *A Boat in the Fog*.

The next round of significant Kong items appeared in the 1960s, when the character's status as a classic character was growing. The first significant item was a plastic model kit manufactured by Aurora in 1964. The model featured a roaring Kong standing on an island-shaped base holding a plastic replica of Ann Darrow. Aurora also put out an unusual model called *King Kong's Thronester*, which (for some inexplicable reason) featured Kong driving a tricked-out drag racer. In 1965, two different sets of trading cards (each containing fifty-five cards) were issued—one by Topps and the other by the Donruss Company. The Topps set was a straightforward set of pictures from the film. The Donruss set was more irreverent and contained a lot of silly jokes and captions. Later in the decade, an abbreviated version of *Kong* intended for home projection was released on 8 mm and Super 8 mm film. In addition, several items related to the Rankin/Bass *King Kong Show* were also released in the mid-1960s, including a board game and a 45 rpm single featuring the show's theme song.

Most Kong products of the time were licensed by RKO-General, but some were authorized by Merian C. Cooper himself. As the credited co-conceiver of the story, Cooper held the copyright on the novel: (Cooper bought Edgar Wallace's portion of the rights from Wallace's estate after he died and Delos Lovelace had no claim on the rights because he wrote the novel as a "work for hire," meaning he worked on the project as Cooper's employee and not as an originator of the material.) Since the novel was a separate piece of intellectual property from the film, this gave Cooper the right to license Kong-related material as long as it was based on the novel and not the film. One of the items Cooper licensed was an oversized comic book adaptation of the story published by Whitman in 1968. Because the comic book was based on the novel and not the movie, illustrator Alberto Giolitti had to change the look of the characters so they did not resemble the actors in the film.

In 1970, Aurora reissued its King Kong model kit, this time with a luminescent "glow-in-the-dark" head. Around the same time, a reprint of one of the posters from the film's initial 1933 run was released and became quite popular (this is apparently the poster Francesca De Laurentiis had hanging on her bed-

TOP: Souvenir picture frame from Universal Studios Hollywood.

BOTTOM: A Kong-themed souvenir from the Empire State Building's gift shop.

room wall). A poster-sized reproduction of the film's most famous publicity still was also released. The poster featured one of the eighteen-inch Kongs looming over the Manhattan skyline, holding a woman in his hand as lightning strikes behind him (the lightning addition came from the ending of the original Edgar Wallace script). In 1975, United Artists Records issued an original recording of Max Steiner's score on LP, conducted by Leroy Holmes. Nineteen seventy-five also saw the publication of *The Making of King Kong*, a well-researched book about the production of the film, written by Orville Goldner and George E. Turner. This was followed in 1976 by the publication of *The Girl in the Hairy Paw*, a collection of articles, stories, and pictures about the film, edited by Ronald Gottesman and Harry Geduld. The book contained original and reprinted articles about the film's production, as well as a generous helping of critical reviews and analyses (many of them offering the kind of esoteric interpretations of the film that Merian Cooper so disliked) and literary riffs on the film's themes and characters. To capitalize on all of the ballyhoo surrounding the release of *King Kong* '76, two different paperback reprints of the Lovelace novelization were published in fall 1976—an illustrated edition from Tempo Books and another from Ace Books that featured a dramatic painting by Frank Frazetta on the cover. With RKO long gone, the credit on the novel was changed to read "Conceived by Edgar Wallace and Merian Cooper. Novelized by Delos W. Lovelace."

In the early 1980s, *King Kong* was released on videotape. Because of RKO's rather indiscriminate approach to licensing, several different VHS editions of the film were put out by different companies, most of poor quality. When Turner Entertainment acquired the rights to the film in the mid-1980s, it released a VHS edition made from a higher quality transfer of the film than the other companies had used. Turner also released a colorized edition of the film. In 1989, *Kong* appeared on a Criterion Collection laser disc, which featured commentary by film historian Rudy Behlmer and contained *The Son of Kong* on the flip side.

On May 13, 1986, Universal opened a King Kong attraction at its Southern California theme park. As previously related, Universal had gained certain merchandising rights to the character in its 1976 settlement with De Laurentiis, including the right to create a theme park attraction. (Some sources close to the company have suggested that the reason Universal fought so hard against De Laurentiis was to obtain this right. Since Universal's theme parks generate as much if not more revenue than its films, the right to produce a Kong attraction was apparently worth a lot more to the company than the right to produce a Kong movie.) Built at a cost of $6.5 million, *Kongfrontation* featured an impressive thirty-foot-tall animatronic Kong equipped with "banana breath," that threatened sightseers as their tour bus drove through an elaborate reproduction of New York City featuring a burning apartment building and an exploding helicopter. A second Kong attraction opened at the Universal's Orlando, Florida, theme park a short time later. A wide variety of *Kongfrontation* merchandise—including T-shirts, sweatshirts, baseball caps, drinking cups, salt and pepper shakers, and picture frames—was sold in the theme park's stores and souvenir stands to promote the ride. *Kongfrontation* closed in both parks in 2004.

In 1990, Monster Comics published a six-part comic book adaptation of the Lovelace novel, written and illustrated by Donald Simpson, and featuring cover art by acclaimed comic book artist Dave Stevens (*The Rocketeer*). The adaptation was authorized by Merian Cooper's estate, which is administered by Cooper's son, Richard Merian Cooper. A few years later, Eclipse Comics published a new set of *King Kong* trading cards. In addition to stills from the movie, the 110-card set also contained facts and information about the making of the film and about its creators. In 1993, Turner Home Entertainment issued a sixtieth anniversary edition of *King Kong* on VHS. Since the original negative was no longer in existence, the tape was mastered from a new negative that had been duped from the best prints of the film that could be found. The tape came in a box equipped with an audio chip. When the chip was activated, it emitted one of the roars Murray Spivak had created for Kong sixty years before. The tape was sold in single units or in a commemorative gift box, along with a copy of *It Was Beauty Killed the Beast*, a poster, and three mounted frames from the film. Nineteen ninety-four saw the publication of *Anthony Browne's King Kong*, a wonderful illustrated storybook version of the tale with exquisite artwork by British artist Anthony Browne. The book was a joint venture between Turner Publishing and Richard M. Cooper. In 1999, two new versions of the film's soundtrack were issued on CD. Marco Polo released a new recording of Max Steiner's score performed by the Moscow Symphony Orchestra, and Rhino Records put out a version culled from the film's soundtrack that also included music, sound effects, and dialogue.

In 2000, the Polar Lights Company reissued Aurora's *King Kong* model from the 1960s (the original version, not the one with the glow-in-the-dark head). Also in 2000, Turner Entertainment (now owned by Warner Bros.) began licensing a series of Kong-related items, including an exquisitely detailed Kong figure pro-

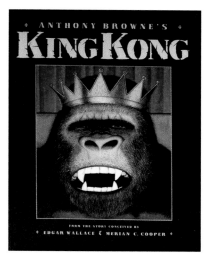

TOP: *Anthony Browne's King Kong.*

BOTTOM: Reissue of Aurora's classic Kong model by the Polar Lights company.

LEFT: Universal Studios Hollywood's Kongfrontation theme park ride.

duced by McFarlane Toys as part of its Movie Maniacs collection. Turner also licensed Kong neckties, notebooks, and even a glass Christmas ornament. To capitalize on the release of Peter Jackson's *King Kong* in December 2005, Richard M. Cooper authorized two new tie-ins to the original film created by painter/sculptor/author Joe DeVito. The first of these is a book, cowritten with Brad Strickland and published in December 2004 by Dark Horse Press, called *Kong: The King of Skull Island*—an elaborately illustrated sequel to the Lovelace novelization in which Carl Denham returns to Skull Island immediately after the events of *King Kong* and then disappears. Twenty-five years later, Denham's son teams up with an older Jack Driscoll and they go to Skull Island to find out what happened to Denham. The new story does not acknowledge the events of *The Son of Kong*, since that film was a sequel to the movie and not the novel. The second authorized item is a porcelain sculpture based on Mario Larrinaga's preproduction drawing

TOP: King Kong figure from McFarlane Toys.

BOTTOM: Monster Comics's 1990 Kong comic, with cover art by Dave Stevens.

RIGHT: Whitman's large-scale Kong comic book. Licensed by Merian C. Cooper.

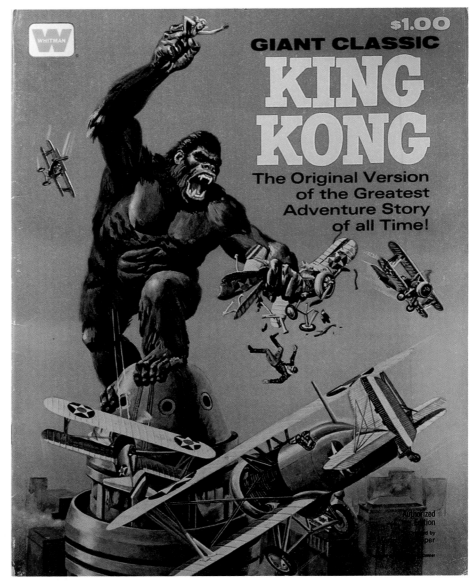

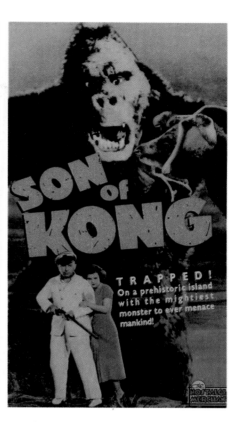

of the Empire State Building climax (to which the Cooper Estate owns the rights). Finally, in November 2005, Warner Home Video will release *King Kong* for the first time on DVD. The disc was mastered from yet another new negative assembled from the best elements and prints obtained from a worldwide search, which were then digitally cleaned and restored. Warner promises that the film will look as good on the new disc as it did when it was first released in 1933.

King Kong has also inspired a series of statues and resin model kits, some of which were sculpted by people like Marcel Delgado and Ray Harryhausen. It has also inspired a great deal of "unofficial" merchandise, including the delightfully tacky knickknacks that can be purchased in the gift shops at the Empire State Building.

THE SON OF KONG

No merchandise tied to *The Son of Kong* appeared at the time of the film's release. In the late 1960s, an abbreviated home movie version of the film was released on 8 mm and Super 8 mm film. As with *King Kong*, *Son* was released on video in the early 1980s in several editions of less-than-sterling quality. In 1989 it was included on the flip side of Criterion's *King Kong* laser disc and in the early 1990s, Turner put out a new VHS edition of the film made from a higher quality transfer than previous editions had used. As yet, it has not been colorized. In 2001, Marco Polo released a new recording of the film's score recorded by the Moscow Symphony Orchestra on a CD that also included music from *The Most Dangerous Game*.

ABOVE, LEFT TO RIGHT:
Christmas ornament from Turner Entertainment. *King Kong Vs. Godzilla* VHS box. *The Son of Kong* on VHS.

KINGUKONGU TAI GOJIRA (KING KONG VERSUS GODZILLA)/ KINGUKONGU NO GYAKUSHU (KING KONG ESCAPES)

No merchandising was done for either of these films at the time of their release. Since then, however, both films have appeared many times on VHS and DVD in Japan. Japanese companies have also produced a wide range of toys, models, and action figures based on characters from both films (although Toho no longer has the right to license the Kong character for any product other than video editions of the films). Compact Disc editions of the music from both movies have been released, also in Japan.

King Kong Versus Godzilla has been released on VHS in the United States in several poor quality editions. A thirty-fifth anniversary DVD was released in 1998 (the cover of which features a picture of the Kong from *King Kong* '76 rather than the one from *King Kong Versus Godzilla*). As previously mentioned, *King Kong Escapes* remained unreleased on home video in the United States until November 2005, when it was issued on DVD along with a new edition of *King Kong Versus Godzilla* in a double pack designed to take advantage of the hoopla surrounding the release of the Peter Jackson *King Kong*. There was no tie-in merchandise produced in the United States, although some of the Japanese items are occasionally available from online sources.

KING KONG (1976)

Merchandising was a key component in *King Kong* '76's promotional campaign. By the mid-1970s, movie merchandising was starting to become an important part of film promotion, especially for big-budget, high-profile films. Paramount Pictures got the ball rolling in 1974 by licensing an unprecedented number of tie-in products for *The Great Gatsby*, but that turned out to be just a dry run for what the company accomplished with *Kong*. Mildred Collins, Paramount's director of special products, made deals with dozens of companies to create tie-in products for the film.

Pocket Books published *The Creation of Dino De Laurentiis' King Kong*—a book about the making of the film written by its publicist Bruce Bahrenburg. The main focus of the book was the production's attempts to get the Big Kong up and running. Since the *Kong* story rights were still in dispute, no novelization of the film was published. Instead, Ace Books published a paperback version of Lorenzo Semple, Jr.'s screenplay, complete with an introduction written by the author. Several other *Kong*-related books were also released, some of them aimed at children. Reprise Records issued a soundtrack album that fea-

ABOVE: Paperback edition of Lorenzo Semple, Jr.'s screenplay for *King Kong* (1976).

BELOW: *Kong* '76 peanut butter cups from Schraft's.

FACING PAGE: A plethora of *Kong* '76 merchandise (clockwise from top left): A Colorforms play set; a key chain from Sedgewick Jeans containing a single strand of hair from the Big Kong, as well as a certificate of authenticity; Jim Beam advertisement featuring a recipe for a King Kong cocktail; a Jim Beam King Kong bourbon bottle; Slurpee cups from 7-11; a collection of Topps trading cards; Kong lunchbox from King Seeley; Premium drinking glasses from Coca Cola; Viewmaster reels from GAF.

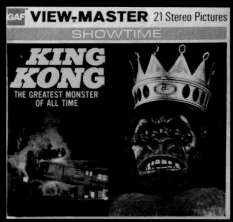

tured John Barry's original score on LP and 8-track tape.

A series of posters, notebooks, and binders were printed featuring John Berkey's illustrations. The King Seeley Company manufactured a King Kong lunchbox and thermos, also featuring Berkey's artwork. Topps published a fifty-five-card set of trading cards and stickers and Schraft's introduced King Kong peanut butter cups. The Mego Corporation produced a plastic model of Kong straddling the World Trade Center and GAF manufactured two sets of 3-D Viewmaster reels, one talking and one not. There were also large and small jigsaw puzzles, a board game from Ideal, balloons, a stuffed animal, a Colorforms playset, a clock, and King Kong wallpaper.

Coca-Cola and 7-11 both offered special King Kong collectible drinking glasses. Plastic cups, plates, and straws were also available, as were T-shirts, pajamas, socks, belts, buckles, and a Ben Cooper Halloween costume. *Family Circle* magazine offered an iron-on T-shirt transfer and Sedgefield Jeans produced a King Kong keychain that contained a few strands of hair, allegedly from the Big Kong. One of the more unusual products was a Kong-shaped bourbon bottle from Jim Beam that came complete with a recipe for a King Kong Cocktail (a mix of bourbon, orange juice, and grenadine with a slice of lime). Finally, some theater owners received a special two-foot-tall resin Kong statue.

By the time the film opened, King Kong merchandise was everywhere. Collectively the tie-in manufacturers spent approximately $10 million to promote their products, which translated into $10 million worth of free publicity for the film. The success of the *King Kong* campaign inspired other studios to use merchandising to promote their films. The practice shifted into high gear the following year with the release of *Star Wars* and has been a key component of motion picture marketing ever since.

Paramount Home Video released the film twice on VHS. In the early 1980s, the film appeared in a two-cassette edition as part of a premiere series of Paramount's top titles. In 1990 it was reissued in a lower-priced, single-cassette version. In the mid-1980s, the film was released on laserdisc and in 1999 Paramount issued *Kong* on DVD in a perfunctory edition with no extras apart from the film's trailer. A few years later, a French company issued a deluxe DVD edition of the film that came complete with a "making of" documentary.

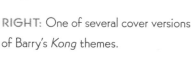
LEFT: Reprise Records soundtrack album featuring John Barry's score for *Kong '76*.

RIGHT: One of several cover versions of Barry's *Kong* themes.

Aside from home video products, a few other *Kong 76*-related products have appeared in the years since the film's release. A poor quality, unauthorized CD version of the John Barry's score was released in Italy in the late 1990s. In the early 2000s, several high-quality resin model kits recreating scenes from the film were produced. Finally, in May 2005 *Film Score Monthly* released an official, remastered version of the score on CD, featuring liner notes by Barry scholars Geoff Leonard, Pete Walker, and Stephan Woolston.

KING KONG LIVES

In stark contrast to *King Kong '76*, there was almost no merchandising done for its sequel. The only significant tie-in product was a soundtrack album featuring John Scott's terrific score. The album was released on vinyl in the United States and on CD in Japan. John Scott himself feels that the Japanese release was the superior one.

King Kong Lives was released on VHS in 1987 by Lorimar Home Video. Several years later, it was re-issued by Anchor Bay. It was released on DVD in 2004, in an edition from Twentieth Century–Fox Home Video that is so bare-bones it doesn't even include a trailer.

■ ■ ■

TOP: *Kong '76* publicist Bruce Bahrenburg's book about the making of the film.

BOTTOM: *King Kong Lives* DVD.

CHAPTER 10

THE RETURN OF THE KING:

Peter Jackson's *King Kong*

Peter Jackson was born on October 31, 1961 in Wellington, New Zealand, and grew up in nearby Pukerua Bay. When Jackson was eight years old, a family friend gave the budding photographer a Super-8 mm home movie camera and young Peter started making short films with his friends in and around his neighborhood. A short time later, he saw an old black-and-white film on television that changed his life. That movie was the original *King Kong*. "I can't tell you what an effect it had on me," Jackson has said. He's also said, "It's my favorite movie." The movie impressed upon Jackson the ability of film to conjour up new and fantastic worlds and to bring to life creatures that had heretofore existed only in dreams. From the moment Jackson saw the film, he knew what he wanted to do with his life. "[*King Kong*] put me on the path to where I am today," he stated.

The new, computer-generated King Kong.

After seeing *Kong*, Jackson became fascinated with stop-motion animation. He studied the films of Willis O'Brien and O'Brien's protégé Ray Harryhausen; he even attempted to make his own stop-motion films, including a remake of *Kong* featuring clay dinosaurs and a cardboard Empire State Building. He later became interested in other types of special effects, including makeup effects and animatronics, and the debut of *Star Wars* introduced him to the possibilities of optical effects. After graduating from high school, Jackson decided to forgo college and attempt to forge a career as a special effects creator.

Unfortunately, there wasn't much opportunity in the minuscule New Zealand film industry, forcing Jackson to take a job as an apprentice photoengraver at a local newspaper. With help from his extremely supportive parents, Jackson purchased a used 16 mm film camera, and began spending his weekends making a short film designed to show off his facility for special effects. Originally scheduled to shoot for only a few weeks, the film—about a man who is attacked and eaten by a group of cannibals that have taken over a small town—soon began to grow. The plotline expanded until the short film became a feature about an attempt by alien cannibals to take over the world. Filled with elaborately gory special effects and outrageously bloody humor, the film would ultimately take four years to complete. After playing at the Cannes Film Festival, *Bad Taste* (1987) was picked up for distribution and became a hit the world over (except in the United States, where it went straight to video). Peter Jackson, special effects man, was now Peter Jackson, film director.

Following *Bad Taste*, Jackson intended his next film to be *Braindead*—another horror comedy about a meek young man who finds his house overrun with zombies—which he cowrote with Stephen Sinclair and Fran Walsh. When the financing for that project fell through at the last minute, Jackson and his crew decided to make an outrageous movie filled with sex, violence, and incredibly gross humor featuring a cast consisting exclusively of puppets. Cowritten by Jackson, Sinclair, Walsh, and Danny Mulheron, *Meet the Feebles* (1990) was less well received than *Bad Taste* and did not do nearly as well at the box office, although it has since developed a cult following on video.

After the release of *Feebles*, new financing was secured for *Braindead* and the long-delayed project went forward. Released in 1992, the film received excellent reviews, although one reviewer also referred to it as "one of the bloodiest films in cinematic history." The film was picked up for distribution in the United States, but objections from the ratings board caused the film to be severely edited, which robbed it of much of its impact. Retitled *Dead Alive*, the film did poorly at the American box office.

During the making of *Braindead*, Jackson and Fran Walsh became romantically involved and decided to work together on Jackson's next film, which was a radical departure from his previous work in both tone and subject matter. Based on a true story, *Heavenly Creatures* was a drama set in the 1950s about Pauline Parker and Juliet Hulme, two New Zealand teenagers who kill Parker's mother. The two shy and introverted girls had met at school and bonded by developing an elaborate mutual fantasy world filled with imaginary characters, landscapes, and adventures. When Hulme's family decided to move

Peter Jackson.

to England, Parker, unable to bear the thought of separation, begged desperately to be allowed to accompany them. Her mother's refusal precipitated the murder. Written by Walsh and Jackson, the script intermixed depictions of real-life events with scenes that brought to life the girls' inner fantasies. To realize the fantasy elements of the story, Jackson established his own special effects company called WETA Limited. (A weta is a large, cave-dwelling insect.) The company was divided into two parts: WETA Workshop, which created mechanical and makeup effects, and WETA Digital, which created computer-generated imagery and composites. Starring seventeen-year old Kate Winslet in her feature debut, the stunning mix of real-life drama and ethereal fantasy was released in 1994 to great acclaim. The film won the Silver Lion prize at the Venice Film Festival, and Walsh and Jackson were nominated for an Academy Award for their screenplay. Miramax Films bought the U.S. distribution rights and signed Jackson to a first-look deal.

In 1995, Jackson made a mock-documentary about a fictional film pioneer called *Forgotten Silver* for New Zealand television and then made his first film for an American film studio. Written by Jackson and Walsh and executive produced by director Robert Zemeckis (*Back to the Future*, *Forrest Gump*) for Universal Pictures, *The Frighteners* was another horror comedy (albeit a much tamer one) about a con man named Frank Bannister (played by Michael J. Fox) who teams up with a group of ghosts. Their scam is an ingenious one: the ghosts invade a location and pretend to haunt it and then Fox's character arrives on the scene and charges the owners to exorcise the unwanted visitors. Trouble arises when Bannister and company encounter a truly malevolent spirit that begins committing murder. To create the films abundant visual effects, Jackson greatly expanded WETA Limited and moved it from the basement of his Wing Nut Films production company to a warehouse he had pur-

Adrien Brody as a literary Jack Driscoll.

chased in the Miramar suburb of Wellington. Jackson has since expanded the complex, which is now named Camperdown Studios.

The early rushes on *The Frighteners* were exciting enough to make the executives at Universal want to work with Jackson on other projects. At the time, the studio was planning to do a remake of their 1954 monster film *The Creature from the Black Lagoon* and offered Jackson the opportunity to direct it, which he declined. The executives were disappointed, but when they learned of Jackson's lifelong love affair with Merian C. Cooper's giant ape, the studio decided that the time had come to exercise the option it had won back in 1976 during its battle with RKO and Dino De Laurentiis. After nineteen years, Universal was finally going to proceed with its remake of *King Kong*.

FIRST TRY

Amazingly enough, when Universal first offered Jackson the project, he turned it down, because he felt that he would be tempting fate by messing with a classic (Jackson knew what a beating sci-fi fans had give *King Kong* '76 over the years for doing just that). However, after thinking it over, Jackson changed his mind. Knowing that Universal was intent on going ahead with the project, he realized that if he didn't direct it, someone else would—someone who might not have the same reverence for the original film that he had would and do an even worse job than he feared he might. Plus Jackson thought that a remake was warranted because, no matter how much of a classic the original film was, he felt that younger audiences were no longer watching it because they weren't interested in black-and-white films. Jackson wanted to give this audience a *King Kong* that would enthrall them as much as the original had enthralled him. Adding these considerations to his great love for the great ape, Jackson accepted Universal's offer.

Universal may have given some consideration to reviving Bo Goldman's 1975 script, but Jackson wanted to start fresh. In early 1996, as *The Frighteners* proceeded through a lengthy post-production period (required to produce the film's prodigious number of visual effects), Jackson and Walsh began writing an all-new Kong screenplay. Set in the 1930s time period of the original film, the result was a curious amalgamation of elements culled from *King Kong, Kong* '76, Cooper's life, *Mighty Joe Young, Raiders of the Lost Ark*, and *Jurassic Park*.

The Jackson/Walsh script begins in the skies over France in 1917, as fighter pilot Jack Driscoll engages in a dogfight with German war planes. Jack's plane crashes and he loses his best friend. The story jumps forward to 1933 Sumatra. An embittered Jack now runs a lumber mill and has frequent run-ins with famed British anthropologist Lord Linwood Darrow and his daughter Ann, who are attempting to excavate some ancient Hindu ruins. Carl Denham, a crass film director from Hollywood, arrives in Sumatra aboard the SS *Venture* to shoot a documentary. While filming, Denham and his crew accidentally uncover an ancient statue of a giant ape. Lord Darrow recognizes the ape as Kong, a legendary god that was once the focus of a fearsome cult that was widespread in the East Indies. The cult was eventually stamped out by the Hindus, although Lord Darrow has heard rumors that a remnant still remains active on an uncharted island somewhere in the Indian Ocean. The statue contains a map of the island that both Ann and Denham manage to copy before the statue is destroyed by the local Hindu authorities. Seeking to eliminate all traces of Kong, the authorities then try to close down Lord Darrow's dig. The stress of arguing with them causes Lord Darrow to experience a fatal heart attack. The authorities then try to arrest Ann and Jack, who escape and take refuge aboard the *Venture* as it sails out of port. Hoping to find a primitive (and preferably naked) tribe that he can photograph to spice up his documentary, Denham decided to go to the island. Ann goes along in order to honor her late father by making the greatest anthropological discovery in history.

The *Venture* sails to the mysterious island, which it finds surrounded by a perpetual wall of fog. A landing party led by Jack, Ann, and Denham explores the island and discovers a primitive tribe living in a village built in front of a giant wall. Watching the natives prepare for a human sacrifice, Ann realizes that the tribe is indeed a member of the Kong cult. The natives capture the explorers and attempt to kill them, but Jack and Ann lead an escape. The landing party makes it back to the *Venture*, whereupon the decision is made to leave as soon as possible. As the *Venture* prepares to set sail, a group of natives sneak aboard and kidnap Ann.

The natives take Ann back to the village and carry her to the top of the wall, where they dress her in sacrificial clothes and tie her to an altar. The altar is then lowered down into a clearing on the far side of the wall. Ann hears something huge crashing through the trees and then Kong—a twenty-five-foot tall silverback gorilla—emerges from the jungle. As Ann screams, Kong snatches her from the altar and carries her back into the jungle. After fighting its way past the natives, a search party led by Jack and a reluctant Denham gives chase.

Kong, a vicious carnivore, carries Ann to his killing ground and is about to eat her when her sacrificial headdress falls off, revealing her blond hair. Kong is fascinated. Ann further entrances him by singing a lullaby. Meanwhile, the search party survives attacks by a variety of dinosaurs before finally being chased by a *Triceratops* out onto a fallen log that bridges a deep gorge. Hearing the commotion, Kong leaves Ann in a tree and goes to the gorge, where he confronts the search party. As Jack climbs down the cliff to a cave, Kong twists the log, causing the rest of the men to fall to the bottom of the gorge, where they are attacked by a variety of giant insects. Kong then attempts to capture Jack. Meanwhile, Ann is threatened by an *Allosaurus* and screams. Her cries alert Kong, who leaves Jack and rushes to her aid. Protecting Ann, Kong battles the *Allosaurus*, who is quickly joined by two of his brothers. Kong is overwhelmed and outnumbered, but is eventually able to marshal his tremendous strength and defeat the three meat-eaters.

Back at the gorge, Jack climbs back to the top of the cliff and encounters Denham, who has also survived Kong's attack. Jack continues on after Ann, while Denham returns to the village to get help. Meanwhile, Kong carries Ann to his lair atop Skull Mountain. Kong brings Ann food and they have a playful encounter before being attacked by a flock of flying batlike creatures. As Kong

Naomi Watts as the new Ann Darrow.

fends off the bats, Jack rescues Ann and they both escape. A furious Kong follows them back to the village, smashes through the wall and tears through the
village looking for Ann. Denham halts Kong's rampage by shooting him in the
kneecaps with a tommy gun, after which the remaining sailors club him into
unconsciousness.

The scene shifts to New York several months later. Denham puts Kong on
display in an ornate theater. Ann, outraged by the way Denham is exploiting
Kong, tries to stop the show. As Denham manhandles her in front of the cameras, Kong breaks loose. The frightened audience flees as Kong stomps down on
Denham, killing him. Jack and Ann escape in a cab, but Kong catches up with
them. Hoping to save the great ape, Ann allows Kong to reclaim her, after
which he carries her to the top of the Empire State Building. Learning that a
squadron of navy planes is on its way to kill Kong, Jack commandeers a working fighter plane that he finds being used as an advertisement in front of a
local movie theater and takes off. He flies interference, preventing the navy
planes from firing on Kong. Jack continues his counterattack until Kong grabs
his plane and trashes it. Jack bails out onto the dome of the Empire State
Building. Finally free from Jack's interference, the navy pilots open fire on
Kong. Mortally wounded, the giant ape caresses Ann one last time as she sings
him a lullaby and then topples from his perch. Ann and Jack embrace as Kong
falls one hundred two stories to the street below.

Full of chase scenes, dogfights, dinosaur stampedes, and derring-do, Jackson
and Walsh's at-times unwieldy script is action-packed and extremely violent. In
stark contrast to *King Kong* '76, it returns to and amplifies Cooper's original
vision of Kong as a fierce and brutal beast. Still, Universal approved the script
and, with Robert Zemeckis as executive producer, the film entered preproduction. The plan was to begin filming sometime in 1997 for a summer 1998 release.

The team at WETA began doing some preliminary design work on Kong and the dinosaurs while Jackson approached Kate Winslet about playing Ann.

At this point, some clouds began to appear on the horizon. First, *The Frighteners* opened in the United States in July 1996 and failed at the box office. At the same time, Disney was producing its remake of *Mighty Joe Young* and Tri-Star had just announced that it was going to produce a big-budget remake of *Godzilla*, which it also planned to open in the summer of 1998. With the studio's confidence in Jackson shaken by the poor performance of *The Frighteners* and worried that the marketplace would not support three giant monster movies at the same time, Universal began to get cold feet. Finally, in January 1997, Universal canceled Peter Jackson's *King Kong*.

MOVING ON

Devastated, Jackson turned to another project he had been developing—a cinematic adaptation of J.R.R. Tolkien's classic fantasy trilogy *The Lord of the Rings*.

Figuring that no studio would be willing to take a chance on an expensive, unproven trilogy, Jackson pitched the concept to Miramax as a two-part epic. Miramax green-lit the project, but, as the budget began to rise, the studio began pressuring Jackson to shrink *Rings* down into a single film. Jackson resisted, feeling it wouldn't be possible to do justice to Tolkien's epic vision in just one movie. Unable to reach a compromise, Miramax gave Jackson four weeks to find a buyer for the project. If he was unable to, Miramax would take over and hire a new director to make *Rings* as a single film.

With the clock ticking, Jackson turned to New Line Cinema, a company he had first worked with in the late 1980s when he co-wrote a (unproduced) script for the studio's *Nightmare on Elm Street* series. To Jackson's happy surprise, New Line chairman Robert Shaye not only agreed to take on the project, but also suggested that the project be expanded to three films—one for each of Tolkien's original books. Joined by screenwriter Phillipa Boyens, Walsh and Jackson expanded and rewrote the screenplays, while WETA began work on the physical and visual effects. Produced by Walsh, Jackson, and Barrie M. Osborne, shooting on all three films began in 1999. The first film, *The Fellowship of the Ring*, was released at the end of 2001, followed by *The Two Towers* in 2002, and *The Return of the King* in 2003. Collectively, the three films won seventeen Academy Awards (including Best Picture, Best Director, and Best Screenplay for *The Return of the King*) and grossed nearly $3 billion. The tremendous success of *The Lord of the Rings* meant that Jackson could now make any film he wanted to. It was not hard for him to decide what that film would be.

THE WHEEL COMES 'ROUND In early 2003, as Jackson was finishing work on *The Return of the King*, the executives at Universal—who no longer had any doubts about Jackson's ability to deliver a box office smash—approached the director and asked him if was still interested in making *King*

Kong. When Jackson indicated that he certainly was, the studio offered him the single highest fee ever offered a filmmaker—$20 million and 20 percent of the gross to write (with Walsh and Boyens), produce (with Walsh), and direct—if he would agree to make *Kong* his next film. He agreed and in March 2003, Universal announced that Peter Jackson's *King Kong* would be the studio's big release for Christmas 2005. Jackson called it "a dream come true."

REVISING THE SCRIPT   In January 2004, after *The Return of the King* had been safely and effectively launched, Jackson turned his attention back to *Kong.*

Reviewing the 1996 script, Jackson found that he was no longer satisfied with it. Working with Walsh and Boyens, he began revising the screenplay to bring it more in line with the original film. The anthropology and fighter pilot angles were dropped. Ann Darrow would once again be a down-on-her-luck actress, and Jack Driscoll was transformed into an idealistic playwright (based on a young Arthur Miller) hired to write the screenplay for Carl Denham's movie. The romance between Jack and Ann would now mirror the romance between Miller and Marilyn Monroe. The character of Denham was revised to make him younger and less crass. Based on a young Orson Welles, Denham would now be a driven, young filmmaker trying to make a name for himself in Hollywood by directing a spectacular film the likes of which no one had ever seen before. The movie Denham is making was changed from a documentary to a dramatic film being shot on location. This allowed the writers to create a clever film-within-the-film in which Ann co-stars with a B-movie actor named Bruce Baxter, whose role requires him to speak many of the misogynistic lines uttered by Bruce Cabot in the original *Kong.*

While the script still contained plenty of action, the *Raiders of the Lost Ark* tone was dropped in favor of an emphasis on realism and character development. The character that Jackson was most interested in developing was Kong, whom Jackson saw as being an ancient, battle-scarred silverback. Like Merian Cooper, Jackson wanted to portray Kong as a fierce, brutal monster, but like Dino De Laurentiis, he was also determined to develop the relationship between Kong and Ann far more than it had been in the original film. However, Jackson was less interested in the romantic aspect of the relationship than he was in the notion that Kong's connection with Ann awakens the great ape's compassion. In an interview in the *Los Angeles Times*, Jackson describes Kong as "a very old gorilla [that has] never felt a single bit of empathy for another living creature during his long…brutal life." Kong's original intent is to kill Ann, "and then he slowly moves away from that and it comes full circle."

PREPRODUCTION   After hiring Jan Blenkin and Carolynne Cunningham to coproduce the film with him and Walsh, Jackson brought back most of the members of the team that worked on the *Rings* trilogy, including cinematographer Andrew Lesnie, production designer Grant Major, art directors Simon Bright and Dan Hennah, conceptual designer Alan Lee, special effects supervisor Richard Taylor, visual effects supervisor Joe Lettieri, editor Jamie

Selkirk, and composer Howard Shore. WETA Limited would, of course, create the special effects.

Although there was speculation that Jackson would again offer the part of Ann Darrow to Kate Winslet, he surprised many by offering it to rising star Naomi Watts instead. Born in England and raised in Australia, Watts came to Hollywood in her early twenties and appeared in a string of forgettable TV shows and movies before she delivered a star-making performance in David Lynch's *Mulholland Drive* (2001). Watts went on to star in the smash hit horror film *The Ring* (2002) and was nominated for an Academy Award for her role in *21 Grams* (2003).

Before Jackson decided to revise the script, actors such as Robert De Niro, Ian McKellan, and George Clooney had allegedly been considered for roles in the film (as Denham, Lord Darrow, and Jack, respectively). After the revision, Jackson chose Adrien Brody to play the new, literary incarnation of Jack Driscoll. A native New Yorker, Brody had appeared in *The Thin Red Line* (1998) and *Summer of Sam* (1999) before winning an Academy Award as Best Actor for his role in *The Pianist* (2002).

Jackson's most surprising casting decision was his choice of actor/musician Jack Black to play Carl Denham. Known for his "gonzo" comedic performances in films such as *High Fidelity* (2000), *Shallow Hal* (2001), and *School of Rock* (2003), Black allegedly modeled his performance of a driven young film director who will stop at nothing to get his vision on film on Peter Jackson in the same way that Robert Armstrong once modeled his performance on Merian C. Cooper.

To round out the cast, Jackson selected Thomas Kretchman to play Captain Englehorn; Kyle Chandler to play Bruce Baxter; Colin Hanks, John Sumner, and Jamie Bell as members of Denham's crew; Evan Parke as Hayes, the *Venture*'s first mate; and Andy Serkis as Lumpy the Cook, a combination of a *Venture* crew member that appeared in James A. Creelman's original script and Delos W. Lovelace's novelization but never made it into the final film and the character played by Victor Wong in *King Kong* and *Son of Kong*.

In all drafts of Jackson's script, the classic closing line from the original film—"It was Beauty killed the Beast"—was delivered by an elderly woman who emerges from the crowd surrounding the fallen Kong's body. After delivering the line, the elderly woman then turns and mournfully walks away. It was Jackson's hope that he could persuade Fay Wray to come out of retirement to play the role. Wray had reportedly agreed, but her death in August 2004 put a sad end to that plan.

PRODUCTION Principal photography on Peter Jackson's *King Kong* began on September 6, 2004. Like Cooper before him, Jackson filmed most of his *Kong* in the studio, primarily at his Camperdown Studios complex in Miramar, New Zealand. Sets for the native village, the Great Wall, and the streets of New York City were constructed on the Camperdown backlot. Interiors were shot on the soundstage on practical sets, some of which will be digitally enhanced in postproduction.

A few of the scenes set on the SS *Venture* were filmed at sea aboard an authentic 1930s era ship called the *Manuia*, which production designer Grant Major refurbished and transformed into Captain Englehorn's venerable old tramp steamer. All of the oceangoing scenes were directed by second unit director Randy Cook because Peter Jackson gets seasick when he is out on the waves. The ship sunk soon after production wrapped. The rest of the *Venture* scenes were shot aboard a full-scale deck constructed in the parking lot at Camperdown Studios and then were backed with a green screen. The ocean was digitally added in postproduction.

Scenes set in the Broadway theater from which Kong makes his escape were filmed in Wellington's Opera House and Auckland's Civic Theatre. The rest of the live-action scenes were filmed on the soundstages at Camperdown Studios.

Principal photography wrapped in March 2005, although, as on the previous Kong films, effects shooting would continue through the postproduction

Jack Black as an Orson Welles–inspired Carl Denham.

process. The film's budget has been reported to be somewhere between $150 and $200 million dollars.

SPECIAL EFFECTS Visual effects are obviously going to play a crucial part in the new *King Kong*, but the types of effects that Peter Jackson is using is very different from those used in the previous versions of *Kong*. Since the early 1990s, the photochemical optical effects that had been in use since the birth of cinema have given way to whole new generation of computer-generated imagery. Image compositing is no longer achieved by photographing separate pictures and combining them on an optical printer or projecting them on a rear or a front screen. Instead, diverse images are now scanned into a database and composited on a computer before being printed out on motion picture film. Monsters are no longer created by building physical models from rubber, cotton, and metal and then brought to life, frame by frame. Instead, creatures are constructed in cyberspace and animated using bytes and cursors. Creature costumes, miniatures, matte paintings, and make-up effects are still being utilized, but rarely as an end in themselves. Instead, they are now but single brushstrokes on a much larger digital canvas.

Computers have revolutionized other aspects of film production as well. Storyboards are no longer drawn, but are now rendered as three-dimensional, moving "animatics." Filmmakers no longer need to build elaborate sets or amass hoards of extras in order to create crowd scenes. Instead, actors can now be filmed in front of a blue or a green screen and then seamless inserted into digitally created sets, and a small group of extras can now be replicated to the point where they become a teeming multitude. *Star Wars* creator George Lucas's Industrial Light & Magic was one of the pioneers of this digital revolution and Peter Jackson was an early and eager convert. WETA has had a digital unit practically since inception, and Jackson has admitted that he could not have made the *Lord of the Rings* trilogy on the epic scale that he did without the help of computer-generated imagery (CGI). For the new *King Kong*, WETA is not only creating a computer-generated ocean for the *Venture* to sail on, but also a digital Kong Island, a digital jungle (reportedly a stylized "jungle from hell" that Jackson's 1996 script specifically directs should be based on the paintings of Gustav Doré), and a digital New York City (based on actual maps, blueprints, and photographs of 1930s Manhattan). Miniature jungle and city sets and several miniature versions of the *Venture* were also constructed and digitally integrated in postproduction. For the first time in the history of Kong films, no giant hand was constructed to hold Kong's leading lady. Instead, Naomi Watts was picked up by a green-covered rig that will eventually be replaced by a CG gorilla mitt.

Kong himself is being created using *motion capture*—the same technique Jackson used to create the character of Gollum in the *Lord of the Rings* films. The motion capture process begins by attaching dozens of small, reflective spheres to the body of an actor. The actor then performs his part in front of a video camera. Once the scene is finished, the video images are then processed in a way that wipes away everything except the reflective spheres. The resulting three-dimensional "map" of the performance is then stored in a database and used by digital animators as the basis for a computer-generated performance.

To create a live-action basis for Kong, Jackson hired Andy Serkis, the actor who so memorably portrayed Gollum, to play the giant gorilla, both in front of a green screen and on set with the other actors (in order to give them a living presence to interact with). In several interviews, Jackson made it clear that the casting of Serkis did not mean that he intended to humanize or soften Kong's character in any way: "The power of the story lies in the fact that this is a savage beast from a hostile environment, and we don't intend to compromise that." To prepare for his performance, Serkis traveled to Rwanda and spent time in the wild observing the actions and behaviors of real gorillas. When the time came to film Kong's scenes, Serkis donned a padded suit created in the shape of Kong and fitted with the reflective spheres. After the scene was taped and processed, the resulting "map" was then given to WETA's digital animators, who built an image of Kong on top of it. By combining the two approaches used to create all of the previous Kongs—animation and man-in-a-suit—with the latest in computer technology, the WETA effects artists are hoping to create a state-of-the-art Kong for a new generation of filmgoers.

Universal will release Peter Jackson's *King Kong* on December 14, 2005—seventy-two years after the original film and twenty-nine years after the De Laurentiis version. The studio is planning a massive advertising and promotional campaign with a tremendous amount of tie-in merchandising, including books, toys, videogames (including one co-designed by Jackson himself), cereal, candy, credit cards, automobiles, fast food, and electronics. It appears that King Kong is once again poised to conquer the world.

■ ■ ■

CONCLUSION

It has now been more than seventy-five years since Merian C. Cooper first conceived of his Giant Terror Gorilla.

Since that time, the great ape has appeared in classics and he has appeared in duds. In the process, he has transcended celluloid and become an indelible part of our cultural landscape. As we prepare to welcome him back to the screen, we know that Kong has become, quite literally, bigger than all of us.

Long live the King!

■ ■ ■

BIBLIOGRAPHY

BOOKS

Bahrenburg, Bruce. *The Creation of Dino De Laurentiis' King Kong*. New York: Pocket Books, 1976.

Burns, Bob, and John Michlig. *It Came From Bob's Basement: Exploring the Science Fiction and Monster Movie Archive of Bob Burns*. San Francisco: Chronicle Books, 2001.

Goldner, Orville, and George E. Turner. The Making of *King Kong*: The Story Behind a Film Classic. Cranbury: A.S. Barnes & Co. Inc., 1975.

Gottesman, Ronald, and Harry Geduld (eds). *The Girl In The Hairy Paw: King Kong as Myth, Movie, and Monster*. New York: Flare/Avon Books, 1976.

Grodin, Charles. *It Would Be So Nice If You Weren't Here: My Journey Through Show Business*. New York: William Morrow & Company, 1989.

Grodin, Charles. *We're Ready for You, Mr. Grodin*. New York: Scribners & Sons, 1994.

Kezich, Tullio, and Alessandra Levantesi. *Dino: The Life and Films of Dino De Laurentiis*. New York: Miramax Books/Hyperion, 2004.

McDougal, Dennis. *The Last Mogul: Lew Wasserman, MCA, and the Hidden History of Hollywood*. New York: Crown, 1998.

Marrero, Robert. *Godzilla: King of the Movie Monsters: An Illustrated Guide to Japanese Monster Movies*. Key West: Fantasma Books, 1996.

Pascall, Jeremy. *The King Kong Story*. Secaucus: Chartwell Books, Inc., 1977.

Perisic, Zoran. *Special Optical Effects*. London: Focal Press, Ltd, 1980.

Pryor, Ian. *Peter Jackson: From Prince of Splatter to Lord of the Rings*. New York: Thomas Dunne Books/St. Martin's Press, 2004.

Semple, Lorenzo, Jr. *The Complete Script of the Dino De Laurentiis Production of King Kong*. New York: Ace Books, 1977.

Smith, Thomas G. *Industrial Light & Magic: The Art of Special Effects*. New York: Del Rey, 1986.

Stallings, Laurence. *The Doughboys: The Story of the AEF, 1917–1918*. New York: Harper & Row, 1963.

Thomson, David. *Showman: The Life of David O. Selznick*. New York: Alfred A. Knopf, 1992.

Turner, George E., with Orville Goldner. Revised by Michael H. Price with Douglas Turner. *Spawn of Skull Island: The Making of King Kong*. Baltimore: Luminary Press, 2002.

Vaz, Mark Cotta. Living Dangerously: The Adventures of Merian C. Cooper. New York: Villard, 2005.

Winters, Ralph E. *Some Cutting Remarks.* Lanham: Scarecrow Press, 2001.

Wray, Fay. *On the Other Hand: A Life Story.* New York: St. Martin's Press, 1989.

PERIODICALS

Beale, Lewis. "The Kong Isn't Dead. Long Live the King." *Los Angeles Times,* 1 June 1986, Calendar section, 5.

"Behind the Scenes of *King Kong.*" *American Cinematographer,* January 1977, 35–36; 76–79; 84; 114.

Berkvist, Robert. "His Specialty Is Comedy with a Cutting Edge." *New York Times,* 20 February 1976, 5; 12.

"Blue Screen on the Silver Screen." *Technology Review,* September 2002.

Burden, W. Douglas. "Stalking The Dragon Lizard on the Island of Komodo." *National Geographic,* August 1927.

Chiari, Mario and Dale Hennesy. "Production Design for the New *King Kong.* " *American Cinematographer,* January 1977, 48–49; 88.

"Danforth Resigns." *Starlog,* 1977.

de Vries, Hilary. "The New Queen of the Big Scream." *Parade,* 4–6 March 2005, 6–7.

Drew, Bernard. "Gorilla Power." *American Film,* December-January 1977, 6–3.

Dunn, Linwood G. "Creating Film Magic for the Original *King Kong.*" *American Cinematographer,* January 1977, 64–65; 96–99.

Fox, Jordan. "Rick Baker: Maker of Monsters, Master of the Apes." *Cinefex,* April 1984, 4–71.

"From Towering Inferno to Towering Gorilla." *American Cinematographer,* January 1977, 44–47.

Gammil, Kerry and Michael W. Davis. "An Interview with Rick Baker." *Enterprise Special Number Three—King Kong Spectacular,* 1977.

Giles, Jeff. "Kingdom Kong." *Newsweek,* 6 December 2004, 82–84.

Goldman, Lowell. "Lord of Disaster." *Starlog,* November 1990, 59–61; 70.

Hammond, David. "Conceiving the Persona of King Kong—In Two Sizes." *American Cinematographer,* January 1977, 42–43; 52–53.

Haver, Ron. "Merian C. Cooper: The First King of Kong." *American Film,* December-January 1977, 14–23.

Horn, John. *"King Kong."* Los Angeles Times, *16 January 2005, E6–E7.*

"*King Kong* Kommercial." *Famous Monsters of Filmland,* July 1976, 43–49.

"King Kong Was a Dirty Old Man." *Esquire,* September 1971, 146–149.

Kline, Richard H. "The Challenges of Photographing *King Kong.*" *American Cinematographer,* January 1977, 36–39; 68–70; 92–95.

"The Making of the Original *King Kong.* " *American Cinematographer,* January 1977, 60–63; 72–73; 80–81; 100–112.

Maryles, Daisy. "Pocket Books, Paramount Beat Chests Over *King Kong* Tie-In." *Publishers Weekly,* 1976, 32.

Murphy, Mary. "The Kong Papers: Ten Days in Dino's Palm." *New West,* December 20, 1976, 26–38.

Oster, Jerry. "The Human Side of Kong." *New York Daily News,* December 26, 1976, 5.

Pourroy, Janine. "After the Fall." *Cinefex*, February 1987, 32–51.

"The Producer Talks about His New *King Kong.*" *American Cinematographer*, January 1977, 40–41.

Reardon, Craig. "Rick Baker Interview." *Close-Up*, March 1977.

Robinson, Glen. "Constructing a 42-Foot-Tall Superstar." *American Cinematographer*, January 1977, 51; 83.

Salmaggi, Bob. "The Invisible Stardom of the Lemon Juice Kid." *New York Daily News*, 27 February 1977, 9.

Sammon, Paul M. "Turn on Your Heartlight: Inside *E.T.*" *Cinefex*, January 1983, 4–49.

Scapperotti, Dan. "The Special Effects of Dino De Laurentiis' *King Kong Lives.*" *Cinefantastique*, January-February 1987, 106–7; 117.

Schickel, Richard. "Here Comes *King Kong.*" *Time*, October 25, 1976, 64–70.

Shay, Don. "Willis O'Brien: Creator of the Impossible." *Cinefex*, January 1982, 5–70.

Shearer, Lloyd. "Kong's New Girlfriend." *Parade*, 12 December 1976.

Siegel, Dick. "The King in New York." *Famous Monsters of Filmland*, March 1977, 20–25.

Tobias, Andrew. "The Battle for *King Kong.*" *New York*, 23 January 1976, 38–44.

Turner, George. "Sailing Back to Skull Island." *American Cinematographer*, August 1992.

Van Der Veer, Frank. "Composite Scenes For *King Kong* Using the Blue-Screen Technique." *American Cinematographer*, January 1977, 56–57; 74–75; 91.

Vertlieb, Steve. "The Man Who Saved *King Kong.*" *The Monster Times*, January 1972.

Wellman, Harold. "*King Kong*—Then and Now." *American Cinematographer*, January 1977, 66–67.

Wilkins, Barbara. "*King Kong*'s Jessica Lange." *People*, 31 January 1977, 40–43.

INTERNET

Erland, Jonathan. "Front Projection: Tessellating the Screen." *SMPTE Website*. http://www.digitalgreenscreen.com/smptetess.html.

Frankish, Brian. "Jack Grossberg Eulogy." *The Jack Grossberg Project*. http://www1.cs.columbia.edu/%7Emdog/jg/index.htm.

Grossberg, Michael. "Jack Grossberg Eulogy." *The Jack Grossberg Project*. http://www1.cs.columbia.edu/%7Emdog/jg/index.htm.

——— "Jagro." *The Jack Grossberg Project*. http://www1.cs.columbia.edu/%7Emdog/jg/index.htm.

"Jessica Lange Biography." *Jessica Lange*. http://home.hiwaay.net/~oliver/jlbio.htm.

Michlig, John. "The 1976 Kong Posters." *John Michlig's Pop Culture Gill Net*. http://www.fullyarticulated.com/KongPosters.html.

Michlig, John. "*King Kong*: Lost and Found." *John Michlig's Pop Culture Gill Net*. http://www.fullyarticulated.com/KongBoomer.html.

SCREENPLAYS

Creelman, James A., and Ruth Rose, from an idea by Merian C. Cooper and Edgar Wallace. *King Kong*. September 1932 Revision.

Goldman, Bo. *The Legend of King Kong*. 1975.

Rose, Ruth (story). *The Son of Kong*. 1933.

Semple, Lorenzo, Jr., based on a screenplay by James A. Creelman and Ruth Rose, from an idea by Merian C. Cooper and Edgar Wallace. *King Kong*. December 8, 1975 Revision.

Shusett, Ronald, and Steven Pressfield. *King Kong Lives*. 1985.

Walsh, Fran, and Peter Jackson, from an idea conceived by Edgar Wallace and Merian C. Cooper. *King Kong*. 1996.

OTHER SOURCES

INTERVIEWS CONDUCTED BY RAY MORTON

Rene Auberjonois

Rick Baker

Jeff Bridges

Robin Browne, B.S.C.

Terry Carr

Jeffrey Chernov

Brian Frankish

Michael Grossberg

Brian Kerwin

Richard H. Kline, A.S.C.

William Kronick

David McGiffert

Gary Martin

Alec Mills, B.S.C.

Barry Nolan

Jack O'Halloran

Robert Pergament

Carlo Rambaldi

Arthur Rankin

Lorenzo Semple, Jr.

Will Shephard

Ronald Shusett

Fred Sidewater

INTERVIEWS CONDUCTED BY TIM PARTRIDGE

Peter Elliott

Collin Miller

Peter Murton

John Scott

INDEX